The King of Adobe

The King of Adobe

Reies López Tijerina, Lost Prophet of the Chicano Movement

Lorena Oropeza

The University of North Carolina Press
CHAPEL HILL

Design and composition by Kristina Kachele Design, llc
Set in Arnhem Blond with Monotype Walbaum display
Manufactured in the United States of America

The University of North Carolina Press has been a member
of the Green Press Initiative since 2003.

Jacket illustration: Reies López Tijerina at UCLA symposium, February 1968.
Photo by Devra Anne Weber.

Library of Congress Cataloging-in-Publication Data
Names: Oropeza, Lorena, 1964– author.
Title: The king of adobe : Reies López Tijerina, lost prophet of the Chicano movement / Lorena Oropeza.
Description: Chapel Hill : The University of North Carolina Press, [2019] | Includes bibliographical references and index.
Identifiers: LCCN 2019009781| ISBN 9781469653297 (cloth : alk. paper) | ISBN 9781469653303 (ebook)
Subjects: LCSH: Tijerina, Reies. | Mexican Americans—Biography. | Political activists—United States—History—20th century—Biography. | Civil rights workers—United States—History—20th century—Biography. | Chicano movement—History.
Classification: LCC E184.M5 O767 2019 | DDC 323.092 [B] —dc23 LC record available at https://lccn.loc.gov/2019009781

Portions of chapters 3 and 7 originally appeared in Lorena Oropeza, "The Heart of Chicano History: Reies López Tijerina as a Memory Entrepreneur," *The Sixties: A Journal of History, Politics, and Culture* 1, no. 1 (2008): 49–67. https://www.tandfonline.com/toc/rsix20/1/1.

Photos of Tijerina as a boy in Texas with his father in the family car (chapter 1) and Tijerina with his first wife, Mary Escobar, in Mexico in 1959 (chapter 4) from Reies López Tijerina, *They Called Me "King Tiger": My Struggle for the Land and Our Rights*, ed. and trans. José Angel Gutiérrez (Houston, Tex.: Arte Público Press, University of Houston, 2000). Reprinted with permission.

For John,

for everything

Contents

Map and Figures

MAP

FIGURES

Note on Terminology and Use of Spanish

Within this book, I use many ethnic identifiers for the people who populate its pages. Consistent with the complicated history of the American Southwest, and of New Mexico in particular, none is perfect. I most often use "*nuevomexicanos*" to refer to people with historic ties to Spanish or Mexican land grants in this region, although that term unfairly excludes land-grant people from Colorado. Depending on the context, I sometimes employ ethnic labels that were once more popular, such as "Spanish Americans" and "Spanish-surnamed people." I usually use "Mexican Americans" and "ethnic Mexicans" to refer to the broader Mexican-descent population in the United States. I tend to employ the terms "Chicanos," "Indo-Hispanos," and, more rarely, "Hispanos," and their gender variations, to capture specific political moments. The words "Anglo" and "Anglo-American" also appear in the text to refer to white people from a non-Spanish-speaking background.

The translations of the Spanish-language sources are mine. As Reies López Tijerina and many land-grant activists could out-talk me in two languages, I decided to forgo "*sic*" except when its use dispelled confusion. Grammatical errors that appear in this book, whether in English or in Spanish, are meant to be true to the original document. I have also often kept the conversational Spanish as it appears in personal letters and sometimes in public comments as the best way to capture the original flavor of these statements.

Finally, regarding accents, I tried to follow convention in terms of Spanish-language place names (Santa Fe not Santa Fé) and honor individual preference in terms of personal names. If uncertain, I usually duplicated the way a name appears in print.

The King of Adobe

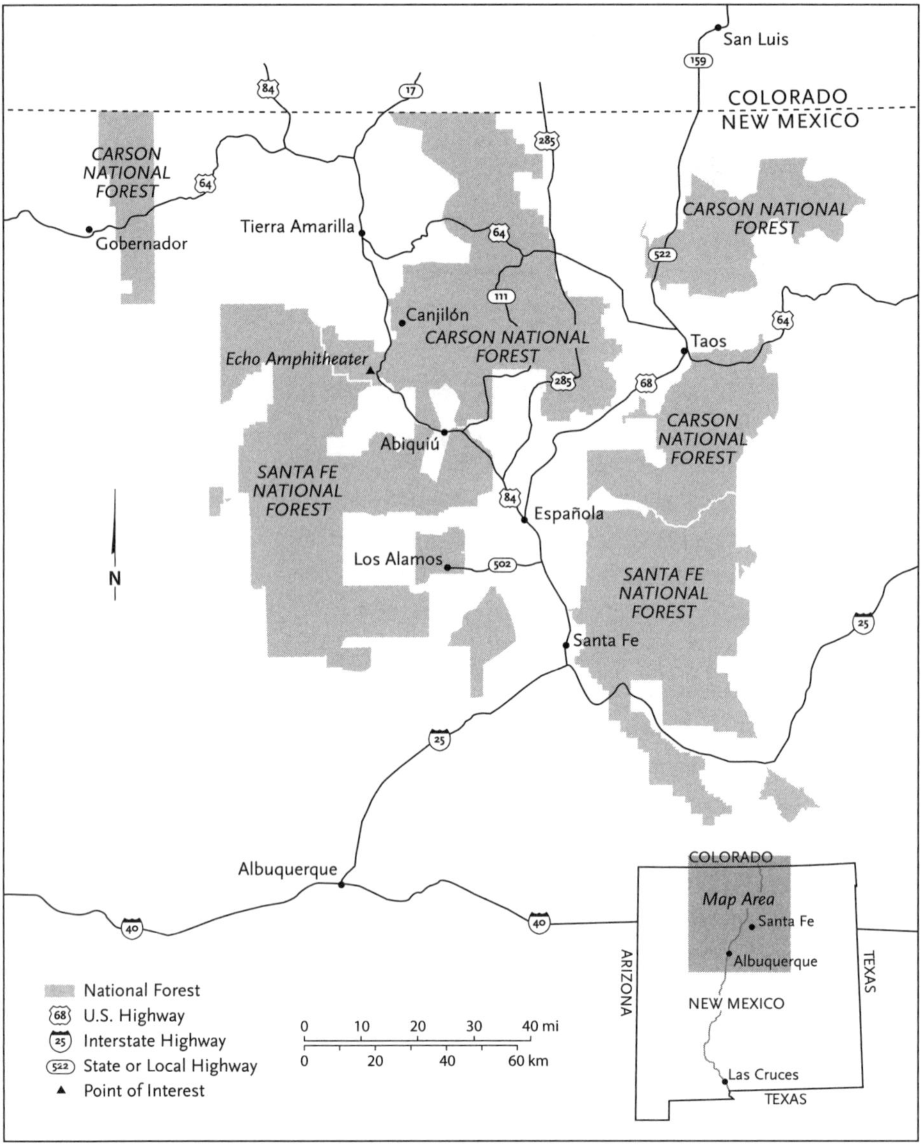

North-Central New Mexico

Introduction

"What did you shoot me for?" Nick Saiz asked just after the bullet shattered his shoulder. "I was going to give you my gun."

Moments before, Juan Valdez had entered the Rio Arriba County Courthouse where Saiz, a state policeman, was standing in the front hallway looking at a bulletin board.[1] When Valdez saw the law officer make a move toward his holster, he determined that he had no choice but to fire. "It came down to I shoot him, or he was going to shoot me—so I pulled the trigger," Valdez recalled. "Lucky for both of us he didn't die."[2] In Valdez's memory of the moment, the alternative meant surrender, not just to Saiz but also to the injustice of land theft in New Mexico, which had brought him to the courthouse that day. In that split second before pulling the trigger, he found himself unable to ignore "the anger . . . in my heart."[3]

Others who joined Valdez in storming the courthouse with loaded weapons on June 5, 1967, displayed equal resolve. They planned to make a group citizens' arrest of the local district attorney, Alfonso Sánchez, whom they accused of violating their First Amendment right to assemble freely. "The Tijerinas are here!" shouted county jailer Eulogio Salazar as he saw Reies López Tijerina and his followers striding into the courthouse that day. Tijerina was the founder and president of the Alianza Federal de Mercedes (Federal Alliance of Land Grants), whose members had decided to conduct this arrest. In an attempt to escape undetected, Salazar moved toward a window when he heard a man—whom he later identified as Tijerina—tell him to stay put or "I will kill you." A frightened Salazar threw himself out of the window anyway. He received a bullet in the jaw even before he hit the ground. Picking himself up, Salazar was hit again, this time in the shoulder, as he fled down the street.[4]

The sound of gunfire sent court officials, employees, and visitors scurrying for cover. Four court employees escaped through another first-floor window. Upstairs in the courtroom, Undersheriff Dan Rivera made a beeline to an adjacent jury room while Judge James Scarborough and several others, including a blind attorney, his wife, and the attorney's seeing-eye dog, all retreated to the judge's chambers along with the court reporter.[5] According to Tijerina, Rivera gave away his location in the jury room when he fired through the closed doorway, presumably upon hearing footsteps approaching.[6] After Alianza members forced the door open, the unfortunate Rivera then received a blow to the head with a rifle butt that nearly cracked his skull.[7] Meanwhile Baltazar Martínez, just twenty-two and easy to spot because he wore a beret and what appeared to be sticks of dynamite strapped to his waist, found Larry Calloway, a United Press International reporter, crouched inside a phone booth, where Calloway had been reporting events as best he could before the line went dead.[8]

As they searched each room, looking for District Attorney Sánchez, the gunmen methodically gathered the people they encountered and put them in the county commission meeting room. "Ahora no están tan bravos!" a gleeful José Madril reportedly crowed at the subdued group. ["Now you are not so brave!"][9] With Juan Valdez's help, the downed Saiz was loaded into an ambulance. A few Alianza members continued to fire their weapons at will. Others decided to ransack the building, vandalizing office equipment, rifling through bookshelves, and even scattering the contents of the county treasurer's vault onto the floor—without taking a penny. Convinced that Sánchez was not in the building, Tijerina ordered a retreat.[10]

Upstairs in the judge's chambers, the blind attorney's wife, Megan Fox, remembered waiting for the shooting to stop and, in the meantime, taking comfort in the fact that her husband's seeing-eye dog, Tawny, stood ready to unleash "150-pounds of enraged German Shepherd" just in case any attackers did burst through the door. An Easterner by birth, she also recalled thinking, "This is not the way we do things in Connecticut."[11]

During a decade when Sergio Leone's spaghetti westerns filled movie theaters and popular television shows included the western-themed *Gunsmoke* and *Bonanza*, a remote part of New Mexico on June 5, 1967, suddenly seemed like the Wild West come to life.[12] The Tierra Amarilla Courthouse Raid, as it came to be known, represented a rare instance in U.S. history when minority militancy went beyond rhetoric to engage in armed confrontation. Like no previous event, the violence that day directed the nation's attention to a little-known but century-long struggle for land within the United States. As Tijerina explained, Alianza members wanted only what "deceit and fraud had snatched away from them," namely land granted to their families by the Spanish or Mexican government before the American hostile takeover of Mexico's far north in 1848.[13] The United States had promised to respect these property rights in the Treaty of Guadalupe Hidalgo, which had ended a war between the two nations. Yet *nuevomexicanos*, if they held onto any land at all, had been surviving on smaller and smaller parcels ever since. Here was a crime, Tijerina insisted, that was "stinking up the pages of New Mexican history."[14]

As the leader of the Alianza, Tijerina emerged as the singular hero of the raid. In the years immediately afterward, writers routinely equated the man and the movement. *Tijerina and the Land Grants* read one title.[15] *Tijerina and the Courthouse Raid* read another.[16] Yet another volume, *¡Grito! Reies Tijerina and the New Mexico Land Grant War of 1967*, escalated the confrontation to a military engagement while keeping its focus squarely on the Alianza leader.[17] All of these early works invested Tijerina with unquestioned masculine power and prestige.[18]

Ethnic variations on this theme further enhanced Tijerina's reputation. At a time when the sociological literature described Mexican Americans as "fatalistic" and "passive," Tijerina struck young participants in the emerging Chicano movement as an impressive action hero.[19] Like their counterparts in other minority movements during the 1960s and into the 1970s, Chicano movement participants sought liberation from political marginalization, economic exploitation, and racial prejudice. At a time when they thrilled to the notion of Chicano power, they took inspiration from Tijerina's Alianza. As one movement participant declared, the courthouse raid represented "the first act of armed insurrection in the Chicano advance toward independence."[20] No other similar acts followed, but that did not stop an early survey of Mexican American history from enshrining Tijerina as one of the "Four Horsemen of the Chicano Movement," along with Cesar Chavez of California, Rodolfo "Corky" Gonzales of Colorado, and José Angel Gutiérrez of Texas.[21]

Evoking the four horsemen of the apocalypse, the label deliberately painted the four men as destroyers of the present corrupt world and harbingers of a glorious new age, one presumably free of Anglo-American oppression. Although early Chicano historians routinely credited Tijerina with sparking a renewed interest in the longer history of Spanish-speaking people in the region, equally or even more impressive to most was his willingness to pick up a gun on June 5, 1967. As "fellow horseman" Gutiérrez noted with admiration as late as 2000, Tijerina "did what Malcolm X and the Black Panthers only talked about."[22] Before the decade was out, the Mexican government honored Tijerina with its prestigious Ohtli Award, an accolade granted to individuals who had significantly improved the lives of members of the Mexican community inside the United States. Although Tijerina received the honor for his lifelong activism, publicity surrounding the award still highlighted the events of one day more than fifty years before.[23]

This book removes Reies López Tijerina from the long shadow of the raid. Although that shadow defined Tijerina primarily as a man of action, he was foremost a man of ideas. No single person did more to shift popular understanding of the history of the American West from a celebratory tale of "manifest destiny" to the now-prevailing notion of a "legacy of conquest" than Tijerina. As early as the 1950s, he accused the United States of operating as a colonial power within New Mexico. As he pressed that point through petition and protest, he rejected the notion, which persists even today, that statehood ended the subordinate status of nuevomexicanos.[24] The process of conquest began with the U.S.-Mexican War, Tijerina asserted, but still had not ended for the region's Spanish speakers. In developing this critical view of westward expansion, and in conceiving of Spanish speakers throughout the U.S. Southwest as a conquered people, Tijerina challenged not only how Americans saw their role within the world but also how Mexican Americans saw their role within the United States.

The magnitude of that change in perspective is easy to underestimate because it has been so thorough. As an organization, the Alianza failed to return even one acre back to land-poor New Mexicans. Equipped with a third-grade education and a Bible, however, Tijerina managed to rewrite the history of the American West. Today, scholars routinely refer to New Mexico as a "colony" alongside Hawaii and Puerto Rico.[25] By choosing to use this term, they recognize that as the American government acquired new territory, it subjugated people living in these areas by refusing them full citizenship rights, by instituting a judicial system that favored the conqueror over the conquered, and by taking away their land. This pattern, of course, broadly defined the Native American experience on the North America continent. During the 1960s, activists and scholars also started writing about the ghetto and the barrio as "internal colonies." They argued that the subordination of black and brown people within the United States was akin to that of colonized people around the globe.[26]

Tijerina laid bare this historical reality in New Mexico. Starting in the 1950s, he denounced the American empire as aggressive and unjust. To him, the Mexican American experience closely paralleled the Native American one. Not since the height of antiwar sentiment during the U.S.-Mexican War itself had anyone so clearly equated the American takeover of Mexico's north with a land grab.[27] At the time that Tijerina first articulated his ideas, moreover, Cold War politics all but demanded the uncritical celebration of the liberating potential of U.S.-style democracy and capitalism. By daring to call into question the legitimacy of U.S. rule in New Mexico and beyond, the Alianza leader toppled, in the words of one scholar, "a conspiracy of silence shrouding" the fate of the conquered population post-1848.[28] Although Tijerina was not alone in pushing forth a more critical view of the American West, he did play an innovative and heretofore unacknowledged role. Inspired by the social movements of the 1960s, including Tijerina's Alianza, scholars of U.S. western history in subsequent decades foregrounded the legacy of conquest and the complexities of race in their own work.[29]

To understand his contribution as a man of ideas, this book reclaims Tijerina's role within the mix of 1960s social protest. The Alianza leader once inspired many as the militant alternative to labor leader Cesar Chavez. In subsequent decades, the nonviolent Chavez emerged as one of the most well known Mexican Americans in U.S. history, the object of state holidays and the focus of sustained scholarly attention.[30] In contrast, the passage of time largely relegated Tijerina to a historical footnote. He rarely earned mention in surveys of 1960s social protest.[31] Indeed, to the extent that Tijerina and the Alianza were remembered at all, the facts were sometimes *mis*remembered.[32]

Tijerina's absence in our memory of the era also reflects just how much the black-white binary still dominates the study of race in the United States. Histories of the civil rights movement, read as black, and histories of the antiwar movement, read as mainly white, dominate. Relatively few scholars of the era have accepted the challenge of integrating multiple racial perspectives into their studies.[33] Yet Tijerina's life story reflects the necessity of just such a broad approach. After the courthouse raid, Tijerina moved in a radical milieu populated by people of all backgrounds. He particularly sought alliances with African Americans and Native Americans. Not by chance did a large mural that appeared on the office wall of the Alianza show three figures, "the Negro, the Indian, and the Hispano," all bound together in their effort to reach a city labeled "Justicia."[34]

A closer examination of Tijerina's politics, moreover, disrupts one of the most enduring narratives about the 1960s: that protest politics moved from "good" to "bad" during the decade. The fate of Students for a Democratic Society stands as a prime example. An organization that began with the hope of the 1962 Port Huron Statement and a commitment to "participatory democracy" ended with terrorist acts of violence committed by former SDS members reconstituted as a sectarian group called the Weathermen.[35] According to a similar declension narrative, the African American struggle moved from triumph to tragedy, as the great legislative achievements of the Civil Rights Act of 1964 and the Voting Rights Act of 1965 were followed by the supposedly self-indulgent violence of the Black Panthers and the self-destruction of inner-city riots.[36] In either the black or the white case, the move toward violence signified failure.

In sharp contrast, the impact of the courthouse raid forces a consideration of the utility of strategic violence. Land-grant claimants had decades of litigation under their belt when Tijerina arrived in New Mexico. Tijerina then pursued land-grant claims peacefully for years in Mexico and the United States to no avail. His efforts met unrelenting dismissal and disapproval until the drama of the courthouse captured the nation's imagination.[37] Of course, law enforcement, from the FBI to local police officers, usually imagined the worst.

Even at the height of his popularity, Tijerina stirred controversy. As one writer noted, contemporaries disagreed as to whether the Alianza leader was a "con man, a folk prophet, a racist, [or an] inspired revolutionary."[38] Hailed as a new kind of ethnic champion by many activists for his willingness to pick up a gun, Tijerina was considered by others an anathema for the same reason. While his impassioned oratory convinced thousands of Spanish-speaking New Mexicans to work together to achieve land-grant victory, law enforcement officials, media critics, and fellow Spanish speakers often labeled him a fraud. "Hero or Evildoer?" asked one Spanish-language newspaper in Albuquerque in the wake of the raid.[39]

Controversy continued to plague Tijerina until his death in 2015. After serving time in prison in the raid's aftermath and still eager to be heard, he turned toward new causes or sometimes refurbished old ones. These included halting nuclear proliferation, reestablishing traditional family values, challenging the field of psychiatry, and, most important to him, warning of a vast Jewish conspiracy to take over the globe. For at least some scholars, Tijerina's post-Alianza activism left one point indisputable: he was less hero than "weirdo."[40] His already severely damaged reputation took an additional beating, moreover, once rumors began to circulate of an extremely troubled family history. As Tijerina himself acknowledged in 2010, his eldest daughter Rose's accusations of sexual abuse constituted an "open secret" in New Mexico.[41]

Drawing on my interviews with members of the Tijerina family as well as archival research, this book extends well beyond what had been my initial interest in land-grant protest during the 1960s. I first found Tijerina fascinating because of his opposition to the war in Vietnam; he drew intriguing parallels between Spanish-speaking New Mexicans and the Vietnamese fighting against U.S. military intervention in Southeast Asia. Unlike scholars who completed their work before the opening of Tijerina's personal archive at the University of New Mexico in 2005, I had the opportunity to explore more than eighty boxes of newly curated material. For this book, I supplemented that research with materials from other collections in New Mexico and Mexico.

My oral history interviews were especially rich. As a result of my earlier work on the Chicano movement, I became dear friends with Enriqueta Vasquez of San Cristobal. Vasquez in turn introduced me to one of her dear friends, Gloria Maes, a longtime land-grant activist, who helped me locate Mary Escobar, Tijerina's first wife. When I knocked on the door of her Albuquerque home, Escobar answered and granted me an interview. The next day I interviewed her daughter Rose, the only woman who participated in the courthouse raid. It was hard to listen to their experiences. It may be hard to read about them. Living through them was no doubt the hardest of all. These interviews made clear that Reies López Tijerina was not the only one who sacrificed and suffered for the Alianza.

The inclusion of women's experiences dramatically changes what has been understood about the Alianza.[42] In writing this book, I have analyzed Tijerina's role as one of the "four horsemen" through the lens of gender. I argue that power relations within the Tijerina family provided the template for how the Alianza functioned. Without the work of women in the Tijerina family, Tijerina would never have had the luxury of developing his thinking on land-grant matters. Indeed, without the work of women, the Alianza may never have existed at all.

Considering the nature of some of the accusations that arose in my interviews with women in Tijerina's life, my decision to employ oral history methodology may invite debate. Some claim such interviews are too colored by memory to serve as reliable evidence. But I embrace their usefulness in contributing to a more complete and accurate historical record even under the messiest of circumstances: when memories directly collide. In writing this book, my original interviews provided a way for me to move beyond Reies López Tijerina's singular recollection of the past as portrayed in his various writings. Given the dearth of archival sources about Tijerina's earliest years, initial chapters rely heavily upon his own memories, albeit ones that he scrawled on paper. Later chapters feature the voices of family members and other Alianza members. Readers will see me acknowledge the role of memory throughout this work, as evinced by such phrases as "he recalled" or "she remembered." As I incorporated these memories, I strove to separate the wheat of historical significance from the chaff of salacious innuendo and unsubstantiated rumor.

The central narrative of this book sets Tijerina's land-grant activism against a longer quest for justice that began in his childhood and accompanied him into old age. The book's title echoes an insight by Fray Angélico Chávez, the priest and historian, who in 1974 noted that the Kingdom of New Mexico after its founding in 1598 failed to generate the wealth of Mexico proper. Instead, "despite its grandiose name," New Mexico survived as an "isolated frontier outpost of adobe for centuries to come," one "sparsely dotted with Hispanic and Indian villages made of mud."[43] Tijerina's land-grant activism began when he substituted this modest earthly kingdom for a heavenly one. As a Bible student, itinerant preacher, and someone who believed he was a prophet, his early life was consumed with preparing for the Kingdom of God. Later, he exhibited the same crusading zeal when he turned to the restoration of the Kingdom of New Mexico, a restoration that he defined as revitalizing those small villages by regaining a viable land base. Borrowing from his preacher days, Tijerina envisioned Spanish-speaking village culture as an ideal cultural and spiritual refuge from Anglo-American immorality and oppression. In advancing this vision, he grappled with the legacy of two conquests in New Mexico—first the Spanish, then the American—to challenge the complicated racial hierarchies that resulted. Yet in either case, whether

Tijerina led a religious flock or a land-grant organization, his kingdom dreams, just like old adobe, turned to dust.

Nevertheless, Tijerina was a remarkable man who constantly reinvented himself in his relentless pursuit of righteousness as he defined and then redefined it. With good reason, his contemporaries often described Tijerina as "mercurial." As leader of the Alianza, he displayed an amazing ability to switch rhetorical gears and political identities. Thus, Tijerina ran the Alianza as a demanding patriarch while he recruited members as an enthusiastic evangelist. He thought of himself as a Mexican pursuing land-grant justice—until he needed to lobby Washington, D.C., as a patriotic American. Eventually, Tijerina adopted an entirely new identity. As an Indo-Hispano, the Alianza leader also decided to move from petition to protest, a shift that culminated in the courthouse raid.

Tijerina's frequent reinvention hints at the resistance that he encountered by daring to demand justice. Time and time again, the courts, judges, scholars, policy makers, and elected officials dismissed Spanish- and Mexican-era land claims as too difficult to resolve and best forgotten. Years before he stormed a courthouse, Tijerina also earned the enmity of law enforcement, who deemed him a threat to the social order by virtue of his ideas alone. Buffeted by constant rejection, Tijerina did not abandon his previous incarnations as much as let another come to the foreground as strategically necessary.

Whatever approach he emphasized, Tijerina maintained his conviction that God was on his side. His religious worldview, and in particular his experiences as a Pentecostal Christian, profoundly influenced his political leadership. Born into a household of believers, Tijerina turned to God to make sense of the harsh circumstances of his youth. As a young man, his faith instilled in him a powerful sense of justice and of his own personal value as a justice warrior. His Pentecostal training gave him practice in the art of public speaking and informed his fiercely critical view of the United States. Moreover, his Pentecostalism shaped him because its practices were frequently scorned by Catholics and mainline Protestants alike. Tijerina learned to embrace persecution as proof that he was doing God's work. Fueled by a sense of moral outrage, he never shied away from challenging mere secular authorities or experts.[44]

Yet this religious through-line in his organizing efforts functioned as a fault line too. Almost as soon as the raid launched Tijerina into the political stratosphere, the limelight began to expose the limits of his style of political leadership. After all, someone who believes that he or she acts in accordance with God's will hardly has reason to compromise or even listen to others. By the time that Tijerina entered federal prison in mid-1969, his inflated sense of self already had cost him friends and allies. Sitting behind bars, a martyr to his beliefs, he identified more than ever with the persecuted Christ.

Such a complex man, with all of his strengths and weaknesses, hardly fits into a simple category of hero or villain. Early on in my research, I shared with two senior colleagues in the field of Chicana and Chicano history my intention to write about land-grant protest during the 1960s and specifically about the Alianza Federal de Mercedes and its leader. Mention of Tijerina provoked an immediate reaction. "You are not going to do a hatchet job on him, are you?" one asked. "You are not going to idolize him, are you?" asked the other.[45]

Ultimately, I wrote this book rejecting both options. A negative portrayal might have been easier to write. Yet merely to denounce Tijerina as "crazy" offers zero explanatory value while casting aside any chance of understanding what motivated nuevomexicanos to join the Alianza. Let us accept, if only for the purposes of argument, that Tijerina often acted in ways that others might view as crazy, or at least unacceptable. What, then, about all the people who placed their faith in him? Were they a bunch of incomprehensible oddballs too? Of course not. In fact, just as this book aims to rescue Tijerina from the long shadow of the raid, I also hope it liberates the land-grant movement from the long shadow of Tijerina. The early and lingering conflation of the man and the movement belied the reality on the ground in New Mexico, and in neighboring Colorado, where land-grant people had fought for their property rights long before Tijerina moved to the state and where they continued their fight after he had gone.

Conversely, to emphasize only the positive required focusing strictly on Tijerina's political ideas in the abstract and avoiding any mention of his personal life or the quality of his leadership. Given how closely Tijerina's family and the Alianza membership overlapped, I found that approach deliberately misleading. It also struck me as intellectually unjustifiable. How could I credit Tijerina with challenging the conventional narrative circa 1960 of U.S. westward expansion while leaving the conventional narrative of him as a heroic ethnic leader undisturbed?

Neither hero nor villain, the "King of Adobe" was a man who from a lifetime of limited opportunities, dashed hopes, and strange, religious dreams promoted a new vision of land-grant justice and a new vision of the American West. Along the way, Tijerina disrupted conventional wisdom in the United States, and among Mexican Americans, about race and white privilege, about the strategic utility of violence, about the inherent fairness of U.S. courts, and about the likelihood of regaining ancestral lands now claimed by others. What follows then is a portrait of a truly fascinating, profoundly flawed, and completely unique crusader within American history.

As the often charismatic and sometimes repugnant Tijerina once stated, "I am nothing but an original."[46]

1

The King of Kings

Reies López Tijerina never forgot the first time that he visited Jesus. The visit occurred during a dream when he was only four years old. As he liked to recount, he had gone to bed extremely hungry and deeply hurt one evening. The son of Texas migrant farmworkers, Tijerina had been upset to discover that dinner consisted of only half a cup of tea brewed from the bark of a pecan tree. He was too young to understand that, as the Great Depression raged, the family had no money with which to buy food. That night, the exhausted and probably malnourished little boy fell into such a profound sleep that his family became convinced that he was dead or dying. His mother sent his brother Anselmo, the eldest and Tijerina's senior by six years, to go fetch a doctor.[1] But Tijerina woke up the next day not only fully recovered but convinced that he had seen heaven and walked with Jesus: "He took me by the hand and was showing me great green pastures and a garden full of flowers, a beautiful place, and then he was pulling me along in one of those small, little toy wagons, a red one, you know—I never did have one—he was pulling me along in that."[2]

In another recounting, Tijerina remembered that he had done the pulling. Otherwise, the central elements of his story remained remarkably consistent over the years: the tea, the hunger, the little red wagon, and the presence of Jesus. Tijerina also repeatedly labeled his deep sleep a "death," a word that suggested his awakening was akin to a resurrection.

In a later interview, Tijerina made sure that no one missed the story's strong connection between himself and Jesus. After he woke up from his deep sleep, Tijerina explained, his uncles used to say about him, "There goes the dead boy . . . there goes the resurrected boy."[3]

As this oft-revisited childhood memory suggested, Tijerina's earliest years were defined by severe poverty and intense religiosity. His first name was a gift from his mother, who wished to name her son after Jesus Christ, the King of Kings, *el Rey de los Reyes*. More common as a surname, Tijerina's first name also featured an unusual spelling, Reies with an *i* versus a *y*. According to the baptismal registry of the Church of the Annunciation in St. Hedwig, Texas, just east of San Antonio, Reyes López Tijerina was born in that town on September 21, 1926.[4] Tijerina, however, always maintained that his mother gave birth to him atop a pile of cotton sacks along the edge of a field in Falls City, Texas, some forty miles to the south. Perhaps his Spanish-speaking parents, Erlinda López and Antonio Tijerina, had a difficult time communicating with the church's pastor, the Reverend S. Przyborowski. In a way, the discrepancies hardly matter. Whichever town marked his actual birthplace, and whatever spelling his parents intended for his name, the meager circumstances of his entry into this world were clear enough. Like so many other Mexican-descent children in the United States at the time, Tijerina was born poor, a member of a despised racial minority, and, like his parents before him, seemingly destined for the backbreaking life of a migrant farmworker.

Yet looking back upon the same set of circumstances, Tijerina saw in himself a boy and then a man destined for greatness. God told him so in dreams and via other signs from above. The visit with Jesus was only the first of many dreams and other occurrences that Tijerina interpreted as close encounters with the divine, a conclusion enhanced by his willingness to read significance in the world around him. As a teen, he also encountered God in the Bible, an experience so profound that it prompted him to go to an Assemblies of God Bible college and become a Pentecostal preacher before he was twenty. Tijerina eventually struck out on his own, certain that formal religion was getting in the way of his faith journey. He married, started a family, and spent more than five years traveling the country as an independent preacher and revivalist.

Only by unlocking the story of Tijerina's early years does their formative, foundational role in shaping the man who later arrived in New Mexico become clear. First, throughout his life a sense of sacred mission inspired and sustained him. Convinced at a young age that history unfolds according to God's plan, Tijerina was equally convinced that, with enough effort, he could determine what exactly God had in store for him. For that reason, in later years, whenever he looked backward, Tijerina saw a straight line running between the boy named after the King of Kings and the man who went on to earn fame as a New Mexican land-grant activist known as King Tiger.

Second, this intense religiosity fed a charismatic and autocratic personality that neither brooked dissent nor depended upon the approval of others. Tijerina always exhibited a ferocious determination to achieve his objectives, never mind what others thought or even how they suffered. As a man of faith, he preached the Bible unimpeded by religious orthodoxy or denominational affiliation. As a husband and father, he pursued a relentless quest to seek God and his righteousness, even when his religious fervor interfered with his ability to feed his wife and children. Although Tijerina later denied mistreating anyone, according to members of his family he was capable of demonstrating considerable cruelty toward those he felt were failing to follow the path of God or who were distracting him from that path.

Third, Tijerina's disgust with the poverty that he witnessed and personally experienced prompted him to cobble together a theology that harshly criticized U.S. society as awash in greed and licentiousness. Such a sinful nation was destined to be consumed by flames in what he warned was a fast-approaching apocalypse. These extreme points of views challenged not only religious but also political orthodoxy in Cold War America. They also made him a powerful but not necessarily popular preacher.

Tijerina did not care. His utter confidence that God had chosen him for a crusading role pushed him to advocate fearlessly for what he believed. Long before he arrived in New Mexico, he demonstrated remarkable tenacity, and questioned the authority of others while rarely questioning his own. And why should he?

He was Reies, the King of Kings.

IN THE BEGINNING

Tijerina's early years coincided with the worst economic downturn in U.S. history. Migrant families like the Tijerinas had barely scraped by during more prosperous times. During the 1930s, their plight became truly desperate. Decades later, Tijerina strove to capture the harsh circumstances of his childhood on paper by describing the same vignettes again and again in his distinctive scrawling longhand and under the heading *biografía*.[5] The resulting repetition in words and on paper hinted at the urgency with which Tijerina wished to convey his conviction that his life amounted to a sacred mission. Yet the vignettes also captured how profoundly poverty and racism framed his life from an early age. To survive, he depended most of all on his family, especially his mother, and on his faith, which she encouraged before her untimely death.

Hunger and want stalked Tijerina's childhood. As a boy, owning the little red wagon that appeared in his dream was just that—a dream. He played instead with what the jackrabbits left behind, their *cagarutas*, or droppings, which he and his brothers used as marbles. Shoes were almost as much of a luxury as toys. While on the migrant trail, home meant a shifting array of one- or two-room wooden shacks or adobe huts that his parents rented on someone else's property. Starting as a little boy, Tijerina worked in the fields alongside his parents and elder siblings. "We moved from town to town looking for work," he recalled. "Poth, Whiteface, Lubbock, Wilson, Levelland, Floresville. We picked beans and melon, we picked cotton, 25 cents a hundred pounds, chopped cotton, 10 cents a row, topped turnips and hoed onions and cultivated broom corn and shelled pecans."[6] Off-season, the Tijerina family returned to San Antonio. There, Tijerina and his brothers scoured the city dump to gather anything of value for resale, from scrap iron to glass bottles. On occasion, Tijerina admitted, they looked for a meal. He fondly recalled the day a friend showed him how to scavenge through garbage cans in the wealthier neighborhoods of San Antonio. Years later, he elaborated in almost mouth-watering detail the sheer abundance of discarded food that he eagerly consumed: "big pieces of fried chicken, roast beef, bread, pieces of fruit, [and] candy." At other times, the family ate what Tijerina called *ratas del campo* or *ratas del monte*, that is, wild rodents. According to Tijerina, the family even once ate wild jackrabbit courtesy of his mother's dexterity with a homemade bow and arrow.[7]

In Tijerina's memory, his mother stood out as a physical and spiritual amazon, a tremendous source of comfort in an otherwise cruel world. Tijerina credited her with giving birth to all of her children without the aid of a midwife or even the presence of her husband. Poverty took its toll: three of his siblings died in infancy. Nonetheless, as he liked to relate, after giving birth to him, his mother jumped up from that pile of cotton sacks and, passing the newborn Reies to an older child, resumed working. Tijerina remembered Erlinda López Tijerina as almost superhuman, catching poisonous snakes using only a stick and her own lightning-quick responses; selling them apparently brought some extra income. His mother was so strong, Tijerina insisted, that she routinely carried 100-pound sacks of cotton on her back, so strong that she even carried her husband to and from the fields when he was unable to walk himself.[8] *Why* his father could not walk at times was unclear: Tijerina once asserted that some Anglo-Americans had slashed his father in his thigh instead of paying him wages; another time he wrote that his father suffered from terrible calluses on his feet, and another time that his father's feet were so bad that he had amputated toes.[9] Consistent in his memory, however, was the notion that his father was a weak and timid man compared to his powerful mother. "My father feared the Anglos very much," Tijerina once wrote; "my mother did not feared them."[10]

According to Tijerina, the source of Erlinda's strength was her extraordinary faith, especially as compared with the weaker Antonio. Tijerina often traced his great desire to be close to God to his mother's influence. Tijerina recalled that his mother prayed before every meal, at times of crisis, and whenever Reies needed soothing as a small boy. He remembered that she spent a lot of time reading the Bible, too. Her religious beliefs evidently shaped how she responded to Tijerina's Jesus dream. In his memory, his mother accepted both the supernatural quality of his dream and his own special standing as its dreamer. Whenever he experienced disappointments afterward as a child, Tijerina liked to recount, Erlinda would gather him in her arms and ask him to tell her again about his vision of heaven. Sometimes she would just ask him to share the story with neighbors and friends.[11]

Erlinda López died when Reies was just seven.[12] One day near Coleman, Texas, Tijerina later explained, the family was "heading toward the cotton fields in a Model-T, [when] my dad had an accident and the car overturned and my mother hurt one breast. Later they operated on her in San Antonio, Texas at that city's Robert Green Hospital [but] it [the injury] became cancer, or more precisely, gangrene, and from that she died."[13] While Tijerina was uncertain about the exact cause of her death, he never forgot listening to his mother's cries of agony before she died; the family was too poor to buy painkillers for her.[14] Always during times of trouble and confusion, he asserted, he would recall her valor and spirituality. "My mother

Undated picture of a young Reies López Tijerina in front of the family car with his father, Antonio, inside. The young man in the background is possibly his brother Anselmo; an unidentified family friend is on the right. The Tijerina family often followed the migrant trail from Texas to Michigan, picking crops along the way. (Photograph courtesy of Arte Público Press–University of Houston)

. . . planted in my blood, soul, and spirit, the seed of justice, of truth, and of mercy," Tijerina wrote many years later. "She was great, robust, and very brave."[15]

The family suffered greatly from her absence. Left a widower with seven children, Antonio Tijerina immediately asked a neighbor to raise the youngest, an infant named Cristóbal. Still, he had troubling providing for the remaining six: Anselmo, Margarito, Ramón, Reies, Maria, and Josefa. On occasion, Reies's two sisters were farmed out to relatives. Sometime around 1940, Antonio Tijerina began to travel with his family to Michigan to cut beets, following a well-established migrant path that bisected the country north to south. For the next several years, the family traveled back and forth between Texas and Michigan.[16]

The poverty that robbed Tijerina of his mother also robbed him of an education. His scholastic career was short and sporadic. Two surviving San Antonio elementary school report cards indicate that Tijerina enrolled in elementary school three times, once every year at the age of ten, eleven, and twelve. In a pattern that plagued migrant families, he repeatedly dropped out to return to work. Tijerina often estimated that he never gained more than a third-grade education, perhaps six months in total. The report cards also listed four different home addresses over the course of three years, strongly suggesting that, even when living in San Antonio, the Tijerina family remained on the move, unable to pay the rent.

Despite these obstacles, the boy whom the teachers called "Ray" earned top marks during his limited schooling.[17] He did so at a time, moreover, when even the best-intentioned teachers assumed that children of Mexican descent were culturally handicapped if not mentally deficient.[18] The Americanization of "Reies" to "Ray" on the report cards underscored the limited value that mainstream society then placed upon Mexican culture and the Spanish language. While Tijerina never commented directly on the imposed name change, he did like to recount how his older brother Ramón, after being spanked for speaking Spanish in the classroom, left school that day in anger and never returned.[19] Poverty reigned as only one of the injustices that framed Tijerina's young life.

Racism flourished in the intense anti-Mexican atmosphere of Depression-era Texas. Across the country, the economic crisis spurred anger toward Mexican immigrants and Mexican Americans alike who stood accused of taking jobs away from "real" Americans. This animosity culminated in a series of repatriation and deportation campaigns whereby local authorities ejected tens of thousands of Mexicans and, in some cases, their American-born children from the country.[20] Texas formed an epicenter for these efforts. One estimate is that more than half of all the people sent to Mexico during the era's deportation and repatriation campaigns were from Texas.[21] The virulence and staying power of anti-Mexican sentiment throughout the decade almost certainly contributed to the Tijerina family's decision to move to Michigan at least on a part-time basis.[22] Indeed, American citizenship offered the Tijerina family only one tangible benefit during the 1930s: Anselmo Tijerina, Reies's oldest brother, landed a job working for the New Deal's Civilian Conservation Corps.[23]

Although the Depression marked a low point in race relations between majority society and ethnic Mexicans, strong antipathy toward Mexican Americans and Mexican immigrants had a much longer history in Texas. Starting with the establishment of the independent Texas Republic in 1836, intertwined racial and economic hierarchies cast Spanish speakers in Texas as a politically suspect, racially stigmatized, and economically exploitable minority. Although many Tejanos (Mexican Texans) had supported Texas independence, afterward they soon lost their political standing and, within a few decades, most of their economic fortune. Key here was the gradual but inexorable loss of land. The legal and extralegal dispossession of property holdings that began in Texas was to have its echoes elsewhere across the new American Southwest after 1848. As David Montejano summarized in his study about south Texas following the American takeover, "Taxes, mortgage debts, legal battles, the effects of the erratic cattle and sheep market, outright coercion and fraud, as well as the cash offer of land speculators, all combined to reduce the number of Mexican landowners."[24]

Consequently, few Mexican Texans were in the position to benefit from the economic shifts that followed the American takeover. Before 1836, Mexican Texas had been a place where Spanish-speaking people made a living mostly through ranching and by growing their own food through small garden plots. It turned out that the vast, flat plains of the state proved as ideal for growing crops as for grazing animals, especially after the introduction of commercial irrigation systems. By the start of the twentieth century, agribusiness had become a mainstay of the Texas economy, along with a booming cattle industry. As a mostly landless population, however, people of Mexican descent, whether they were born north or south of the Rio Grande, rarely rose above the position of farm laborer in the state's economic hierarchy. To agribusiness, the value of Mexican-origin people was that they kept hiring costs down. A 1928 advertisement boasted as much. Showing seven dark-skinned men standing with their hoes in front of row upon row of cabbage plants that faded into the distance, the accompanying text bragged, "MEXICAN LABOR—Cheap and plentiful—wages $1.50 a day, ten hours—efficient, loyal and plentiful."[25]

Just as the advertisement drew no distinction between immigrant and native-born, neither did the tremendous amount of violence, much of it officially sanctioned. First formed in the 1870s, the Texas Rangers acted as "an army of occupation" in south Texas, dispensing their form of vigilante justice against Mexicans and Mexican Americans alike.[26] One of the worst episodes occurred between 1915 and 1917 when Texas Rangers and other law enforcement agents aggressively responded to a far-fetched plan to return the U.S. Southwest to Mexico. Although the Plan de San Diego attracted only a few adherents on either side of the border, law enforcement engaged in suppressing this perceived threat indiscriminately killed as many as 5,000 people of Mexican descent in Texas over this two-year period.[27] As late as 1922, just four years before Tijerina's birth, the *New York Times* noted in an oft-cited editorial that in the Texas border region, "the killing of Mexicans without provocation is so common as to pass almost unnoticed."[28] At the time, Texas was home to tens of thousands of members of a reinvigorated Ku Klux Klan.[29] Not until the end of the decade did segregationist practices imported directly from the South begin to replace violence as the new means of keeping the state's Mexican-origin population contained.[30]

Although much of this violence predated Tijerina's birth, family lore and Texas history often met and merged in his recollections. He looked to his paternal grandfather, Santiago Tijerina, to trace a genealogy of persecution and heroic resistance within his own family. According to Reies Tijerina, both the Tijerina and López families had been landowners until the arrival of the Americans. As he often recounted, one day the Texas Rangers murdered his great-grandfather, a terrible crime that young Santiago witnessed. In Reies's estimation, Santiago went on to become a "lion" of a man, someone who spent the rest of his life fighting against an oppressive racial order. According to his grandson, Santiago escaped across the border from the Texas Rangers three times and, when fleeing was impossible, fought them with his bare fists. He even survived vigilantes stringing him up in a tree. Luckily for him, the story went, a judge told the crowd that they had the wrong man, and he was cut down.[31]

In contrast, Reies Tijerina seemed to view his father's life as a cautionary tale of the failure to resist injustice. His son maintained that Antonio Tijerina suffered more than a knife wound to the thigh. As a young family man, Reies wrote, Antonio had tried to make a living as a sharecropper, but three times he was run off the property before being paid at the end of the harvest. The last time, the landowners ordered him at gunpoint to depart the field and, when Antonio refused, dragged him away by a rope. Even after his father had descended the economic ladder from sharecropper to migrant worker, his son recalled, Antonio still had to worry about anti-Mexican hooligans. Another of Reies Tijerina's childhood memories was of his father and fellow fieldworkers keeping close watch, especially after payday, in case members of the Ku Klux Klan decided to visit them.[32]

Although impossible to confirm in every detail, these family narratives were in keeping with the violence that marked Texas during the first decades of the twentieth century. They also injected a mythic quality to Tijerina's own origin story. In revisiting stories about his youth, Tijerina repeatedly cast himself as a fighter in the mold of his paternal grandfather and his own mother. For example, later in life, he recalled challenging a teacher who proclaimed the United States the home of the brave and the land of the free. After all, it was not a land of freedom for people like him![33] In another recollection, the teenage Tijerina stood up to some landowners who were trying to cheat the family of their wages. Meanwhile his timid father cowered in the background. The memories must have contained an element of truth as his brother Anselmo designated him an *abogado sin libros*, literally a lawyer without books or formal education but also meaning someone who acted as an advocate for the downtrodden. Thus, Anselmo paid tribute to his younger brother's penchant for speaking out in defense of what he believed was right.[34]

According to Tijerina, his personal bravery extended beyond a willingness to confront economic or racial injustice. While as a child he had met Jesus in a dream, as a teen he had a chance to act like a savior one day in Michigan. There, according to state labor regulations, he was too young to work in the fields. According to Tijerina, he spent many dull days stuck in a big, old house that his family shared with other farmworkers until one day a fire broke out on the roof. "No one was home except old women and children," he later wrote. "I ran out to the roof, the ladies raised buckets of water to where I was, the pitch was very high and steep. I had to walk to the middle of the roof. My mother catching rattlesnakes came to my mind in a flash. . . . [Yet] I felt very natural, no fear. We poured about 25 gallon-cans of water and the fire was out."[35] Tijerina's account calls to mind the New Testament story of Jesus on the rooftop of the temple of Jerusalem rejecting Satan's overtures: in dousing the flames, Tijerina metaphorically triumphed over hell and Satan's dominion.

Tijerina's faith deepened after a traveling Baptist preacher, Samuel Galindo, came knocking at the door one day while the family was in Michigan. Many times he recounted how receiving a Spanish-language Bible from Galindo changed his life. As Tijerina later wrote, "As soon as he left, I began to read the bible from the first page of Genisses. That afternoon I asked Josie [his sister Josefa], who was 12 years old, to make supper for the family because I didn't want to brake my reading." Once free of his obligations, Tijerina conquered the challenge before him: "The language was difficult but with my already advanced Spanish reading ability, I managed to pull through page after page," Tijerina recalled. That night after supper, he then read passages from the Bible out loud to his siblings and then read some more "until far past midnight." The next day, he wrote, "as soon as the family left for the beet field, I went straight to the book called

Bible. Josie went back to bed, but I read all day long." Enthused, Tijerina recalled reading the Bible cover to cover and then reading it again.[36]

In its pages, the teenager discovered a way to understand the world around him. "Here for the first time I got acquainted with the importance and meaning of the words Justice, Mercy, [and] Truth," Tijerina later wrote, recalling how he underlined key passages and took particular inspiration from the Old Testament prophets.[37] That the Old Testament struck a strong chord with Tijerina is relevant given his later career as a land-grant activist. Starting with Genesis, the books of the Old Testament primarily tell the story of God's special relationship with humanity as mediated through the possession of land.[38] As Tijerina recalled, "I read . . . about . . . Abraham, David, Ishmael, and Moses, who led his people to the Promised Land, and there through the prophets I saw satisfaction for the yearning of my heart for justice and peace." He continued, "I found the word justice used as many times as words like love."[39] The word *"justicia"* in Spanish conveys both what is technically fair and what is morally righteous. Taken with both meanings, Tijerina undertook a spiritual quest that brought him back to a church of his youth.[40]

While Erlinda had been a devout Roman Catholic, Antonio Tijerina always leaned Protestant, according to their son.[41] After his wife's death, Antonio and the Tijerina children briefly attended services at Templo Cristiano, a Spanish-speaking Assemblies of God church in San Antonio.[42] Now, on his own, Tijerina began attending Baptist and Methodist church services in Michigan and then, once the family returned to Texas that winter, in San Antonio too. All this searching culminated with him being, as he put it, rebaptized "Protestant" via full immersion. By then Tijerina likely had returned to Pentecostalism.[43]

In turning toward this faith tradition, Tijerina joined part of a distinct minority among the broader population of overwhelming Catholic Mexican American faithful.[44] Scholars usually point to the 1906 Azusa Street Revival in Los Angeles as marking the birth of modern Pentecostalism in the United States, with ethnic Mexicans among the initial participants.[45] The movement took its name from the Feast of Pentecost, which in the Christian tradition was the day that the Holy Spirit descended upon the apostles and granted them the power to preach the gospel to many different nations. Best known for the charismatic practice of speaking in tongues, most adherents to Pentecostalism also viewed dreams and visions as possible modes of communication with the divine. Striving to recapture the spirit and enthusiasm of the earliest Christians, members of the Assemblies of God and other Pentecostal groups eagerly awaited the imminent return of their savior. Accordingly, the truly devout rejected manifestations of popular culture, from music (except for hymns) to theater to alcohol and tobacco, as so many worldly distractions.[46] Rooted in a backlash to massive industrial and cultural change, Pentecostalism's central supposition that anyone, no matter his or her race, gender, or level of education, could directly experience God appealed greatly to those who felt most ill prepared to compete in modern society.[47]

Pentecostalism plugged Tijerina into a vibrant network of believers that straddled the U.S.-Mexico border. In the decades following the Azusa Street Revival, Mexican-descent people spread Pentecostalism from Los Angeles to mining and agricultural camps across the American Southwest and into northern Mexico. Unburdened by the institutional structures of more established churches, Pentecostalism and its preachers traveled "light" across the border and back again.[48] Almost as soon as it was founded in 1914, moreover, the Assemblies of God, the country's largest organized Pentecostal group, took steps to evangelize among the Spanish-speaking by establishing Spanish-speaking congregations, a Spanish-language missionary press, and a school to train Spanish-speaking ministers for missionary work in the United States and Latin America, the Instituto Bíblico Latino Americano, or Latin American Bible Institute (LABI), in Saspamco, Texas.

In 1943, Tijerina enrolled in LABI. The choice was a practical one. Tijerina knew the school's superintendent, Kenzy Savage, who had been a pastor at Templo Cristiano in San Antonio. As the school was located just outside of San Antonio, Tijerina was returning to the closest thing he had to a hometown. Culturally, too, the school felt like home. At the time, "Latin American" was considered a polite substitute for the more racially charged "Mexican." The student body, in fact, was overwhelmingly of Mexican descent, and classes were offered in Spanish. As far as admission, moreover, LABI imposed no minimal educational requirements. Not yet seventeen, the largely self-taught Tijerina qualified for entrance based solely upon his earnest desire to grow close to God.[49]

The school provided an ascetic and strict environment. Its facilities offered unheated dorm rooms, cold-water showers, and outhouses in lieu of indoor plumbing. Its schedule emphasized hard work. Students attended classes on weekday mornings, worked in the fields on weekday afternoons to earn money for their tuition, and studied in the evenings.

Multiple worship services then filled their weekends. Teachers forbade romantic interactions among the seventy students who attended the co-ed school. In the interest of modesty, school rules further dictated that young women wear a skirt that reached at least four inches below the knee, with the measurement beginning precisely from the middle of the kneecap.[50] After graduation, male students looked forward to becoming ministers, while female students expected to become ministers' wives.

Despite all the rules and regulations, Tijerina professed to find the school a severe disappointment on moral and theological grounds. His memory recorded a series of clashes with school officials and fellow students. The impossibility of confirming these accounts exposes the complications inherent in mining memory to gather information. In this case, the memories of school disputes placed Tijerina in a superior light compared with other students and even his teachers. He had hoped to enter a "most holy of places," he later wrote, but was shocked to witness students "stealing . . . cursing, swearing, and fighting."[51] Tijerina also wrote of repeatedly clashing with the school's teachers. As he recalled, the teachers spent their time explaining the tenets of faith according to the Assemblies of God (as might be expected), while he was interested in fostering unity among all Christians. Years later he insisted that even as a young man, doctrine mattered less to him than deeds and actions.[52] In fact, his vision of religious unity apparently extended beyond Christianity to include Islam, which he first learned about in a "Religions of the East" course. From that moment, Tijerina wrote, he became a great admirer of the faith.[53]

Ironically, given his complaints about other students offending his sense of propriety, Tijerina's LABI career ended badly when he dated a student in violation of school rules. Her name was Vicky Rivera. Tijerina met her during his second year at the school. "We talk[ed] twice. I kissed her once. And that was the beginning of my first problem—[with] Mr. Kenzy Savage," he later explained.[54] Claiming Savage immediately expelled him for dating, Tijerina maintained that he nonetheless reapplied and was reaccepted the following year. By then, he wrote, Rivera was no longer in attendance. When she returned to see him graduate, however, and they went off campus without permission to eat lunch, Tijerina apparently was caught breaking the rules again.[55] Exemplifying Tijerina's desire to portray himself as a man fated for greatness, he later wrote that he and Savage dueled verbally at that time. Savage labeled him "a lost case," to which Tijerina supposedly countered that Savage would one day hear the younger man's name "ringing from coast to coast."[56]

Documents from the school confirm Tijerina's account of being kicked out twice.[57] In later years, Tijerina always insisted that Kenzy Savage tried to make amends by offering to send him his graduation certificate after Tijerina's rancorous departure. Yet an unrepentant Tijerina liked to boast that he rejected this attempt at reconciliation, preferring that his diploma stay at the school "as a witness to my rebellion."[58]

The exact nature of this rebellion, however, is unclear. In a later retelling of the same incident, Tijerina suggested that he suffered from a racial double standard. In contrast to his swift punishment, he alleged, Anglo-American students engaged in open displays of affection without penalty.[59] For his part, former school superintendent Savage merely recalled that Tijerina displayed atypical fervor. He described Tijerina as "fanatical, more peculiar, in his thoughts. I guess . . . he was not orthodox . . . [although] when he went to school he was a very sincere student."[60]

Indeed, *some* of Tijerina's more controversial political views emerged during these years. Unlike two of his older brothers, Anselmo and Margarito, who both served during World War II, for example, Reies, who turned eighteen in the fall of 1944, never entered the military.[61] Contrary to many Mexican Americans of his generation whose participation in World War II heightened their sense of belonging within U.S. society, Tijerina later insisted that he was glad to have missed the fight. "Me? Go across the Atlantic and kill people I had never met before?" he queried rhetorically. In this same 1970s-era reminiscence, Tijerina wrote that he did not even understand hating Hitler, who, after all, had never set foot in the United States, whereas Americans had crossed the Atlantic to invade Germany.[62]

Tijerina's remarks about Nazi Germany foreshadowed later accusations of anti-Semitism. In 2010, Tijerina, when asked what he had learned about Jewish people while a student in Saspamco, instantly responded, "They were the Christ-killers!"[63] By the time that Tijerina entered the Latin American Bible Institute, however, most Pentecostal faithful accepted the Jewish people as God's chosen people and therefore likely converts.[64] "Christianity does not destroy Judaism but completes it," read an August 1941 article that appeared in the *Pentecostal Evangel*, the weekly newsletter of the Assemblies of God. Equally important, the article forcefully decried the Hitler regime. "Germany will have to pay, and that dearly, for the persecution of God's own people. Hitler and his men will have to give an account before the living God," the *Evangel* thundered.[65] It is thus questionable that LABI contributed much toward the anti-Semitism that Tijerina voiced later in life.

Tijerina's early opposition to the atomic bomb appears more straightforward. He recalled he had been making his way back to LABI from Michigan in August 1945 and was passing through northern New Mexico when he heard about the bombing of Hiroshima. "The bomb didn't shock me as much as to see the 'Christians' thanking God for what the atom bomb had done in Japan," Tijerina later wrote. As he correctly noted, the early reaction of most Americans to the dropping of the atomic bomb was overwhelmingly positive (with approval rates hovering at 85 percent before month's end). In contrast, Tijerina insisted that he had been immediately horrified at the mass suffering of the Japanese, particularly of women and children, who were noncombatants. The failure of his LABI teachers later that fall to condemn the use of atomic weaponry, he also wrote, greatly outraged him. For the rest of his life, Tijerina tended to see the atomic age as ushering forth Armageddon.[66]

SEEKING GOD ABOVE ALL ELSE

Despite such apocalyptic concerns, Tijerina decided to get married.

In July 1946, Reies Lopez Tijerina wed Mary Escobar. For seventeen years she stood by her husband, first as he pursued his spiritual visions and later as he became involved in the land-grant cause. But in the literature about the Alianza, she remains a shadowy figure, in part because she and Tijerina were divorced in March 1963, just one month after the land-grant organization was officially founded. In his own writings, Tijerina rarely mentioned his first wife, whom he always called Maria, despite the length of their marriage. When asked about these years, however, Mary Escobar told a tale of unrelenting misery and woe.[67]

She had expected a more placid existence. Born in San Antonio on April 8, 1927, the fourth of thirteen children, Escobar remembered growing up in a poor family but one that was united and loving in their Christian faith. "*Muy* [very] close *la familia*," she explained in 2006 in her characteristic mix of Spanish and English. "We always went to church to sing praises to God," she added. "The house was filled with prayer, it was a Christian house." She recalled first meeting members of the Tijerina family at Templo Bethel, another Assemblies of God church in San Antonio, which she, Reies, and most of their respective siblings attended as teenagers. Like the Tijerinas, the Escobar family followed the crops, from Texas to Michigan and back again. At fifteen, however, Escobar, with only a sixth-grade education, enrolled at the Latin American Bible Institute with the blessings of her devout parents. She returned to Michigan to work during the summers.[68] In fact, Tijerina once wrote that he first learned of LABI from a fellow fieldworker named Maria. In this recollection, he failed to mention that this Maria was his future wife.[69]

LABI provided the opportunity for the two to get to know one another better. Escobar was a second-year student by the time Tijerina arrived at the school. By then, they were also related through the marriage of their respective siblings: her sister Esther and his brother Ramón had wed. After Esther and Ramón decided to enroll at LABI too, the couple often recruited Mary and Reies for babysitting duties of their young daughter. Once she graduated from LABI, Escobar found work at a San Antonio drugstore, where she continued to encounter Reies. Although he was then dating Vicky Rivera, Escobar recollected that Tijerina used to stop by to offer her advice, warning her that the job was leading her astray from "*el camino de Dios*" (the path of God) because young men were stopping by the store's soda fountain just to see her. Quiet and reserved, Mary Escobar, as her pictures reveal, was also quite beautiful. Indeed, when her engagement photo appeared, Escobar remembered, a woman dropped by her work and asked her if she wanted to be a Latin dancer in the movies, even offering to train her for such roles. But she refused. "I had graduated to do God's work, not be a dancer," she explained in Spanish. She also recalled fearing God's punishment if she chose otherwise, for a dancer had ordered John the Baptist's head cut off (as told in the New Testament books of Matthew and Mark).[70]

Sharing a common ethnic and religious background, the pair began their union contentedly enough, according to Escobar. Initially, her husband worked at the General Motors plant in Pontiac, Michigan, alongside his father. Although still inclined to pursue a religious life, Tijerina, like most newly minted ministers with the Assemblies of God, needed a day job to keep afloat economically.[71] On the assembly line, however, Tijerina soon suffered an accident in which he fell and injured his back. He received limited compensation and insufficient medical attention. Decades later, in his eighties, he traced his difficulty walking to that workplace injury.[72] Mary Escobar remembered long-term consequences as well. "He would cry like a baby because of his head hurting so much," she recalled. She posited that the original injury to his spinal column had extended upward and affected his neck and head. Her supposition mostly rested upon personality changes that she detected in her husband. After the accident, Escobar recalled years later, Tijerina became more aggressive and easily irritated. Although Savage described Tijerina as "fanatical" during his student days, Escobar stated that he embarked on an uncompromising spiritual quest only after the accident. "That's where he started," she recalled; "he had to seek God and seek God."[73]

Even as a newlywed, Tijerina agreed, his greatest desire was to achieve "illumination," by which he meant obtaining a deeper grasp of his relationship to God. Devoted to that proposition, he had married, he later wrote matter-of-factly, only because "I was tired of being alone." Mary Escobar seemed like a good candidate because she "had been reared in a religious environment" and was, like himself, "a field worker." Nonetheless, Tijerina later insisted that the couple had different priorities from the start. Whereas his wife kept pressing him for a son, his "obsession" was to grow closer to God. Despite working on a temporary basis as a pastor in Pontiac and then in Saginaw, Michigan, he recalled that nothing satiated his religious hunger, his sense that he ought to be doing more as a man of God. "I kept on having a struggle with my conscience, my soul. I was not satisfied. I was always finding that the Bible rebuked me. I found things, not outright things, but that I was a hypocrite, that I was not doing what I could do," he later stated. Finally, after being married just three months, Tijerina gave away all his possessions, meager as they were, and set out on a journey to find God or die.[74]

Tijerina always recorded that 1946 California trip as one of the "*pilares en la historia de mi vida* [milestones in the history of my life]."[75] According to "El Libro de la Vida de Reies [The Book of Reies's Life]," his handwritten manuscript, he and Escobar took a Greyhound bus together from Michigan to Texas but parted ways in Dallas. Escobar went on to stay with extended family in San Antonio, while Tijerina traveled to Los Angeles. Arriving in the middle of the night with only a dime in his pocket, Tijerina boarded a streetcar, rode it to the end of the line to a town named El Monte, and disembarked. He walked for several blocks until he found a hill covered in brush, which provided a place where Tijerina could stay undisturbed. He then found a clearing within the brush and dug what he alternatively called a hole or cave in the ground in which to sleep. There, he waited.[76]

A few days later, as Tijerina often described, he suddenly felt an overwhelming sense of joy and a sense of release from all the doubts that had plagued him. Perhaps the emotional euphoria stemmed from hunger. Like Native Americans who experienced a sacred vision after several days of ceremonial fasting, Tijerina, who had not eaten since Dallas, suddenly gained clarity that bordered on ecstasy. The greatest obstacle between man and God was the church itself, he decided.[77] "I saw that those of different religions were all the same. . . . They were all full of pride and coveted the same things," Tijerina later stated. "I learned that there was no difference between Protestant and Catholic after all." From then on, Tijerina liked to recall, he was determined to share his "new interpretation of the Bible, just literally, the way it was."[78] From then on, Tijerina's faith also chafed at the bonds of organized religion.

Nevertheless, Tijerina initially chose to preach this antiestablishment message within the faith tradition that he knew best. The local district council offered Tijerina—his clashes with school authority apparently forgiven—a steady job serving several Spanish-speaking churches in southwestern Texas.[79] Tijerina preferred an itinerant path. Over the next five years, he crisscrossed the country with his wife and growing family visiting Assemblies of God churches and traveled south of the border too. After making his peace with Kenzy Savage, Tijerina also preached with him for a short while. As Savage remembered, his younger colleague "was a very good speaker, with spunk and spirit."[80] Characterizing Tijerina's preaching as "hard," Savage also endorsed it as "what we needed, and God blessed."[81]

For his part, Tijerina credited Savage with reintroducing him to the topic of land-grant fraud by recounting to him the sordid history of the Tierra Amarilla land grant in northern New Mexico. Savage knew the area well because he had ministered there for several years prior to his tenure at LABI, and, as Tijerina noted, his sympathy lay with the dispossessed.[82] In his 1978 memoir, *Mi Lucha por la Tierra* (My Struggle for the Land), Tijerina wrote that he first heard stories of land loss while passing through Tierra Amarilla in 1945 (perhaps during the same trip that coincided with the dropping of atomic bombs over Hiroshima and Nagasaki). Tijerina later explained that he had been so intrigued at the time that he almost joined the land-grant cause right then. While he decided to continue on to Texas to finish his education, the first thing he did upon arrival in Saspamco was to visit the local library to find out more about the treaty that had concluded the war, the Treaty of Guadalupe Hidalgo. He later took note that his daughter Rose was born on February 2, 1949, the 101st anniversary of the signing of the treaty, a coincidence that he invested with great significance. About Rose's birth, Tijerina later wrote,

"I saw her as a living memorial to remind me of the treaty and its implications. . . . However, I felt no impulse [at the time] to go into the legal history of the treaty." Subsequent pastoral trips through northern New Mexico in 1951 and 1952, however, continued to stoke his interest in land-grant matters.[83]

Tijerina, moreover, interpreted two chance meetings with Anglo-American men as suggesting that God might have a greater role for him. As Tijerina described the first encounter, he was traveling with his family from Dallas to Fort Worth, hoping to hitch a ride because his wife, pregnant with their second child and carrying their first, was having "a hard time" walking. Fortunately for her, just a few miles outside of Dallas, a man drove up alongside Tijerina and asked, "Why do you carry that big Bible and no suitcase?" At the time, the family was so poor they had no other clothes but what they wore. "I talk to people about God and his ways of justice," Tijerina explained. The man then countered, "I don't like preachers," to which Tijerina quickly replied, "I don't agree with them either, that's why I'm walking and trying to take a different direction." This initial exchange apparently led to hours of conversation between the two. Before the talking was over, Tijerina wrote, the stranger had given his family food, clothing, a ride all the way to their destination, and some advice. Specifically, the man urged Tijerina to forget the ministry and to study law and politics instead because the "Mexican people in the United States have no one to speak for them." Years away from heeding this advice, Tijerina nevertheless contended that this man's "words and deeds kept coming back to me."[84]

Even more important to Tijerina was a conversation he had with "the man from Cuero," as he referred to a blue-eyed, older Texan he met in Victoria during the summer of 1949. In telling this story, Tijerina always offered that the man came from Cuero, just in case others wanted to try to verify the information. He admitted it sounded like a "made-up story—too horrible to accept." As Tijerina explained, this stranger had come to hear him preach. Afterward, the pair spent hours sitting on a park bench conversing, the man desperate to confess, in Tijerina's wording, "the sins of my people and [the] crimes committed against your people." Those crimes rested in the distant past. Several decades before, this man's father and uncles had coveted nearby land owned by a Texas Mexican family. To get that land, the man from Cuero continued, his relatives had conducted a coordinated and successful campaign of harassment, arson, murder, and theft, all the while pretending to be great friends of their besieged neighbors. Later Tijerina credited this man for teaching him "the truth that has never been written in the history books." He refused to assign the encounter to chance. "I [k]new beyond any doubt that the God of Justice was educating me. The Great Depression had deprived me and my brothers and sisters of an ordinary education, but now I didn't regret this anymore."[85] Like his 1946 California trip, this conversation merited the designation "*pilar*" or "milestone" in the book of his life.[86]

Mary Escobar offered a less sanguine interpretation. She saw these encounters not as evidence of divine guidance but as a testament to Tijerina's strong will and the family's vagabond lifestyle. If she was tired walking from Dallas to Fort Worth, she had good reason to be: their journey on foot had begun long before, specifically in Illinois. In his enthusiasm to emulate the "prophets of old," Tijerina had decided walking from Chicago to San Antonio was a good idea.[87] Escobar's preference was to take a bus. As she recalled, she had gone to the Salvation Army and "me iban a dar mi pasaje. Yo ya iba a la oficina a recoger el cheque a pagar el bus fare [They were going to give me a ticket. I was already on my way to the office to pick up the check to pay the bus fare]." But then, "Someone was tugging at my suitcase. It was Reies." According to Escobar, Tijerina demanded that she accompany him, and so she did. Sometimes strangers offered rides, including the man who picked them up outside of Dallas. Escobar's memory, marked by an air of chastisement, again differed from her former husband's. As she recalled, "A man, a drunk, picked us up along the road and asked Reies, 'Hey, you know you are a preacher. Why do you have your wife and kid walking like that?'" As for the man in Victoria, Escobar remembered that "he told Reies things, like about how they had mistreated the Mexicans. He put a lot of things into his head." To Escobar, the upshot was that Tijerina was now inspired to learn more about these sorts of injustices in addition to seeking God. Eager to satisfy both yearnings, Tijerina decided to leave Victoria, where he had a steady post, and hit the road once more. "So, there we go again," Escobar recalled about the family's constant movement.[88]

In 2006, Escobar struggled to remember all the places the family had passed through during the decade that Tijerina worked as a minister. A partial list included Michigan, Illinois, California, New Mexico, Arizona, Colorado, and Texas. The family also took several trips into Mexico and had an extended stay in New York City, where Tijerina ministered to Puerto Rican congregations. In Texas, the family often returned to San Antonio, which continued to function as a home base of sorts because both Tijerina and Escobar could count on extended family there to be a source of support in times of economic crisis.[89] Not coincidentally, three of the couple's first four children were born in San Antonio: Reies Hugh in 1947, whom the family called David, Danny in 1951, and Rachel in 1953. Of the four, only Rose, the oldest girl and second child, born in 1949, called Victoria, Texas, her birthplace. Without money for medical care, Mary Escobar often delivered her children with only her husband's help.[90] About her former spouse and the transient life they once shared, she told an interviewer during the late 1960s, "He didn't care about luxuries. All he wanted to do was preach. Preaching, reading, fasting. When we were traveling, I had to wash clothes on the rocks sometimes, and when the car broke down, we would just leave it there. But when the kids were growing up, I started to want to settle down, and that's when our arguments started."[91] By far the worst times, Escobar recalled, were when Tijerina deposited his family with relatives, friends, or even virtual strangers so that he could continue his journeys alone.

Ironically, Tijerina ended up replicating the same impoverished and unsettled circumstances for his wife and children that had once framed his own youth. All too often, according to Escobar, she and the children would find themselves living in the homes of other church people, dependent on their charity, waiting for Tijerina to return. Escobar, for example, remembered an extended stay in Kansas City under these circumstances because her eldest daughter, Rose, probably four at the time, had gotten pneumonia and needed to be hospitalized. Escobar also insisted that Tijerina did not even see his daughter Rachel until the baby was almost three months old. As Escobar recalled with some horror, she and her three, and then four, children ended up staying so long at the home of "*la hermana Hernández*" (Sister Hernández) that this woman started to hint strongly that she wanted Danny Tijerina, then an adorable toddler, as payment. To escape, Escobar finally called her father, who came to her rescue. While impossible to confirm in every detail, Escobar's memories of "a terrible history" of deprivation and instability coincided with those of others.[92]

As Tijerina freely acknowledged, his needs and desires almost always trumped his wife's concerns. While his wife had wanted to stay in Victoria, for example, Tijerina felt compelled to move in part because the local public library "was running out of good books." Inspired by his conversation with the man from Cuero, Tijerina claimed that he had spent all his free time in the local public library reading history and philosophy, among other topics.[93] At the same time, this congregation, like others elsewhere, did not collect enough offerings to sustain the family economically. Time that Tijerina spent studying was time that he did not spend working for wages. While his wife sought a measure of financial security for the family, Tijerina truly did not care about money or material goods. To Escobar's dismay, twice more he divested himself of everything he owned in order "to feel at ease with my heart's desire," he later explained. When his wife accused him of taking bread away from his own children through this endless generosity, Tijerina took comfort from an ancient story, that of how Xanthippe, the wife of Socrates, once threw hot water at the philosopher because her husband was so preoccupied with his own pursuits. "When I read that Socrates' wife threw a bucket of hot water on him," Tijerina once told an interviewer, "I would rejoice. Because my wife was always angry that I gave everything away."[94]

At the same time, Tijerina described economic conditions that went beyond precarious. Although he did not specify whether he was referring to his solo travels or those with his family, Tijerina once told a newspaper reporter that as a preacher he grew accustomed to sleeping under bridges and on the floors of other people's homes.[95] When he and his wife found temporary quarters, they frequently confronted awful conditions. In 1947, he wrote, an Anglo-American rancher in Texas allowed the family to stay in an abandoned garage surrounded by tall weeds and plagued by mosquitoes. There they remained, stuck ten miles away from the nearest town, without a car and without money.[96] Tijerina recounted how grateful he was that, while the family lived in Victoria in 1949, one church member would bring produce past its prime for the family to eat. The produce was food the man gathered to feed his pigs. But his family partook, Tijerina remembered, his wife bringing a long-handed pan to scoop the slop out of the truck.[97] "Sometimes he brought very good pieces of cabbage, heads of lettuce, fruits," Tijerina wrote about his benefactor; "I considered him the angel appointed to feed us."[98]

To Tijerina, such deprivation was a critical means to an important end. "My heart needed, as I saw it, bleeding, tears, pains, and agony," he wrote about this time period. "To reach the poor," he continued, "I had to walk on their path, live their life and be like them."[99] A full belly was not a priority. "I was only 22. I didn't care so much about the present. My eyes and hope were on the future."[100]

On the altar of this future, he sacrificed his children's well-being. "I was hitchhiking before I could walk," a teenaged David Tijerina once revealed to an interviewer. "[The] people who used to feed us were winos and hobos."[101] Decades later, Rachel Tijerina could not think of the time that the family had lived "as gypsies," as she put it, without crying at the memory of so much hurt and want.[102] And despite the passage of decades, Rose Tijerina could still conjure up the details of doing without. She recalled once staying in a one-room dilapidated house and at another time in a beat-up trailer on someone else's property. She also remembered being constantly hungry: a typical meal for the Tijerina children, she said, was half a banana between two pieces of bread. To make ends meet, once the children were old enough, they joined their parents in the fields. As Rose Tijerina also stated, "I remember him [her father] taking us to cotton, to potatoes, mostly to cotton. So, we were never given a chance to start school, especially David and I [the two oldest children]."[103]

While the lack of money and lack of education echoed the circumstances of Tijerina's own childhood, in one respect the experience of the Tijerina children appeared to differ greatly from their father's. In all his reminiscing of his childhood, Reies López Tijerina never mentioned being struck physically. To the contrary, his soft-spoken father could make Reies feel repentant about his youthful misdeeds by a few well-chosen words.[104] In contrast, Rose Tijerina remembered a heavy hand. She was about five when the family lived in a New York City apartment. As she recalled, one day her parents took Rachel and Danny with them to run an errand, leaving David and Rose alone in the apartment.

> I got lonely because my brother was in the living room playing with a little neighbor, a little boy. So, I went in there to watch them play. I sat on the couch. I was so careful about my dress, because my dad was very, very strict so I tucked my dress under my legs like that, so it wouldn't come up. And even like that, I got into trouble. When my dad came home, my brother told my dad, "Papi, Rosa was sitting here in front of me and my little friend and she had her dress above her knees." And my dad just took me in the bathroom and told me to sit on the toilet bowl so I did and he whipped me and whipped me and I must have been about five and I remember that when I cried out loud he would say you better not because I'm going to keep whipping you so I learned to cover my mouth and cry within.[105]

Another time, after Rose Tijerina trimmed some little bothersome wisps of hair that framed her face, she recalled that her father whipped her so badly that she almost passed out. One interpretation of 1 Corinthians 11:6 is that a woman who cuts her hair is disgraced. Tijerina had forbidden his daughters from cutting theirs.[106]

Proving these accusations is all but impossible. Once her father's favorite by everybody's account, Rose Tijerina in middle age had entered a bitter dispute with her father.[107] The feud may have charged her allegations, yet the memory of what triggered the beatings certainly rang true. Throughout his life, Tijerina demonstrated a preoccupation with female modesty and sexual purity. Furthermore, in 2010, when asked directly if he ever beat his children, Reies Tijerina, while initially taken aback by the question, finally answered, "I don't know, maybe. A *coscorrón*, *un pellizco* [a rap on the head with the knuckles, a pinch]."[108] His daughter Rachel, who was also in the room during the interview and who demonstrated sympathy and concern toward her father throughout, then contributed a clarifying comment about changing social norms: "Nowadays it would be called child abuse, but back then there was no such thing." Or as she said when her father was not nearby, "He used to beat us real bad."[109]

Accusations of physical abuse aside, Kenzy Savage's own memoir about his life as an itinerant Pentecostal preacher at midcentury is instructive here. Like Tijerina, Savage was also frequently on the move. Borrowing from a Bible verse (Acts 11:12), he titled his memoir *The Spirit Bade Me Go*, subtitling it *Rambling with Kenzy*. Savage roamed throughout the Southwest, into Mexico, and as far away as Cuba. Always trusting in the Lord to provide, Savage and his family made do with old cars, donated food, and often less than a dollar in his pocket. Also revealing were Savage's comments about women in church. In 1956, for example, he was shocked to see a woman with short hair and a sleeveless dress leading the choir. Worse, he wrote, "All around me there were women who had the appearance of having eaten raw meat and then not wiped their lips to get the blood off! The newfangled Assembly of God churches!" Yet Savage also recognized that change was inevitable. "It used to be that a woman would not be considered modest if she allowed her ankle to show," he wrote, but "a dress that long now would be ridiculous." His advice for preachers was to seek a happy medium between respecting tradition and operating in the modern world.[110]

Tijerina's inclination, however, lay toward extremism. According to his own recollections, Tijerina spent much of his early ministry blasting the Assemblies of God for failing in the denomination's original mission to be a refuge for the poor and the marginalized. Specifically, he preached that churchgoers should give their money directly to the needy and not to any established religious group. He delivered this unusual message, moreover, vehemently. Once Tijerina took out a hammer during a sermon and smashed the collection plate flat to make his point.[111] On another occasion, Tijerina apparently flung the collection plate at a man who dared to walk out of his sermon and narrowly missed striking his target.[112] As Tijerina admitted in one of his writings, "Very few sympathized with what I was point[ing] out. Others were cold."[113] Essentially, Tijerina was asking churchgoers to follow the same standard of sacrifice he had set for his family. In fact, once Tijerina had decided the collection plate was tainted, he refused to accept money from it. That decision naturally compounded the family's poverty, as "love offerings" from congregants made up a critical means of income for young Assemblies of God ministers.[114]

Intrinsic in Tijerina's rejection of the collection plate was a rejection of church authority. The final rupture occurred in 1950 or 1951. Savage and Tijerina told two different stories about their parting of the ways. According to Savage, Tijerina "began to get those rather far-out ideas about how people ought to conduct themselves."[115] Without divulging more, Savage asserted that the Assemblies of God formally revoked Tijerina's ministerial credentials based upon his "unorthodox attitude."[116] His point may have been wholly theological, as doctrinal differences soon divided Pentecostalism into what were termed orthodox and heterodox branches.[117] Or perhaps Savage simply found Tijerina's heated behavior unacceptable. In either event, Tijerina insisted that he never obtained any formal credentials because of his reluctance to commit himself completely to the Assemblies of God and that this ambivalence displeased church officials.[118] Tensions mounted, he recalled, until one day he found himself locked out of a church in Eden, Texas, where he had been acting as the pastor.[119]

Years later, Tijerina explained that he initially had been drawn to Pentecostalism because it "lay on the outer boundaries of the religious world."[120] The description accurately captured the essence of a religious tradition that was relatively young and crusading. By the early 1950s, however, Tijerina had moved far beyond those boundaries. Rejecting all organized religion as corrupt, soft, and sinful, he decided to preach his "new interpretation for the Bible, just literally the way it was."[121] For Tijerina, that meant preaching a unique social gospel.[122]

In 1954, Tijerina provided a snapshot of how he saw the world at midcentury by publishing a collection of forty-two of his sermons. Poorer than ever, having eschewed what little financial security the Assemblies of God had to offer, he doggedly acquired the resources to type his sermons up, collect them in pamphlet form, and distribute them under the title *¿Hallará Fé en la Tierra?* (Will Faith Be Found on Earth?).[123] The apocalyptic content of these sermons left little doubt that the answer was no. Not enough faith flourished on earth to stay the hand of an angry God, Tijerina repeatedly warned. Already he could see the fiery glow of the forthcoming conflagration just over the horizon.[124] A few good people might "be lifted up into the clouds and escape the wrath that comes," he predicted, but most would not.[125] Speaking from experience, Tijerina offered that the cries of the damned were going to sound like those "of a woman giving birth."[126]

The decadence of modern U.S. consumer society was to blame. Tijerina compared the country to the whore of Babylon, who appears in the book of Revelation, the final book of the Bible that describes the apocalypse. Fittingly, he depicted women as particularly susceptible to sin. Most of all, he expressed disgust at how such a rich people treated poor people in their midst. At a time when the United States championed its economic abundance as proof of its superiority over the Soviet Union, Tijerina's strident religious views directly fed some iconoclastic political ones too. These stayed with Tijerina long after he changed his mission from saving souls to recovering land grants.

Tijerina's starting point was to rail against the sin of greed and the plight of the poor. He constantly berated "so-called Christians" for turning their back on those in need. Indeed, he emphasized charitable acts so much that he nearly abandoned a central tenet of Protestantism: justification by faith alone.[127] Yet with equal force, Tijerina scoffed at the aid available, contending that it aimed only to alleviate the consciences of the rich. In a rebuke that called to mind his displeasure at his wife turning to the Salvation Army for help, Tijerina wrote, "There is only the work of Satan and everyone excuses themselves [for failing to help the poor] with mention of the 'Red Cross' and the 'Salvation Army' and 'the Well Fare.'"[128] Complicating matters further, he condemned salaries, never mind that receiving one provided one sure way to enrich the poor.[129] Between equating wealth with temptation and railing against insufficient charity, Tijerina in these sermons implicitly seemed to favor only one solution to the problem of poverty: a radical restructuring of society to ensure enough for all.

Having broken with the Assemblies of God over the problem of poverty, Tijerina expected no help on this front from organized religion. Instead, he revamped the biblical metaphor of the church as the bride of Christ to label the modern church "an unfaithful spouse." Originally, he wrote, the church had been an ideal mate who "obeyed her holy husband in everything" and who "strove to please her husband in everything that he ordered." Jesus, Tijerina pointed out, never had a home of his own and was considered a beggar, the poorest of the poor. The true bride of Christ, he insisted, eagerly joined him in his tribulations, grateful to have been lifted out of the darkness. Admired before all women for her good works and modest disposition, this bride of Christ "was content in her possessions." Yet all too soon, Tijerina complained, the church grew tired of constant sacrifice and became "a rebel Church," seduced by power, wealth, and vanity.[130] At this point, Tijerina sounded less like he was scolding lapsed believers and more like he was scolding Mary Escobar for her long-standing complaints about the family's economic insecurity. Yet if Escobar was akin to the poorly behaving bride, then the analogy made Tijerina the groom, Christ himself.

Mention of a badly behaving bride, like Tijerina's reference to the whore of Babylon, revealed his low opinion of women's moral fiber. In *Hallará Fé*, Tijerina repeatedly warned that they were great temptresses. Across the centuries within Christianity, the notion of women as naturally inclined toward backsliding was common enough. Tijerina added to this perspective by arguing that modern-day materialism had destroyed female modesty. He condemned perfumes and cosmetics because adorned women all too easily—and willingly—became "objects of lust, of lasciviousness, of concupiscence, and of adultery."[131] Filled with the desire to be desired, these women not only compromised their own salvation but also the salvation of those who looked upon them with lust. "Woe to women who have been placed as traps to ruin men," Tijerina thundered, adding with an air of disgust, "What adornment do women *not* use?" More rhetorical questions followed. "Perhaps there are men who are clean of heart who are not affected by such women?" And then in a slam against more revealing modes of dress: "Perhaps they [these men] are so clean that they are not affected by female nudity?"[132] In short, Tijerina lambasted contemporary beauty products and fashion styles because he believed that they had increased the likelihood of sexual sin.

Tijerina proposed that female virtue was best protected when women stayed in their place at home. Echoing his earlier opposition to Mary Escobar's job at the drugstore, Tijerina strongly objected to women working outside the home. In one sermon passage, he suggested that an insatiable hunger for more consumer goods prompted fathers to gamble with their daughters' virtue. "[Fathers] put their daughters in the public marketplace, young daughters, who in olden times were in the kitchen or at their needlework [at home], now they can be found in the Kress [the name of a chain drugstore] or in the shops, passing their tender youth in the lowest and most detestable work that a woman can do," he scolded.[133] He advised women to "return to God and do good work." They should also do so quietly. "The woman who speaks as much as her husband must watch her mouth and her honor will be restored to her," he counseled.[134]

Similarly, Tijerina worried that children no longer listened to their parents. That troublesome development Tijerina blamed on the dangers of education. Although Tijerina had once visited libraries and boasted an extensive reading habit, in *Hallará Fé* he disputed the value of secular knowledge. Outside the orbit of their parents' supervision, children at school risked eternal damnation. Referring to compulsory education laws, Tijerina lamented, "Our children have to attend, by force, schools where the . . . [danger of] hell lurks."[135] Specifically, children spent the day in co-educational classrooms "being devoured by haughtiness and lust."[136]

Tijerina likewise disputed the priorities of institutions of higher learning, asking, "Where is the school of justice? Where is the college of mercy?"[137] Book learning did not matter, he asserted, because, with the single exception of the Bible, books amounted to meaningless distractions, given that the world was about to end.[138] Newspapers were even worse because they carried what Tijerina called "announcements for the vanities of life," in other words, advertisements for material goods—like cars, televisions, and radios—that became luxurious pitfalls.[139] In Tijerina's worldview, new inventions all too soon became desirable marketable goods and thus dangerous temptations too. He thus questioned the very notion of scientific progress.[140]

By far the greatest sin that Tijerina laid at the feet of science was the invention and use of weapons of mass destruction. Horrified by the dropping of the atomic bombs in 1945, Tijerina overwhelmingly blamed the United States for the escalating arms race. How a nation that produced and used such weapons could even claim to be a Christian nation was beyond him. "Previously, Christians all gather[ed] to build the atomic bomb, to build airplanes, to fortify the defenses of war. And who among them protests? Who will be able to withstand the result of the preparation [for war]? . . . There is no one to protest and rebel against the deadly work that occupies a people who profess to fear God," he wrote.[141] That war between the two superpowers risked mass annihilation only confirmed the immediacy of Tijerina's apocalyptic visions.

In this regard, Tijerina shared something in common with many of his preacher peers, even as he struck an independent path. Starting in the late 1940s, a religious revival swept across the United States, spurred in part by fears of atomic catastrophe.[142] This revival led to a surge in attendance at worship services and in church expansion, including in evangelical and Pentecostal denominations. By the early 1950s, the Assemblies of God alone had founded some 500 new congregations.[143] The Assemblies of God, however, firmly denounced another aspect of the revival that may have appealed to Tijerina, the Latter Rain movement. Latter Rain Pentecostals asserted that Christianity had lost its zeal, and, like Tijerina, they proclaimed with new vigor that the end times really were approaching. Most intriguing, in a new theological development, Latter Rain folks also believed in the existence of contemporary prophets to hasten the restoration of the Kingdom of God.[144] Quite possibly, Tijerina counted himself among this select group.

Otherwise, Tijerina diverged significantly from his religious contemporaries. First, whether willingly or not, he apparently lacked what many Pentecostals celebrated as within their grasp, specifically, glossolalia and the ability to heal the sick. Latter Rain adherents looked upon these "gifts of the spirit" as proof of the outpouring of the Holy Spirit upon the earth before the Second Coming of Jesus. In his writings, however, Tijerina never mentioned ever speaking in tongues or curing anyone. In contrast, Oral Roberts, who became one of the most famous Pentecostal ministers in the country by the time of his death in 1993, first rose to fame during the post–World War II religious revival as a faith healer.[145]

Tijerina also stood far apart from an incipient prosperity gospel that was then gaining popularity. By the 1950s, constant anxiety associated with intertwined fears of atomic and apocalyptic destruction had prompted some preachers to dispense a more positive and uplifting message, often one with an economic edge. New York City pastor Norman Vincent Peale, for instance, hit the best-seller list by championing the power of positive thinking.[146] Similarly, Roberts promoted "seed faith," a promise that God's blessings for the faithful included not only good health but also economic gain.[147] Certain that material prosperity doomed the nation, Tijerina preferred to blast the capitalist class.

Going one step further, he voiced admiration for the Soviet Union. No opinion that he offered in his collection of sermons placed him more at odds with post–World War II Christianity. In what one scholar termed the "spiritual-industrial complex" of the Cold War, political and religious leaders together condemned the "godless communists."[148] Most famously, Billy Graham, who also rose to fame during the postwar religious revival by conducting enormous evangelical gatherings in stadiums and auditoriums across the country, crusaded not only for Christ but also against communism as the devil's religion, "a malevolent attempt to usurp the sovereignty of God on earth."[149] In an indication of the mainstreaming of their religious tradition, the overwhelming majority of Pentecostal faithful similarly offered a rousing endorsement of the era's anti-communism.[150]

Placing consumerism and greed at the rotten heart of the American way, Tijerina rejected the hyper-patriotism of the 1950s. Unlike the much-persecuted radical Left in the United States during the 1950s, Tijerina never advocated communism or socialism per se. As he once admitted, the one time that he tried to read Marx, the text failed to hold his attention.[151] As a man of faith, moreover, Tijerina's favorable view of the Soviet Union ended where the country's endorsement of atheism began. "I'm not saying that communism can take the place of the government of God nor that it can create a lasting peace much less that Christ is visible in the government of the [Soviets]," Tijerina explained in one of his sermons.[152] To Tijerina, however, nothing occurred by chance. Just as he tried to discern God's plan for himself through portents and dreams, Tijerina also searched for the hand of God at work in human history. He strongly suspected that God had assigned the Soviet Union the task of ushering forth the downfall of the United States. Thus, he pointedly asked in one sermon, "Why have we left God? And why has God lifted up a great enemy against this nation?"[153]

While others might champion the United States as a beacon of liberty, Tijerina knew better for two distinct reasons. At home, he dismissed democracy as overrated: democracy meant freedom, and freedom meant choice, and choice too often meant pursuing pleasure. "The Devil, seeing that the time was ripe and opportune, gave us democracy, under which system we can do whatever we want, and under which system was born the hunger to possess," Tijerina intoned.[154] At the same time, Tijerina also doubted that the United States was spreading democracy and freedom abroad. His antipathy toward the United States therefore extended to the nation's actions on the world stage. Tijerina opposed U.S. entry into the Korean War, which broke out in 1950. He strongly supported Puerto Ricans' independence from their *yanquí* overlords, even going so far as to sympathize with a group of *independistas* who in 1950 tried to assassinate President Harry S. Truman.[155] Disinclined to accept Cold War assumptions that the United States, as compared with the communist Soviet Union, automatically stood on the side of right, Tijerina also was predisposed to question media accounts about the "red enemy."[156]

Tijerina showcased all his divergent Cold War attitudes, as well as his extreme ones regarding female modesty, in an oppositional reading of a 1952 article published in the *Ladies' Home Journal*. "Letters from Moscow" contrasted the prosperous lifestyles of American women to those of their Russian counterparts. The author, Lydia Kirk, the wife of a former American ambassador to the Soviet Union, used the popular women's magazine to paint a dismal picture of Soviet society. Food scarcity, cramped housing, and a dearth of fashionable clothing all afflicted Russian women, she wrote, and even in the best hospitals in Moscow, women gave birth without the benefit of anesthesia.[157] Yet Tijerina, who alone had attended Mary Escobar during several childbirths, dismissed each of Kirk's criticisms. He commented approvingly upon the humble lifestyle of the Russian people. What Kirk viewed as dearth, Tijerina celebrated as freedom from temptation. Never having visited the country, Tijerina had no comment about greater Soviet female participation in the labor force as compared to U.S. women. Instead, Tijerina chided Kirk for not recognizing the "modesty" and "humility" of Russian women. If Russian women wore long and loose dresses in somber and dark colors, Tijerina argued, then such clothing demonstrated their innate "honor" and "decency," especially as compared to vanity-plagued American women.[158]

As Tijerina soon discovered, however, his way of interpreting the world found few takers. Despite, or perhaps because of, his zeal, he proved to be an unpopular preacher. His daughter Rose, who might have been five or six at the time, remembered falling asleep once during one of his endless harangues and hitting her head as she fell backward from the outdoor bench that substituted for a pew.[159] Mary Escobar recalled that Tijerina's preaching might last an entire day.[160] While as a land-grant leader, Tijerina earned acclaim as an orator, as a preacher, if the sheer length of his sermons was not off-putting, the content of his message almost certainly was. At a time of unprecedented prosperity in the United States, which included, for the first time, significant progress for Mexican Americans, he upheld poverty and self-abnegation as the truest signs of holiness.[161] Next to Christ, Tijerina continued to look to Old Testament prophets as models for correct living. As he saw it, these men "did not lack bread because God failed to bless them. [Instead] in times gone by, they voluntarily kept themselves away from those [material] things that have always been the ruin and downfall of the avaricious."[162] After years of depending upon the kindness of strangers to survive, by this measure Tijerina clearly stood in good stead with the Almighty. But he also set a standard that few rushed to embrace.

With some foresight, Tijerina expected his message to fall on deaf ears. "I will be called big fat critic by [some] and fanatical and stupid by others," he acknowledged at one point.[163] As he also recognized, "I know that the man who reprimands is not appreciated on this earth. . . . The same One who put these words in my mouth made me see that there are many who would abhor them."[164] Despite predicting such failure, Tijerina eventually grew disheartened at his meager harvest. In five years of independent ministry, and ten years total of preaching, he had convinced fewer than ten families to join his flock.[165] As he told an interviewer years later, he finally reached the conclusion that "a man could preach the word of God forever and never change a thing."[166] The man named after the King of Kings decided to follow a new course: to retreat into the desert with a few like-minded followers. Soon they considered him a prophet, sent from above.

They called him Iratéo, or Wrath of God.

2

The Prophet

In late 1955, Tijerina and a small group of devoted followers pooled their meager resources to buy 160 desert acres some six miles outside of Casa Grande, Arizona. With only the outline of some low-slung mountains in the distance to break the monotony, the harsh landscape mostly featured gray-green shrubs, stunted trees, and hard-packed earth. In this place, which he later described as "the wildest spot I could find," Tijerina sought to build a community where he and his followers "wouldn't trouble others and we wouldn't be bothered ourselves."[1] He named the settlement Valle de Paz, or the Valley of Peace.

Working "like ants moving the earth," Tijerina recalled that he and the other men literally used their hands to begin to carve out a new life for themselves and their families. They constructed subterranean homes, using the hoods and trunk lids of abandoned cars that they found at local dumps to reinforce the ceilings.[2] It took Tijerina probably two months to carve out a room-sized bunker for his wife and children, deep enough to allow everyone to stand upright.[3] Determined to make their religious utopia a reality, Valle de Paz members pooled their money together to stock a common pantry. "Our lives in the Valley of Peace were simple," Tijerina asserted years later, but together residents strove to create a "paradise."[4]

The following spring, a torrential rainfall threatened to undo all their progress. At the time, Tijerina was away in Visalia, California, where he had been invited to preach at a local church and hoped to find new recruits for his utopian experiment. A phone call from a Valle de Paz resident informed him that massive flooding had swept through the community. The water had completely inundated the bunker that housed Mary Escobar and their children and had swept away the family's possessions. His wife was now living beneath a tree with all five of their youngsters, including a newborn, whom she had just delivered, again with only Tijerina's help, the week before. Drenched and desperate, Escobar awaited her husband's return.[5]

Upon hearing this bad news, "I cried, I cried," Tijerina remembered years later. He was moved to tears not by concern over the plight of his family but by worry about what this tragic turn of events portended about his relationship with God. He thought, "My God, how could you do this to me? For ten years, I have dedicated myself to you and this is how you reward me?"[6] That night he received an answer in the form of another vision, one that he infused with so much significance that Tijerina always referred to it as a "revelation" or "super-dream" and included it among the major milestones (*pilares*) in his life.[7] More than fifty years later, he could still recount details of the dream. "Three angels flew down from space, one after the other, coming down at an angle toward me," he recalled in 2010. "They had come to take me to an ancient kingdom." In the dream, Mary Escobar grudgingly asked the angels, "Why him?" The angels responded, "He is the only one who can do this mission."[8] In this 2010 version, Tijerina portrayed Escobar as particularly shrewish. Also new was that she was sweeping, an archetypical domestic task. Literally and metaphorically, Tijerina had put his former wife firmly in her place.

Otherwise, his recollection paralleled almost verbatim the description of this vision that he had offered many times before. The dream-Tijerina asked the angels, "What is the mission?," and the angels answered, "Secretary." Before Tijerina awoke, he said, he experienced the sensation of being lifted through the air to that ancient kingdom. He saw tall pines and a cemetery of frozen horses. He entered a walled city. Finally, he met an old man dressed in white robes who told him that Tijerina was to reign over the kingdom. "Above you, only me," said the figure. In 2010, when asked if the figure was God, Tijerina only smiled coyly and shrugged his shoulders as if to say the answer was so obvious that he did not need to speak it.[9]

The dream account sheds light on the significance of the Arizona experiment, one of the most hidden chapters of Tijerina's life. Most important, in his dream, heavenly figures communicated directly with him. Similarly, in Valle de Paz, Tijerina claimed to have direct knowledge of God's will because, as he told his followers, he was no longer a preacher but a prophet. The distinction mattered. Whereas preachers proclaim the word of God as found in the Bible, prophets profess to discern the will of God through divine revelation. As the prophet Iratéo, Tijerina launched Valle de Paz with the great hope of building a haven for believers who embraced the values and priorities that he outlined in *¿Hallará Fé en la Tierra?* In Valle de Paz, he would make those Old Testament dreams of finding the promised land, a land where God's will and justice prevailed, come true.

Yet the two years that Tijerina spent in Valle de Paz marked an important turning point in his life. Conveniently, at a moment when the future of Valle de Paz seemed most precarious, the angels in his dream handed Tijerina a new mission. As Tijerina later interpreted his dream, the pine trees evoked northern New Mexico's forests, and the frozen horses, which in his dream were beginning to thaw, signified individual land grants that were awakening to a new surge of activism. As for his angel-appointed role as "secretary," Tijerina heard a direct order from on high that he needed to investigate and record the true history of the land grants.[10]

What the super-dream failed to elucidate was how Tijerina should navigate this transition. In Valle de Paz, Iratéo constantly collided with local residents, school officials, law enforcement, and, eventually, some of his own followers. Dashed hopes all around made these years of sorrow and pain for many residents. Under these adverse conditions, Tijerina displayed a limited capacity for self-criticism and an even more limited tolerance for dissent. Yet he also exhibited a skill at survival and a knack for reinvention. All of these traits stayed with him long after he fled the state.

THE VALLEY OF TEARS

When Tijerina moved to the Casa Grande Valley with a few families and big dreams, the area was still mostly rural and agricultural. Once home to the ancient Hohokam people, the Jesuit missionary Father Eusebio Kino had given the arid and shallow valley its name in 1694 after seeing ruins of once thriving villages. He called one especially impressive structure the Great House, or Casa Grande.[11] By the time that Tijerina and his followers arrived, the introduction of irrigation systems in the twentieth century had transformed this section of desert between Tucson and Phoenix into a leading area producer of pima cotton, named after the Native American group that first cultivated it. Nearby fields thus provided work when needed for Tijerina and his followers. Some six miles away from Valle de Paz, the town of Casa Grande boasted a population of just over 4,000.[12]

Valle de Paz residents sought a measure of isolation to create their vision of an ideal community. In *Mi Lucha por la Tierra*, Tijerina explained that the families who joined him deliberately "left behind the cities with all their vanity and corruption" to live where "neither the church nor the school would condition the minds of our children."[13] Tijerina fondly recalled how residents of Valle de Paz sought to "create a community of justice and harmony, with our language and our customs. A place—well, a *pueblo*."[14] The switch to Spanish was telling. Tijerina and at least some of his followers took inspiration from the Mexican countryside. According to Simón Serna, one of Tijerina's California recruits, Tijerina's followers hoped "to prepare a *pueblo* of God so that when the wrath of God starts to come we are all united."[15] With even more specificity, Serna stated that Valle de Paz residents intended to model their holy city after "*un povladito tipo Mexic[an]o*," that is, a little Mexican-style pueblo (*pueblecito*).[16]

Tijerina's work on behalf of the Kingdom of God was always ethnic-specific. Although he referred to race just once in *Hallaré Fé*, as Tijerina later confessed, "At the time I believed all Anglos to be the enemy."[17] His antipathy clearly spilled out in his condemnation of the privileged rich. Conversely, impoverished Spanish speakers like himself understood through bitter experience that the divide between rich and poor in the United States was a racial divide as well. Mostly poor farm laborers, they were not the ones luxuriating in a sea of consumer goods. Nor were they in danger of becoming members of any educated elite. Serna, for example, always wrote forcibly but phonetically and with minimal use of grammatical notations. For all these reasons, by the time they decided to found Valle de Paz, Tijerina's followers could take perverse pride, if pride were not a sin, in their poverty and lowly status. They led lives that rejected the white-dominated wealth and wickedness that they saw flourishing elsewhere. To them and to their prophet, Valle de Paz offered an escape not only from modern society but from the Anglo-dominated world too.

Other religious utopias dot American history. Perhaps best known are the Shaker separatist communities in New England founded before the Civil War to uphold the values of celibacy, simplicity, and communalism.[18] In 1847, Brigham Young led his fellow Latter-day Saints into the desert of Utah in order to build a faith-based society free from outside harassment and interference.[19] In its infancy, Pentecostalism similarly flirted with utopianism. In 1900, an early church leader launched a Christian city outside of Chicago called Zion, whose residents eagerly awaited the restoration of God's kingdom.[20] Arguably, Valle de Paz also foreshadowed the hippie communes of the 1960s and 1970s. Although Tijerina was never going to endorse the sexual revolution, the countercultural youth closely echoed his rejection of modern consumer society and similarly advocated returning to the land. Despite outwardly questioning hierarchy, moreover, many of these countercultural communes were organized around the vision of a single charismatic male leader.[21]

In the Valle de Paz, Tijerina fit the bill of an Old Testament prophet. In 1946 in California, he had gone into a cave like Elijah; nine years later, he now led his followers into the desert like Moses.[22] In accord with Max Weber's classic definition, Tijerina had rejected formal religion by leaving the Assemblies of God, had eschewed monetary gain by giving away all his belongings, and had experienced dream revelations. Most important, he wielded a certain measure of charisma through his "vital, emotional preaching."[23] How else was he able to convince his followers that they could transform a small patch of desert into a holy land?

As their prophet, Tijerina took the name Iratéo, a name that was neither Spanish nor Latin but one that he insisted meant "the wrath of God." His followers believed that Tijerina's new status mandated their respect and obedience. "We are at your orders, Prophet of God, Iratéo, precious rock for the poor and humble of this world," Serna assured Tijerina in a 1961 letter. "How much I feel in my heart your words."[24] Serna was offering the highest praise. To label Tijerina "a rock" suggested the pontifical image of Peter, the rock upon which Jesus built his church. Another Valle de Paz resident, Rudy Marez, consistently referred to Tijerina as an "angel" of the Lord.[25] Indicative of his great faith in Tijerina, Marez and his wife, Sadie, also sold a piece of their own property in Fruita, Colorado, to provide the bulk of the money to purchase the acreage for Valle de Paz.[26] In return, Tijerina called male followers like Serna and Marez his *valientes*, meaning brave ones. Not all of his recruits were men, however. The justice-for-the-poor emphasis of *Hallará Fé*, along with Tijerina's ability "to explain the word of God," greatly appealed to a California farmworker named Maria Moreno, according to her eldest daughter. Against her husband's wishes, Moreno decided to relocate her entire family, which then probably numbered ten children, to partake in the Valle de Paz experiment.[27]

Unfortunately for community members, outside forces soon intruded upon their attempt to build an earthly "paradise." First, state education officials insisted that Valle de Paz residents comply with Arizona state law and send their children to the local public school, which was a three-mile bus ride away. The community had been founded in large part to escape this specific mandate in accord with the warnings contained within *Hallará Fé*. In his memoir, Tijerina reiterated this primary objection: public schools undermined "the unity and discipline of the family" by introducing the "perversion" of sex education.[28] According to Mary Escobar, a shocking crime that occurred shortly after the founding of Valle de Paz increased the determination of residents to keep their children removed from the outside world: a young girl who lived nearby was attacked, raped, and beaten one morning while waiting for the school bus.[29] Assigned in 1956 to investigate the lack of school attendance by Valle de Paz children, Sheriff George D. Pickerel recalled that Tijerina "told me that he was perfectly capable of teaching the children and they would never attend public schools."[30] In his memoir, Tijerina lamented that the ongoing conflict with the school board was most responsible for converting what had been "our paradise of peace into a concentration camp."[31]

Local landowners posed another problem, according to Tijerina. Specifically, he recalled, they did not like that Valle de Paz operated as a refuge for other marginalized folks who called this stretch of desert home. These included Native Americans who occupied reservation land nearby; African Americans who lived in a tiny nearby hamlet named Randolph, founded by Dust Bowl refugees; and ethnic Mexicans, both U.S.-born and immigrant.[32] A 1952 letter to the *Casa Grande Dispatch* about a recent trip to the city dump revealed the depth of poverty in the area among all three groups, as one family's discards provided treasure for others. As the letter writer sympathetically noted, "There were Indians who pounced on the boxes. There were Mexicans who looked for bottles and other things. A little Negro boy grabbed my son's old tryke. It had three wheels missing but it brought a smile to his face."[33] In his memoir, Tijerina maintained that he lent a helping hand to all but that he earned a reputation for "riling up the Mexicans" in particular because he demanded justice for braceros, agricultural workers temporarily imported from Mexico under a binational agreement. Despite the existence of contracts meant to protect them, braceros often faced harsh working conditions and low pay. In Arizona, as elsewhere, they accused local growers of cheating and mistreating them.[34] Still operating as an *abogado sin libros*, Tijerina spoke up on their behalf.[35]

Before long, and not coincidentally, according to Tijerina, Valle de Paz residents confronted a rash of vandalism. Problems began when local youth from a nearby ranch—sons of an aggrieved rancher who hired braceros, Tijerina contended—took to riding horses across the property and over the roofs of the underground homes. Once, the pounding hoofs caused dirt to drift down from the roof of the Tijerina home and upon their family meal, Tijerina wrote; another time, while Valle de Paz residents were out picking cotton, these rides succeeded in causing two other bunker roofs to collapse completely. Not content with this amount of destruction, vandals also burned down two aboveground structures along with everything inside them.[36] Mary Escobar similarly remembered widespread opposition from outsiders to Valle de Paz. "Everyone was against us. They did not like that we were very private there," she recalled.[37] Although the local newspaper failed to provide contemporary coverage of Valle de Paz, the *Casa Grande Dispatch* made clear that a negative reaction to it still lingered years later. Writing after Tijerina had made headlines as a land-grant activist, the newspaper observed that Tijerina had been well known in the area during the 1950s in part because he had led such a strange group. Residents of Valle de Paz had "lived in solitude and had little relation with the outside world," according to the newspaper. Still, outsiders could not help but notice that some two dozen people were living in the middle of the desert in what the paper described as "shacks, weird leaf-covered caves, and other rudimentary dwellings."[38] The estimate suggests a rapid decline in the number of residents from Tijerina's original ten or so families.

In fact, Valle de Paz quickly became Valle de Lágrimas, a valley of tears. Sadie Marez, whose husband, Rudy, was a faithful valiente, first offered that play of words, according to Rose Tijerina, but the sentiment struck her as accurate. A little girl of six and seven during this time, her perspective varied greatly from her father's. Instead of seeing Valle de Paz as a potential paradise, she always equated the Arizona experiment with "ugliness," beginning with the harsh desert climate. In addition, Rose Tijerina dreaded those rare moments of interaction with the outside world. "My dad had all the women wear these long dresses, long all the way to the floor," she recalled, adding that the women and girls also covered their heads. As a result, she complained that "my dad and the [other] men would take us women to the store to buy groceries [and] everybody would stare at us, because we were not with the fashions and to top it off [we were] dressed like way back in Pilgrim times." Rose Tijerina hated the clothing not so much because it was out of style but because it attracted so much attention. "I felt so humiliated," she recalled.[39] Years later, Reies Tijerina insisted that the women in the community dressed the way they wanted to dress.[40] Mary Escobar concurred. Looking back, she voiced no complaints about the ankle-length dresses that the women wore.[41]

When asked what she thought of Tijerina being perceived as a prophet named Iratéo, however, Escobar professed ignorance. While seemingly implausible for a wife not to know of the revered status of her husband, Escobar's comments were in keeping with Tijerina's many admonishments about women remaining subordinate to men. As Escobar explained, the men of the community were always huddled together talking among themselves, leaving the women out. In times of crisis, all the residents would meet together to ponder their next steps, Escobar said. Yet if she dared to speak at these gatherings, her husband would typically snap at her in front of everyone, "Who asked you [to offer an opinion]?" Her husband seemed no more inclined to obtain information from her than he was to share information with her. Still, she recalled fully supporting the community's values and enjoying living with like-minded folks. "I was very happy to be surrounded by a lot of brothers and sisters [in faith]," Escobar remembered. "We all believed in God in the same way."[42]

Escobar also recalled that Valle de Paz represented a marked improvement for herself and her children as far as their living conditions. Most important to her, the time that she spent in Valle de Paz meant an end finally to imposing upon others. After years of constant travel, "I had a permanent place, so I was very content and gave thanks to God," she said, adding, "It says a lot to have your own place in which to raise your kids, to not have any one going around giving you dirty looks or anything." Thus, when asked whether Valle de Paz was peaceful for her, Escobar responded with an immediate "For me, it was. I had a home!"[43] Her comments indirectly underscored how chaotic her life and the lives of her children must have been in the years preceding. The ability to sustain herself and her family, even at the most minimal standard, offered a sense of peace.

For desert living was anything but uneventful for a family with small children. Escobar summed up the time she spent in Arizona as "me and the kids in the middle of the rattlesnakes." Compelled by other obligations, Tijerina was often away from Valle de Paz. He was gone so much, in fact, that he never got around to building an aboveground structure for his family. On occasion, Escobar and the children were able to use a structure that another family had vacated temporarily. Most of the time, however, they stayed in that underground bunker. Being underground, however, meant living with the likelihood of a snake inside their home. Years later, Escobar could still remember the exact tally of snakes killed during the community's short tenure: eighty-seven. One even appeared shortly after she had given birth in that underground room attended only by her husband. Tijerina saw a snake appear near the head of the bed where Escobar and his newborn daughter lay. He quickly moved the pair out of the way and killed it.[44] An admirer of Islam since his Bible college days, Tijerina named his new daughter Ira de Alá, that is, another version of "Wrath of God," by using the Arabic "Allah" ("Alá" in Spanish).[45]

Visiting California immediately following the birth, Tijerina was devastated to hear news of the flood's devastation. Yet the super-dream that he experienced that night erased his sense of defeat and instilled within him a renewed sense of hope and of destiny. "From that day, I began to see many new things and comprehend other things that before I had not understood," Tijerina later wrote. "From then on I felt alive in my breast the weight of the new mission that they [the angels] had just given me. Now, my life had a purpose."[46] As he understood it, he had been chosen by God to further land-grant justice. Yet where this new mission left his old mission of creating a peaceful valley was something that Tijerina was going to have to figure out.

TWO MISSIONS

That work started immediately. In the wake of the flood, Tijerina's most pressing task was rescuing his wife and children and earning some money to get by. Returning to Arizona the day after he learned of their plight, he decided to travel immediately with his flock to Fruita, Colorado, in time to harvest beets. As Tijerina wrote in his memoir, while there he saw a magnificent rainbow appear on an otherwise clear day, an anomaly that he interpreted as another sign, literally from the heavens, to him. Although Tijerina later wrote that he "saved in his heart" the precise significance of the rainbow to him, as a student of the Bible, he was acutely aware that God's promise to Noah, after the flood, came in the form of the rainbow. Convinced that God was sending him messages, Tijerina spent much of his time in Fruita surveying his entire life and, in doing so, kept returning to the times he had spent in northern New Mexico learning about how Spanish speakers in the area had been pushed off the land that their ancestors had once owned.[47]

He decided to travel there with a handful of his valientes in June 1956, a trip that marked the beginning of his new crusade. Tijerina first met with several men who were members of the Penitente Brotherhood, a lay religious organization that had protected nuevomexicano faith practices after 1848 despite strong opposition from the Catholic Church in the United States.[48] As his memoir made clear, older Penitentes became his first teachers in understanding what Tijerina accurately termed the "long, sad, and violent history" of land usurpation. "I felt a stab in my heart," he later recalled. "These humble elders had a holy, just, and sacred cause." In return, Tijerina remembered telling everyone whom he met in New Mexico that, although he knew "absolutely nothing" about land-grant affairs, he was willing to travel to Mexico to learn all he could in support of people's claims. Looking back, Tijerina also portrayed the Penitentes as timid and beaten down, the result of their "conditioning" by an Anglo-American educational system. He recalled them complaining, "We have asked Washington and heaven for justice for more than 100 years, but no one hears our pleas."[49]

According to his memoir, Tijerina concluded that he needed to dispel not only their fear but also their ignorance. They were confused about the 1848 peace treaty that concluded the war, he wrote, telling him, "We thought Guadalupe Hidalgo was a man who had been president of Mexico."[50] That last comment directly clashed with Tijerina's admission that New Mexicans were his first and best teachers. It was entirely in keeping with his newfound sense of mission, however. Eager to get started, Tijerina returned to Fruita only long enough to arrange for his followers to head back to Arizona while he traveled south with his wife and children. Dropping his family off with Ramón and Esther Tijerina and their children in San Antonio, Tijerina continued on to Mexico City.[51]

The trip instilled a sense of awe regarding the country's long history. As Tijerina later wrote after visiting the ancient ruins of Teotihuacán, just outside of Mexico City and already abandoned for centuries by the time of the arrival of the Europeans, "I felt like a stranger on this great planet. It was so old, and I did not know the history of my own people much less the history of the world."[52] While in Mexico City, Tijerina also toured Chapultepec Castle, where young Mexican cadets had famously thrown themselves off a balcony rather than surrender to superior American forces during the U.S.-Mexican War. Probably the most meaningful excursion to him, however, was the visit he took to Villa de Guadalupe Hidalgo, the tiny village now enveloped by Mexico City, where representatives from both countries had signed the document that ended the state of war between their two nations.[53]

Tijerina was extraordinarily pleased to find a copy of the Treaty of Guadalupe Hidalgo within a volume of international law that he discovered at one of Mexico City's open-air markets. For a mere twenty-five cents, Tijerina now had the luxury of poring over his own personal copy of the treaty, as he put it, "letter by letter."[54] Indeed, demonstrating what religious studies scholar Rudy V. Busto termed an "obsession with text-based authority," Tijerina scrutinized the treaty with the same intensity with which he read the Bible.[55] The treaty clearly spoke of land rights. Article 8 promised that the property of former Mexican citizens was to be "inviolably respected." Article 9 stated that the conquered population was to "be maintained and protected in the free enjoyment of their liberty and property."[56] Also of special significance to the preacher-cum-prophet, representatives of the United States and Mexico had signed the treaty "in the name of the Almighty God."[57]

At the massive Archivo General de la Nación, Tijerina made another important find: the multivolume *Recopilación de las Leyes de las Indias* (1680), which compiled a total of 6,500 Spanish laws used to govern the Americas over centuries of colonial administration.[58] Again investing the written word with overwhelming authority, Tijerina read the Laws of the Indies to understand the privileges of Spanish colonists, the proper formation of towns and settlements, and the regulations regarding conduct with indigenous people. For years to come, Tijerina was to invoke Ordenanza 99, which declared in 1543 that all settlers in the Americas were to become *hidalgos* (literally *hijos de algo*), that is, minor noblemen with land. In addition, he was taken with a 1514 law that sanctioned intermarriage between indigenous people and Iberians. In settler colonial nations, intermarriage often serves as part of the logic of eliminating the native.[59] Yet Tijerina admired the Spanish crown for promoting the familial coming together of the conquerors and the conquered.[60] Later, as Tijerina sought to navigate between competing nuevomexicano and Native American land claims, this law grew increasingly important to him.

By his own account, Tijerina stayed in Mexico until January 1957. He left behind a classic, and flattering to him, complication in the form of a young woman who had grown enamored of him. As Tijerina asserted in his published memoir, during his months in Mexico City, he lived with a family whom he had known since his Pentecostal days. During his stay, he grew close to a young woman of twenty, a niece of the family. At first, he saw their relationship as one of shared dedication to the same land-grant cause. "It was as if she wanted to embody the visions and dreams that had brought me to Mexico," Tijerina recalled. Unbeknownst to him, he wrote, she also had fallen in love. As his awareness of her "irrational love" for him grew, Tijerina experienced what he described as an "internal conflict within my heart" for this unnamed woman, aggravated no doubt by her being, as he described, a great mestiza beauty who exhibited "all the characteristics of the Indian women painted in almanacs and calendars in Mexico." When he left her, he promised to return to Mexico, and implicitly to her, although he knew even then that "in my heart there was no room for competitors." Tijerina made clear in his memoir that by competition he referred not to his wife and children but to his "mission": to secure the "liberty and justice for my people."[61] It was this mission that he now described as "holy, just, and sacred."[62]

On his return to Arizona, Tijerina collected his family as well as his brother Margarito from San Antonio. In later interviews, Reies Tijerina described his older brother as a hard worker, a slow learner, and a troubled loner.[63] That he would invite Margarito to join him revealed a powerful sense of familial loyalty and fraternal responsibility shared by the Tijerina brothers. Convicted of manslaughter in 1947, Margarito Tijerina had killed a man during a drunken brawl in Indiana. His prison records indicate that Indiana authorities expected little better from a man they described as a "feeble-minded Mexican" who "had lived the life of an alley cat; drinking; running with bad women." His incarceration, they concluded, "was the inevitable result of his way of life and his low intelligence."[64] As much as racially charged notions of criminality and depravity infested Margarito Tijerina's prison records, the same records revealed that his behavior in prison (and away from alcohol) was exemplary. Once shipped to Texas in early 1950, however, Margarito Tijerina resumed his drinking and worse. By the time that Reies Tijerina stopped by Texas on his return trip from Mexico, his older brother was a suspect in three serious crimes: a homicide, an assault on a female, and a case of arson.[65] Meanwhile Reies Tijerina was a proud teetotaler without a criminal record (yet). A loyal brother, Reies invited Margarito to join him in Valle de Paz.

The extended Tijerina family stayed in Valle de Paz for only a short while, however, before Tijerina abruptly decided that he wanted to return to New Mexico. Still listening to their prophet, the remaining Valle de Paz residents agreed to follow. The ragtag group arrived there with little money and no plan in February 1957.[66] As Tijerina recounted, he and his followers traveled as far as Gobernador, a ghost town that sat on the edge of the Carson National Forest, about seventy miles by road west of Tierra Amarilla. Hungry and enduring "bitter, severe, cold weather," in Mary Escobar's recollection, they took shelter in an abandoned church.[67] In desperation, Rudy Marez and Simón Serna, as trusted valientes, went out into the mountains to look for food and, according to Tijerina, found the carcass of a deer.[68]

Fortunately, more aid arrived after Tijerina encountered an older man named Manuel Trujillo, who owned a ranch nearby. Shocked to hear that entire families were in such desperate straits, Trujillo gave Tijerina fifteen dollars to buy food. With his permanent home closer to the Colorado border, he also allowed the group to use his otherwise empty ranch house. Considering Trujillo "a guardian angel" for his generosity, Tijerina also appreciated the older man's knowledge about local history.[69] Trujillo claimed a share of the Tierra Amarilla land grant.[70] Through Trujillo, Tijerina began to renew and expand his acquaintances with land-grant folks during this trip.[71]

Financial necessity, however, soon compelled the Valle de Paz group to return to their 160 acres—as apparently did a desire to stay one step ahead of the law. Disputing the assertion that Serna and Marez had discovered a frozen carcass, U.S. Forest Service rangers had arrested the pair for killing a deer, presumably on charges of hunting without a license or out of season.[72] Or as Tijerina later put it, Forest Service rangers "had no room in their hearts for mercy or justice" and thus refused to consider that the deer had already been dead, that his two followers in New Mexico had only scavenged the meat.[73] According to Richard Gardner, who compiled one of the earliest accounts of the Alianza and its leader, other problems brewed. The arrival of this group of strangers in the town of Lumberton (where Manuel Trujillo had his permanent home) aroused curiosity and then suspicion. A screenwriter by profession, Gardner stated that the men who traveled with Tijerina stood out because they wore long, white robes, sported long beards, and called themselves the Heralds of Peace, hailing as they did from a place called the Valley of Peace.[74] The description may have been more fanciful than actual: neither Mary Escobar nor Rose Tijerina, for example, remembered any long robes. They did remember that all the men tried to grow beards, some more successfully than others, apparently inspired by Leviticus 19:27, which forbade the trimming of beards.[75] (As a preacher, Tijerina had offered that a man's face without a beard was as bad as a woman's face covered in cosmetics.)[76] Yet Gardner also provided a reason for the group's swift departure from New Mexico. "A series of petty thefts appeared to coincide with the comings and goings of *los barbudos* [the bearded ones]," he wrote. The local sheriff launched an investigation before deciding that he lacked sufficient evidence to make any arrests.[77]

Arizona officials, however, reached a different conclusion.

LEAVING ARIZONA

On March 19, 1957, the Pinal County sheriff's office in Arizona arrested Reies Tijerina, his brother Margarito, and a recent recruit from northern New Mexico named Sevedeo Martínez on charges of grand theft. The previous night, a local rancher had reported that the tires on two of his vehicles were missing. Deputies found a distinctive set of tire tracks leading to the Valle de Paz settlement, where they discovered not only the missing property but several items marked USFS (U.S. Forest Service), including a first aid kit, batteries, and two canvas tarps. Further investigation yielded saws, axes, canteens, grinders, and pans and plates, all stamped USFS.[78] On April 5, authorities filed additional grand theft charges against all three men.[79] Once arrested, none had the money to post bail. To the contrary, Martínez had exactly one cent in his billfold at the time of his arrest.[80]

In his memoir, Tijerina accused the rancher of filing a false report. This man was the father of the misbehaving teens, he wrote, and had sought to cause trouble for the people who had accused his children of vandalism.[81] Still, Tijerina stayed in the county jail in nearby Florence until mid-June, when a superior court judge dismissed all the charges for lack of any evidence linking the three men directly to the stolen items.[82] Martínez was released too. Margarito Tijerina, however, remained behind bars because leaving Texas had violated the conditions of his parole. Remarkably, Reies Tijerina risked his own freedom in an apparent attempt to break his brother out of jail the following month.

"Soap-Slick Jail Breaker Foiled in Pinal County," read the *Tucson Daily Citizen* headline on July 8, 1957.[83] The newspaper named the jail breaker as Antonio Diaz but did not clarify whether he was a resident of Valle de

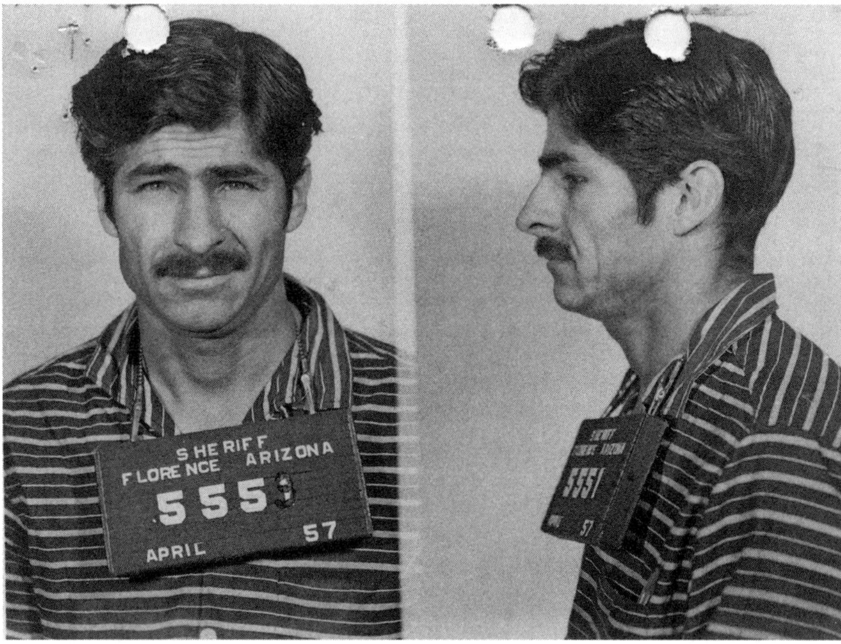

Tijerina's April 1957 mug shot from Florence, Arizona, the site of the Pinal County jail, where he spent three months on charges of grand theft after deputy sheriffs found stolen tires as well as U.S. Forest Service items in the religious community that he founded, Valle de Paz, outside of Casa Grande, Arizona. (Box 1, folder 1, Alfonso Sánchez Papers, Center for Southwest Research, University of New Mexico, Albuquerque)

Paz. He may well have been, given his close relationship to the Tijerinas. According to the sheriff's report, the incarcerated Diaz, using smuggled hacksaw blades, had cut through one of the bars covering a jailhouse window and managed to squeeze through the resulting eleven-inch-wide opening after making his body slippery with soap. As cutting through the bar had occurred bit by bit over the course of several days and possibly weeks, Diaz had also used the soap to help affix the bar into place each day. After all that effort, Diaz enjoyed the briefest taste of liberty. Sheriff's deputies, who had learned of the plot in advance, arrested Diaz almost as soon as he was outside. Another accomplice, Margarito Tijerina, evidently never even left his cell. Deputies also arrested Reies Tijerina, whom they found nearby sitting behind the wheel of a waiting car.[84] In his memoir, Tijerina again insisted that he had never tried to bust his brother or anyone else out of jail but instead was the victim of more false accusations.[85]

In this case, not only did police and news reports tell a different tale, so did Mary Escobar. Barred as a woman from her husband's inner circle of confidants, Escobar could not recall much about Tijerina's legal woes except that the police appeared to follow him from New Mexico to Arizona. She did, however, remember those instances when her husband's problems intersected with her life and the lives of her children. She angrily recalled the events of Mother's Day 1957 when she had gone to visit her husband during his ninety-day stay. She brought him a basket of fried chicken that another Valle de Paz couple (also named Martínez) had cooked for him. Little did Escobar know that they had slipped some hacksaw blades beneath the food. The timing suggests that the original plan called for Reies Tijerina to make a break for freedom too. Only later did Escobar realize her unwitting participation in the escape attempt. "I wanted to die," she recalled when realization finally dawned. She resented being drawn into criminal activity. "The Martínezes made that arrangement with your dad," Mary Escobar told Rose Tijerina in 2006.[86]

In trouble with the law again, Tijerina jumped bail rather than face trial on the jailbreak charges. According to Escobar, Manuel Trujillo of New Mexico, the man whom Tijerina had called a "guardian angel," lent Tijerina money to post bail as he awaited trial. She recalled Tijerina rushing home and saying to her, "Let's go. Let's go." His lawyer had just told him he was going to be sent to prison if he did not leave immediately, she remembered him saying.[87] In his memoir, Tijerina maintained that his lawyer had advised him to flee Arizona because local hostility toward the Valle de Paz community had intensified to such a level that Tijerina's life was in actual danger.[88] In particular, Tijerina cited a nefarious connection between the developers of a planned community called Arizona City, which was about to be built, and his continuing legal troubles as further proof of his persecution. Yet the developers had the option of buying the Valle de Paz land, which they in fact did a few years later. Much more likely, Tijerina simply wished to avoid conviction and more incarceration.[89] As the county sheriff noted, referring to Tijerina as "subject," "The above-named subject was out on a $1,000 bond, appeared for jury trial, and when court recessed for noon, subject jumped bail and never returned."[90]

By then, Rose Tijerina maintained, most community members had lost faith in their leader. Although only a child at the time, she remembered the lack of residents. While her father was in jail, she recalled, her mother had no choice but to work in the fields to earn money to support the family, leaving Rose and her siblings to stay with an elderly couple who were among the few community members remaining. According to Rose

Tijerina, the old man sexually molested her repeatedly during that three-month period. She was too ashamed to say anything at the time to either parent and instead just felt "like the dirty one . . . [like] this very ugly person."[91] Granted that the death of the couple years before rendered Rose Tijerina's recollection both uncontested and uncontestable, the disjuncture between her account of molestation and the community's constant emphasis on sexual morality was both jarring and familiar. By virtue of living in Valle de Paz, residents conveyed their agreement with a strict moral code. Yet the phenomenon of champions of family values becoming embroiled in sexual scandal is common enough. These accusations, were not, moreover, the only indications that Valle de Paz had become a valley of tears.

Mary Escobar recalled how Tijerina's incarceration affected the family. Left with five children to support, she said, she had no choice but to apply for government aid for the first time in her life. The county supplied a small sum that supplemented her field wages. Furthermore, while her husband was in Florence in jail, Escobar began to retrieve the family mail that came to a local post office box address, a task that usually fell to Tijerina himself. She was encouraged to do so by other *hermanas* who, as she put it in 2006, wanted her to "open her eyes." Escobar said that they were already partially open because a love letter from Mexico had arrived directly at the house not long before. Escobar did not share details but merely offered, "That letter did not come from a Christian woman." Worse, at the local post office, she found many more letters. Escobar said that when she asked Tijerina about these letters after he was released from jail, he got so angry that "he wanted to burn my face." Rose Tijerina remembered a similar violent altercation. After her mother confronted her father, she said, "My dad grabbed my mother's braids and he had the idea of trying to put her face on the wooden stove we had. David and I were grabbing him. We were little, but we were grabbing him as best we could." Pulled away from his wife, Tijerina ordered Escobar to leave, Rose Tijerina recalled. Escobar added that she did pack a suitcase but got only as far as the highway before deciding that, even if she managed to reach her mother's house in Texas, she would be leaving the children alone with Tijerina, whose number one priority had never been child care. Escobar turned around.[92]

Letters that Simón Serna wrote at the time provide additional evidence that Tijerina betrayed Escobar's trust and violated the law. Initially, at least some valientes believed that the best course of action for Tijerina in the face of his mounting legal troubles was to flee Arizona.[93] In *Mi Lucha*, Tijerina specifically credited Serna with helping support him and his family once Tijerina became a fugitive from Arizona law. The generosity was even more remarkable given that Serna had his own family of nine children to feed.[94] The support evidently continued for years. As late as July 1961, Serna sent a telegram to "Roy López," one of the false names that Tijerina adopted while a fugitive, with the apologetic words "No pude más [I could not (send) more]," a clear reference to a monetary donation.[95] Yet Serna clearly thought he was helping sustain his prophet only until Valle de Paz could be reestablished. Apparently Tijerina did not discourage that belief, as Serna revealed in a letter dated November 1962. Long after Tijerina had turned his attention completely to land-grant affairs, Serna was still detailing plans for bringing back a religious community in the desert. The now-scattered population of Valle de Paz could regroup, build a successful pueblo, and thus escape the wrath of God, Serna wrote, if only the faithful dug a deeper well, built stronger adobe houses, and planted a profitable carrot crop![96]

However slowly, it finally dawned on Serna that the man he had been financially supporting as his prophet had moved on to another mission. Although the quantities of money involved may have been small, the deceit was thorough. Even more troubling to Serna, he and the other valientes, whom he referred to as "the sons of the Kingdom," had risked their own salvation by performing criminal acts to support Tijerina while he was a fugitive. Serna specifically regretted stealing $153 from a gas station.[97] In January 1963, just one month before Tijerina officially founded a land-grant organization called the Alianza Federal de Mercedes, Serna wrote a series of letters that captured his deep sense of betrayal by a man whom he had once considered a prophet. Referring specifically to the time that Valle de Paz residents spent in New Mexico in early 1957, Serna wrote, "You made us steal, [you said that] God told you in Gobernador not to work and you started stealing from the Forest Service," continuing, "You said that we weren't sinning against God but against the rich man." Serna also alluded to a failed political aspect to Tijerina's original mission. "You said that God had spoken to you and that you were going to go to the White House to denounce the iniquity of this nation," he complained, but that never happened.[98]

Serna spoke, moreover, confident that God was on his side and not on Tijerina's. He too had just had a dream in which "God had removed you

[Tijerina] from your place of guiding his pueblo toward his Kingdom" and given Serna the job instead. To Serna, Tijerina was no prophet but "a hypocrite, son of the devil, [and] enemy of the justice of God." The ultimate proof for Serna: Tijerina had broken the spirit of "the woman who helped you in every way that she could." He warned Tijerina to "leave behind the carnal knowledge that comes from the devil and in which you have enmeshed yourself" and pointed out the hypocrisy of Tijerina preaching against adultery, querying, "How can one bad man rebuke another especially when God sees all?" Releasing years of accumulated frustration, Serna signed off a final letter to Tijerina by calling him "a miserable worm before our Lord."[99]

Like Serna, Maria Moreno also moved on from Valle de Paz while keeping her faith in God intact. Compared to Serna, Moreno lost her regard for Tijerina fairly quickly. According to her daughter, Moreno came to understand that Tijerina wanted to pursue a new mission centered on land grants and treaty rights, but this kind of mission did not interest her. After hearing rumors of sexual impropriety, she then "parted ways" with Tijerina.[100] Moreno returned to California and became deeply involved in farmworker unionizing until she ran afoul of her union bosses, who apparently did not appreciate a woman in a position of leadership. In a decision that echoed Tijerina's seeking God, suddenly one day Moreno decided to retreat to the desert with her two youngest children and wait until God revealed his plan for her. She spent the rest of her life as a traveling Pentecostal minister along both sides of the border.[101]

The religious journey of both Serna and Moreno provide a greater context for Tijerina's own evolution from preacher to prophet. According to Daniel Ramírez, the lack of institutional structure coupled with the immediacy of the divine gave Pentecostalism its emotional vitality. The same circumstances also produced a "chaotic mix" that generated not only independent preachers but sometimes "self-styled prophets" who pushed the faith tradition beyond "recognizable boundaries."[102] One of the most controversial and successful Pentecostal offshoots, for example, the Luz del Mundo Church in Mexico, which in the first decades of the twenty-first century counted perhaps as many as a million members globally, shared much in common with Valle de Paz. Founded by Eusebio Joaquín González in 1929 after he had a vision from God, the church privileged male authority, promoted modest dress for women, and even confronted rumors of sexual scandal. Just a few years before Tijerina founded

Valle de Paz, moreover, González launched La Hermosa Provincia, the Beautiful Province, on the outskirts of Guadalajara and for the same reason: to separate from secular society.[103]

Valle de Paz also invites consideration with another religious community in Arizona, Colorado City. In 1913, members who broke away from the official Church of Jesus Christ of Latter-day Saints after the church forbade polygamy founded the town near the Arizona-Utah border. There, extreme devotion, again as manifested outwardly in long hair and long dresses for women, joined the twisted theology of a self-proclaimed male prophet to result in the sexual exploitation of minors.[104]

In 2010, Tijerina vigorously defended his leadership in Valle de Paz against these multiple allegations of impropriety and criminal activity. He specifically denied that he had ever physically hurt Escobar or violated his marriage vows in any way. Emphasizing his own moral fiber, he insisted that he had stuck to Pentecostal social mores for most of his life, avoiding smoking, drinking, and cursing and acting with utmost respect toward other men's wives.[105] In contrast, he asserted that Escobar had always been an insanely jealous woman who, moreover, had not been a virgin on their wedding night.[106] While mention of any wedding night seemed off-topic, his comment exemplified the connection that Tijerina had long drawn between honor and sexual purity in women. Essentially, he was offering me as the interviewer what he considered irrefutable proof that Escobar was not to be trusted. Escobar meanwhile heatedly accused her former husband of being incapable of telling the truth.[107] More accurately perhaps, Tijerina could not separate how he saw the world from his overarching sense of mission.

As his memoir revealed, Tijerina demonstrated little patience for those whose viewpoint differed from his own. He saw them as enemies constantly conspiring against him. Local school officials harassed the community instead of allowing them to proceed with an independent school. The rancher sought revenge. Every accusation of criminal behavior was false. Rich developers plotted against him. And law enforcement refused to take the concerns of Valle de Paz residents seriously. On this point, he offered a telling detail about what no doubt was quite likely an unfair double standard. In tallying the suffering that Valle de Paz residents endured at the hands of antagonistic outsiders, Tijerina always included the day "a high-flying airplane flew down into our property. . . . Because of that accident one pregnant girl lost her child and an old woman went crazy."[108] Yet even more important to Tijerina than the fact of the jet crash was the disparity between how promptly the local FBI agent had investigated the accident and the lack of interest that he and the local sheriff had displayed when investigating the constant harassment of Valle de Paz residents. In his memoir, Tijerina included the names of both law enforcement officers, albeit with misspellings, almost as if he wished to still chastise the two officials publicly for failing to come to the aid of Valle de Paz residents all those years before.[109]

The rapid collapse of the Valle de Paz experiment after Tijerina fled Arizona nearly erased its history entirely. Years later the *Casa Grande Dispatch* commented that the few remaining residents departed so quickly that it appeared that "the population of the entire village disappeared overnight," leaving behind "clothing, cooking utensils and other personal belongings."[110] In addition, Tijerina always presented an edited version of the years in Arizona. Neither in his massive memoir nor in any interview did he mention that some of the Valle de Paz faithful considered him a prophet named Iratéo. Nor did he reveal that he had predicted the imminent end of the world. No doubt Tijerina surmised that few would understand the level of religious conviction that most Valle de Paz residents had shared. Plus, contrary to his predictions, the globe kept on spinning.

Even as Tijerina shook the dust of Arizona off his feet, the experience there left a mark on him. In Arizona, Tijerina had been driven to undertake the extraordinary task of building a religious utopia centered on land and justice. Also in Arizona, whenever conflict arose he accused his opponents not so much of disobeying God than of blocking the true spirit of justice as carried forth by one of his prophets. Finally, despite the widespread misery that accompanied his years in Arizona, Tijerina never lost his audacious certainty that God, as the author of human history, had selected him for some great role.

And if his days as Irateó had come to an end, then he was free to pursue his new mission south of the border in Mexico.

3

The Mexican

On Thanksgiving Day 1961, Jack Taylor and two of his ranch hands were harvesting Christmas trees on Taylor's 77,500-acre spread in southern Colorado when they came across vandalized ranch property: a burned-out trailer and a tractor with its radiator riddled with bullet holes. Seeing fresh hoof prints in the snow, Taylor and his employees tracked the prints for several miles until they discovered three men eating lunch in a clearing, their horses tied up nearby. Eduardo Medina, twenty-six; his brother, Gilberto, twenty-nine; and Tomás Rael, also twenty-nine, explained that they had been looking for a stray heifer and had just stopped to eat. Taylor told the men to leave his property. When they refused, Taylor took the law into his own hands. According to Gilberto Medina, Taylor struck him multiple times with a wooden post, each blow hard enough to knock him down. Medina kept struggling to his feet until one of the ranch hands advised him to stay put or, as Medina recalled, "Taylor would kill me." The two Medinas and Rael later testified that Taylor and his ranch hands also took potshots at them, stripped them of their hunting rifles and knives, and then tossed them in the back of a pickup truck and hauled them to the Costilla County Courthouse in nearby San Luis, Colorado. There, Taylor dumped the three captured men on the steps of the county jail and waited for the sheriff to arrest the trio for arson and trespassing.[1]

Taylor waited in vain. Sheriff Ruben Navarro sent the men to the hospital, not to jail. Worse for Taylor, town residents had noticed his truck driving through town with the injured men in the back. While Taylor and his men waited inside the courthouse, an angry mob began to form outside. Demanding that Taylor and his ranch hands be turned over to them, some threw rocks and others fired their weapons against the wall of the building. Sheriff Navarro went outside to calm the situation. When words failed, he fired his weapon into the air in an attempt to disperse the crowd. That did not work either. Finally, Navarro decided that the best course of action was to arrest Taylor and the two ranch hands on charges of assault, kidnapping, and robbery and to keep them in jail overnight for their own protection. Only then did deputies successfully convince everyone outside the jail to go home.[2]

Open hostility between Taylor and the descendants of some of the first Spanish-speaking settlers of the region had been the order of the day ever since Taylor had purchased what longtime residents called La Sierra, or the Mountain Tract, two years before. La Sierra comprised some of the last remaining unfenced acreage within the Sangre de Cristo land grant, which straddled the New Mexico–Colorado border. The Mexican government had issued the grant in 1844 to encourage settlement in what was then the farthest reach of northern New Mexico. In 1860, Congress confirmed the grant as private property, after which La Sierra passed through a string of absentee owners.[3] Without anyone around to dictate otherwise, Spanish speakers in the area maintained a tradition of collective use—pasturing their animals and collecting wood—for nearly a century.

Taylor's arrival and his determination "to keep those damned Mexicans from taking over" changed that scenario.[4] A native of North Carolina who had accrued a fortune in the timber industry, Taylor purchased the Mountain Tract for the bargain rate of just $6.40 an acre. The cheap price reflected the "little cloud upon the title," meaning the competing claims of locals. Dismissing those claims, Taylor saw evidence of an "inferiority complex" at work. Spanish speakers who knew that they were "not equal, mentally or physically, to the white man," in his words, stuck together and made outrageous demands.[5] Taylor responded by throwing up fences. He also took legal action to keep people out. In 1961, he filed a restraining order against Mariano Vigil, the local school board president, to prevent him from grazing his sheep on La Sierra. Nonetheless, Taylor soon saw Vigil again—as he put it, "on a horse . . . going across my mountain."

Adopting a mocking accent when he later told the story to a North Carolina newspaper reporter, Taylor said that he asked Vigil what he was doing. Vigil reportedly retorted, "Theese is not the United States. Theese is Mexico."[6] Even assuming that he had been quoted correctly (and that his accent had been so thick), Vigil certainly knew as well as Taylor where the border between the two countries actually fell. Yet the fact that this part of Colorado once had been part of Mexico mattered greatly to land-grant claimants like Vigil.

It also mattered to Reies López Tijerina. After fleeing Arizona, he immersed himself in the land-grant cause. Tijerina took more trips to Mexico and learned from people who still called themselves land-grant heirs about a painful history of widespread land dispossession. All of this research pushed him toward one central conclusion: Spanish speakers in northern New Mexico, southern Colorado, and implicitly throughout the Southwest were a conquered people. Denouncing the U.S. war against Mexico as a blatant act of aggression, Tijerina accused the United States of betraying the promises embedded in the Treaty of Guadalupe Hidalgo, including most prominently a promise to respect property rights. By 1961, his expert reputation on this topic had grown to such an extent that San Luis residents asked him to visit and offer his advice in the wake of the Taylor incident.[7] In response, Tijerina envisioned a grand crusade to tackle an enormous injustice: the American government and individual American citizens had stolen the land of former Mexican citizens and their descendants through deceit, fraud, and questionable court decisions.

Forget Taylor's "inferiority complex"; Tijerina blamed the United States for the contemporary circumstances of a people devastated by war and conquest. "Here is the root of our misery and poverty," he insisted. "All of a sudden . . . in the year 1848 we were left . . . without any protection for our lands . . .without any protection for our cultures."[8] At a time when severe poverty, low educational levels, and social marginalization characterized the lives of many, Tijerina reassured Spanish speakers in the region that their difficult circumstances were not the result of personal failing or of a backward culture but instead a direct result of colonization.

They were all Mexicans trapped inside the belly of the beast.[9]

In May 1958, Ubaldo C. Martínez invited Tijerina to speak to a gathering of members of La Corporación de Abiquiú, Merced de Tierra Amarilla (*merced* meaning "land grant"). Formed in 1937, the group represented an unprecedented attempt, sustained over decades, to recover what was one of the most highly contested land grants in all of New Mexico. Martínez was the latest president of the organization. His invitation suggested that Tijerina had earned a measure of acceptance among local folks just a few months after moving to the state. In honor of the occasion, Tijerina brought along a few loyal valientes who had followed him from Arizona as well as his older brother Anselmo, whom he had recently recruited to the land-grant cause.

Tijerina had barely started speaking to the crowd of about 100, however, when an audience member began to whisper agitatedly to the sergeant at arms that Tijerina and his friends needed to be expelled from the gathering because they were not corporation members. But when the sergeant at arms asked Tijerina to stop talking, Tijerina refused to comply. The sergeant at arms then hit a surprised Tijerina on the head with a wooden club. Rushing to his brother's defense, Anselmo Tijerina grabbed the club and struck the sergeant at arms. Soon others joined the melee. Before the fight was over, one of Tijerina's friends lay flat on the floor, felled by a stranger's punch; Reies needed treatment for a bleeding scalp; and Anselmo faced arrest on assault charges.[10]

A less-than-propitious launch to any public-speaking career, the episode indicated how deeply some members of the Corporation of Abiquiú were inclined to distrust Tijerina. Over the course of a century, land-grant families had heard many self-proclaimed experts promising to help them protect their property. Over the course of that same century, these families had seen their landholdings inexorably shrink on account of court rulings, acts of Congress, and shady deals by crooked lawyers. Estimates are that Spanish-speaking New Mexicans lost title to 80 percent of their landholdings in the fifty years following 1848.[11] In addition, in northern New Mexico, where families tended to live in the same village for generations, the Texas-born Tijerina raised suspicions as an outsider. For all these reasons, Tijerina initially counted on the support of only a handful of land-grant claimants.

Still, along with the few remaining Arizona faithful, this small circle helped Tijerina and his family weather his fugitive years and launched him on his new quest. At various times, Tijerina counted upon his old valientes to provide a car, a place to sleep, and ready cash.[12] When he first arrived in New Mexico, Tijerina also greatly depended on Manuel Trujillo, who first had come to his rescue the year before when the remnants of the Valle de Paz community had visited New Mexico. After the Tijerina family left Arizona, Trujillo once again opened up his ranch house in the northern portion of the state to them. They stayed there until Tijerina grew concerned that law enforcement was zeroing in on his location. The family then fled to San Antonio, where Mary Escobar that April gave birth to the couple's sixth child, a son that Tijerina named Noe.[13]

Meanwhile, Tijerina exhibited familiar patterns: he relied upon others for support, often lived apart from his family, and enjoyed spending days deep in study. Once again, he alone attended Mary Escobar during the delivery of Noe. Once again, Tijerina chose a name for his child that reflected his sense of mission. The name Noé, or Noah, recalled not only God's promises to his people after the biblical flood but also the moment when Tijerina in Colorado had viewed a rainbow and interpreted it as a sign from above that he should pursue land-grant justice. Immediately after the birth, he left Escobar and the children to stay with extended family in Texas while he delved into the history of land confiscation. Returning to New Mexico, he took to hiding out in a cave near Manuel Trujillo's ranch. He furnished the cave with an old mattress and some blankets and appreciated the time to read and reflect.[14]

Tijerina particularly relied upon the generosity of Fernanda and Juan Martínez of Tierra Amarilla. He stayed with them intermittently for more than a year. "He read all the time those law books," Fernanda Martínez remembered. "He never drank, he never swore, just worked and worked."[15] A great part of that work was to listen to Señora Martínez "school him mercilessly" on land-grant history.[16] In his memoir, Tijerina acknowledged his debt. "That woman helped me day and night, for weeks and months," he wrote. Offering the highest praise that he could, Tijerina compared Fernanda Martínez to his mother, Erlinda. She was an "electric spark of courage" who not only knew the history of "every one of the Anglos" who had taken over portions of the Tierra Amarilla grant, he wrote, but, along with her husband, made sure that all their children, fourteen in all, learned this history too.[17] That years later Tijerina still remembered Señora Martínez so positively—especially given his generally low opinion of women—spoke volumes about her helpful and influential role in deepening his understanding of land-grant affairs.

As Tijerina was the first to admit, he had a lot to learn. Spanish-speaking settlement in the area stretched back centuries. The explorer Francisco Vázquez de Coronado and his troops first crossed the region in the 1540s. Permanent Spanish-speaking settlement began in 1598, long after the founding of the Pueblo "sky city" of Acoma but nine years before English colonists founded Jamestown. In 1680, Pueblo Indians from different villages united in an astonishing act of coordinated revolt to kick out Spanish-speaking colonists and missionaries. Twelve years later, Don Diego de Vargas reconquered the Kingdom of New Mexico for a Spanish crown still burdened by a sense of obligation to spread the Catholic faith. Otherwise, the region, on the far frontier of empire, primarily served as a buffer between the rich mining regions of Mexico proper and Native Americans hostile to Spanish-speaking expansion. Throughout the 1700s and first half of the 1800s, Spanish speakers continued to push northward. Just as often, indigenous groups pushed them back. For most of the Spanish and Mexican eras, intermittent warfare and widespread slavery characterized life on this far frontier.[18]

Indeed, the Corporation of Abiquiú took its name from the village of Abiquiú, which originally was founded in 1754 some fifty miles north-northwest of Santa Fe to serve as a village for *genízaros*, a word that referred to Navajo, Apache, or Plains Indians who had previously been captured and enslaved and thus detribalized. For *genízaros* especially, a piece of land on the frontier represented the opportunity to start anew. Risk-takers and refugees from earlier settlements likewise found their way to this region. The Tierra Amarilla land grant, which Tijerina knew best, drew its original settlers from this pool of adventurers and their descendants. In 1832, the Mexican government deeded the grant to Manuel Martínez, a leading landowner, who asked for the *merced* (the grant but literally a "mercy," meaning a gift or favor) on behalf of himself, his eight sons, and "some others who voluntarily desire to accompany me."[19]

Building on earlier Spanish traditions, Mexican-era land grants deeded land in common and to private individuals. The distinction between the two types of land grants tended to fade in practice because individuals granted land often brought other settlers with them, as had Martínez. In addition, land-grant documents routinely recognized the rights of these settlers to their own small plots and to the commons. In the case of the Tierra Amarilla land grant, the Mexican authorities demanded that Martínez grant the settlers who accompanied him a plot (measured in ancient *varas*) to situate their homes and fields.[20] In the high desert of northern New Mexico, everyone knew that a community's survival depended on residents sharing land to pasture animals, collect timber, and provide water for crops.

As Tijerina discovered, none of this complicated and tradition-bound history mattered to the U.S. Congress. Before signing the Treaty of Guadalupe Hidalgo, Congress had rejected Article 10, which would have automatically recognized the validity of all property held by Mexican citizens. The deletion meant that, unlike the residents of Florida and Louisiana, whose property rights were automatically recognized when those territories entered the United States, the former citizens of Mexico had to prove that they owned the land. Meeting that requirement was hard enough given the age of some of the land grants and the quality of the documentation surrounding them, but Congress made the job much harder. First, Congress failed to set up any adjudication mechanism in New Mexico until 1854, meaning that for more than six years, uncertainty reigned. When Congress finally established the New Mexico Office of the Surveyor General, it charged the office with the monumental task of "ascertaining the origin, nature, character, and extent of all claims of lands under the laws, usages and customs of Spain and Mexico" but seriously underfunded the endeavor. Not surprisingly, a succession of surveyors failed in their assigned task. Working alongside members of the notorious Santa Fe Ring, a group of lawyers and speculators, a number did, however, succeed at corruption. "Land-Stealing in New Mexico," summarized a disgusted George W. Julian in 1887, the last man to hold the post of surveyor general. Julian favored an end to rampant corruption. Like many Americans, he also favored an end to any claim to common lands by Spanish speakers. Established in 1891, the Court of Private Land Claims adhered to what one scholar called a "technical, rigid process" that advanced that goal. In the end, it rejected two-thirds of the claims brought before it to approve a grand total of just 6 percent of the land area in question.[21]

The fate of the Tierra Amarilla grant, Tijerina learned, fit within this sorry pattern. In 1860, Congress recognized Francisco Martínez, one of Manuel's sons, as the sole owner of a 594,515-acre Tierra Amarilla grant. Without regard to the other sons or other settlers, the decision granted Francisco Martínez the unilateral right to sell the land, which he started to do bit by bit. Reflecting earlier traditions, Martínez in 1861 also began handing out a type of document called a *hijuela*, or deed, reaffirming the rights of settlers to use the land grant communally.[22] Like the Spanish speakers in Colorado who continued to claim La Sierra as their own, land-grant folks around Tierra Amarilla used the land mostly without restriction for decades afterward. Only after new owners started putting up fences did local Spanish speakers begin to feel squeezed off the land. In 1937, Tierra Amarilla land-grant claimants, many who shared the last name Martínez and many who held *hijuelas*, founded a new Corporation of Abiquiú determined to fight for their rights in court. In four separate cases between 1938 and 1957, however, New Mexican courts rebuffed their claims.

For a student of history like Tijerina, these cases collectively highlighted some of the primary mechanisms that American courts employed to sever Spanish speakers from their ancestral holdings. The courts refused to recognize *hijuelas* as conveying any right to use the land. They also refused to recognize long-term land use by Spanish speakers as constituting evidence of adverse possession. In addition, the courts insisted that if Congress had confirmed a grant as private, as in the case of the Tierra Amarilla grant, then reversing that decision was up to Congress as well. Finally, in lieu of an act of Congress, the courts repeatedly favored private ownership rights over communal ones. In 1953, for example, a judge not only ruled in favor of a ranch owner named Bill Mundy but also added that corporation members were "barred and forever estopped from having or claiming any right, title, or interest" to any disputed property within the historic boundaries of the Tierra Amarilla land grant. In 1956, the New Mexico Supreme Court upheld the judge's sweeping pro-Mundy, anti-corporation decision.[23]

By the time that Tijerina arrived in New Mexico, the discontent of Tierra Amarilla land-grant activists centered on Mundy. Similar to Jack Taylor's story in Colorado, Mundy in 1951 had scored a "freak deal" on some of the last unfenced portions of the Tierra Amarilla grant precisely because the land had been the focus of so much legal wrangling. Unlike Taylor, who inherited considerable wealth from his father, Mundy, a native of southern New Mexico, was a self-made man, "a hard worker and a hard hitter" who became a "land baron," according to his admiring family.[24] Like Taylor, Mundy immediately started putting fences on his original 11,000-acre purchase to keep others out. Over time, he also increased his holdings to 25,000 acres.[25] By 1953, the property Mundy had purchased extended right up to Los Brazos Creek and the land-grant village of Los Brazos, where José María Martínez, then president of the Corporation of Abiquiú, had been born in 1896.[26]

Like many land-grant heirs, José María Martínez viewed Mundy's purchases as encroachments upon a shared inheritance. Both viewed the other as a trespasser. Their mutual hostility sometimes erupted into violence. On one occasion, Martínez and some of his friends stationed themselves on one side of a creek and took potshots at Mundy and a work crew on the other side.[27] On another occasion, Mundy got the better of Martínez. As Bill Mundy's son Jim recalled years later, his father surprised Martínez and about a dozen armed "granters" who were trying to sneak their cattle on land that Mundy and his men had just fenced. Before Martínez could react, according to Jim Mundy, "Bill grabbed Jose Maria by the collar and jerked him up on his horse with [Martínez's] back on the saddle horn."[28] Unfortunately for Martínez, Mundy also triumphed in court.

Unable to gain any traction on their land claims over the course of twenty years, Corporation of Abiquiú members thus had every reason to feel down and defeated by the time Tijerina arrived in New Mexico. "Bill Mundy was fencing off the last of the grant land . . . and we couldn't get anywhere in the courts," recalled Juan Martínez, José María Martínez's nephew and Fernanda's husband. "So we were ready to listen to just about anybody who had a good idea of what to do, just as long as we could be sure he was with us and would stay with us."[29] Despite his initial less-than-warm reception at the May 1958 Corporation of Abiquiú meeting, Tijerina's determination to learn land-grant history had impressed at least some land-grant activists. Before the year was out, Tijerina returned to Mexico to build support for their cause.

SOUTH OF THE BORDER

"My father loved Mexico and loved Mexicans," Rose Tijerina recalled.[30] As late as 1960, she estimated, her father proposed moving the entire family to an undeveloped island off the coast of Mexico, inspired by the notion that they would grow up in an environment uncontaminated by modern society or "the Anglo-Saxon's ways." Her father had toyed with the idea before, Rose remembered, but this time Mary Escobar prevailed. As she recalled, "That's when my mom put her foot down finally for once and said [in Spanish]: 'You go . . . but I don't want the children growing up in a place where there is not even a book for them to learn how to read.'" With that dream deferred, Tijerina maintained his commitment to the land-grant cause. Nevertheless, his love affair with Mexico continued. He spent nearly a year there between September 1958 and September 1959. Between 1960 and 1964, he continued to take trips south of the border, often visiting more than once a year.

Tijerina's identification with Mexico began in childhood. Throughout his life, Tijerina tended to identify more with his ethnicity than with his nationality. The inclination originated in the near destitute conditions of his youth and the widespread discrimination that he experienced. These overlapping structures of segregation and exploitation routinely labeled him Mexican, despite his U.S. birth. But Tijerina also truly idealized his Mexican heritage. According to Rose Tijerina, the only time her father raised no objections to his children attending school was when the family was in Mexico. Her father also never allowed any language but Spanish to be spoken at home, she recalled. (Thoroughly bilingual, Tijerina nonetheless spoke English with a heavy accent.)[31]

Although written decades later, a scrap of memoir about one of Tijerina's pastoral trips south of the border still brimmed with enthusiasm for the Mexican countryside. "We went deep into the mountains, to the little *rancherias* [small ranches]" reachable only by horseback, Tijerina later recalled. "I fell in love with the humble, meek lifestyle of the . . . people." Commenting approvingly of sex and gender matters, Tijerina continued, "The men were dressed simple . . . but their *coraje* [courage], was unbelievable"; the men were rich in honor.[32] Small Mexican towns—where he often stayed for months at a time—provided the template for Valle de Paz. After that failed experiment, Mexico still appealed to Tijerina for cultural and linguistic reasons.

For the fugitive Tijerina, being in Mexico provided another advantage: it maximized the distance between himself and the people who wanted to apprehend him. By Tijerina's count, he managed to elude law enforcement at least seven times before taking his first extended trip to Mexico.[33] In his memoir, he specifically credited Eulogio Salazar, a Corporation of Abiquiú member and the Rio Arriba County jailer, for keeping him informed of the ongoing hunt for him so that he could always stay one step ahead. He also maintained that a friendly Salazar had facilitated Anselmo Tijerina's escape from jail following that disruptive Corporation of Abiquiú meeting and had often provided food and clothing to the Tijerina family while Tijerina was a fugitive.[34] As we shall see, Tijerina in later years had every reason to portray Salazar as an ally and a friend.

In the late summer of 1958, Tijerina experienced his closest call yet. Along with his brother Anselmo, Tijerina had joined Mary Escobar and their children to work in the fields near the town of Plainview, New Mexico. One day, the two brothers noticed that police had surrounded three sides of the house that the Tijerina family was renting. To escape, the pair quietly entered the bathroom in order to sneak out of a bathroom window that was on the unguarded fourth side of the house. Rose, nine, was taking a bath at the time. "If they open up the door," she recalled her father telling her, "stand up and lift up your arms and start to scream so that they can see that you are naked." Already greatly embarrassed to be unclothed in front of her father and uncle, Rose Tijerina was greatly relieved that the police never opened the bathroom door. Meanwhile, when asked where her husband and brother-in-law were, Escobar lied to police. "I said they had gone back to work," she recalled. Hitting the ground outside after jumping through the window, "I ran like a deer being hunted," Reies Tijerina later wrote. He kept on running all the way to the Mexican border.[35]

Tijerina arrived in Mexico City on September 1, 1958, by all indications a sorry-looking champion for land-grant affairs. Staying with old Pentecostal friends to save money, he depended on donations trickling from friends and family north of the border to fund his research. He immediately got to work. He hit the archives again in Mexico City and also traveled to the city of Guadalajara in the state of Jalisco, which had administered New Mexico for much of the colonial era. He also took advantage of his time in Mexico to court new allies. A testament to his power of persuasion, Tijerina soon collected a broad array of supporters in the nation's capital.

Most important, Tijerina launched a friendship with Agustín Cue Cánovas, a historian and educator who offered a critical view of the U.S.-Mexican War, or what the Mexicans called *la intervención estadounidense*. Long viewed as a national humiliation, the war attracted limited scholarly attention in Mexico, none of it focused on the fate of the conquered population.[36] Unique among his colleagues, Cue Cánovas took an interest not only in the conflict but in what he called "forgotten Mexico," the Mexican-origin population within the United States. His analysis of this population's fate began with violations of the Treaty of Guadalupe Hidalgo and the devastating loss of property suffered by the former citizens of Mexico and their descendants as a result.[37] Deeply impressed, Tijerina invited the historian to meet with land-grant activists in New Mexico and made it a point to share his work.[38]

While in Mexico City, Tijerina also made the acquaintance of Benjamin Laureano Luna, one of Mexico's leading human rights activists and the founder of a group called the Frente Internacional de Derechos Humanos (International Human Rights Front). Known in high government circles, Luna agreed to lobby within Mexico on behalf of nuevomexicanos seeking land-grant rights.[39] For example, when Tijerina found out that Luna had the occasion to meet Milton Eisenhower at a high-level meeting, he asked Luna to hand-deliver a memo to him to give to his brother, President Dwight Eisenhower. Luna did just that, but whether Milton Eisenhower ever bothered to read the memo, much less pass it on to the president, is unclear.[40]

The January 1959 memo that Tijerina drafted marked his first attempt to marry his deeper appreciation of land-grant injustice with his critical perspective of American empire. Addressed broadly to "every tribunal of justice and every nation that preserves 'respect for the rights of others,'" the memo started by invoking Benito Juárez, one of Mexico's most admired presidents, who famously said, "Among individuals, as among nations, respect for the rights of others is peace." The quotation perfectly underscored Tijerina's main complaint, that the United States had failed to respect the 1848 Treaty of Guadalupe Hidalgo. "On that day, our smiles and our happiness ended. In that year, our liberty ended," Tijerina wrote.[41]

The rest of the memo reflected Tijerina's outrage at that fact. Whereas once Tijerina had warned of a forthcoming Armageddon, he now characterized the land-grant struggle as another epic battle between the forces of good and evil. He accused the United States of committing "savage and black crimes" against former Mexican citizens and their descendants. "We were left surrounded by hangmen and gunmen," Tijerina wrote of the American takeover. "Our lands have been robbed, our daughters raped, and our fathers buried alive." Even more wildly, Tijerina wrote of multiple massacres and killings of Mexicans by Americans in Texas, claiming that as many as 130 cadavers were secretly buried at one spot, 90 at another, 30 at still another. Like references to daughters raped and fathers buried alive, Tijerina's sources regarding such gruesome findings were unclear. Even during the worst episodes of anti-Mexican violence in Texas early in the twentieth century, no one incident resulted in that many bodies dumped—and then later discovered—in one place. In fact, the numbers he cited more closely approximated U.S. Army massacres of Native Americans. Perhaps that history encouraged Tijerina's exaggerations. Through such sweeping indictments, Tijerina strove to rally sympathy for "the oppressed Mexican people" now living throughout the entire U.S. Southwest.[42]

Still fuzzy on the details of land dispossession, Tijerina in the rest of the memo recycled and expanded upon ideas from his preacher days to make his case against the United States. He not only faulted U.S. public schools for encouraging moral laxness but also accused them of seeking "to brainwash the minds of our children and erase the historical deeds" of a land-hungry nation-state. Similarly, Tijerina provided a list of crimes that the United States had committed on the world stage. Although the list still prominently featured the use of the atomic bomb, it also included a war of aggression against Mexico. In another continuation, Tijerina expressed sympathy for those countries that the United States viewed with grave suspicion during the Cold War. Writing less than three weeks after Fidel Castro and his followers had deposed of Fulgencio Batista, the U.S.-backed dictator in Cuba, Tijerina offered his warmest regards to the island's new leader. "We congratulate the valiant Cubans. . . . Blessed is the man who broke the yoke upon Cuba and happy are his faithful followers who have reached . . . liberty," he gushed.[43]

As the rest of the memo made clear, the yoke was the yoke of U.S. imperialism. Within this early document, Tijerina clearly identified the land-grant struggle with Mexico and defined land-grant activists as Mexicans. After 1848, Mexican citizens above the river were "sold to the enemy," he charged, leaving "the life of a Mexican valued and respected south of the Rio Grande only." Having suffered "110 years of opprobrium" and "110 years of servitude," Tijerina asked, "How can we ever say that we are content [being] Mexicans [north of the border]?" In what was to become a familiar metaphor, the text labeled Mexico "mother" while the United States was a "stepmother," and an evil one to boot. If nuevomexicanos were really Mexicans, then they were by definition not Americans. Suggesting instead that they constituted a conquered and subjugated Mexican population in the United States, Tijerina urgently implored friends south of the border to seek justice on behalf of their "blood brothers" to the north. "Is there no one in all of the land who will come to our aid?" he asked.[44] The answer, apparently, was no. Tijerina's lengthy memo failed to elicit any response from the Mexican government.

An indefatigable Tijerina continued to expand his circle of contacts south of the border to include some of the country's most well known leftists. Tijerina, for example, met with Vicente Lombardo Toledano, who headed Mexico's national labor union for decades, although a disappointed Tijerina later complained that Lombardo Toledano wanted money in exchange for any support.[45] Tijerina visited with other union men, including Demetrio Vallejo, who had organized a series of national railroad strikes in 1958 and 1959, and Jacinto López, who during those same years had led land invasions against vast holdings of the American-owned Cananea Cattle Company in the Mexican state of Sonora. Vallejo evidently lent Tijerina a sympathetic ear.[46] Finally, he met Lázaro Cárdenas, who during his tenure as the nation's president had nationalized the oil industry and enacted land reform. A student of Mexican history, Tijerina no doubt understood the significance of both events. Years before, as a preacher, he had made it a point to make a pilgrimage to the hacienda that Pancho Villa had called home while visiting Mexico. Tijerina also stopped by the town of Parral, where the Mexican revolutionary general, crusader for land distribution, and enemy of the United States had been shot and killed.[47] "Entering Mexico as an itinerant religious leader," one scholar wrote about this early visit, "[Tijerina] left it deeply motivated by the philosophy of the Mexican Revolution."[48] Like a modern-day Pancho Villa, Tijerina sought to pursue justice on behalf of landless Mexican-origin people, albeit a population *north* of the border. On this point, Cárdenas offered helpful advice, reportedly warning Tijerina to expect massive resistance to any land reclamation effort.[49]

Even more intriguing was Tijerina's association with obscure fringe groups. These included the mysterious Movimiento Nacional por la Reintegración Territorial, a name that strongly suggested that members looked upon the U.S. Southwest as a Mexican Sudetenland.[50] Tijerina likewise cultivated friends among members of the Comité de Anáhuac, Anáhuac being a reference to the region that the Aztec Empire had once occupied. Also known as the Movimiento Confederado Restaurador de la Cultura de Anáhuac, its followers favored the restoration of pre-conquest civilization. Taken with a composite mythical history, committee members contended that the Aztecs originally hailed from India and had stopped by ancient Egypt and Greece on their way to Mexico. Still, their greater goal of societal renewal must have struck a familiar chord with Tijerina. The committee expressed disgust with the present decadent world. Sounding a lot like Tijerina in his preacher mode, the group's founder, Rodolfo Nievas, a Mexico City lawyer, even bemoaned the immodesty of modern-day women. Most important, the movement's anti-imperialist views echoed Tijerina's own critical perspective. As early as 1930, Anáhuac adherents denounced "Tío Sam's" ongoing economic and cultural invasion of Mexico.[51]

To his delight, Tijerina discovered that his attempt to forge relationships across the border, despite the lack of any discernible payoff, won him additional Corporation of Abiquiú support. Like Tijerina, many northern New Mexicans proudly recognized their Mexican heritage. Although technically New Mexico had formed part of the Spanish empire for two and a half centuries, whereas it was a part of an independent Mexico for only two and half decades, across the years administrative and trade connections had always oriented the region toward Mexico City. After 1821, an independent Mexico also actively cultivated a sense of national identity among the people dispersed along the northern frontier.[52] Certainly Tijerina's efforts in Mexico met the corporation's stamp of approval. When his wife and children came to visit Tijerina in December 1958 for the Christmas holiday, Mary Escobar brought with her $200, a gift from the Corporation of Abiquiú, which wished to support his research efforts.[53] By the following summer, the corporation recognized Tijerina as its official representative in Mexico City.[54] In addition, an August 1959 letter from another corporation member specifically addressed Tijerina as "*mi caro amigo*," my dear friend. The letter included an unspecified amount of cash for Tijerina's use.[55] After Tijerina's return to the States the following month, he credited Corporation of Abiquiú members for supplying him and his family with donations of food and clothing to help them survive another winter.[56]

COLONIZED IN NEW MEXICO

In the immediate aftermath of the 1967 courthouse raid, when the nation's focus suddenly turned to northern New Mexico, the *New York Times* struggled to convey the level of economic destitution there to readers unfamiliar with the region. It drew a series of comparisons. Consider Rio Arriba County, one *Times* reporter wrote, like "Appalachia with a language problem," or like "Spanish Harlem with clean air [and] cool, summer nights."[57] In a more troubling analogy, given that emancipation had occurred a century before, another writer offered that "the helplessness of the Spanish-speaking peasants rivals that of plantation negroes who have been replaced by machines in Mississippi."[58] In each case, journalists writing for one of the nation's leading newspapers turned to some of the deepest pockets of poverty in the country to convey the extent of socioeconomic woes found in northern New Mexico.

Tijerina knew them firsthand. Returning to New Mexico in late 1959, he and his family wintered in the tiny village of La Ensenada, near the county seat of Tierra Amarilla. Adding fuel to his anticolonial fire, there he observed the fragility of northern New Mexican rural village life up close. While life on the far frontier had often been precarious during the Spanish and Mexican period, the U.S. takeover, by severing Spanish speakers from the land, undercut traditional industries such as lumbering and cattle and sheep grazing. As Tijerina increasingly understood, a cascade of socioeconomic woes resulted. By the post–World War II period, conditions had become so dreadful that many northern New Mexican villages teetered on the brink of demographic collapse.

Census data bared a series of inequalities. In 1960, the average annual income of "Spanish-surnamed" families in New Mexico was $3,291, whereas "white" families in New Mexico earned nearly double that amount, or $6,082.[59] Meanwhile, nationwide the average family income approached $8,000.[60] These average figures, moreover, masked the fact that the U.S. Census categorized Spanish-surnamed individuals as "white." If information pertaining to Spanish-surnamed families was removed from the "white" category, then the discrepancies would be even greater, according to a state report that crunched the numbers. With that caveat, the same report estimated that the nuevomexicano unemployment rate, hovering at 20 percent, was nearly twice that of the state's "white" population.[61] Other statistics added to the grim picture: high infant mortality rates, high tuberculosis rates, and a profusion of substandard housing. Like Tijerina, moreover, many Spanish-surnamed New Mexicans lacked schooling. In Rio Arriba County, which was 70 percent Spanish-surnamed, nearly half of the population over the age of twenty-five had less than an eighth-grade education.[62]

Confronted by these desperate circumstances, people kept leaving the region. Between 1940 and 1964, Tierra Amarilla saw its population shrink from 2,200 to 500. The smaller villages of Truchas and El Rito during this same period experienced similarly dramatic declines in the number of residents, from 900 to 200 and 1,300 to 200, respectively.[63] In La Ensenada, where he was staying, Tijerina noted that only thirty-three of seventy-nine houses were occupied.[64] While many nuevomexicanos moved to Albuquerque, the state's largest city and a major economic engine, others left the state entirely. In another telling set of statistics, from 1950 to 1960, the state's overall population increased by 39.2 percent, whereas the number of Spanish-surnamed New Mexicans increased by just 8.3 percent.[65]

Added together, these demographic trends and socioeconomic data raised grave concerns about the long-term viability of the historic heartland of Spanish-speaking New Mexico.

Once back in New Mexico, Tijerina also witnessed the difficulties that Tierra Amarilla land-grant claimants faced in court. Just one year after the New Mexico Supreme Court affirmed that Corporation of Abiquiú members were "barred and forever estopped from having or claiming any right, title, or interest" to the Tierra Amarilla grant land, the Payne Land and Livestock Company filed suit against the corporation members. The company wished to negate any claim on the part of local Spanish speakers to a measly 70 acres that fell within the 7,000-acre Payne ranch. The claim dated back to 1883, when the land was sold with an exception allowing local residents to utilize these 70 acres. Since then, Spanish-speaking residents had used the exception to draw water from two local creeks and to irrigate their farms. The Payne Company sued in an attempt to end that access, a move that put corporation members on the defensive. While they wished to assert their collective rights not just to the 70 acres but to the entire grant, they lacked the deep pockets necessary to counter Payne's lawsuit, much less to stake a broader claim.[66]

Aware that the legal deck was stacked against them, in December 1959 local land-grant claimants opted to send a letter directly to President Eisenhower to convey the urgency of their situation. Although Tijerina was not among the more than eighty signatories, he authored the letter on behalf of the corporation.[67] In tone, the letter mimicked that of earlier letters the corporation had sent to the Department of Justice and the Department of the Interior requesting aid. "At all times it has been our intention to honor our citizenship and to cover with prestige our nation in which we feel pride," began one typical sentence. In what appeared to be a Tijerina touch, however, this letter also paid attention to current events, noting that Eisenhower had sent federal troops two years before to Little Rock, Arkansas, to enforce the U.S. Supreme Court's desegregation ruling. In that case, the letter queried, could not the president similarly come to the rescue in New Mexico? "This matter we likewise consider an emergency because the situation has reached a crisis point and from one moment to the next things might result that only you can prevent."[68] An implicit threat thus accompanied the deferential tone. The White House issued a perfunctory response, a few "cold" lines, in Tijerina's recollection.[69] The news from the bench likewise disappointed. In February 1960, the U.S. District Court ruled entirely in Payne's favor, the fifth time in a row that the courts had refused to countenance Tierra Amarilla land-grant claims.[70]

Not coincidentally, during the first half of 1960, a spate of violence broke out in Rio Arriba County. In New Mexico, where the enclosure of grant land by unwelcome newcomers gave rise to the saying "Cuando llegó el alambre, también llegó el hambre [When the (barbed) wire arrived, so did hunger]," fence cutting amounted to a resistance tradition. In Rio Arriba County, episodes of fence cutting along with haystack burning had occurred throughout the twentieth century, with clusters of anonymous vandalism breaking out in the 1940s and 1950s, often in response to court defeats.[71] This time, sporadic fence cutting and threatening anonymous phone calls were only the beginning of the illegal activity. Jim Mundy recalled how his father, after receiving one of these phone calls, placed a bulldozer blade in front of his dining room window to act as fortification in case a firefight broke out.[72] The defensive move failed to prevent the Mundy home from being burned to the ground in late February 1960, when Bill Mundy was gone from the property.[73] Unknown assailants also set fire to one building on each of three other ranches owned by Anglo-Americans who had likewise purchased land that fell within the historic boundaries of the Tierra Amarilla land grant. Suspecting a conspiracy of night raiders, angry Anglo-Americans threatened to form a vigilante group to pursue the culprits, at which point Rio Arriba County district attorney Walter Kegel expressed his concerns. "If people start taking the law into their own hands up there, I'm afraid that someone is going to get killed," Kegel told the press. "A lot of people are carrying guns again."[74]

Privately, Kegel and other law enforcement officials suspected Reies López Tijerina of being not a letter writer but an outside agitator.[75] They had been keeping an eye on him and his brother Anselmo since 1958 and that disruptive Corporation of Abiquiú meeting. The police report filed at the time dubbed Anselmo Tijerina "either a communist or a communist sympathizer" while describing Reies as an "intimidating" man who pressured those in attendance "to join his crusade to take land away from the gringos."[76] Yet these suspicions of criminal activity likely were misplaced. Although years later Tijerina admitted that he did once participate in fence cutting, he was back in Mexico during the worst of this violence in 1960.[77]

There, Tijerina looked forward to broadcasting a central conclusion that he had drawn as a result of all his studies, observations, and archival investigations: the land had been stolen from its rightful owners. On his return trip to Mexico, he wrote, he came bearing land-grant documents that indicated that the U.S. was not honoring the Treaty of Guadalupe Hidalgo. In his memoir, he also provided an excellent summary of what he had learned about land-grant history thus far: "The treaty was signed on Feb. 2, 1848, but it was not until 1891 that the Congress of the United States established the Court of Private Land Claims to adjudicate land claim. During these 43 years, the Santa Fe Ring [a corrupt group of land speculators and lawyers] stole all the land grants. In 1891, when the Court of Private Land Claims began its process, they insisted on proof of title to the land. Each land grant heir was to present his or her deed. But how could she or he?" As Tijerina noted, by then, key documents had fallen into the hands of others, or biased courts refused to recognize them as legitimate. Tijerina also described as unfair the burden the United States had placed upon the former citizens of Mexico to prove their property rights. Finally, Tijerina claimed unique credit for grasping the scope of the problem at hand.[78] Upon his arrival in Mexico in 1960, Tijerina dashed off a letter to the Mexican president informing him that under this treaty, the president had the both the authority and the responsibility to intervene on behalf of "*el Pueblo de Nuevo Mexico*."[79]

Despite his boast, the following year Tijerina had company when it came to petitioning the Mexican government. In June 1961, José María Martínez, the Corporation of Abiquiú leader who had challenged rancher Mundy in court and outside of it, also sent a letter to the president of Mexico. He asked the president's "sound advice" about land-grant affairs and also inquired whether Mexico had any documents relevant to matter of the mercedes. Perhaps Tijerina's south-of-the-border journeys inspired Martínez to contact Mexico. If so, the lines of influence probably ran both ways. Martínez wrote not as president of the Corporation of Abiquiú but on behalf of a new group called the Alianza de las Mercedes México-Españolas, General Headquarters, Tierra Amarilla. This land-grant group, he explained in his letter to the president, sought to unite land-grant claimants from all over New Mexico and then take their case to "world tribunals" in the near future.[80]

In 1963, Tijerina formed his own Alianza and endowed it with a similarly broad mission. Although Tijerina always stressed the independence of his organization from any precursor group, including the Cooperation of Abiquiú, Gregorita Aguilar, another woman who had "mercilessly schooled Tijerina" about land-grant history, contended otherwise.[81]

Once an enthusiastic supporter of Tijerina, years later she conveyed her disappointment at his failed promises when she denounced him as a thief who had stolen all his best ideas from Tierra Amarilla activists, including the idea to form a broad-based Alianza.[82]

Whoever first thought of forming one great alliance of land grants, Mexico did not care. It flatly rejected both supplicants. To his initial delight, Tijerina promptly received a telegram from the president's office informing him that his letter had been passed on to the secretary of foreign relations. He then waited in vain for additional action on the part of the Mexican government.[83] A year later, Martínez, whose inquiry was also rerouted to the secretary of foreign relations, fared little better. Although a government official in that office informed Martínez that he might want to pursue his investigations at the national archives in Mexico City, the official also suggested that such a visit would be a waste of time. Mexico and the United States already had convened two general claims commissions to settle land and other disputes between the two countries, in 1923 and 1941, the letter noted.[84] In other words, Martínez's inquiry was at least twenty years too late.

While Martínez's Alianza then faded from the archival record, Tijerina continued to press ahead south of the border in person. In the spring of 1962, for example, Tijerina called a press conference and invited the Mexico City press. Referring to Colorado rancher Jack Taylor and the notorious beating that he had delivered, Tijerina asked rhetorically, "Is it possible [that such an event occurred] in the 20th century?" He urged friendly journalists throughout Latin America to investigate the fate of their northern brethren.[85] Some did. "Thousands of Mexican Descendants Insist That the United States Should Return Their Lands to Them," read one Mexico City headline.[86] No longer so fuzzy on the details, Tijerina also claimed that precisely 1,715 land grants in New Mexico were at stake. He had gleaned the number from an 1855 surveyor general report charged with tallying all those contested "grants, conveyances . . . , and . . . claims to land."[87] Over time, that number whittled down significantly. Ultimately, the surveyor general's office considered only about 180 claims (minus Pueblo Indian ones).[88] The larger number, however, corresponded with the vastness of Tijerina's anticolonial vision.

Unlike most land-grant heirs who sought to recover land associated with one particular grant, Tijerina expressed little interest in the details of dispossession from grant to grant. He wished to make broader points. In 1848, the American takeover of the north of Mexico had cleaved an entire people from their property. It had also savagely divided the Mexican people, Tijerina insisted. The imposition of a new border in 1848, he asserted, had failed to break the bonds of culture that still united land-grant heirs to Mexicans. "We have kept the manners of speech, traditions, methods of organization, and the folklore [of Mexico]," Tijerina contended in a typical appeal. "We have stayed culturally Mexican."[89]

In an attempt to prove that contention, Tijerina promoted the idea of organizing a car caravan between Albuquerque and Mexico City in a patriotic pilgrimage. The route would follow that of the yearly caravan of goods that had been New Mexico's major link with Mexico proper throughout the colonial era. Plans called for caravan participants to "symbolically kiss the ground" the moment they stepped upon Mexican soil. During a series of "civic ceremonies" along the way, caravan participants were also supposed to don "Mexican attire" and carry a standard with the Virgin of Guadalupe like that carried into battle by Father Miguel Hidalgo y Costilla, the hero of Mexican independence. Each stop would serve as an occasion to exalt Mexican national heroes like Hidalgo and his fellow independence leader, José María Morelos, as well as Mexican Revolution leaders Emiliano Zapata, Pancho Villa, and Venustiano Carranza and the Aztec prince Cuauhtémoc. (In the only nod to the United States, Tijerina's list of heroes also included Abraham Lincoln and the recently slain John F. Kennedy.)[90] The entire effort was to culminate with as many as 200 cars arriving in Mexico City on the sixteenth of September, Mexican Independence Day, and gathering for a massive celebration in front of Mexico City's Palacio Nacional, which housed the offices of the Mexican president.[91] Perhaps defeated by the logistical challenges, Tijerina soon placed the caravan idea on a back shelf. Privately, one land-grant activist wondered whether that was not for the best, given how much money and time such a trip would cost.[92]

Still, Tijerina expressed a cautious optimism concerning the success of his Mexican strategy overall to his wife. Perhaps most surprising, given his later reputation as a militant, his definition of success defied the suspicions of U.S. law enforcement. "Maria, you and Holy God are witnesses to my convictions, that I don't believe in violence," he wrote in a May 1962 letter to Mary Escobar. In lobbying south of the border, Tijerina hoped to elicit the sympathy of other Mexicans so that they might pressure their government to pressure the United States to take meaningful action. He therefore urged his wife "to pray to God that our fight and supplication will be heard by our oppressors," meaning the Americans. If only the

United States would grant freedom to New Mexico just like European nations had granted freedom to (the formerly colonized) Africa, he continued, a crisis might be averted. "I don't want to see my people in rebellion," he warned.[93] For New Mexicans who continued to flirt with violence, Tijerina offered his anticolonial analysis as both a summation of their plight and the basis—through appealing to the signatories of the Treaty of Guadalupe Hidalgo—of a new way forward.

In tracing the root of the problems confronting Spanish speakers to the American takeover, Tijerina owed an intellectual debt to George I. Sánchez, a leading Mexican American academic and civil rights activist during the middle decades of the twentieth century. A professor of education and New Mexican native, Sánchez in 1940 published *The Forgotten People*, a slim but influential volume with an apt title. When it was published, the book provided one of the few sources of information available anywhere in any language about Spanish-speaking New Mexicans. Sánchez focused upon the population of Taos County, heavily Spanish-speaking and, as Sánchez noted, poorer and less educated than the rest of the state. Sánchez knew why. "In the march of imperialism," he explained, "a people were forgotten, cast aside as the byproduct of territorial aggrandizement."[94] Tijerina kept a copy of Sanchez's book in his personal library.[95] Although born twenty years apart, both men looked back to 1848 to explain contemporary circumstances.

As much as Sánchez and Tijerina agreed upon the enduring significance of the 1848 war, their proposed solutions moved in completely opposite directions, underscoring the distinctiveness of Tijerina's anticolonial politics. A year after the publication of *The Forgotten People*, Sánchez was elected the national president of the League of United Latin American Citizens, or LULAC.[96] Founded in 1929, LULAC emerged as one of the leading Mexican American civil rights organizations of the postwar era. Along with the American GI Forum, a civil rights organization and veterans' group, LULAC during the 1950s accrued a number of significant courtroom victories aimed at ending segregation directed at Mexican-origin people. The victories did not come easily. In the 1930s, Sánchez's dedication to advancing racial equality gained him so many enemies that the professor carried a gun for self-protection.[97] Nevertheless, the quick-witted Sánchez once labeled the trouble that Mexican-origin people had in finding acceptance within the United States a problem of "cultural indigestion."[98] The metaphor captured his integrationist perspective. Despite the obstacles, Sánchez never wavered in advocating the incorporation of Mexican-descent people within the American body politic as equals. Tijerina, in contrast, was never particularly interested in civil rights per se. Whether a preacher, a prophet, or a land-grant activist, he expressed zero interest in integration. Tijerina wanted justice and retribution. He wanted an end to colonization. He wanted the land.

Although wisdom dictated keeping a low profile, at least until an Arizona warrant for his arrest expired the following year, Tijerina could not wait to share his determination on this point. In August 1962, he drafted an open letter to the Spanish-speaking people of New Mexico that succinctly showcased his anticolonial thesis. "We declare that the treatment that the Anglo-Saxon has given us over the past 120 years, is the same as the treatment he has given to the poor and humble peoples of Africa, and Asia, as well as of Latin America," Tijerina announced. Across the Southwest at the time, the term "Anglo-Saxon" popularly referred to a person of European extraction versus someone of African or Mexican origin. Tijerina's choice of ethnic identifier, however, deliberately melded British imperial history with the history of the American empire. Just as European nations had colonized areas of the globe, Tijerina maintained, the United States had operated and continued to operate as a colonial power in New Mexico and across the Southwest. Consequently, nuevomexicanos had spent the past 114 years being treated as "despised insects" by those who had conquered them.[99]

The rest of the statement angrily detailed the suffering inflicted by conquest. A proud people who had once grazed their own cattle without restriction now received federal food subsidies in the form of "LECHE DE POLVO," that is, powdered milk. Still antagonistic toward the very concept of welfare, Tijerina used capital letters to scream the injustice. No doubt tapping into bitter personal experience, he also lamented the sense of humiliation that so often surrounded poverty. He excoriated members of the "Saxon race" as well as of the U.S. federal government for "making fun of our economic state" and for "scoffing at our children, [saying] that they are inferior to their own."[100] The conqueror since 1848, he complained, "has disdained us in thousands of ways and [on thousands of] occasions." Tijerina continued to view military service as a form of exploitation, bluntly stating that "nothing has come of the sacrifice of thousands of fathers and brothers in these [American] wars." The only solution to this sad state of affairs: "to resurrect the legal value of the Treaty of Guadalupe Hidalgo." Just like José María Martínez, Tijerina proposed the formation of a single "great alliance" dedicated to that singular task.[101]

After five years of hiding, multiple trips to Mexico, and critical early support from Tierra Amarilla grant residents, Tijerina finally founded the Alianza Federal de Mercedes on February 2, 1963, the 125th anniversary of the Treaty of Guadalupe Hidalgo. Its purpose: "To unite all of the land grants into one single body of land grants to demand of the two governments that signed the Treaty of Guadalupe Hidalgo a complete investigation of all of its violations."[102] Coming out of the shadows did not initially shift his orientation toward Mexico. Throughout 1963 and much of 1964, he continued to take trips south of the border and to welcome Mexican visitors to the Alianza's offices in Albuquerque. To the delight of many, a labor activist visiting one of the first Alianza meetings, for example, assured members that their cause was known throughout Mexico and that it enjoyed the support of millions.[103]

Founding an organization, however, made new demands upon Tijerina. Answering phone calls, replying to correspondence, taking minutes of meetings—in short, all the tasks of running an office—awaited. Not at all inclined toward this sort of drudgery and still convinced that he was fulfilling his God-given destiny, Tijerina turned to family members for support. Invoking his patriarchal authority, he imposed on them to sacrifice for the Alianza cause.

4

The Patriarch

The same day that the Alianza was incorporated, Rose Tijerina turned fourteen years old. Shortly thereafter, Mary Escobar and Reies López Tijerina divorced, and Rose and her father went to Mexico for three months. The purpose of this trip, Tijerina wrote in his memoir, was to rally support for his idea to arrange that automobile caravan from Albuquerque all the way to Mexico City.[1] But Tijerina had another motive for the trip, according to his daughter: he intended to find her a husband in Mexico.

Both agree that, shortly after arriving, Tijerina introduced her to a young man named Mauricio. Rose Tijerina remembered that she instantly developed a crush on her intended fiancé, a handsome nineteen-year-old. She also remembered that her girlhood fantasies were destroyed late one evening when she and her father entered a restaurant and Tijerina explained that he had something extremely important to tell her. According to Rose Tijerina, he told her that he had to train her body in preparation for her husband, so that she would not feel sensations, and that was because God had revealed something to him: that Rose was to be the cup of sacrifice from which the cause would drink. "And then, *esa misma noche* [that same night], when we got home he started molesting me. Every night . . . but I fought him off by crying and crying. And only a curtain used to separate our bedroom from the bedroom of . . . the owner of the house."[2]

Although Rose Tijerina never spoke with Mary Escobar about what happened in Mexico City until years later, her mother remembered receiving a series of phone calls at the time. They were only partially enlightening. At home in New Mexico with her other five children, Escobar recollected, she heard from Dolores "Lolita" Rebelde, who, along with her husband, was hosting the two Tijerinas. The Rebeldes had known the Tijerina family for years through their shared Pentecostal faith. "Dolores Rebelde didn't tell me [anything specific]," Mary Escobar recalled. "She said to me, 'Send for Rosita. Send for Rosita. She needs to go back with you, *hermana*.'" Escobar remembered then trying to talk directly to Rose twice over the phone, to little avail.[3] "I couldn't talk because I had this lump in my throat," Rose Tijerina confirmed. "I didn't want anyone to know. I was so ashamed. And so my mom finally goes, '¿Quieres que mande por ti? [Do you want me to send for you?]' And I just went 'ummhmm.' That's all I could say. She said, 'Bueno, te voy a mandar cinquenta dolares y que tu papi te ponga en el bus para que vengas a la casa [Okay, I'm going to send fifty dollars and have your dad put you on a bus so that you can come home].'" Mary Escobar did send the money, but, according to Rose, Reies Tijerina intercepted the fifty dollars and told her how he planned to spend it. Newly divorced from Mary, Tijerina was already dating a woman in Mexico City. Rose recalled her father telling her that with this money, she and her fiancé and he and his girlfriend could all enjoy the sights of Mexico together.

Asked about these allegations in 2010, Reies Tijerina explained that his daughter had "talked all over the state [of New Mexico]" making accusations but that he was going to take the opportunity to provide "the real story." He had a point about the rumor mill. In New Mexico, allegations of sexual molestation by Tijerina had circulated for years. According to Reies Tijerina, however, he took his eldest daughter to Mexico only upon her mother's request. He said that at the time Mary Escobar also warned him, "'Don't you forget if something happens to Rosa, you are going to be fully responsible.'" Reies Tijerina then clarified, "She was talking about her virginity." After Rose Tijerina suggested that she and her boyfriend and he and his girlfriend visit a wilderness park on the outskirts of the capital, he said, he had reason to grow concerned. The young couple did not return to the car when Reies Tijerina started calling for them, he recalled. "I didn't know what to do. I was thinking about what Maria had told me, 'You be responsible,'" Reies Tijerina remembered. "But I said to myself, if she [Rose] was raped by Mauricio, her panties had to be bloody." He needed to check whether she had engaged in sex, forcible or otherwise. In other words, the allegations of molestation emerged from his vigilance and concern as a father. As far as Tijerina was concerned, moreover, any deviations from this story were false memories that psychiatrists had foisted upon his daughter in the intervening decades. When asked whether he had ever told his eldest daughter that she was the sacrificial cup from which all would drink, Tijerina abandoned his typical aversion to cursing. His response: "That's bullshit!"[4]

Ultimately, the only two people who ever will know exactly what happened during those three months—or single night—in that Mexico City bedroom were the two people there. Certainly, the circumstances that Rose Tijerina described raise suspicion. According to the literature on incest, the classic profile of abuse has a powerful father turning to an eldest daughter in the absence of the mother and explaining that he needs to train her sexually.[5] Yet, as memory experts claim, in delving into the past, we cannot forget what happened in the intervening years. That deep divisions and mutual recriminations haunted the Tijerina family decades later was also beyond debate.

The difficulty of disentangling memories from lingering hurts compounds the challenge of ever reconciling these two accounts. In 2010, Rachel Tijerina, Rose's younger sister, was present during her father's interview and, speaking in defense of him, noted that she had heard the same version of events from him years ago. "You notice [that when] people lie, they change their stories, [but] he told me what he's telling here," she pointed out.[6] For her part, Rose Tijerina spoke with me first with her mother present and then alone. Like her father, she demonstrated a willingness to share her story. After years of therapy, she said, her doctor had told her that to "vomit it all out" would be a path toward healing.[7]

Nonetheless, the two accounts are fraught with a converging significance. In Rose Tijerina's memory of an extended episode of sexual abuse, her father appears incredibly powerful and demanding. Reies Tijerina's version of events likewise highlighted a patriarchal and commanding personality at work. He did not deny touching his daughter intimately; instead he insisted that he had the right and obligation as a father to verify physically whether his daughter was still a virgin. Here was the most important common denominator amid the multiple versions of the past: Tijerina arrogantly viewed himself as invested with tremendous authority from God, authority that both justified and explained his actions within his family. A similarly inflated sense of self-importance was to guide his behavior within the land-grant organization that he founded.

In fact, the Alianza and the Tijerina family extensively overlapped. With few resources to his name in terms of education or money, Tijerina relied on family members to make up the backbone of the organization throughout its existence. He continued to depend on Mary Escobar even after the pair divorced in March 1963, just one month after the organization's founding. Their older children were likewise active in the Alianza, especially his sons David (Reies Hugh) and Danny, who operated as Tijerina's steadfast lieutenants, and Rose, who worked as an unpaid secretary for ten years. Each of Tijerina's four brothers also supported the organization, particularly his youngest brother, Chris (Cristóbal), who usually held a formal position. In fact, only a handful of people not related to Tijerina ever entered the inner circle of Alianza advisers.

As a patriarch, Tijerina expected to rule the Alianza with the same absolute authority that he so often exerted within his own family. The patriarchal structure that dominated the Alianza both spurred its success and contributed to its failure. On the one hand, the day-to-day operations of the Alianza greatly depended upon the contributions of those family members closest to Tijerina. Indeed, without the unpaid labor of Mary Escobar and Rose Tijerina and their commitment as activists to the land-grant cause, the Alianza might never have existed at all. On the other hand, in accord with the constitution that flatly pronounced dissent divisive and reason for expulsion, the Alianza never developed any mechanism for criticism or even any real organization beyond what Tijerina as its supreme leader dictated. Decision-making power always rested with the organization's founder and president, as did the potential to abuse that power.

THE SACRIFICIAL CUP

The sacrificial cup that appears in Rose Tijerina's recollection also appears in a letter that she wrote in 1967. In this letter, the then eighteen-year-old Rose begged her father's forgiveness for her involvement with a young man named Gilbert. "Yo todo lo que quiero ser es la soldada de mi pueblo umilde [humilde] or mas bien un baso [vaso] para que mi Dios y tu junto con mi pueblo tomen de el [All I want is to be a soldier for my humble people or better a cup from which God and you and my people may drink]," she wrote. More troubling in light of her allegations, Rose Tijerina in this letter seemed to be willingly offering herself as a sacrificial victim for the Alianza. Yet children of abuse often employ a strategy of being good.[8] And if in 1967 a teenage Rose was making a determined effort to return to her father's good graces, that effort was entirely consistent with attempting to avoid what all family members had experienced or witnessed: the explosive force of his anger. As if reminding her father where she stood in the family pecking order, she closed the letter, "Sin más, tu hija favorita, Srta. Rose Tijerina [Without further adieu, your favorite daughter, Miss Rose Tijerina]."[9] Her closing lacked conceit. Rachel Tijerina agreed that while they were growing up, Rose had been by far their father's favorite.[10]

In the New Testament, the cup of sacrifice refers not only to the cup of wine that Jesus lifts up during the Last Supper but also to the very notion of Jesus as a sacrificial victim. In the letter, the imagery seems familiar enough to father and daughter. More important, the cup of sacrifice serves as an apt metaphor for how members of Tijerina's family suffered on his behalf as he pursued land-grant justice. Contributing to the success of the organization no doubt allowed them to placate a temperamental man. At the same time, their assistance also deserves to stand apart from the specter of abuse. As activists in their own right, they were a part of the Alianza's success.

Mary Escobar's role in building the Alianza has been overlooked primarily because she was a woman and because she had been divorced from Tijerina for several years by the time the organization received national attention. Yet it was Escobar who supported Tijerina during those critical five years before the Alianza was officially founded. As a fugitive, Tijerina understood that securing steady employment risked creating a paper trail that could lead to his capture. Using the alias "Roy López," he occasionally found odd jobs. He also worked in the fields alongside his wife and children when he was not in Mexico.[11] In the fields, families could work as a unit, which provided the opportunity for male heads of households to keep a close eye on their wives and daughters. That mattered to Tijerina, who generally objected to women working outside the home. Once the Tijerina family settled in Albuquerque, however, Escobar had no choice but to find a job in the city. Relatives and friends provided at best scattershot aid, and she had six children to feed and clothe.

Escobar's hard work essentially provided Tijerina a five-year sabbatical to pursue his land-grant studies. To avoid alerting authorities as to her husband's location, Escobar returned to using her birth name upon entering the workforce. At first, she cleaned houses. Soon, however, she decided to take secretarial classes, which allowed her to land a better-paying job at the University of New Mexico hospital downtown. She typically worked the 3 P.M. to 11 P.M. shift and remembered her eldest son, David, who was a young teen at the time, getting out of bed on school nights to ride his bicycle to meet her when her shift ended so that she would not be alone late at night while walking home from the bus stop. She had purchased a car with her wages, but Tijerina had taken it to Mexico on one of his extended trips and she never saw it again.[12]

The fate of another car had even more severe repercussions for the family. They were traveling from Farmington, New Mexico, to Tierra Amarilla along a desolate road one night when the car that Tijerina was driving, which one of his followers had given him, was rear-ended. The accident probably occurred during the winter of 1959–60, as Mary Escobar remembered being in the backseat with Noe and his slightly older sister, Lalita (Ira de Alá). In his memoir, Tijerina mentioned that he got $750 from the insurance company of the other driver, money that he immediately used "to further the cause of my oppressed community."[13] As Escobar recalled, Tijerina told her to tell the insurance agents that the children were bruised in the accident. She did. She did not tell them that she had started bleeding. She thought it was her period, but the bleeding did not end.[14]

Instead, it got worse. Instructed by her husband to stay in Tierra Amarilla while he was away (probably in Mexico), Escobar eventually traveled to San Antonio, more than 800 miles away, upon the insistence of her brother Efrain, who escorted her and the children. In San Antonio, a doctor told her that she needed surgery. But Reies Tijerina, now reunited with his family, told her no. Escobar recalled Tijerina saying something like, "No hay que operar ni que nada, vámonos. Ay vengo con el otro carro, piscamos algodón antes de llegar a Albuquerque [No operation, no nothing, let's go. I'm coming with the other car, and we'll pick cotton on the way back to Albuquerque]." She continued, "And he would get mad because I wouldn't pick [cotton] because a lot of blood would come out of me." For months she bled, and every time she stood up from a seated position, the smell of dead animal would escape her body. A likely scenario is that Escobar was suffering what doctors term a missed abortion, meaning that the fetus had died but was never expelled from the body. "I was rotting from the inside," she recalled.[15] Missed abortions often result in sepsis, blood poisoning, and even death, but sometimes the infection is contained and the woman either feels fine or suffers from flu-like symptoms.[16] Mary Escobar recalled feeling so sick that she could not get out of bed. In a separate interview, Rose Tijerina remembered her father insisting that her mother work. "That's when he got really angry. That's when my mom was bleeding so much because they had had the car accident and she wanted to stay home because she was hemorrhaging, and she had a fever too," she recalled.[17] Finally, Escobar got medical attention and, ultimately, in 1961 a hysterectomy.[18]

From all appearances, it seems as if the operation gave Tijerina an excuse to divorce Escobar and marry a land-grant heir. The hysterectomy, while probably saving her life, left Escobar vulnerable to replacement. Or so she believed. As she told a friend at the time, she felt "dead inside."[19] Looking back decades later, Escobar shifted to Spanish and the present tense: "No siento lo mismo, como una mujer completa [I no longer feel the same, like a complete woman]." She offered as a way of explanation, "They had taken out my uterus."[20] More forthcoming than her mother, Rose Tijerina explained that Escobar believed that without a uterus, she no longer could give a man sexual satisfaction.[21] Escobar herself did not elaborate on this point. If she so surmised, however, one reason may have been that, after her hysterectomy in 1961, Tijerina evidently started hinting that he needed a new wife. Escobar remembered that her husband began to complain that, because he was not a land-grant heir, he needed to marry someone who was in order to gain legitimacy as a land-grant leader.[22] According to Escobar, Tijerina's favorite Bible passage even before the car accident was Isaiah 4:1 (here from the King James Version): "And in that day seven women shall take hold of one man, saying, We will eat our own bread, and wear our own apparel: only let us be called by thy name, to take away our reproach." In short, the passage had women embracing polygamy as a means of saving themselves from sin. After her hysterectomy, which ended her childbearing capacity, Escobar may no longer have qualified in Tijerina's estimation to be even one of the seven. Escobar recalled that Tijerina started insisting, "La esposa debe estar viente años menor que el marido para que el esté contento [A wife should be twenty years younger than the husband for him to be happy]."[23]

Despite the long-troubled state of the marriage, Escobar's devotion to the Alianza and to her husband never wavered. In fact, she said that she divorced Reies upon his instructions only because she thought that divorce was to be in name only, a way to secure more money for their children and for the newly founded Alianza. According to Escobar, Tijerina had told her that as a single mother Escobar would be eligible for welfare, and from that welfare check she could send the Alianza fifty dollars a month. She recalled doing just that.[24] In addition, she sent money to Tijerina while he was in Mexico. "Reies, aquí te envio unos centavos [here I send you a few cents]," she wrote him, probably just after their divorce.[25] Another letter mentioned, more as an inquiry than as a complaint, that Tijerina had been quiet on a certain point: "No mencionas en las cartas el recaudo que te envío [You don't mention in your letters the provisions (financial?) that I send]."[26] The fact that the two lived together when Tijerina was not in Mexico only furthered Escobar's initial conviction that the divorce was a sham. For nearly a year, the divorced couple and their children lived in the same building that housed the Alianza's Albuquerque office. "Finally, the welfare lady said, 'You have to leave the building,'" Escobar remembered, "because it [cohabitating with her ex-husband] was unlawful." Not until Reies Tijerina was on the verge of remarrying in 1965 did Escobar, a woman in her late thirties, allow herself to accept the reality of the divorce. By then, she said, she mostly felt a sense of relief, asking herself, as she recalled, "Why am I waiting for this *hombre* who has me starving to death with my kids?" Indeed, when interviewed years later, Escobar repeatedly referred to herself as a "*tonta*" and a "*tontera*," a dummy and a big fat dummy, for sticking with Tijerina for such a long time.[27]

Yet if Escobar judged herself harshly when looking back across the decades, at the time, her desire to further land-grant justice extended to esteeming the man behind the mission. A picture taken in March 1959, when Mary Escobar and the children were visiting Tijerina in Mexico, hinted at a close connection between the pair despite their difficulties. In the photo, Tijerina is extending his hand outward toward Escobar; she grasps it and places it on her heart while looking directly, and arguably adoringly, at him. As Escobar once explained to an interviewer during the 1960s, "I married him because I believed he was chosen by God for a special purpose. I still do, but now I think he was chosen for this cause [the land grants], for the poor of the earth."[28] Thus a letter that she penned probably in 1964 wished Tijerina well. "Bueno que Dios te ayude a engrandecer el trabajo de la Justicia, y te de más iluminación para su Reino [May God help you make great the work of Justice and give you more illumination for his Kingdom]," Escobar wrote. "Yo no te pude seguir ayudando como una esposa pero con mi trabajo voy a ser [hacer] todo lo posible para cumplir con el porque la causa es todo lo mas grande que hay [en] mi corazón [I could no longer continue helping you as a wife but with my work I'm going to do all that is possible to meet my obligations regarding *el* (the masculine pronoun, "it" meaning the work, or possibly "he" referring to El Señor, that is, God) because the cause is what most occupies my heart]."[29] Perhaps Mary Escobar defended land-grant rights the only way she knew how, by supporting the man whom she married. Or perhaps continuing to back the land-grant cause was the only way she could stay connected to the one she still loved. In either case, only the level of alleged abuse makes her case unusual. Otherwise, the way in which she expressed her political commitment—by standing by her man—fit the activist profile of many women of her generation.[30]

Tijerina, in turn, initially relied upon Escobar for not just financial but also moral support. In her interview, Rose Tijerina kept mentioning that the two fought loudly and often before the divorce, but early letters from Tijerina to Escobar nevertheless brim with declarations of love and fidelity. Exhibiting a possessive streak, for example, Tijerina in April 1960 closed a letter to Escobar with the words, "Así que Mi Dios te guarde fiel y viva para mi nada mas para mi. Todo mi corazón para ti y mis hijos que tanto deseo verles [So may my God keep you faithful and alive for me and only for me. All of my heart (is) for you and for my children whom I so much wish to see]."[31] In another letter, Tijerina urged Escobar to find a way to get to the border so that the pair could reunite. He also dismissed Escobar's suspicions that he was less than faithful to her: "Y ya no me andes con tus celos. Tu sabes que soy de ti y que a ti solo pertenesco [And quit bothering me with your jealousy. You know that I am yours and that I only belong to you]."[32] Whether he was as faithful as he declared to be, Tijerina clearly depended upon Escobar. At a time when he was still new to the world of land-grant politics, she offered a familiar emotional connection as well as a constant sounding board. Tijerina regularly provided updates concerning his progress in lobbying Mexican officials and wrote to her about his plans for a just land-grant future.

Subsequent correspondence, however, shows Escobar quickly transitioning from "*amada esposa* [beloved spouse]" to Alianza administrative assistant.[33] In a May 1962 letter from Mexico City, for example, Tijerina wrote to Escobar that he understood that an opportunity had arisen to sell the Valle de Paz property in Arizona, and he charged her with overseeing the arrangements until he returned to the States. He also told her

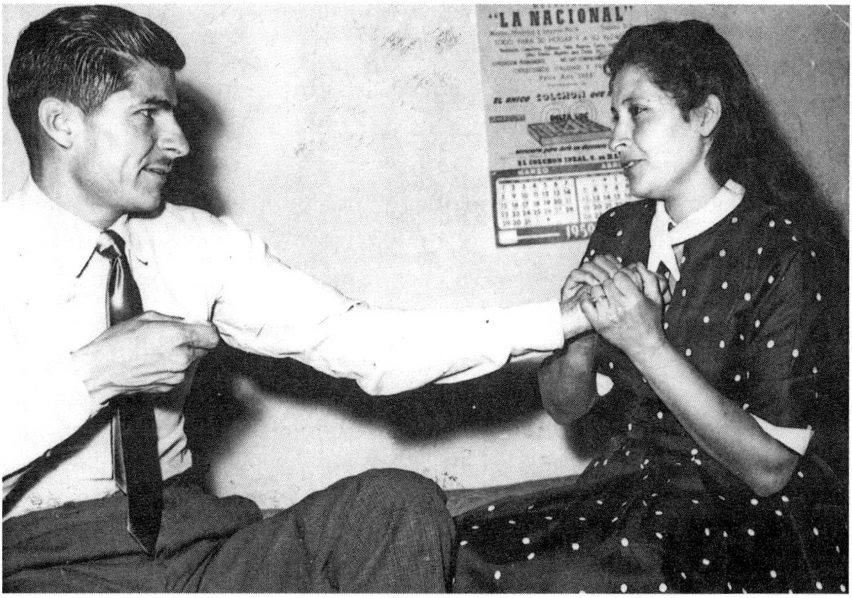

Tijerina spent nearly a year in Mexico researching land-grant history between September 1958 and September 1959. His wife at the time, Mary Escobar, paid him a visit, probably in March 1959, according to the calendar behind them. Despite troubles in their marriage, in this photo she holds his hand over her heart. (Photograph courtesy of Arte Público Press–University of Houston)

how to avoid striking the keys of the typewriter with so much force the next time around.[34] Confirming some of Escobar's recollections, Tijerina mentioned in another letter that he owed Mexican authorities $160 for bringing Escobar's car into the country. As he did not even have the money to pay these customs duties, he wrote, she was going to have to figure out May's rent on her own ("Así que María, procura juntar para la renta el mes de mayo").[35] After the divorce, the commands continued. In one of his oddest odd jobs, the summer after founding the Alianza Tijerina was hired as a movie extra on the set of a western called *A Distant Trumpet*. But the horse he had been riding stumbled and fell. From his hospital bed where he was nursing his back, Tijerina instructed Escobar to take care of canceling or finding adequate substitutes for all his pending appointments so that he could rest a few days.[36]

Fittingly, at least one early version of the Alianza's stationery formally acknowledged Escobar as the organization's secretary. In addition to responding to Tijerina's specific instructions, Escobar performed other tasks: she shared the latest Alianza member news with Tijerina while he was in Mexico, made copies of important documents, and augmented the Alianza's collection of reference books.[37] Throughout 1963 and 1964, moreover, the minutes of most Alianza gatherings appeared in Escobar's neat script.[38] Finally, at least once Escobar fulfilled another traditional gender role, that of being a cook. She recalled preparing an enormous dinner at a local restaurant, El Comedor de Julia, to introduce the new land-grant organization to interested Albuquerque residents soon after the Alianza's founding.[39] Escobar divorced the man but not the organization.

Although Escobar never claimed to be more than a helpmate, her daughter, Rose, insisted that her mother should also be credited with pushing Tijerina to do something more than study and investigate land-grant matters. Rose correctly saw her mother as an activist in her own right. "Pues nadie quiere hacer nada de esto de las mercedes [Well, no one wants to do anything about these land grants]," Rose Tijerina recalled her mom saying one day. "Yo voy a empezar a tocar puertas y recoger nombres para ser una organización para pelear por las mercedes [I'm going to start knocking on doors and collecting names to start an organization to fight for the land grants]." As Rose Tijerina recalled in 2006, her father then told her mother to wait, that he was on the verge of opening the Alianza office.[40] This recollection dovetailed with a statement that Rose Tijerina had made nearly forty years before to a reporter. Complaining that her mother's critical contribution to the founding of the Alianza had been overlooked, Rose asserted sometime in 1968, "My mother still supports the Alianza and does whatever she can. . . . There isn't much she can do because she is on welfare and because of the children in school. But she is the one who started the office. She did [underlining in the original]. She helped my father and the Alianza a lot and she had to suffer a lot to do it."[41]

In his memoir, Tijerina concurred that his mission placed a tremendous burden of responsibility upon Escobar. She was the family's main economic support.[42] He recalled that harvesttime once interrupted a happy family reunion in Mexico because Escobar needed to return to the States to pick cotton with the children while he stayed behind to continue his investigations.[43] Tijerina recognized that his decision to pursue land-grant justice meant that Escobar and their children often went without. The responsibility of keeping the household afloat fell entirely to her. Nevertheless, Tijerina credited Escobar with sympathizing with his priorities despite the economic insecurity that the family suffered. Whenever he tried to set aside the land-grant cause to concentrate solely on earning money, Tijerina wrote, "after a few days or weeks, my spirit would decay and I would feel like a prisoner. My wife herself would tell me, 'Your heart is not here, it's better if you follow your mission.'" Even after the divorce, he acknowledged, "My wife continued helping the Alianza a lot."[44]

Yet in contrast to Escobar, Tijerina explained the divorce as a function of Escobar escaping the orbit of his patriarchal control. Although Tijerina preferred that mothers stay home with their children (a preference Escobar shared), financial necessity drove him to abandon his opposition to Escobar seeking employment outside the home.[45] Given his long absences and fugitive status, Tijerina also had to abandon his opposition to Escobar literally taking the driver's seat. How else was she to get to work or perform errands? "In Albuquerque, I started to let her drive the car," he noted. "As I was a fugitive, I preferred not to go out much."[46] Whereas Escobar maintained the divorce was Tijerina's idea, Tijerina attributed it to Escobar's emergence as a professionally trained working woman who wanted more money than he could provide. "She started to study to become a secretary and the difficulties [between us] multiplied. For the first time, she mentioned divorce. I felt like I had been hit by a car," he wrote.[47] Yet the timing of Tijerina's explanation is off. The end of the couple's marriage and the expiration of the statute of limitations for Tijerina's alleged crimes were nearly concurrent. In other words, the divorce occurred when the Alianza needed supporting, not when Tijerina was still undercover. Tijerina's jumbled chronology did, however, neatly place the blame for the divorce entirely upon Escobar. Just like the misbehaving bride of Christ in his long-ago sermon, Escobar refused to conform to the role of a subservient wife that Tijerina wanted.

In his memoir, Tijerina expressed regret that he failed to be a good provider for his children and his spouse. It "broke his heart" to leave his family behind when he headed to Mexico for an extended stay in September 1958, just a few months after Noe's birth. His "soul hurt" whenever he denied his children new clothes or a toy. Every extra cent went toward "the struggle for the land," he explained, and his children had to make do with secondhand things. He also felt "much regret and tenderness," knowing how hard his children worked in the fields to earn money for the family and, indirectly, for the land-grant cause. David, the eldest, would pick up to 100 pounds at a time, while Rose, the next oldest, would come close to that amount, Tijerina wrote admiringly.[48] In an interview, Rose Tijerina recalled her father as a demanding taskmaster. "He used to work us really hard," she said.[49] Yet in *Mi Lucha por la Tierra*, Tijerina maintained that for the sake of his mission he had no choice but to harden his heart.

"From what I saw, I was the only man who profoundly understood who the Anglo was and how he had grabbed those 100 million acres of land that belonged to the pueblos that our ancestors had founded," he wrote. "It was this truth and this awareness that tormented me the most whenever I denied my children new things."[50]

Tijerina recounted one disturbing episode in which he felt he had no choice but to inflict suffering upon Lalita, then just four years old. Trying to cross the border back to the United States, Tijerina had attracted the attention of border agents, who, after discovering a box of bullets with him, had called the city police of El Paso. Afraid that his fugitive status was about to be discovered while he was being detained with his family, Tijerina wrote, he began to pinch Lalita so that she would cry loudly. The idea was to raise such a ruckus that border agents, believing the little girl was hungry and needed milk, would let the family go. Tijerina pinched his daughter even harder until border agents did just that.[51]

Otherwise—with the exception of Rose, who frequently went with him to Mexico—his memoir mentioned his other children only in passing. Apparently, he felt obliged to offer an explanation about why Rose traveled with him. She accompanied him to Mexico, he wrote, because the Rebeldes, their host family in Mexico City, liked her so much. "'Bring Rosita with you,' is what they would tell me every time I did go to Mexico. So I always brought her with me."[52]

Actually, once Tijerina began organizing publicly on behalf of the Alianza, he brought Rose with him not just to Mexico City but everywhere. During the early years of the organization, Tijerina spent most of his weekends traveling to villages and towns throughout New Mexico, seeking supporters. "I would always have to be there. If I didn't show up, oh boy I would be in trouble," Rose recalled. "One time . . . I lied to my dad [by] not going with him out of town for a meeting and I told him I was feeling sick. And when he came home he saw me, [he saw] that I wasn't in bed, and he just took off his belt and started whipping me." The violence, and threat of violence, provided another reason to demonstrate her devotion to her father's cause. At Alianza meetings, Rose recalled taking notes, issuing membership cards, recording dues payments, and distributing literature. After the 1963 visit to Mexico, moreover, she recalled doing so quietly.[53]

Although her father never again touched her inappropriately, she said in a later interview, she nonetheless spent the following years acting like a virtual "zombie." Her relative silence even attracted the notice of the men who gathered for early Alianza meetings, she recalled. "This older guy would say, 'Well, Rosita already talked her eleven words for the day so we're not going to hear from her again for the rest of the day.'"[54]

Rose says she spent almost every weekend of her teenage years in her father's company attending meetings. Given her travel schedule and her father's protective tendencies, school provided only a rare reprieve. While she loved school and loved to read, she attended only up until the ninth grade of high school and then only after her older brother David promised his father that he would supervise her.[55]

Pinpointing the reason why her father wanted her close to his side is difficult, but her physical appearance almost certainly played a part. In many ways, the attractive Rose Tijerina became the "face" of the Alianza, next to her father. When Tijerina organized a parade to honor the 350th anniversary of the arrival of the Spanish language to New Mexico in 1969, one *aliancista* offered her a white horse to ride at the head of the procession. When the Alianza cast Christmas dramas, her role was to be the Virgin Mary. And she was the only woman to participate in the courthouse raid, "the beautiful girl in very tight pink trousers striding past," according to one account.[56]

Forty years later, one journalist remained deeply impressed by Rose's presence. Larry Calloway, a writer for United Press International, had been inside the Rio Arriba County Courthouse on June 5, 1967, and was one of two people taken hostage for a brief time. Subsequently writing about that experience, he cast Reies Tijerina as a man driven by a spiritual fury and his daughter as his heir apparent. "She was 18 at the time of the raid, with long black hair and a perfect figure and a modest but defiant expression. Mystical," Calloway rhapsodized. According to an old Native American legend, he continued, a warrior emerges out of the flames followed by a beautiful woman. "Similarly, as Tijerina emerged from the court house raid as a militant activist of global proportions, a girl of 18 came out of the flames too."[57]

Although not comfortable labeling herself "beautiful," Rose Tijerina surmised that her father decided that she was his favorite largely based upon how she looked. The slightly darker-skinned Rachel, five years Rose's junior, remembered much the same without a trace of bitterness. To their father, she once commented, "Rose was the beautiful princess. I was the ugly Indian."[58]

Calloway nonetheless erred in characterizing Rose as emerging from the flames as a leader of her people. Instead, she occupied a subservient and usually isolated role. Among the organization's papers, the name

Rose (sometimes Rosa, sometimes Rosita) Tijerina appears on countless letters in English and in Spanish in which she is writing to members requesting dues payments, sending letters of thanks for donations, or answering inquiries.[59] As she remembered, after her father's remarriage, she did her best to fill her mother's secretarial shoes: "My mom had a typing book. When she stopped working [for] *la* Alianza, I asked her if I could have it so I could learn and she says, 'yeah.' So, I started learning with it. [Until then] I was still handwriting the letters. I used to type a lot of stuff for my dad." Rose took on the role of obedient daughter. Yet like her mother, she also sacrificed on behalf of the land-grant cause because she supported it. "At age fourteen, I started learning of the Alianza from my mom," she remembered. "Then my mom left, and I stayed."[60]

Limited by her gender in a male-dominated organization, however, her contribution was largely confined to administrative tasks. Though she attended countless meetings, she recalled that she remained in the dark about the histories behind the documents she often handed out to attendees, such as references to Ordenanza 99. Rose once asked her father why she knew so little about their content. Her father responded that she had been so busy working that she had not had time to read anything. "It was true," she said. "All I had time for was work, work, work." It all took a toll. Years later, she theorized that her silenced demeanor gave classmates as well as Alianza members the impression that she was a snob.[61] The upshot was that being her father's favorite also meant being lonely.

Her father's second marriage in September 1965 introduced a new set of troubles for her and her brothers and sisters. Reies Tijerina married eighteen-year-old Patricia Romero, an Albuquerque native whose family traced its lineage all the way back to the original settlers of the 1739 Tomé grant located south of town. In fact, Romero met the requirements that Mary Escobar recalled Tijerina listing as essential in his ideal spouse: she was fully twenty years younger than he and a land-grant heir.[62] "I know, to you Anglos, my marrying an heir would be charged as self-interest, but you see, my people think differently," Tijerina later admitted to a reporter about his marriage. "They believe that if I have a genuine self-interest in the cause, I am far more likely to do the job for them."[63] In his memoir, Tijerina added that the marriage solved another problem. Despite his reputation as a non-swearing, non-drinking man who was unfailingly polite to women, he wrote that, as a divorced man, "I could not visit homes if the husband was at work or away from the house. Suspicion was undermining the harmony of the Alianza. I started to think it preferable if I marry."[64]

Yet on a strictly utilitarian level, choosing Patricia Romero, called Patsy, as his bride made no sense at all. "She cannot read or write. You know what that means? You know what that means? She is retarded," Tijerina bluntly divulged in a 1968 interview. A 1961 school report for fourteen-year-old Patricia Romero had labeled her "mentally deficient" based on her low scores on the standard IQ test for children. The report also stated that the teen had dropped out of Washington Junior High School "because of the subject's unfortunate school experiences due to her inability to function in a regular academic classroom."[65] In the 1968 interview, Tijerina referred to these scholastic difficulties. "I thought they were making fun of her in school and I decided to marry her and put her above all women," he noted in a comment that also revealed his own sense of self-worth. "Modern wisdom is foolishness," he continued.[66] As inspiration for the union, Tijerina remembered consulting with the same angels that had visited him in Visalia, California, at the time of his super-dream. They did not block his path.[67] Indeed, as a newlywed, Tijerina wrote Romero many letters that declared her to be "my heart," "my consolation," "my life," and, in another revealing comment, "worthy of all my love."[68]

Decades later during an oral history interview, however, Tijerina bypassed any mention of affection, or of angels, to share a more sordid tale of trying to break off the relationship as soon as he found out that Romero could not read or write: "Instead of writing P-A-T-S-Y, she would write P-A-S-T-Y," he recalled. But Romero's family pressured him into marrying her after she made it clear that she wanted to wed. The couple did so just two months after first meeting in an Albuquerque restaurant. Tijerina resolved to make the best of a bad situation. "She blackmailed me. I was too much of a man to let her down. So I started praying to God, what am I going to do Lord, let me know," Tijerina recalled. At this point, however, this private looking- backward began to echo the earlier public version that Tijerina had presented for so long. "In my mind and spirit, I felt she was a symbol of all my people. A symbol. Because that's the way my people were, ignorant," he continued.[69] The characterization of nuevomexicanos—and of his new bride—stung. At the same time, the comment confirmed the extent that Tijerina years later still saw himself as superior not only to the woman whom he married in 1965 but also to other Alianza members.

At the time, Tijerina's personal life yielded political implications. First, the new Mrs. Tijerina was never going to serve as secretary of the Alianza. Instead, Rose Tijerina continued in that supporting role for ten unpaid years. Unfortunately, Rose and her new stepmother, who was only two years Rose's senior, did not get along. Years later Rose suspected that Patricia could sense Tijerina's particular favoritism toward his eldest daughter and resented it.[70] During a separate interview, Rose's sister Rachel offered a similar insight. Weighing her words carefully, she proposed that Patsy had a "mental jealousy problem" that drove a wedge between the first and second Tijerina families.[71] Meanwhile, Romero's reasons for marrying Tijerina are open to speculation. Coming from a land-grant family, she may have been attracted to him or his cause—or both.[72] Whatever the case, during the years that Tijerina headed the Alianza, tensions among his different relations constantly boiled and bubbled out of public view. "It was a problem," he recalled about the constant family drama. "It was a big problem."[73] As a patriarch, Tijerina's solution to any problem was the same: to concentrate power in his own hands.

The symbols and structure that surrounded the founding of the Alianza conveyed that building his own power was his intent from the start. In one of the first Alianza meetings, for example, Tijerina unilaterally announced that the rainbow was to be the organization's official symbol. As Tijerina explained, alluding to the rainbow that appeared after the story of the flood in the Bible, the rainbow represented the arrival of an entirely new social order.[74] Equally important, however, Tijerina understood the rainbow to be a sign of his own anointed status ever since he had seen one in Fruita, Colorado, in 1956. Similarly, Tijerina selected the secretary bird, a native of sub-Saharan Africa, as the Alianza's official avian symbol. The choice, as well as the need to have an official bird at all, seemed inexplicable except that Tijerina had been told in his 1956 super-dream that his role was to be "secretary." Conveniently, moreover, the secretary bird is a type of raptor that preys upon snakes, which, like the serpent in the Garden of Eden, biblically is associated with evil or the devil. Again, the choice spoke to Tijerina's supreme role in the Alianza's great battle for justice.

Fittingly, the Alianza's original constitution acknowledged a single "*executivo supremo*." To be sure, the same document mandated an organizational structure consisting of six additional posts. These ranged from a "secretary of fiestas and symbolic rites" to a "secretary of land" to, in an ominous portent given the extent to which Alianza activities later came under police scrutiny, a "secretary of security."[75] The constitution, however, failed to ascribe any duties to these secretarial offices, which, in any event, soon collapsed into the more traditional roles of vice president, secretary, and treasurer. Tijerina felt free to ignore the constitution when it suited him—for instance, when he worked to secure his brother Cristóbal a top spot in the organization's hierarchy.[76]

Tijerina's brothers were part of a small circle of handpicked advisers. Most important from a public relations aspect, Cristóbal, the youngest, joined the cause—occasionally at first and then full-time by 1965 when the Alianza stationery formally recognized him as the organization's first "Secretary of the Interior." Growing up apart from his siblings and evidently having enjoyed the opportunity to receive more schooling, Cristóbal Tijerina employed impeccable spelling and syntax in English as compared to Reies Tijerina's more idiosyncratic and phonetic approach. The younger brother took charge of writing to federal bureaucrats and legislators. Even before accepting a formal role in the organization, "Chris," as he often signed his letters, had made it a point to share his income from his job as a beer distributor with Reies Tijerina's family and accompanied his brother on trips to Mexico.[77]

Anselmo Tijerina rededicated himself to the cause in 1961. Initially among his brother's earliest recruits, Anselmo's decision to escape the Tierra Amarilla jail had resulted in a two-year absence from any political involvement after police caught him at the border in 1959 and he ended up serving time. Shortly after his release, a jobless Anselmo wrote to Reies. "I am ready for what you order, that is, if there is a place for me," he pleaded. "If you think there is a hope of something [some position or some work], well, you tell me what I should do."[78] Although the main base of the Alianza's operations was always Albuquerque, Anselmo eventually ran a satellite office in Hernandez, north of Santa Fe. There he once brought Rose Tijerina for a time when the relationship between Rose and her stepmother became particularly volatile. As for Ramón Tijerina, although he lived in San Antonio with his family during the early years of the Alianza, he supported the organization too, even acting as its president at one time.[79]

Incarceration delayed Margarito Tijerina's arrival in New Mexico, but he also wished to contribute to his brother's mission. First, however, he needed Reies's help understanding precisely what that mission was. After the fiasco in Arizona, Margarito ended up in Indiana serving time for violating his parole. In letters to Reies Tijerina, he frequently asked his brother for his financial assistance while pledging his support to his cause. Expanding his efforts, in January 1961 Margarito wrote to Juan Martínez of Tierra Amarilla, a prominent Corporation of Abiquiú member. He explicitly asked him to pressure Reies to provide the soon-to-be-released Margarito some cash.[80] Evidently Margarito Tijerina knew enough about Reies's activities to contact this land-grant ally. At the same time, he did not seem to realize that the mission had changed. A few months later, Margarito Tijerina wrote to his brother to complain about the situation in Illinois, where he was living after his release: "Here all the people are blind. They don't understand about the wrath of God that is about to arrive."[81] Reies Tijerina must have clarified at some point that the mission had switched entirely from awaiting the end of the world to seeking land-grant justice, for Margarito Tijerina eventually made his way to New Mexico.

Once there, however, Margarito created problems. According to police, in the early evening of October 2, 1965, a couple stopped at a gas station in Rutheron, New Mexico, just west of Tierra Amarilla. The male driver got out while his female companion stayed inside the car. Once inside the gasoline station, the male driver punched the owner, stabbed the owner's wife, and took $300 before fleeing. Two months later, the victims positively identified Anselmo, Reies's oldest brother, as the culprit. When Anselmo's alibi proved airtight (he had been in Chicago at the time), the couple then positively identified Margarito. In late July 1966, with Rio Arriba County district attorney Alfonso Sánchez in charge of the prosecution, Margarito Tijerina was found guilty of robbery and assault and was sentenced to ten to fifty years. Sánchez also worked to ensure that afterward the courts recognized Margarito Tijerina as a "habitual criminal."[82]

Certainly, the incident threatened the Alianza's reputation and that of the Tijerina family. Just as important, however, the entire episode suggested the extent that Reies Tijerina exerted considerable sway over members of his increasingly complicated family. He may, for example, have convinced his eldest son to testify on his uncle's behalf. In August 1966, the local district attorney filed perjury charges against David (Reies Hugh) Tijerina, then nineteen, the eldest son of Reies Tijerina and Mary Escobar. Just two weeks before the case against his uncle went to trial, David had come forward to say that he had seen his uncle in Albuquerque when the crime had occurred. David explained that he had kept silent up until this point because he had been up in a tree with a girl at the time and, expecting that others could vouch for his uncle's location, wanted to protect the girl's reputation.[83] Whether or not the story was true, ultimately David Tijerina risked his own freedom to try to save his father's brother from imprisonment. Escobar too was pulled into this drama via the female companion in the car, a woman named Beatrice Hofrice. Her exact role in this story varies, depending upon the source. The lead prosecutor painted her as a victim who needed new teeth because Margarito Tijerina had beaten her so badly. In this telling, Margarito Tijerina committed the robbery to get the money to purchase false teeth.[84] A defender of the Tijerina family, in contrast, portrayed Hofrice as a shiftless character who, to avoid jail, cut a deal with the prosecution to frame her former lover.[85] In either case, Hofrice's involvement in the court case often left her six children unattended. Escobar—even though she had been divorced from Reies Tijerina since early 1963—increasingly took primary responsibility for caring for them.[86]

Although Tijerina mentioned his two eldest sons only in passing in his memoir, they stood by Tijerina throughout the 1960s and into the 1970s.[87] David's willingness to provide an alibi for his uncle in particular fit a long-term pattern that began in childhood of doing his part to help the family. Just ten when his father became a fugitive, David had served as a daytime lookout in the winter cold of northern New Mexico.[88] Following his father's incarceration, moreover, David, as the oldest, tried his best to hold the organization and family together. In letters to his father, he wrote of navigating a series of power struggles within the Alianza that occurred in Tijerina's absence, provided updates regarding the latest efforts he was spearheading to secure legal and medical help for his imprisoned father, and offered repeated reassurances concerning the welfare of his stepmother, Patsy, and her children, who were, of course, his half-siblings. All of this work reflected the absolute esteem in which the son held his father. "Well, Papi, everyone here sends their greetings and affection to a leader who forever will be recorded in the history books," he wrote in Spanish. "Receive all the honor from a son who is proud to have a father [who is] so humble and rich in wisdom."[89]

The Tijerina children also demonstrated loyalty to their father, and to their own political commitments, by participating in protests that echoed their father's priorities. In 1967, David and Daniel both took part in the courthouse raid along with their sister Rose. In 1968, when Tijerina traveled to Washington, D.C., as part of the Poor People's Campaign, he brought these three oldest children along with Rachel. During a protest at the U.S. Supreme Court, Daniel, sixteen, climbed atop a statue of Athena, the goddess of justice and mercy, much to his father's admiration. Later, he got into a scuffle with police in front of the Supreme Court building that ended with him being beaten and jailed while his sister Rachel, fifteen, was also struck.[90] To their father, his children's willingness to suffer for *his* beliefs made them "soldiers of justice, *valientes*."[91] That same year, Rachel and Daniel participated in a school protest at Washington Junior High School in Albuquerque that captured many of her father's concerns regarding discrimination in public education. The students' demands included a greater emphasis on Mexican American history and culture, an end to corporal punishment, and the ability to fire teachers who demonstrated racial prejudice. For their activism, both Rachel and Daniel were arrested and suspended from school.[92]

In 2010, Rachel voiced no regrets. Instead, she echoed her brother David's high opinion of Reies Tijerina circa 1970. "Until this day I can't find him to be wrong," she stated about her father. "To me he is the best historian in the world, the most knowledgeable historian in the world."[93] A few years later, however, she conveyed that her relationship with her father had frayed after the two had a minor disagreement.[94] That too fit a broader pattern that dated back decades. As family members knew and Alianza members soon found out, a good relationship with Reies Tijerina depended upon acquiescence to his ideas and demands.

Alianza members who failed to uphold that standard of loyalty soon left or were expelled. Frank Treviño, for example, the owner of El Comedor de Julia restaurant, initially was so taken with the land-grant cause that, in addition to providing Tijerina and Escobar the space to hold a fund-raising dinner, he loaned Tijerina temporary office space next door to his establishment. The Mexican-born Treviño also did translation work for Tijerina for which he said he was never paid. The two men then had a falling-out for that reason, Treviño recalled. Tijerina called him a "parasite" because Treviño had no familial connection to any grant. In return, a disenchanted Treviño found fault with Tijerina's oratory, scoffing that the Alianza president "just said the same things over and over again." His central complaint, however, revolved around how Tijerina ran the organization. "The officers are just 'puppets,'" the restaurateur reportedly told a state investigator who had to interview him in 1967. "When [Tijerina] says jump or even insinuates it, they jump and follow his instructions to the point that they don't even ask questions."[95]

Eunice Lovato Myrick likewise discovered that Tijerina's authoritarian personality operated as much within the new organization as it did at home. Hailing from the nearby Atrisco land grant, just across the river in Albuquerque, Myrick boasted a nearly encyclopedic knowledge of local land-grant history. She joined the Alianza in 1963, and for a short while she replaced Mary Escobar as the Alianza's official secretary. One day, however, Eunice Myrick asked Tijerina to account for his expenses. The quantity involved was paltry—the Alianza originally collected dues of just one dollar a month per member. Nevertheless, according to Myrick, Tijerina angrily responded that membership dues were collected to support his personal welfare and therefore were not a matter under her purview.[96] Myrick, along with another early member, Paul Vigil, soon broke with the Alianza because Tijerina refused to "disclose the membership list or the income of the Alliance" and instead "kept all files under his control."[97] Later, sharing the incident with a police investigator seeking information about Tijerina, Myrick portrayed Tijerina as quick to take umbrage. As she recalled, "Tijerina would go into a long tirade, discrediting [her] or anyone else who would question him."[98] Clearly, the Alianza leader also proved willing to hold a grudge. A year later, still upset about this woman's willingness to question his authority, Tijerina in a letter to his brother Chris dismissively referred to Myrick as "an ignorant person."[99] Chris Tijerina's reply was even less charitable. Instead of using Myrick's name, he disparagingly referred to her as "*la pansona*," that is, "the potbellied woman."[100]

Tellingly, Alianza members rallied around their leader at the time of the Myrick incident. At the meeting directly following Myrick's request for more financial transparency, attendees voted unanimously to boot Myrick out of the Alianza. They accused "*la* Señora Myrick" of threatening to "ruin or divide our noble cause." The position of secretary would remain vacant until a person who was more "dignified and grateful" was found to occupy it.[101] In taking these actions, moreover, Alianza members were operating in accord with the organization's 1963 constitution. Should any land-grant claimant, man or woman, work against the Alianza's interests, or even independent of them, the document declared, that person was to be considered "persona non grata" and "a traitor to the Forgotten People."[102] For good measure, in the wake of Myrick's expulsion, Alianza members reaffirmed the need for unity under the leadership of the Alianza president.[103]

Both Treviño and Myrick spoke to police after Tijerina's protest politics had turned violent and they had every reason to keep their distance from the controversial organization. Nevertheless, their conflicts with the leader of the Alianza make clear that Tijerina's authoritarian manner permeated the organization just as it profoundly affected his family. Not coincidentally, Tijerina once described his central mission as uniting all land-grant claimants into "one great family" dedicated to the pursuit of land-grant justice for all.[104] "We have been like sheep. We have never opened our mouths as a unified pueblo," he lamented.[105] As leader of the Alianza, Tijerina was determined to be a father to this family, a shepherd to those sheep.

Without apology, although with some regret, Tijerina felt he had no choice but to exploit his own family members in service to the land-grant cause. Dissent was intolerable because dissent threatened to disrupt his God-given destiny. His first wife and their children therefore questioned his authority at their peril. Although the story of families suffering because of a political leader's all-consuming dedication to a cause is familiar enough, even by this measure, the suffering of the Tijerina family was impressive.

This family model operated within the Alianza too to its ultimate detriment. At the most basic level, if a leader refuses to accept criticism or even suggestions, then how can that person find a way forward under difficult circumstances? What if the path selected is providing diminishing returns? How can the course be corrected? And what happens when the leader is suddenly gone? Tijerina ended up behind bars. How does an organization that is so dependent upon a single individual function in that person's absence? Eventually, Tijerina's patriarchal tendencies undermined the organization that he founded precisely because these sorts of questions, by challenging his authority and his vision, were completely irrelevant to him.

Initially, however, Tijerina's strong personality benefited the Alianza. Whatever his personal failings, Reies Tijerina possessed the ability to convey tremendous charisma and inspire intense devotion. The magnetic aspect of his personality operated in New Mexico as it had in Arizona. Indeed, the earliest minutes of Alianza meetings indicate a dozen or so people already in attendance, a testament to Tijerina's enthusiastic recruitment efforts. A handful of these original members, moreover, were to form part of an enduring inner circle of Alianza supporters, sometimes called Los Caballeros de las Indias (The Gentlemen of the Indies) and, later, the Mesa Cósmica (Cosmic Table).[106] To his credit, Tijerina had a knack for distilling generations of convoluted lawsuits, countless complicated land-grant histories, and the pain of poverty and discrimination into a single story of conquest and injustice. The immense popularity of that message had begun to reinvigorate the land-grant movement across the state. The Alianza was poised for explosive growth.

5

The Evangelist

In the fall of 1960, Tijerina, still a fugitive, donned a wig and dress to travel to Arizona in the guise of a woman. Successfully avoiding detection by law enforcement, he arranged to sell the Valle de Paz property during this trip.[1] Tijerina then used the $32,000 from this sale to purchase a concrete industrial building near downtown Albuquerque.[2] He and his family had been renting part of the building as rudimentary living quarters; the rest, until recently, had housed the production facilities of the *Albuquerque News Chieftain*, the "Most Thoroughly Read Newspaper in New Mexico," according to its masthead.[3] The sale severed Tijerina's last connection with his prophet days in Arizona and, with the building allocated as the Alianza's new headquarters, marked the start of his public career as an activist.

As Tijerina went about the task of trying to convince land-poor New Mexicans to take a chance on supporting his new organization, the purchase carried several benefits. First, in deciding to establish the Alianza in Albuquerque, Tijerina chose a centrally located city no more than a day's drive from anywhere in New Mexico. Albuquerque also boasted a population of dispossessed land-grant heirs who over the years had migrated to the state's largest city looking for work. With good reason the Alianza leader extended his recruitment efforts to "all those who are to be found away from the mercedes working at jobs or in factories because the land was stolen from them."[4]

Second, while short on beauty, the building ranked high in functionality. Featuring a main hall large enough to seat 200, the Alianza's headquarters soon became a social and political hub for land-grant heirs throughout the state. As Peter Nabokov—one of Tijerina's first chroniclers and then a reporter for the *Santa Fe New Mexican*—noted, weekly Alianza meetings drew a crowd and combined the flavor of "a Spanish-American family reunion, a Saturday night evangelistic tent meeting, a cantina on a Friday night, and a cautious deliberation among embittered villagers."[5]

Third, as part of the purchase agreement, Edwin Stanton, the owner of the building and the editor of the *Albuquerque News Chieftain*, agreed to publish "La Alianza Informa," a weekly column that appeared in every issue of the newspaper from March 1, 1963, to January 14, 1966.[6] Written in Spanish by Tijerina, "La Alianza Informa" served as a critical recruitment platform, a means to reach people beyond face-to-face interactions. As more individuals joined and membership dues rolled in, Tijerina could afford to spread news about the organization via Spanish-language radio. Touting Tijerina's status as a gentleman and an expert, a printed advertisement for Albuquerque station KARA promised ten minutes of "historical and legal truth" courtesy of *el caballero* Reies López Tijerina. "All questions answered," declared the bilingual advertisement.[7] For a short while during the mid-1960s, the Alianza budget even stretched enough to afford a five-minute weekly spot on television.[8]

Whatever the format, Tijerina's political proselytizing reflected the years that he had spent pastoring and researching, his lifelong veneration for the written word, his intimate familiarity with the pain of discrimination and want, and his roiling anger toward economic and racial injustice. "Hablaba con huevos [He showed real balls]," Juan Valdez stated years later about Tijerina. "He was the first person to speak about the matter of the mercedes with real force and vigor."[9] Transcending mere politics, the land-grant cause to Tijerina amounted to a "*santa misión*" or "*santa cru[z]ada*."[10] His dreams for Valle de Paz had died in the desert, but in New Mexico, these same aspirations—to secure a piece of land, to find ultimate justice, and even to establish and protect a cultural haven—hit fertile ground. "Do your part" and join the Alianza, Tijerina urged. "Soon you will be living on lands that have been liberated, where you will be able to hunt, fish, and gather wood without anyone bothering you."[11]

The ten minutes a day that Tijerina spoke on an Albuquerque radio station helped him recruit Alianza members. Although the advertisement was bilingual, he broadcast mainly in Spanish during the early years of the organization. This photograph captured Tijerina during what he referred to as his "prime looking period." (Box 2, folder 19, Peter Nabokov Papers, Center for Southwest Research, University of New Mexico, Albuquerque)

Thousands did. In February 1963, when the Alianza was officially launched, it counted representatives from fourteen land grants among its members.[12] That September, an estimated 800 people attended the organization's first annual convention.[13] By January 1965, membership files tallied at least 3,000 members with ties to 130 different mercedes.[14] Estimates soon climbed to 6,000 members or even higher.[15] While still only a tiny fraction of the total Spanish-surnamed population in the state, the organization's membership quickly surpassed that of any other land-grant group by a factor of ten at least.[16] In understanding land as a sacred cause, Tijerina breathed new life into the efforts of northern New Mexicans to reclaim property now owned by others.

No longer seeking souls to save, he was an evangelist for a more earthly justice.

On September 20, 1963, the *Albuquerque News Chieftain* announced the first annual convention of the Alianza Federal de Mercedes, to take place at a local high school gymnasium. A row of three photos accompanied the article. One was of Alton A. Davis, an African American businessman and civil rights activist from Chicago whose friendship Tijerina had cultivated during visits there. Davis had traveled to Albuquerque to attend the convention. The other photo was of U.S. attorney general Robert F. Kennedy, who had not. Tijerina, however, had lobbied Kennedy briefly during two recent public appearances by the attorney general in Chicago and Albuquerque. An unflattering headshot of Tijerina appeared between these two photos. The Alianza leader stared unsmiling directly at the camera, a toothbrush moustache resting atop the grim line of his mouth.[17] In the 1920s, this style of facial hair would have evoked the silent film star Charlie Chaplin. Any time after World War II, it inevitably evoked Adolf Hitler.

Although Tijerina during the 1970s sometimes sported a big, bushy moustache (equal parts Burt Reynolds, the decade's most popular movie star, and revolutionary hero Emiliano Zapata), the toothbrush version never appeared in any other photo of the Alianza president. In a later interview, his daughter Rose recalled her father reading "Hitler's book," presumably *Mein Kampf*, during the early 1960s.[18] If that was the case, then the title of Tijerina's memoir, *Mi Lucha por la Tierra*, seems suddenly less generic and more an eerie echo of *Mein Kampf*, German for "my struggle." Yet nothing about Tijerina's writing during the 1960s offered any hint that he esteemed Hitler or wanted to look like him. To the contrary, as Tijerina launched a campaign to encourage Spanish-speaking New Mexicans to join the Alianza, he frequently expressed his admiration of Jewish people. As he saw it, in 1947 with a little help from the United Nations, they had gotten their land back after 2,000 years.[19] By this measure, the Alianza goal of regaining land after only a century-plus of American rule appeared infinitely achievable.

Tijerina brought unbridled enthusiasm and all his oratorical savvy to this new crusade. Onstage, the Alianza leader would often raise and lower his voice theatrically, move his hands about emphatically, and, as if his face were made out of rubber, scrunch and re-scrunch his features into one intense expression after another.[20] As a public speaker, Tijerina displayed an unfailing ability, Nabokov noted, to "arouse a pitch of enthu-

Spanish Land Grant Heirs To Meet Here

Dr. Alton A. Davis, Executive Director of the American Emancipation Centennial, held in Chicago August 16 to September 2, will address the A.F.D.M. Convention in Albuquerque, this Saturday.

Mr. Reyis Tijerina, President of the Federal Alliance of Spanish Land Grant Heirs.

READ AND USE THE CLASSIFIED ADS

The president of the A.F.D.M. Mr. Rayis Tijerina, interviewed and discussed the problem of the Spanish land grant heirs with Attorney General, Robert Kennedy, in preparation for the coming convention this Saturday.

The First Annual Convention of the Federal Alliance of Spanish Land Grant Heirs (La Alianza Federal de Mercedes) will be held in the gym of Rio Grande High School, at 2300 Arenal Road SW in Albuquerque. The convention will begin at 8 a.m. this Saturday, and last until 6 p.m. Lunch will be served and those attending are being urged to bring their entire family. Preparations are being made for a crowd of more than one thousand people.

The Federal Aliance of heirs was formed last February in Albuquerque with heirs of 14 different grants represented. Approximately 50 grants have now joined in to back the organization. Principal discussion at the First Annual Convention will be the Guadalupe Hidalgo Treaty.

The basic purpose of the Alliance is to unite, into one organization, as many of the estimated five million heirs to Spanish land grants in the United States as possible, for the purpose of mutual aid in obtaining lands and rights which have been illegally or wrongly lost by these heirs.

Front page of the September 20, 1963, *Albuquerque News Chieftain*, a local weekly that covered the activities of the Alianza Federal de Mercedes. Here the newspaper announced the organization's first convention. Tijerina's picture appears between that of Alton A. Davis, an ally and businessman from Chicago, and Robert F. Kennedy, the U.S. attorney general, whom Tijerina had met briefly when Kennedy gave speeches in Chicago and Albuquerque.

siasm though a masterly exhausting exhibition of folk rhetoric, savage mimicry, lapses into his backlog of fundamentalist tales and an actor's shifting of emotional levels."[21] And he always stood ready to speak for his cause. As Felix Martínez (son of activists Juan and Fernanda Martínez of Tierra Amarilla) once told an interviewer, "If he stopped for gas, he would talk to the man on the pump. At the store he would talk to customers. And the owner. I once saw him try to convert a state cop while the guy was making him out a ticket."[22]

Of course, the content of Tijerina's message mattered as much as the delivery. As the leader of the Alianza, he needed to persuade poor New Mexicans that despite a century of evidence to the contrary, they could still regain their land and protect their culture. His message featured three main arguments designed to encourage and embolden the dispirited. First, Tijerina invoked Spanish colonial documents to assert that only the descendants of the original settlers were the legitimate owners of the mercedes. Years of study convinced Tijerina that God, the pope, and Spanish law all stood on the side of the Alianza. Second, Tijerina emphasized the fundamentally fraudulent basis of American rule. He drew that conclusion based on a close reading of still more documents, including, of course, the 1848 treaty that ended the war between the United States and Mexico. Third, Tijerina maintained that, beyond land theft, nuevomexicanos suffered discrimination and "cultural genocide."[23] He defined the land-grant cause as revolving around cultural rights as much as property ones from the start. "In absolutely nothing have they protected us. . . . Not a single one of our rights have they respected," Tijerina thundered in a typical passage. "They uprooted our language, they threatened us with hunger, their judges twisted the law."[24] Refusing to apologize in case he sounded monotonous (and sometimes he did), Tijerina preached this gospel with the same intensity and relentlessness with which he had once warned that the world was rushing toward destruction.

Ironically for someone who was so proud of his Mexican heritage, Tijerina first looked to Spain in formulating his message's authority. Strategically, he claimed all the majesty of imperial Spain on behalf of Spanish-speaking New Mexicans. "Come and see for yourself; Come and hear for the first time in 117 years [since 1846] your true rights, and royal Heritage that truly belongs to you," trumpeted the Alianza invitation to the organization's first convention. "If you fail to appear," it cautioned, "you will regret it when your co-heir tells you about it."[25] The organization's original 1963 constitution offered variations on this regal theme, repeatedly referring to "royal rights," "royal decrees," and "royal heirs."[26] The last term especially resonated in New Mexico, where the use of the word "*heredero*" or "heir" to refer to those with historic ties to land grants prevailed among English- and Spanish-speakers alike. Tijerina wrapped a royal cloak around this long-established practice. "It should be understood that every [land-grant] heir is a royal heir because the grant is royal, donated by a royal crown," he contended in a typical statement from 1963. "We are, well, a royal seed."[27]

To bolster these aristocratic assertions, Tijerina invested new significance in an archival discovery that he had made four years before in Mexico. Tijerina's earliest addresses as Alianza president were littered with references to Ordenanza 99 of the Laws of the Indies, which had offered settlers enticements to come to New Mexico and elsewhere. In one early statement, Tijerina even quoted the 1543 text in its entirety. "The King of Spain, Don Felipe II, in Ordenanza 99 of Book IV, Title VI and Law VI decreed the following," he began in a speech in Cuba, New Mexico. According to the ordinance, Tijerina read, all settlers and their children were to be "hidalgos and persons with noble lineage and with *un solar conocido*." Generally referring to a plot of land, the phrase "*solar conocido*" actually conveyed much more in terms of permanence and privilege as the land (*suelo*) in question was known (*conocido*) because historically it had belonged to a nobleman whose ancestral estate was seated in a particular location and handed down from generation to generation. In addition, Tijerina noted, the Spanish Crown had promised to award settlers in New Mexico "all the honors and pre-eminences that all the hidalgos and gentlemen of these kingdoms of Castile should have and enjoy, according to all the *fueros*, laws, and customs of Spain." "*Fueros*" was another word that rooted a people to a place. Although commonly translated as "jurisdictions," *fueros* were also privileges that the Crown extended to certain people often from specific towns or areas.[28] Significantly, in his personal copy of this speech, Tijerina literally underscored with the typewriter keys the words "*fueros*, laws, and customs." Thus, Tijerina contended that the massive legal weight of centuries of Spanish empire protected the mercedes, the original settlers, and all their descendants.[29]

Always more inclined to pay attention to text than to context, Tijerina's emotional appeal in this case outstripped his historical knowledge. He seemed unaware that hidalgos traditionally had occupied the absolute lowest rank of nobility in Spain. They enjoyed freedom from taxation; otherwise the Crown restricted their "honors and pre-eminences" to the right to use the honorific "don."[30] Far removed from Madrid or even Mexico City, the New Mexican aristocracy of the 1600s was a feebler version yet.[31] Similarly, Tijerina overestimated the relevance of the Laws of the Indies in protecting land-grant rights. American judges had used these same laws to take land away from villagers. In the devastating 1897 *Sandoval* decision, for example, the U.S. Supreme Court ruled that land that had been used in common always belonged to the Spanish king according to the Laws of the Indies and therefore now belonged to the U.S. government and not to the settlers who had lived there for generations.[32] Still obsessed with textual authority, Tijerina concentrated upon the laws as they were drafted in Spain versus how they actually operated across the ocean. The tremendous gap between the intent and application of these laws mattered less to him, moreover, than appealing to potential Alianza members. Shrewdly, Tijerina recognized the tremendous pride that nuevomexicanos took in their long presence in the region, a powerful counter to the weight of discrimination they faced. As Tijerina wrote, "Of course, this noble status prompts jealousy among those who arrived very late to New Mexico."[33] Deflecting any notion of Anglo-American superiority, his talk of noble lineage reminded members of a cultural minority that to be treated with dignity was their birthright. "We are not only making claims to the land," Tijerina contended, "but also to the honor with which our forefathers and their descendants were crowned."[34]

Historically, that honor had stemmed from doing the dirty work of defeating Indians. Into the 1960s, therefore, nuevomexicanos often staked their property claims upon their ancestors' military sacrifices and accomplishments. "The struggles, the sacrifices, the troubles, the efforts to settle and live here were indelibly written in the blood of hundreds of our people," José A. Lucero from the Alameda land grant north of Albuquerque reminded his fellow *aliancistas* in one early letter.[35] On rare occasions, Tijerina parroted this point of view. "The price the GRANTEES paid for the mercedes was exceedingly high, [as] many thousand settlers perished or were killed by the different tribes that inhabited these lands," Tijerina wrote in one 1963 missive.[36] In another early address, Tijerina lauded "those first settlers who placed their life in peril . . . to come and receive [the mercedes]."[37] In general, however, as we shall see, Tijerina preferred to view Native Americans as potential allies versus historical antagonists. His earlier discovery that the Catholic Church had sanctioned intermarriage between indigenous people and Spanish colonists as early as 1514 profoundly influenced Tijerina's thinking in this regard.

Surprisingly, in light of his Pentecostal training, Tijerina also looked to the authority of the Roman Catholic Church to confer legitimacy upon the land grants and upon himself as a leader. He had returned to Catholicism shortly after arriving in New Mexico. An apparently waning belief in an imminent Second Coming contributed to Tijerina's general disenchantment with his former life as a preacher. "I waited a long time for that man. He is not coming," Tijerina purportedly told his daughter Rose after she once asked him why he no longer preached the way he used to do about Jesus.[38] Learning more about New Mexican history, he later wrote, likewise prompted him to move away from Protestantism in general and toward Catholicism. Not only were the Americans who arrived after 1848 mostly Protestants while nuevomexicanos were traditionally Catholic, but as far as Tijerina was concerned, the newcomers also had "never raised their voice" against the unscrupulous land grab that followed the American takeover.[39]

As an outsider, Tijerina gained another advantage by returning to Catholicism. From feast day observations to Penitente Lenten rituals, Catholicism formed an integral part of village life in New Mexico. As a Catholic, Tijerina occupied the same side of that cultural divide as the vast majority of his followers. In the end, it served the same purpose as marrying a land-grant heir: it made him more familiar. As Tijerina once succinctly yet arrogantly asserted to an interviewer, "My people expect it. They are like children about such matters."[40]

As a Catholic, the Alianza president sought to harness what he now viewed as an unparalleled sacred authority. As he once noted, Roman Catholicism was nearly 2,000 years old, making the church "the most powerful, the longest [lasting], authority on earth" and, better yet, one "established by Christ."[41] Now recognizing the authority of the pope as the Vicar of Christ, Tijerina zeroed in on a papal bull "issued by his Holiness, Pope Alexander VI," on May 4, 1493, as particularly significant to questions of land rights. The *Bula Inter Caetera* awarded sovereignty over Columbus's discoveries to Queen Isabella of Spain and King Ferdinand of Aragon.[42] The following year Spain and Portugal ratified a version of this declaration in the Treaty of Tordesillas, which secured Portuguese dominion over Brazil but left the rest of the Americas under Spanish rule.[43] To Tijerina, these details mattered less than placing authentic ownership of the mercedes within a thoroughly impressive chain of command. This chain began with God, whose representative on earth was the pope, who by "Divine Decree" had awarded sovereignty over New Mexico to the "Royal Crown of Spain," which then had granted the land to Spanish-speaking settlers in the region and their descendants. The 1493 papal bull thus joined Ordenanza 99 as documents that Tijerina constantly invoked as providing irrefutable proof that the land belonged to nuevomexicanos.

This outstanding pedigree, both royal and sacred, Tijerina insisted, made the mercedes different from other types of property holdings. "These mercedes were not granted to just anyone," he elaborated in a 1963 radio address.[44] Instead, "the land of the mercedes and the title of nobility are inseparable."[45] Like the landed estates of European nobility that were passed down from generation to generation, Tijerina contended that the Crown had granted an irrevocable inheritance, a "perpetual possession," a phrase found in colonial-era documents and in Mexican colonization laws.[46] The same phrase appeared in the Old Testament too; the ancient priests of Israel could not buy or sell their land but held it in "perpetual possession" (Leviticus 25:34). Wherever Tijerina first encountered this concept, he cited it constantly now. Nuevomexicanos, he asserted, enjoyed "perpetual security," "perpetual protection," and "perpetual rights" over what amounted to a perpetual landed inheritance.[47] Consequently, any subsequent American action aimed at separating a people from their land was automatically null and void. "It should be understood clearly that . . . the mercedes . . . at no time and for no reason can be lost," he proclaimed. Even if the land had been sold or possessed by the state for failure to pay taxes, he stated, it had not been lost forever but only "temporarily taken away from us."[48] The "foreigners" who had done the taking, Tijerina declared, were legally obligated to return the land.[49]

Accordingly, the second part of Tijerina's land-grant gospel condemned the conquerors of 1848 for failing to uphold their promises. Exhibit A in this regard remained the Treaty of Guadalupe Hidalgo. The treaty earned mention no less than sixteen times in the Alianza's original 1963 constitution, which was only ten pages long.[50] "The Treaty of G.H. is the guarantee and most powerful law that the heirs have to obtain all their rights and all their lands," Tijerina emphasized in his addresses.[51] Unfortunately, "for more than one hundred years . . . the Treaty of Guadalupe Hidalgo has been ignored completely," he argued.[52] Fault rested with the United States. "There is no pardon nor excuse for the nation that violates the rights of its citizens, nor for the nation that violates international accords," Tijerina insisted.[53] Lest others dismiss land-grant claims at this late date as minor matters for local courts to solve, the Alianza leader correctly reminded all New Mexicans that meeting treaty obligations was a matter of international law.

Only the significance that Tijerina assigned to the Laws of the Indies matched his high opinion of the Treaty of Guadalupe Hidalgo. Indeed, he once declared the Laws of the Indies "our only defense and hope," a declaration that appeared to make this body of laws a rival of the 1848 treaty in terms of significance.[54] Tijerina's belief in the irrevocable nature of Spanish-era privileges reconciled the apparent contradiction. In promising to uphold the rights of former Mexican citizens, Tijerina argued, the Treaty of Guadalupe Hidalgo automatically guaranteed the rights outlined in the Laws of the Indies. Connecting the different elements of his land-grant gospel, Tijerina interpreted the 1848 treaty, which he never forgot was signed in the name of Almighty God, as affirming the inviolable, perpetual nature of nuevomexicano land claims.[55] "This great and powerful nation takes the name of God in vain in order to deceive a defenseless, humble, and meek people," he rebuked.[56]

As Tijerina evangelized for the Alianza's cause, he marshaled additional documents to reinforce his main point about broken treaty obligations. In keeping with his reputation as an *abogado sin libros*, a lawyer despite his lack of formal education, Tijerina rescued from obscurity another text signed by the United States and Mexico, the nearly forgotten Protocol of Querétaro. As noted in chapter 2, and as Tijerina often repeated in his land-grant gospel, the Treaty of Guadalupe Hidalgo included two important articles that guaranteed the property rights of the former citizens of Mexico: Article 8, which stated that this property was to be "inviolably respected," and Article 9, which declared that the conquered population was to "be maintained and protected in the free enjoyment of their liberty and property." In addition, the original version of the treaty also included an Article 10, which had promised that "all grants of land made by the Mexican government or by competent authorities . . . shall be respected as valid." The U.S. Senate upon ratification, however, reduced the protections contained within Articles 8 and 9 and deleted Article 10 entirely. Concerned Mexican negotiators immediately called for clarification. The protocol was the result. Drafted by Mexicans but signed by Americans, it stated that the removal of Article 10 "did not in any way intend to annul grants of land made by Mexico" in Texas, New Mexico, or California.[57] Within six months, however, U.S. officials were also insisting that the protocol had no legal standing but was simply a record of conversations between U.S. and Mexican diplomats.[58] To Tijerina, however, the protocol offered further evidence of the sacrosanct nature of the treaty overall.

As did, he insisted, the U.S. Constitution and the state constitution of New Mexico. The Alianza president diligently mined both documents for pertinent citations. Most important, he noted that a section of Article VI of the U.S. Constitution stated that "all treaties made, or which shall be made, under the Authority of the United States shall be the supreme Law of the Land." In 1789, the article's intent was to establish that the power of the new federal government exceeded that of the states. Tijerina's interpretative takeaway stressed the preeminent status of the Treaty of Guadalupe Hidalgo as "the supreme Law of the Land."[59] Taken with that fact, Tijerina, first in addresses to Alianza members and later in petitions to heads of state, started noting every additional appearance of the word "law" in the U.S. Constitution that he could use. Article I, for example, charged Congress "to make all Laws which shall be necessary and proper" and the president to "take Care that the Laws be faithfully executed." Of particular relevance, given that New Mexicans often found the land sold out from under them, the Fourteenth Amendment forbade depriving any citizen "of life, liberty, or property, without due process of law." Perhaps aware of the tangential nature of some of these references, Tijerina atypically refrained from quoting them verbatim but instead usually presented the citations together in a single list.[60] In this way, they drove home his main point: the United States was constitutionally obligated to defend the treaty.

As Tijerina noted, a similar promise bound the state of New Mexico, according to its own constitution. Although the Alianza leader liked to chide New Mexicans for having forgotten the Treaty of Guadalupe Hidalgo, Spanish speakers who attended the state's constitutional convention in 1910 enshrined it in the state's founding document.[61] Article V, Section 2, of the document specifically promised to uphold the guarantees contained within the 1848 treaty. Still other articles defended racial equality and endorsed the use of Spanish and English in the classroom and in the courts. These provisions reflected the demographic clout of Spanish speakers at the time. They made up 32 of the 100 delegates at the constitutional convention and nearly 40 percent of the new state's population overall.[62] An incensed Tijerina contended, however, that none of these constitutional provisions had been adequately respected.[63]

As the self-trained lawyer made way for the former fire-and-brimstone preacher, Tijerina's oratory boiled over as he denounced the "savage injustices" committed against the Spanish-speaking people of New Mexico as a result of conquest.[64] "A hundred years ago, those who were the strongest and most violent wrenched the land away," Tijerina fumed. "The most powerful established new laws to slake their desire and greed and to gain that which JUSTICE would have denied them."[65] The Alianza leader kept a long list of transgressors. He was appalled to discover, for example, that in 1870 cartloads of documents, including land-grant papers, were either burned or sold as scrap in an effort to carve out more space in Santa Fe's crowded Palace of the Governors. Worse, the territorial governor at the time, William Pile, had been a Methodist minister and, so Tijerina implied, surely must have known better.[66] Pile immediately earned a top spot among the Alianza's pantheon of land-grant villains, along with lawyer and land speculator Thomas B. Catron of the Santa Fe Ring.[67] By the mid-twentieth century, many of these documents ended up in the hands of a Kansas City bookseller named Kenneth D. Sender, who then tried to make money by selling them to the state of New Mexico.[68] Sender soon joined Tijerina's list of conspiracy participants. Curious about what other contemporary scoundrels abounded, Tijerina on occasion asked land-grant folks to share their ongoing grievances.[69] The names of individual landowners in New Mexico whom he labeled trespassers and thieves would then dot his speeches.[70]

Tijerina directed particular venom toward the U.S. Forest Service. His first teachers regarding land-grant matters, members of the Corporation of Abiquiú, had tangled in court with private landholders only. Many nuevomexicanos resented the Forest Service even more. Through ownership of Carson National Forest and the Santa Fe National Forest alone, the federal agency controlled nearly three million acres in northern New Mexico.[71] Even before the Forest Service's founding in 1905, court decisions secured the federal government's claim to the land against that of longtime residents. In the aforementioned 1897 *Sandoval* case, for example, the U.S. Supreme Court ruled that, after 1848, ownership of all communal landholdings devolved to the U.S. government.[72] During the first decades of the twentieth century, moreover, the U.S. Forest Service rapidly increased its holdings by purchasing former land-grant property that the federal government had deemed "private," no matter how questionable that designation, ultimately swallowing up large swaths of some twenty different land grants.[73] The upshot for local Spanish speakers: a federal agency now mediated their relationship with the land. As Tijerina noted with dismay, one heredero was arrested for cutting firewood on public land, another for fishing along a stream, and yet another for killing a deer, although in each case the land had once belonged to the mercedes.[74] While nuevomexicanos complained about their lack of access to grant land once held in common, the Forest Service maintained that it was indeed protecting "the commons"—on behalf of the entire population of the United States.

Charged with supervising the lumber harvest, protecting the watershed, and curtailing erosion, Forest Service personnel for most of the twentieth century operated from the assumption that professionals knew how to protect natural resources better than locals, whose concerns posed a "danger" to the efficient execution of policy.[75] Tensions rose dramatically starting in the 1940s, when the Forest Service unilaterally began to slash the number of grazing permits that it issued. The decision devastated local nuevomexicanos, who, fenced out by private owners, increasingly depended on access to federal lands to maintain their subsistence lifestyles. "The 'rangers' who take care of these MERCEDES CONVERTED INTO FORESTS . . . prohibit us from grazing the few cows that we have left. Our animals are skinny from the scarcity of water and fodder. This is one of [the] greatest calamities that has plagued us since we were stripped of our mercedes," Tijerina acidly observed.[76] Lest the Forest Service portray nuevomexicano land use as threatening a valuable natural resource, the Alianza president countered that government policies undermined something equally endangered and priceless: the heritage of an entire people. He pledged to his brothers and sisters (*hermanos*) "of blood [and of] culture" to stand firm against this onslaught.[77]

The third part of Tijerina's land-grant gospel provided a vigorous defense of traditional nuevomexicano village life against the pain of prejudice and discrimination. Unlike an earlier generation of Mexican American civil rights organizations that endorsed the use of English as an integral step toward obtaining first-class citizenship, the Alianza declared Spanish its official language in its 1963 constitution. The same document affirmed that the bonds of land *and* culture forever united land-grant heirs.[78] By 1965, the slogan "La Tierra es Nuestra Herencia y la Justicia Nuestro Credo" appeared on Alianza stationery. Although usually translated as "The Land Is Our Inheritance and Justice Our Creed," in Spanish the word "*herencia*" also means "heritage." The motto therefore proudly upheld the mercedes as a precious depository of culture as much as a physical piece of property. "Our poverty is not due to . . . some natural disadvantages of our culture . . . but because we were violently and against our will . . . deprived of our culture," Tijerina insisted.[79]

In making this assertion, moreover, he refuted decades of academic wisdom that disparaged Spanish-speaking culture as an obstacle to assimilation. In its rawest form during the 1920s and into the 1930s, this school of thought accepted speaking Spanish as prima facie evidence of mental incapacity.[80] Cutting-edge scholarship endorsed the notion of cultural determinism, which in northern New Mexico directly fed Forest Service attitudes toward Spanish-speaking New Mexicans, as evinced by a 1935 report that said, "[New Mexicans] are sedentary in character living in the present and with no thought for the future. They accept conditions as they are and make the best of them with no idea of conserving the natural resources much less enhancement of them."[81] By the time the Alianza was founded, these same ideas had been regrouped under the presumably neutral and widely influential "values orientation theory." The work of Harvard academics who spent considerable time in New Mexico, the theory proposed that Anglo-Americans valued independence, hard work, and future-oriented goals, whereas Spanish Americans valued the collective, more immediate gratification, and tradition. Ostensibly, values were neither good nor bad but simply different. Yet in each case "Spanish Americans" lacked the necessary attributes to succeed in middle-class American society.[82] Holding an extremely low opinion of Anglo-American society in the first place, Tijerina questioned that definition of success.

Instead, the Alianza leader drew a direct line between the indignities, ironies, and inequities that framed the everyday lives of nuevomexicanos and the American takeover. All too often, he asserted, Spanish-speaking New Mexicans found themselves at the mercy of tightfisted bankers, crooked judges, and biased politicians, as well as uncaring Forest Service rangers.[83] Aided, he admitted, "by a few [nuevomexicano] traitors," these so-called elites routinely "blocked justice."[84] In a similar vein, the Alianza leader accused law enforcement of employing a double standard in the administration of their duties. "There are police and officials who arrest our brothers because they passed a stop sign or a red light and there are thousands of police officers who arrest a guy who drinks a bit," protested the teetotaler. "Whatever infraction they commit, the full force of the law comes down upon our brothers and sisters while the foreigners escape punishment."[85] In short, Anglo-Americans "not only took away our land but now they discriminate against us" and "treat us like we are a stupid and inferior race."[86]

As if to emphasize the extent of oppression suffered by nuevomexicanos, the Alianza leader often described village life under Spanish-speaking rule in almost Edenic terms. "Before the American conquest," Tijerina insisted, "all of our [fore]fathers had every kind of wealth, they had abundant cattle. They had access to water and grasslands in abundance, [and to] silver and gold in abundance." Here the Alianza leader literally gilded the past. The upper Rio Grande Valley offered significant natural resources, including timber, pastureland, rivers filled with trout, and plenty of game animals, including, deer, elk, bears, and turkey. Yet New Mexico never duplicated the mineral wealth of old Mexico. Tijerina insisted, however, that the wealth of nuevomexicanos before 1848 extended beyond mere material possessions. His low opinion of American consumer society evident by comparison, the Alianza leader enthused about a time when "our people were morally strong, healthy physically, without needing anything. Our people lived happily, content, and their fiestas, they celebrated with pomp and joy."[87] Inclined to downplay the matter of settler-indigenous conflict, Tijerina was free to uphold traditional village life as a fount of economic security, cultural harmony, and, in a legacy from his preacher days, a reservoir of traditional family values and moral virtue. This nostalgic portrait stood in vivid contrast to his portrayal of American perfidy post-1848.

In the context of the land-grant movement, such nostalgia amounted to a political act. Indeed, Tijerina's tendency to look backward prompted some early writers to label him a "primitive rebel," a term coined in 1957 by Eric Hobsbawm, the British historian, to describe Robin Hood–like characters.[88] Other writers borrowed from the American anthropologist Anthony F. C. Wallace to argue that Tijerina led a backward-looking "revitalization movement."[89] While only mentioned in passing, combined, these references suggested a type of leader who sought a return to better times without much of a vision for the future. To be certain, Tijerina did lead a movement whose members recalled with longing a time when they had enjoyed the use of the land without restriction. His romantic portrayal of settler life as well as his overwhelmingly positive view of Spanish-era colonialism lent further credence to the "primitive rebel" interpretation. Such a conclusion, however, shortchanged the utility of invoking history.

Acting as what Argentine sociologist Elizabeth Jelin calls a "memory entrepreneur,"[90] Tijerina tapped regularly into the power of the past. "Every merced," he once noted, "has its bitter history inscribed in the heart of every heredero."[91] Yet he looked backward not merely to idealize the past as some golden age but to understand better the contemporary conditions afflicting Spanish-speakers in New Mexico and, implicitly, across the Southwest. His brand of nostalgia spoke directly and powerfully to people who remembered how they had once controlled their land, and with it much of their own destiny.

Ironically then, Tijerina sometimes echoed stereotypes of passive nuevomexicanos to urge action. Conquest, he argued, had inflicted a final indignity upon Spanish-speaking New Mexicans. They were beaten down and defeated, unable to muster the will to make a change for the better. Overlooking the long history of land-grant struggle, Tijerina even appropriated the state motto, which declared New Mexico the "Land of Enchantment," to assert that Spanish speakers had not experienced enchantment so much as fallen under an evil hex that prevented them from pursuing, or even knowing, their rights. "The mercedes cannot be defended or rescued by an ignorant pueblo," he scolded.[92]

Yet Tijerina also tempted with the promise of better times. If only all land-grant heirs would awaken to their responsibility, then a new day of justice was certain to dawn. The land-grant crusade became a new arena for his vision of a postapocalyptic heaven. In his newspaper columns, radio addresses, and television appearances, Tijerina spoke of the world made anew. "After [more than] a hundred years, . . . the SUN OF JUSTICE begins to shine for all the royal heirs," he enthused. "The grace of God is raining down on the earth of New Mexico and like new green grass, JUSTICE is sprouting forth."[93] Once land-grant justice reigned, the bitterness produced by more than a century of discrimination would simply vanish. "Every race will feel proud of itself and no one will feel embarrassed to be who he [or she] is." Perhaps just as thrilling to some *aliancistas*, the sinful too were to receive their ultimate judgment. "The day is coming when all the black crimes committed against the poor ROYAL HEIRS are going to come to light and the evil ones will be punished," Tijerina affirmed in 1963.[94] "The thieves and the liars are going to feel embarrassed and truly ashamed, [and] those who flout the law will have to return all that they that have stolen and . . . the land will come back to its legitimate owners," he wrote.[95]

Although coy at first, Tijerina understood his role in summoning forth this glorious new era. "My people have a guide. Someone to direct them," he hinted in 1962. By 1965, he could no longer contain his sense of pride and wonder at his chosen status.[96] In an address that he labeled "Confesiones Personales," Tijerina wrote, "I see it as a necessity to confess before all who surround me, and who will surround me, and also for those who will never meet me in person, to confess that in everything that I am doing, and will do in the future, results not because of my own abilities . . . [but because] the divine hand of God is what has guided me."[97]

The passage contained a double message. On the one hand, Tijerina professed to be nothing more than a humble servant of the Lord. "I don't want anyone someday to try to give me credit, for without the strength of God or His will, I could do nothing," he wrote. On the other, he always knew that he was something special. "Always from the start, although I kept it hidden in my heart . . . I knew, and am now well persuaded, that a supernatural force selected me, but for what purpose exactly, I did not initially understand," Tijerina explained. In New Mexico, however, "I began to discern and to comprehend the task and the responsibility that the hand of Destiny had placed upon my shoulders, had nailed into my heart, in such a way that I could never escape this charge." Despite Tijerina's expressed humility, the parallels to the Christian Messiah were impossible to miss. Nails had crucified Jesus; nails pierced Tijerina's heart. And just like Christ had come to save sinners and bring forth the Kingdom of God, Tijerina sought to rescue land-poor nuevomexicanos and restore the Kingdom of New Mexico. Such was his "sacred obligation," he insisted, to bring forth "the SALVATION OF A NEW PEOPLE."[98]

FERTILE GROUND

As Gregorita Aguilar liked to point out, she did not join Tijerina's Alianza; rather, Tijerina joined one started by Tierra Amarilla land-grant activists, the Alianza de las Mercedes México-Españolas. Still, her own land-grant story holds clues as to why so many Spanish speakers in the region responded positively to Tijerina's evangelizing efforts. Along with her husband, Cruz Aguilar, Aguilar had been deeply committed to seeking land-grant justice since a child. Growing up in the 1930s, she remembered her grandfather showing her *hijuelas* that outlined the property rights of land-grant heirs. Long after U.S. courts had ruled that these informal deeds lacked any legal value, Gregorita and Cruz continued to hold onto their *hijuelas* as proof of their rightful claim to the land and the claim of all their descendants. Engaged in land-grant activism for decades, she and her husband managed to raise a family of ten in northern New Mexico despite the difficulties posed by a shrunken land base. To Gregorita, the land was a sacred trust, something to be treasured for future generations, not something to be bought and sold. Describing a connection to the land that was so profound that it was nearly biological, she spoke of the day her body would return to the earth that had nourished her for so long. "The land is our mother," she explained.[99] To land-grant folks like herself, the Alianza leader's insistence upon the sacred nature of the mercedes and of land-grant rights echoed familiar and cherished ideals.

Several writers have observed a profound connection to the land among Spanish speakers in the region. In his sweeping volume about the legal history of New Mexican land grants, Malcolm Ebright called attention to "that intangible quality that develops between the land and those who work it."[100] Similarly, Richard Nostrand, the author of *El Cerrito, New Mexico: Eight Generations in a Spanish Village*, argued that among Spanish-speaking New Mexicans, "attachment to place" was "uncommonly strong," a characteristic he attributed to their long tenure in the region.[101] Popular writers found the topic ripe for romanticization. One author named Frank Waters likewise wished to convey what he termed the "psychological and spiritual relationship of early settlers to their land." Best known for his books on Native American prophecy, Waters nonetheless correctly noted the many ways in which nuevomexicanos traditionally had made use of the land: by "planting, irrigating, harvesting, [and] tending their flocks and herds." They even lived *in* the earth in that their adobe homes were constructed of mud. Sounding very much like Aguilar, Waters concluded that a Native American saying, "The earth is our mother," best captured the significance of the land to nuevomexicanos.[102]

Perhaps if the land had been less beautiful, the connection would have been less intense. State tourism boosters settled upon the nickname "Land of Enchantment" as early as the 1930s, but the description hardly seemed like hyperbole when applied to the northern portion of the state.[103] Situated along the Continental Divide, northern New Mexico boasts stunning rock formations, broad valleys between high peaks, and vast skies. Much closer to its headwaters in southern Colorado, the Rio Grande carves a deep gash in the earth before winding its way through picturesque mountains. Centuries before, Spanish-speaking colonists selected names that reflected the vivid landscapes that they encountered: Tierra Amarilla for yellow earth; Sangre de Cristo, or Blood of Christ, because the mountains appeared red at the break of dawn. The high desert air showcased all of this splendor with an extraordinary quality of light that attracted artists throughout the twentieth century, most prominently Georgia O'Keeffe.

For much of the colonial period, however, the region was as dangerous as it was beautiful. Far from the military garrison in Santa Fe, colonial settlements on the New Mexican frontier were particularly vulnerable to Indian attack. Even as they engaged in and benefited from the slave trade, settlers, or *pobladores* in Spanish, also understood that to tend a field or to go collect water was all too often to risk being kidnapped, killed, or, worst of all, tortured and left to die. Some 200 years after the first conquistadores had passed through the region, Spanish-speaking settlement in New Mexico remained clustered along the Rio Grande within a narrow corridor of safety extending north and south of the colonial capital of Santa Fe. As Robert J. Tórrez, the former state historian of New Mexico, once wrote, "In order to own property under the Spanish and Mexican land grant system, you had to physically step on the land, run your fingers through the soil, and make a public commitment to live on it, cultivate it, and, if necessary, defend it with your life."[104]

The bold ceremony of possession invested the start of settlement with ritual and meaning. After a flurry of paperwork up the colonial administrative hierarchy and back down again, the interested parties gathered at the site selected and, as in a marriage ceremony, the local alcalde, or mayor, asked if anyone had any objections. Sometimes neighboring Pueblo Indians did. Next came an attempt to walk the perimeter of the grant. Along the way, the alcalde set up stone markers or, if rugged terrain or physical distance made the tour impossible, noted the natural landmarks along the edges of the grant: the black mesa to the south, the rocky hill to the east, or that big white ridge to the west (the imprecision of these descriptions augmenting property problems after 1848). The act of possession concluded with a flourish: members of the procession "plucked up grass, threw stones to signify their dominion over the land, and shouted, 'Long live the King!'" The words changed a bit during the Mexican era to "Long live the president and the Mexican nation!," but the sense of bravura remained.[105]

Against difficult odds, the ancestors of Alianza members made the ceremony of possession into a reality. In his study of the economic development of colonial New Mexico, Ross Frank linked the ascendency of Hispano society over indigenous ones to the evolution of settlers into citizens, or, in Spanish, their shift from being *pobladores* to *vecinos*.[106] Notably, in Spanish, the word "*vecino*" means "neighbor" too. Invested with certain rights and obligated to carry out certain duties in their own villages, a *vecino*, above all, was a person from a specific community, a specific place. In the vocabulary of geographers, nuevomexicanos transformed what to them initially was abstract space—a series of lines imposed upon an unfamiliar terrain—into a specific place imbued with identity, memory, and meaning. Such was the "power of place" in New Mexico.[107]

The "power of place," moreover, reverberated with sacred significance. To eke out a living in such a region required fortitude and faith. Or so many New Mexicans believed. Constantly strengthening and sanctifying the bond between a people and a locale, religious tradition infused everyday life. For example, villages relied upon water delivered by acequias, a system of irrigation ditches that crisscrossed the land. In contrast to the American style of water distribution that generally followed a doctrine of "first come, first served," acequias truly were *acequias de común*, as their formal titles boasted. In good times, the mayordomo, or ditch captain, allocated water according to the amount of land under cultivation and the amount of water available. In times of drought, however, the mayordomo's first responsibility was to ensure that every individual and livestock animal had sufficient water to survive. Spanish-speaking New Mexicans living in this high desert region referred to the lateral ditches as "*sangrias*," from the word "*sangre*" or "blood." In Catholic practice, water invokes the water of baptism and renewal; blood is synonymous with the blood of Christ and salvation. Thus, according to Sylvia Rodríguez, the mere act of watering one's fields bound villagers to each other and to what she termed a "sacred hydroscape."[108]

Equally important, according to Rodríguez, Catholic New Mexicans marked their faith and territory through religious procession. By the nineteenth century, one of the most important throughout the year was the springtime procession along fields and acequias in honor of San Isidro Labrador, or St. Isidore the Farmer, the Catholic saint of farmers and field hands. According to Catholic hagiography, San Isidro (ca. 1070–1130) was so immersed in prayer that he neglected his crops until God sent him an angel to help him complete the plowing. In the New Mexican version, however, San Isidro refused to abandon his farming even though it was Sunday, the day of rest. He worked despite God directly telling him to stop. He worked even after God sent hail and locusts to force San Isidro to leave the fields. San Isidro abandoned his work only after God threatened to inflict him with "a bad neighbor." Honoring San Isidro via procession thus reminded villagers of the sacred bonds of community and place within *vecino* society and that in the high desert "survival requires cooperation."[109] Similar to the spring procession in honor of San Isidro, on Good Friday the entire village participated in a ritual led by the Penitentes, the lay brotherhood that served local spiritual needs for decades after the American takeover. Women and children followed the cross-bearing Penitentes across a sacred topography singing alabados, or hymns of praise. The Penitentes boasted a repertoire of hundreds of different songs, some specifically about the land. One stanza of the popular "Adios, Acompañamiento" went this way:

Tierra soy, tierra ha de ser
porque de tierra Dios me hizo
y dondequiera que piso
piso lo que hemos de ser
[I am earth, I will one day become earth again
from earth God made me
and wherever I walk
I walk upon what we all must become][110]

Tijerina's tendency to portray the land-grant struggle as a sacred crusade, therefore, resonated perfectly with a cultural background that upheld a sacred connection between a people and a place.

In fact, one scholar has suggested that the most compelling part of Tijerina's message was precisely its religious character. According to Mario Joaquín Encinias, a powerful faith sustained nuevomexicanos as they carved out a living on the far rim of empire. A native New Mexican himself and a grandson of a Penitente, Encinias described a population whose members "had always turned to God in moments of crisis and truth." Echoing Tijerina's analysis, he wrote that by the 1960s, the crisis was one not just of tremendous poverty but of cultural disintegration as a direct result of land loss. Under these circumstances, Tijerina's characterization of land-grant conflict as a final showdown between the forces of good and evil resonated with the spiritual predispositions of many Spanish-speaking New Mexicans. Not only did Penitente Easter week rituals commemorate death and rebirth, Encinias argued, but older villagers subscribed to other traditional religious beliefs, including the belief that world destruction was a prelude to a more just future.[111]

While knowing relatively little about Tijerina's experiences in Arizona, a sociologist writing about the Alianza in 1967 invoked the word "prophet" to describe Tijerina's appeal as a land-grant leader. Nancie L. González conducted interviews with Alianza members as well as with Tijerina to conclude that "super-natural elements" infused the membership's belief structure. She noted the importance that Tijerina placed upon dream visions and how this former preacher talked about the return of the land in millennial, end-of-the-world terms. When addressing a Spanish-speaking crowd, González wrote, Tijerina eagerly alluded to a time when evil Anglos would be violently punished for their sins. Meanwhile, she asserted, Tijerina's followers reinforced the prophetic narrative, repeating how "their ancestors foretold a time when large numbers of persons would come 'laughing' from the east and take their land by force, thus destroying the happy life of the Hispanos. They would suffer for many years, but they were urged to maintain courage and to watch for a leader who would also come of out of the east to lead them against the enemy who would be forced to return 'crying' to their original homes."[112] Although the story vaguely resembled a Hopi legend about two brothers, one of whom, Pahána, or "White Brother," was to return from the east, González remained uncertain about its origins.[113] According to González, however, the legend predisposed some nuevomexicanos toward Tijerina's message. "Incidents have been told of old men who, after hearing Tijerina speak at public gatherings, have gone to him on their knees to kiss his feet, proclaiming him the messiah of legend," she wrote.[114] Plenty of people had heard of the legend and knew it to be very old. Tijerina was among them. Lucky for him, his birth state of Texas fell almost entirely to the east of New Mexico.[115]

Of course, not everyone was moved to join the Alianza for supernatural reasons. Much of Tijerina's charisma rested in his ability to give voice to the anger and frustration felt by many land-poor New Mexicans. In Tijerina's fearless, accusatory thunder, Juan Valdez heard someone who finally spoke courageously and uncompromisingly on behalf of people like his family. Born in 1938, he had grown up hearing the story of how the U.S. Forest Service had encouraged his grandfather Juan Ysidro Valdez to move away from pasturelands near Cañones, which the agency had determined were overgrazed, in exchange for permission to pasture his flocks in Canjilón. According to family lore, that promise was forgotten.[116] A tiny hamlet some twenty-three miles south of Tierra Amarilla, Canjilón was entirely surrounded by Forest Service land. As if to underscore that state of dependency, the only road into Canjilón went right by a U.S. Forest Service office before entering the village.

Juan Valdez resented the agency's role as an instrument of U.S. colonial authority. His grandfather had been an active member of the Corporation of Abiquiú, but his father, Amarante Valdez, confronted the problem of grazing permit reductions. Interviewed in 2007, Juan Valdez pulled from beneath his bed a small metal box containing two letters that his father had received from "*la floresta*," as locals call the Forest Service. The first, written in the midst of the Great Depression in 1937, told his father, who by then had five children to support, that his grazing permit was about to expire and he was not going to get a new one. Nearly twenty years later, another letter likewise denied Amarante Valdez permission to graze cattle "because there was no surplus range" and because, the letter explained, the responsibility of the Forest Service was to manage the forest "for the greatest good to the greatest number in the long run."[117] For Amarante Valdez, the long run had been a long refusal.

For his son, the family's resulting economic plight was a long-simmering injustice that deserved redress. In defiance of the Forest Service, Juan's father taught him starting as a young boy "how to trespass on what were former common lands, to graze animals surreptitiously, [and] to hunt, fish, and cut wood" so that the family might supplement its meager income.[118] Going to work, however, meant not going to school. "Poverty stole my education," Valdez insisted in 2007. "If I had gone to school . . . I would have been a lawyer working to recapture our lands." Trying to support a growing family on wages earned as a wood harvester instead, Valdez during the 1960s found himself at the mercy of the U.S. Forest Service like his father and grandfather before him. Resenting the agency's ability to dictate the relationship between Canjilón residents and the land, Valdez recalled that he "carried anger in his heart."[119] When he heard Tijerina speak on the radio, he heard someone who gave voice to all of his years of accumulated frustration.

Valdez soon joined the Alianza. So did other young men attracted by the fighting spirit of Tijerina's appeal. As in Arizona, Tijerina called his closest followers, almost all of them men, "valientes." They were the brave ones. "It is now or never," Tijerina insisted at one point. "Do your part. These rights and land claims of the mercedes belong to all of us. . . . Act now for your children's sake."[120] In keeping with his concept of the Alianza as "one great family," the patriarchal Tijerina also appealed to men in their role as fathers and husbands. "Now the time has come to display our valor on behalf of what belongs to us," he urged at one point. "Remember that we are defending the rights of our families, [and] of our wives."[121]

Although still a teen, and a girl, Tina Valdez also found Tijerina's message inspirational. She was born in San Luis, Colorado, on the Sangre de Cristo land grant, home to the Taylor ranch, but economic necessity forced her entire family to move to Denver while she was still a girl. Like many dispossessed Spanish speakers with ties to ancestral lands, her parents had been pushing for the recovery of the merced since before the founding of the Alianza. Valdez initially dismissed their activism. As she recalled, when her father, Luis, talked about "how the government stole the land grants or that the government helped to cover up th[is] history . . . I thought he was crazy." But after the emergence of the Alianza and hearing Tijerina speak multiple times, Valdez decided that this "crazy" version of history explained why her family had been uprooted. Inspired, she volunteered in high school to do a report on the Treaty of Guadalupe Hidalgo. A recent television special on the Spanish-speaking people of the American Southwest, which explained their poverty as springing from cultural deficiencies, prompted the school project. "I not only covered the land grants and the Treaty of Guadalupe Hidalgo . . . [but] I said . . . that our people weren't poor because they were lazy, ignorant, and superstitious. I said that they were poor because they got their land stolen and because they worked the hardest jobs for the lowest pay."[122] As soon as she graduated from high school, Tina Valdez, just seventeen, became a full-time volunteer for the Alianza. Upon Tijerina's suggestion, she also started using her full first name, Valentina, as she was now a "valiente" too.

Not everyone experienced such a conversion experience. To detractors who considered the chances of recovering any grant land nil, the Alianza leader's powers of persuasion were precisely the problem. Later in the decade, the media compared Tijerina to Elmer Gantry, Sinclair Lewis's fictional fast-talking preacher who cares little for morality but uses the pulpit to get rich.[123] The comparison made sense to some nuevomexicanos who suspected Tijerina of leading nothing more than a huckster scheme aimed at separating poor people from what little money they had. Even if they agreed they had been robbed of their inheritance, this group just as firmly believed that the time had long passed to do anything about it. In that case, what purpose did those membership dues serve except to enrich the Alianza leader? According to one early chronicler, Tijerina alone among the top officials of the Alianza could be counted upon to raise money merely by asking for it.[124] Other observers noted with some disquiet that the Alianza president ended nearly every speech and letter to members with just such a request.[125] One witness recalled older men slipping Tijerina $100 bills, usually in the fall after they had sold their cattle and precisely when their children needed the money for books and other school supplies.[126] The lack of financial transparency that dated from the earliest days of the Alianza left the organization vulnerable to criticism.

It also fueled gossip and speculation. Critics noted, for example, that every column that Tijerina wrote for the *News Chieftain* ended with him urging readers not only to join the Alianza Federal de Mercedes but also to buy a subscription to the newspaper.[127] Rumor had it that Tijerina received a one-dollar "kickback" on each newspaper subscription sold. Based on a swift calculation of membership size times monthly dues, rumor also had it that the Alianza was rolling in the dough. One police informant reported that the organization boasted a six-figure bank account and thus stood poised to launch eighty-two different lawsuits.[128] Actually the organization operated very close to the bone because many members paid upon joining and then sporadically after that, if ever again. In April 1964, Chris Tijerina felt flush with cash because, as he happily reported to his brother, dues payments had totaled $230 in March, compared to just $50 in February.[129] Despite occasional infusions of cash from true believers, the Alianza barely kept one step ahead of financial insolvency throughout its existence.

Tijerina employed all his oratorical flair to counter the negativity. His critics were infidels, traitors, pessimists, and cowards.[130] They went around "*soplando orejas*," that is, making baseless charges (literally "blowing ears") only because they did "not want their own crimes exposed." He directed a particular wrath at nuevomexicanos who claimed that the "mercedes can no longer be redeemed," accusing them of wanting "to change sides and their jacket every day."[131] As working-class men donned a jacket and tie for special occasions only, the comment implicitly painted the Alianza's critics as economically successful Spanish-speaking New Mexicans who did not care about their poorer brethren. Regarding money matters, he offered angry defiance. "Bad individuals are poisoning the minds and the heart of many innocents, saying that I, Reies López Tijerina, am from Mexico and that I am receiving money from the people that I am sending to a bank in Mexico," he announced in early 1965. Declaring "I am not from Mexico" and "I'm not a thief," Tijerina told anyone who did not believe him to go ahead and ask the FBI.[132] On rare occasions, his rebukes turned to pleading. In February 1965, for instance, Tijerina urged members to avoid those "quarrels, hatreds, jealousies and suspicions" that had plagued previous land-grant efforts. In an indication that the reverse had occurred, he also requested that Alianza members treat the organization's officials with respect, given that they "work without pay and for the good of all."[133]

The amount of criticism sometimes weighed on Tijerina. In June 1965, he instructed his brother Chris to take over the planning for the upcoming convention that September. Visiting friends in Independence, Missouri, the Alianza leader was unsure when, or whether, he would return to New Mexico. Tijerina wrote that he felt "really bad, in body and soul, [because of] the responsibilities before me, [and because of] the destruction of my home [an apparent allusion to a social worker's order that Mary Escobar and the children leave the Alianza's premises]. . . . Maybe I'll just forget about everything and stay here."[134] A month later, a still dispirited Tijerina wrote from a hospital bed in San José, California, where he had taken another trip. He was suffering from severe pain in his throat, a malady that would become a recurrent problem for him. Perhaps stress-related, the location of the pain literally rendered him unable to give voice to his crusade.[135]

Charisma describes a relationship as much as a quality. Charismatic leaders attract followers but need to deliver on their promises to keep them. Operating almost entirely in Spanish and largely out of the limelight, Tijerina through his land-grant gospel convinced hundreds and then thousands of New Mexicans to join the Alianza and his holy crusade. As the land-grant organization grew more popular, however, pressure mounted upon Tijerina to do something more than say "the same things over and over again," in the words of one erstwhile supporter.[136] Other land-grant heirs suspected that Tijerina's main talent was lining his own pockets. Clearly, the Alianza leader was at least as polarizing as he was mesmerizing. "The reaction to the cause of the Alliance ranges from sympathy to outright hostility, with these extremes reflected in Latins and 'Anglos' alike," commented one reporter as early 1964.[137] Thus, even as he enjoyed early success, Tijerina faced extraordinary pressure to deliver on his promises before his followers began to lose faith. The question for the Alianza leader was what to do next.

He decided to try his luck as an American citizen and petition Washington, D.C.

6

The American

In July 1964, Tijerina accepted an invitation from university students in Chihuahua, Mexico, to speak about land-grant matters. Much to his surprise, state police detained him the day after his speech and held him overnight for questioning before allowing him to continue to Mexico City. There he met with a future president of Mexico Luis Echeverría, who was then an assistant secretary of "Gobernación," a cabinet-level department in charge of the nation's internal affairs and security. In his memoir, Tijerina remembered thinking that the meeting, centered on how to publicize the land-grant cause, went well. He called a press conference to share that sentiment. Afterward, reporters from two leading Mexico City dailies wrote articles that implied that the land-grant cause had the support of the Mexican government.

It did not. As Tijerina also recorded, at 7 A.M. on August 4, 1964, immigration agents descended upon the Mexico City home of Dolores Rebelde, where he was once again staying with his daughter Rose. Without even allowing him to finish dressing, they whisked him away to an office for interrogation. There, they called him a communist, accused him of interfering with the internal affairs of the nation, and threatened him with ten years of jail. The interrogation was brief, however, because, just as suddenly, Tijerina was rushed to the Mexico City airport. Still shirtless, the Alianza leader was put on a plane bound for San Antonio, Texas, and unceremoniously deported.[1]

As much as Tijerina claimed to be a Mexican, to the Mexican government he was a troublesome American. Investigating the fate of land ceded long ago mattered less than avoiding the risk of antagonizing a powerful neighbor to the north. Three days after Tijerina's forced departure, Echeverría ordered consulates throughout the American Southwest to be wary of issuing travel permits to anyone associated with the Alianza in case members were still planning to organize a car caravan into Mexico. The same memo complained that Tijerina had "intervened" in a meeting of the student group that had invited him to speak on campus in Chihuahua and noted warily that Tijerina had met with other political groups too. Although a later report by Echeverría's office acknowledged that Tijerina always stuck to the topic of the land grants, the Alianza leader still meant trouble, as far as the Mexican government was concerned.[2]

His deportation deeply upset Tijerina. Financially, the trip was costly: police sequestered Mary Escobar's 1957 lilac-colored Pontiac sedan that Tijerina had borrowed to drive to Mexico.[3] Emotionally, the Alianza leader labored to understand why a country that he had esteemed so highly had rejected him. His response was to compartmentalize. Insisting that he had many good friends in Mexico, Tijerina blamed a few "bad and traitorous elements" for his deportation.[4] Politically, Tijerina braced himself for the reaction stateside. "I thought with horror how the Anglo press would make fun of us," he admitted in *Mi Lucha por la Tierra*. Sure enough, he wrote, the talk around the town soon became "Nobody wants Tijerina, not even his own country, Mexico."[5] Yet Tijerina's "home country" was actually the United States.

The deportation left the Alianza leader with no other choice but to seek redress from the U.S. government, whose actions he had so vigorously condemned. Maintaining his key argument regarding violations of the Treaty of Guadalupe Hidalgo, Tijerina revised his rhetoric to address a new audience of U.S. academics, policy makers, and politicians. Angry condemnations in Spanish became polite pleading in English as Tijerina sought to present the organization's sweeping goals as modest, nonthreatening, and legitimate. The Alianza president did his best to assure potential allies in Washington, D.C.—and potential members closer to home—that the organization shunned subversion and violence. Or as Eddie Chavez, a World War II veteran and one of Tijerina's most loyal followers, chirped at the first Alianza meeting in February 1963, "There is nothing anti-American in this Alianza."[6]

Even as he shifted toward accepting an American identity, however, Tijerina redefined what it meant to be an American. The nation's founding documents upheld private property rights as fundamental to the functioning of democracy. Tijerina promoted the commons. In the United States, the courts formed a primary avenue to settle disputes. Tijerina's historically grounded mistrust of the legal system led him to seek some other forum to investigate land-grant grievances. The United States clung to a vision of itself as a fundamentally fair and democratic nation. Tijerina told a tale of war and conquest. Inevitably, Tijerina also challenged existing notions of equality. He did not want "his people" treated like just any other group of Americans; Tijerina wanted their historic land claims recognized by the federal government. He also wanted protection of the unique cultural heritage of Spanish speakers in the Southwest.

Consequently, Tijerina could never appear American enough to satisfy most policy makers or politicians. They deemed his ideas preposterous. Despite his best effort to adhere to the law and, as was his constitutional right, to peacefully petition his government for redress, Tijerina also encountered strong opposition from law enforcement. J. Edgar Hoover, head of the Federal Bureau of Investigation, deemed Tijerina dangerous and foreign. Closer to home in New Mexico, Rio Arriba County district attorney Alfonso Sánchez emerged as Tijerina's chief nemesis. Like Hoover, Sánchez worried that the Alianza leader posed "a constant threat to the peace and dignity of the State."[7] At both the federal and the state level, such dire conclusions emerged in the absence of any evidence of wrongdoing. In such circumstances, what utility did Tijerina's professed allegiance to the United States serve?

Soon, the Alianza leader concluded that the answer was "none." As much as he acted like a model—and even patriotic—American, Tijerina received official responses that ranged from polite rebuffs to intense law enforcement scrutiny. Not surprisingly, Tijerina's season of foregrounding his American identity proved brief and frustrating and ultimately provoked within him an even harsher assessment of the land of his birth.

In August 1964, just a few weeks after Tijerina's deportation from Mexico, a reporter dropped by the Alianza's Albuquerque headquarters on the eve of the organization's second convention. Nigel S. Hey of the city's *North Valley News* noted that the humble decor spoke to Tijerina's political interests. Posters of the incoming Mexican president Gustavo Díaz Ordaz shared wall space with a weathered copy, in Spanish, of the U.N. Declaration of Human Rights. The number of U.S. flags scattered about, however, outnumbered the single Mexican one relegated to a corner. Otherwise, the adornment consisted of a few yellowing newspaper clippings taped to the wall. These recounted either the Alianza's activities or instances "in which Latins [or] Jews have been victimized by ethnic discrimination." As Hey noted, however, the magnitude of the Alianza's agenda belied the main office's modest appearance. Although "the consensus of land grant experts is that 'what's done is done,'" he wrote, the organization had set its sights on recovering more than 100 million acres across the U.S. Southwest, an acreage that exceeded the size of the entire state of New Mexico.[8]

To some critics, that lofty goal alone told them all they needed to know about the Alianza. Not by coincidence did writers compare Tijerina to Don Quixote tilting at windmills. Just like the lead character of *Man of La Mancha*, which opened on Broadway in 1965, Tijerina appeared to chase an impossible dream.[9] Such skepticism placed enormous pressure upon him to present the Alianza crusade as entirely respectable. Indeed, the Alianza president reassured his followers that they were better Americans than those "thieves and assassins" who had plagued them for so long. "Our rights and our property for many years have been in the hands of advantage-taking foreigners who know nothing of Democracy nor anything about what it means to be an AMERICAN," he intoned. While the phrasing was awkward, the message was clear: compared to *aliancistas*, those who undermined property rights were "false citizens."[10]

Given that the Alianza's agenda called for massive land redistribution, a priority was to protect the organization's reputation from accusations of communism. Tijerina's own views toward communism shifted dramatically following the assassination of President John F. Kennedy in November 1963. Although he had spoken admiringly of the Soviet Union in his years as a preacher, Tijerina shuddered to learn that killer Lee Harvey Oswald had proclaimed to be a communist. A fearful Tijerina urged *aliancistas* to stay away from "Communists or Marxists who go around riling

Tijerina standing in front of the Alianza headquarters in Albuquerque in April 1966, by all appearances a scholarly and upstanding citizen. The photograph originally appeared in the *Denver Post* with the headline "The Part-Time Preacher Dreams of Forcing Uncle Sam to Return 100 Million Acres." The words on the window read "Justice [Is] Our Creed." (Nancy Tucker Pictorial Collection of Southwest Materials, Center for Southwest Research, University of New Mexico, Albuquerque)

up and perverting the right [to claim justice] of the poor and oppressed." "The just man is never safe in the United States," he concluded. "*Hombres malos* [bad men]" lurked everywhere. After all, if Kennedy, surrounded by the Secret Service, had been assassinated, how much more vulnerable were Alianza members?[11]

Tijerina also understood that the Alianza itself was vulnerable to attack if it did not take a firm stand against communism. Influenced by Cold War propaganda, nuevomexicanos often hurled the word "communist" as the worst kind of insult.[12] After hearing Tijerina speak for the first time, for example, one distrustful Atrisco land-grant heir reportedly denounced him as a "communist wetback."[13] Similarly, Tijerina's contacts with former Mexican president Lázaro Cárdenas raised the suspicions of an erstwhile Alianza member who described Cárdenas as a "communist" with "close connections to Communist Cuba." (Also in the dark as to Cárdenas's identity, the state police officer gathering this information described Cárdenas as someone who "supposedly heads an organization of collective farms in Mexico.")[14] More broadly, Tijerina understood that those opposed to land-recovery efforts might also make use of anti-communism to shut down the organization. "They will want to call us communist to avoid turning their face toward JUSTICE; they will accuse us falsely to avoid making reparations and paying [us] what they owe," he wrote.[15] Like so many political organizations during the Cold War, the Alianza early on adopted by-laws that formally forbade "all Heirs or members suspicious of treason or communist infiltration" from voting or partaking in any Alianza activities.[16]

The most powerful elected official closest to the matter of the mercedes, U.S. senator Joseph Montoya, kept his distance nonetheless. A descendant of eighteenth-century Spanish immigrants to New Mexico, Montoya was first elected to the U.S. House of Representatives in 1957 and then to the U.S. Senate in 1964, where he proudly served as "the only U.S. Senator of Spanish heritage" until 1977.[17] Initially, Montoya extended to Tijerina the same courtesy he provided all his constituents. He met privately with the Alianza leader in Albuquerque shortly after the organization's founding. Afterward, the press noted, Montoya "gave token approval" to the possibility of sponsoring a bill to investigate land-grant concerns.[18] Montoya also diligently responded to all correspondence that he received from Alianza members. Yet he remained wary of the organization overall, and no bill emerged. Montoya declined every invitation to attend an Alianza convention. While polite, his responses to correspondence were often perfunctory.[19] After two years of back-and-forth communications, for example, Montoya in a letter to a constituent referred to the "Federal Alliance of Mercy," a literal translation of the Alianza's name. As the proudly bilingual Montoya knew better, the response, perhaps crafted by an office staff member, suggested that Alianza concerns merited glancing attention at best.[20] Even more telling, Montoya warned family members to stay away from the Alianza. Or so his younger brother, Ted Montoya, also a lawyer, told *aliancistas* at a January 1964 meeting. According to the minutes of the gathering, the younger Montoya formally withdrew a previous offer to help the new organization. Although still happy to give advice in private, he was adamant that "under no circumstances could he help publicly because doing so would harm the next electoral bid of his brother."[21] Ironically, Tijerina had just informed the Alianza membership that Congress boasted three Mexican American representatives—including Montoya—who as Democrats were perfectly positioned to secure the Alianza an audience with the occupant of the Oval Office.[22]

Another of the three, Representative Henry B. González of Texas, likewise dashed Tijerina's persistent hope that ethnic bonds might translate into political capital. The son of Mexican immigrants, González lacked any ties to a land grant, but Tijerina nonetheless labeled him a *heredero*, or land-grant heir, too. Dialing González directly, Tijerina offered to share "the constitutional facts and federal documentation that has elevated the spirit and revived the legal value of the Treaty of Guadalupe Hidalgo" with one aim in mind: "Can you get us an interview with the President?" González, however, sidestepped that request. Citing protocol and professional courtesy, he advised Tijerina, in a suggestion that already had led to a dead end, to "contact Representative Montoya right there in Albuquerque" instead.[23]

Tijerina preferred to pepper official Washington with letters and phone calls, pressing for an audience. After receiving a letter from Tijerina, the Department of Justice professed confusion without seeking clarity. "We were unable to ascertain from your letter which provisions of the treaty you were referring to and the circumstances under which rights have been allegedly violated," the official response read.[24] Tijerina had better luck contacting the Department of the Interior, which oversaw the Bureau of Indian Affairs. In imperfect but earnest English, Tijerina's letter first introduced the Alianza as "a Corporation, compose of all the Heirs of the more than one thousand spanish and mexican land grants." The rest of the Alianza letter drew a powerful parallel between land-poor New Mexicans and Native Americans in that both groups had seen their land base shrink under American rule. Tijerina's point: Spanish-speaking New Mexicans were equally deserving of federal attention. "We[,] like the Indians, have many legal rights through the treaty [of Guadalupe Hidalgo] and land titles, but for lack of economic support we cannot prove it," the letter explained.[25] In response, Interior Department officials issued an invitation to visit their offices if members of the Alianza were ever in Washington, D.C.[26]

Tijerina did just that during a ten-day visit to D.C. in April 1964 that he took with new president of the Corporation of Abiquiú Amarante Ray Serrano. In updates that he sent back home, Tijerina accentuated the positive results of this trip for Alianza members. The Department of the Interior had proved true to its word: Tijerina met with Charles H. Stoddard, who headed its Bureau of Land Management, which controlled even more public land in New Mexico than did the U.S. Forest Service. Another highlight of the trip was his meeting with Democratic representative Edward Roybal of California, who served in Congress along with Montoya and González. Born in Albuquerque to a Spanish-speaking family whose roots in the region went back to 1598, Roybal had moved to Los Angeles as a young boy. According to Tijerina, an intrigued Roybal admitted that he had never heard of the Treaty of Guadalupe Hidalgo but, sincerely interested in land-grant history, had suggested that a bill on the issue be drafted and introduced in Congress.[27] Tijerina also met with Montoya and González despite their initial unhelpful attitudes. Finally, Tijerina wrangled appointments with lower-level functionaries in the White House and at the Department of State as well as a brief chat with U.S. attorney general Robert F. Kennedy, whom he had met briefly twice before by attending public speeches that the attorney general had delivered in Chicago and Albuquerque.[28]

Afterward, Tijerina confidently pronounced the trip a success overall. He confided to his brother that those who had heard him speak would remember his words for as long as they lived.[29] News of the Alianza had provoked "great alarm and surprise" in the nation's capital, he similarly assured delighted Alianza members: "No longer can Washington, D.C. ignore our situation and our pleas."[30]

In fact, Washington could and did. The strategy of petition reflected the politically weak position of the Alianza. Like vulnerable dependents, Tijerina and other Alianza members pleaded for policy makers and politicians to pay attention to their cry for justice, with no tangible result.

Both geography and demography worked against them. At a time when the African American civil rights movement was reaching a national crescendo with the 1963 March on Washington and subsequent civil rights legislation, Mexican Americans constituted, in one reporter's telling phrase, "a minority that nobody knows."[31] Concentrated in the Southwest, most Mexican Americans lived far from the centers of governmental and financial power in the United States. Comparatively speaking, moreover, their numbers were small. According to the 1960 census, whereas African Americans numbered about 19 million, or nearly 10 percent of the overall U.S. population, Mexican Americans numbered only about 3.5 million. New Mexico's Spanish-surnamed population, to employ the terminology of the official census, was smaller yet, hovering just over 250,000.[32] Consequently, few Americans, even Americans of Mexican decent, knew much, if anything, about land-grant history. Indeed, some Americans even questioned whether New *Mexico* was a foreign country. With good humor, the state's residents collected anecdotes of their fellow citizens wondering whether they needed visas to visit or if the water was potable.[33]

To draw attention to the Alianza cause, Tijerina embellished the organization's prestige and his own reputation by claiming the largest possible potential political constituency. He routinely claimed that he represented half a million Spanish-speaking New Mexicans, a number nearly double the census estimate. Likewise, the Alianza leader often asserted that he spoke on behalf of all Mexican Americans, a population that he estimated to be not 3.5 million but 5 million and sometimes even 10 million.[34] Even though the vast majority of the Mexican American population descended from immigrants who arrived after 1848, Tijerina's assertion suggested that the general U.S. ethnic Mexican population and the population of land-grant claimants were one and the same. Implicitly then, it extended to all Mexican Americans a claim to the land in the Southwest. Thus, Tijerina casually bestowed *heredero* status upon Representative Henry B. González.

Tijerina tried his best to cultivate liberal Democrats like González by emphasizing common goals. Theoretically at least, the Alianza's goals of achieving economic independence and ending racial discrimination could both be met by working beneath the umbrella of American sovereignty. The latter goal especially echoed the priorities of a generation of Mexican American activists like the aforementioned George I. Sánchez (chapter 3). These activists fought to end anti-Mexican discrimination in schools, in the workplace, and in public accommodations, mostly by suing in court. At the time of the Alianza's founding, the handful of Mexican American elected officials in the country came from this tradition, which emphasized assimilation but could be feisty. With oratorical skills that arguably topped Tijerina's, González, for example, as a state senator in Texas spoke for twenty-two hours straight to filibuster a set of bills delaying the implementation of the 1957 *Brown v. Board of Education* decision outlawing segregation.[35] That effort perfectly exemplified the politician's commitment toward "influencing policy from the inside."[36] An optimistic Tijerina initially hoped to tap into precisely that sort of influence. The question of land ownership at the heart of the Alianza crusade, however, sharply distinguished it from previous civil rights efforts.

Wisely, Tijerina left the question of sovereignty for a later date. Instead of demanding the immediate return of the land, he pressed for an investigation into land-grant grievances in 1964 and 1965. Utterly convinced of the righteousness of the land-grant crusade, he argued that exposing injustice was the first step to victory. "Now that all the heirs are aware of their rights, now that they know how to defend themselves . . . not a tribunal in the world will deny us justice," Tijerina predicted.[37] As an interim measure, an investigation offered several advantages. It boiled down the Alianza's monumental agenda into one seemingly reasonable request. More important, calling for an investigation indefinitely postponed the infinitely more complicated topic of how exactly land recovery was to proceed. In the meantime, Tijerina had time to find out more about land grants beyond New Mexico. As late as 1964, Tijerina's knowledge of land-grant affairs essentially stopped at the New Mexico state border. No one in the organization, and few scholars beyond it, for that matter, knew much of Spanish and Mexican land-settlement patterns or the history of land dispossession after 1848. Aware of this knowledge deficit, in 1964 Chris Tijerina dashed off a series of letters to the Department of the Interior asking for any available maps or other pertinent details regarding land grants in Arizona, California, Texas, Colorado, and Nevada.[38] Under these circumstances, the organization's emphasis upon an investigation inevitably amounted to a plea for information as much as for justice.

Tijerina considered multiple forums. The Alianza's constitution cited a planned appeal to the United Nations as a "last recourse." When it was founded in 1945, one of the United Nations' top objectives was "to establish conditions under which justice and respect for the obligations arising from treaties and other sources of international law can be maintained."[39] The next year, the National Negro Congress attempted to appeal to the United Nations under this provision.[40] Although Tijerina may not have known of this precursor action on the part of African Americans, any talk of meeting treaty obligations was bound to catch his attention. Tijerina even imagined one day appearing in front of the U.N.'s top court, the International Court of Justice in The Hague, Netherlands.[41] Despite his oft-expressed lack of confidence in the U.S. judicial system, Tijerina also entertained taking land-grant demands directly to the U.S. Supreme Court. But this effort was soon abandoned for lack of funds.[42]

The Alianza president also decided to press his case directly with President Lyndon B. Johnson. Three letters that the organization sent between November 1964 and September 1965 all appealed on patriotic grounds. Written the day after Election Day, the first letter congratulated President Johnson on his "historic triumph" at the polls. A second in January 1965 sympathized with the president's heavy responsibilities globally, including the ongoing war in Vietnam. Accompanying these letters were a petition signed by 150 land-grant heirs and a series of polite queries. Might the president extend the same courtesy to Spanish-speaking people in New Mexico that the federal government had extended to Native Americans throughout the nation by at least acknowledging their property rights? What about issuing a presidential executive order that would allow land-grant heirs to pasture their flocks on U.S. Forest Service land and to remove wood from there too?[43]

Written in English by Chris Tijerina, a third letter tried even harder to "Americanize" the land-grant movement by linking it to the more familiar civil rights movement. The letter began by quoting from the speech that Johnson had delivered upon signing the 1965 Voting Rights Act. The president had referred to his first job as a schoolteacher in a segregated "Mexican" school in Cotulla, Texas, nearly forty years before: "Somehow you never forget what poverty and hatred can do when you see its scars on the hopeful face of a young child." Chris Tijerina pushed for more than personal memories. "Mr. President, these are beautiful words," he wrote, "but we wonder if they have any meaning that can help us."[44] His appeal failed to budge the federal government from its position that land-grant matters were settled. "All the land grants which were examined and considered by the federal government were confirmed many years ago," read the only response that the Alianza received.[45]

To the extent that legal and government experts contemplated the Treaty of Guadalupe Hidalgo at all during the mid-1960s, they considered it a promise fulfilled. Although no less a historical luminary than Frederick Jackson Turner acknowledged at the turn of the last century that the American territorial system was colonialism by another name, Turner's focus was almost exclusively upon Euro-Americans moving west. According to this line of analysis, the subjugated status of people in a territory always ended with statehood, in New Mexico's case in 1912.[46] Consequently, into the 1960s many Americans in New Mexico and beyond looked upon their nation's westward expansion as an extension of, in Thomas Jefferson's phrase, an "empire of liberty."[47] Up until the 1960s, scholarly interpretations of the U.S.-Mexican War tended to fit into this "winning of the West" framework. "American expansion across a practically empty continent despoiled no nation unjustly," intoned one of the dons of the history of U.S. foreign relations as late as 1965.[48]

Ironically, Tijerina's lack of formal education may have provided him the intellectual freedom to come to a more critical viewpoint. He certainly did not have to disregard what he learned in school about how the United States had come to stretch from sea to shining sea. Absent any conception of colonialism, for example, Senator Montoya responded to another land-grant query in 1965 by asserting that any resolution to the problem of contested land "must be undertaken through the available legal machinery under our system of jurisprudence."[49] As land-grant activists knew all too well, however, the courts had operated as a primary mechanism for land-grant dispossession. Indeed, Tijerina had traveled to Washington precisely to circumvent this problem. "One hundred years of bitter experience with American courts has left us disillusioned," he observed. "Only united can we receive real protection from the federal government."[50]

AROUSING SUSPICION

Despite Tijerina's best efforts to cultivate allies in Washington, D.C., only one agency did not immediately dismiss the Alianza—the Federal Bureau of Investigation. Initially, federal agents sought to determine any possible connection between land-grant activism and the Communist Party in Mexico. As head of the FBI, Hoover had waged a crusade against communism for decades by the time the Alianza was founded. Convinced that foreign meant radical and Mexican meant both, the bureau under Hoover had placed even highly patriotic Mexican American civil rights organizations under scrutiny during the 1940s and 1950s.[51] By the 1960s, the success of the civil rights movement, and Hoover's conviction that the movement was riddled with communists, arguably conditioned the FBI to rely even more upon race as a proxy for subversion. Although the FBI never found any evidence of international communist connections, documents obtained through the Freedom of Information Act reveal that the bureau began keeping a close eye on the Alianza in January 1964 and, with the help of a confidential informant, continued to do so for ten years.[52]

Ironically, whereas Mexico's internal security police had rejected Tijerina because he was an American, the FBI viewed him as someone who was really a Mexican despite the place of his birth. Specifically, Hoover wondered whether Tijerina had violated the 1938 Foreign Agents Registration Act, which required any person in the United States working in a "political or quasi-political capacity" on behalf of foreign interests to register with the federal government. To gather more information, in February 1964 an agent with the Albuquerque field office of the FBI showed up at Alianza headquarters to interview the Alianza leader, only to discover that Tijerina was on another extended trip south of the border.[53] In April 1964, the FBI director personally ordered agents to investigate Tijerina's connections to Benjamin Luna's Frente Internacional de Derechos Humanos, the group in Mexico City that had offered early support to the Alianza. The next month, Hoover wished to know why Tijerina was associating with members of a Mexican group that advocated "territorial reintegration." Agents in New Mexico repeatedly told their higher-ups that they found no indication that the Alianza was operating at the behest of any Mexican group or any evidence of subversion. Unrelenting in his suspicions, Hoover ordered that FBI surveillance of the Alianza's headquarters continue.[54]

Aware that the land-grant group was under scrutiny, Chris Tijerina in July 1964 dropped by the local FBI office in Albuquerque and made a plea as an American. Announcing that the Alianza had nothing to hide, he invited agents to attend the Alianza's upcoming second convention that August. Surprised field agents declined in part because the FBI already planned to be there, albeit undercover.[55] As it turns out, Rio Arriba County district attorney Alfonso Sánchez had devised a similar plan.

Sánchez had nursed suspicions about the Alianza and subversion from the moment he first met Tijerina back in October 1963. Trying to follow the letter of the law, the Alianza president had sought the legal advice of the Rio Arriba County district attorney concerning how to incorporate the Alianza as a nonprofit, which was a useful status for seeking donations and applying for grants. According to notes that he took that day, Sánchez immediately noticed the sway of the former preacher's speech with some trepidation. "Very convincing!" he scribbled. "Bears watch[ing]!" The DA wondered whether this was the same organization that his wife's uncle had recently joined. (It was, although Paul Vigil would soon leave along with the Alianza's first official secretary, Eunice Myrick.) Before long, Sánchez had fingered Tijerina and his followers as "communists and rabble rousers."[56] The reason? From their conversation, Sánchez gleaned that Tijerina not only hoped to unite all land-grant claimants against the Anglos but also was willing to use force if necessary. Sánchez remembered telling Tijerina during this initial meeting that he, in his role as DA, would be the person to stop him from doing that. Or as Sánchez recalled with considerable pride during a 2013 interview, "I tried to get everyone to put the brakes on him."[57]

Despite their adversarial positions, the two men shared much in common. Born in 1928 in Belen, New Mexico, Sánchez, like Tijerina, had grown up during the Great Depression in a large and impoverished family. He also lost his mother as a young boy. Although Sánchez went off to the military and then law school, both men also entered the Corporation of Abiquiú's orbit by the late 1950s. Their paths never crossed then, but Sánchez represented corporation members who were being sued by the Payne ranch at the same time that Tijerina was lobbying on behalf of the corporation in Mexico. In fact, the DA's demonstrated support of the land-grant cause had prompted Tijerina to choose Sánchez's counsel in October 1963. A clash was nearly inevitable, however, not just because they advocated different approaches to land-grant woes but also because each tended to think that he knew best. Like Tijerina, Sánchez boasted a proud personality mixed with more than a dash of paternalism. In later years, he, like Tijerina, often referred to Spanish-speaking New Mexicans as "my people," by which he also meant a people in need of guidance.[58]

In 1957, Sánchez tried to guide Corporation of Abiquiú members to accept the letter of the law. In the Payne case, corporation members as the plaintiffs were required to prove their right to use just 1 percent of the land that the Payne Land and Livestock Company claimed as its own, 70 acres out of 7,000. The best way forward, Sánchez decided, was to trace a chain of title from one owner to the next, starting in 1832, when the Mexican government issued the original grant. This approach required extensive—and expensive—genealogical and legal research. The young lawyer put the price tag at $4,000. In the end, the Corporation of Abiquiú managed to cough up just $20. The piddling sum reflected tactical differences as much as poverty. Corporation of Abiquiú members favored using the Payne case to argue for their collective right to access not just 70 acres but all of the grant's resources, that is, they sought to revive the commons.[59]

In opposing that goal, Sánchez had an ally in Gilbert Espinosa, a New Mexican lawyer, who declared the very concept of the commons un-American. Perhaps prompted by early rumblings of the Alianza, Espinosa wrote an article for the *State Bar of New Mexico Journal* that attempted to undercut land-grant activists. His article underscored just how deeply Tijerina's approach, even when wrapped in the best behavior, challenged the conventional wisdom within New Mexico and beyond. Espinosa began by emphasizing that shared access to mutual resources was "alien to other systems of land tenure that we have" in the United States. He had a point.

Americans had long idealized the small, independent farmer as the bedrock of democracy. That ideal had justified the 1887 Dawes Act that, in a disastrous attempt to transform indigenous people into farmers, had divided millions of acres of tribal lands into individual allotments and dramatically shrunk tribal holdings. Now Espinosa proposed a similar remedy to the land-grant question. The best way to resolve lingering land-grant disputes, he insisted, was to get rid of community land grants altogether and make "land-grant heirs" into "owners" and "proprietors of interest," with the ability to sell the land portion by portion, or not, according to individual wants.[60] Thus, whereas Tijerina advocated a mass movement to right a gross injustice, Espinosa proposed an act of redefinition to address what he considered a lingering legal artifact. Unlike Tijerina, Espinosa encouraged his fellow nuevomexicanos to accept the status quo gracefully.

Frustrated individuals around Tierra Amarilla refused. The summer of 1964 ushered forth a dramatic ratcheting up of vandalism around Tierra Amarilla targeting the property of large landholders. Unknown culprits slashed tires, cut fences, and burned barns and haystacks in an attempt to stop what they saw as encroachment on grant land. In one case, someone poured sugar into a car's gas tank; in another, someone stole and then slaughtered a cow. In addition, land developer Kenneth Heron complained that an irrigation ditch on his property had been blown up to the tune of $1,500 in damages, and, particularly frightening to his wife, someone had kicked in the door while she was at home alone.[61] Two days before Tijerina was deported from Mexico, a suspicious fire at the Chama Land and Title Co. nearly caused a major explosion in town and cost the company an estimated $70,000 in damages.[62]

In addition to these suspected acts of vandalism mostly occurring under the cover of night, that summer the Corporation of Abiquiú members again began, in David Correia's phrase, to "perform their property claims," meaning that, to send a message to authorities, they started acting in public like the landowners they claimed to be. In one instance, for example, a land-grant heir impounded a man's cow for trespassing and then asked the owner to pay him seven dollars to get the animal back, the exact fee that the U.S. Forest Service charged to return cattle that had trespassed on federal lands. Other corporation members demanded that tourists purchase hunting and fishing licenses from them and not from state officials, although, tongue placed firmly in cheek, they promised "lower prices for Mexicans." Land-grant activists also blanketed northern New Mexico with eviction notices.[63] Recipients ranged from individual property holders like land developer Heron to government agencies, including the State Game and Fish Department, the U.S. Forest Service, and even the Peace Corps, which had established several training operations in northern New Mexico precisely because conditions there mimicked those that volunteers expected to encounter in Latin America.[64]

Before the summer was out, Sánchez found all his suspicions confirmed in a gossip-laden law enforcement report detailing the presumed activities of "Reyes López Tijerina a/k/a King Tiger." A mistranslation of Tijerina's name (the Spanish word for tiger is "*tigre*"), the epithet became popular after the 1967 courthouse raid when, to many, it captured the spirit of a leader who so fiercely defended land-grant rights. The report revealed that Tijerina's supporters were employing the nickname as early as 1964. To the extent that Tijerina spoke in millennial terms about ultimate justice and punishment of the evildoers, however, at least some police informants heard a man who frightened them with visions of racial strife and social division.

Otherwise, the report relied upon rumor to castigate the Alianza leader. "Rumor has it that he is a cult leader and a school teacher and has been on the scene for many years," the report stated. "He is considered a crackpot by many who have come in contact with him." Plus, according to the latest gossip, Tijerina leaned far left. "The original rumor . . . was that he and another man were up here at the instance of the Communist Party," this "Partial Report on Tierra Amarilla Dispute" stated. Contending that "a great many people in the Tierra Amarilla region seem to be afraid of him," the report concluded that on one point, universal agreement reigned: "The inhabitants on both sides [of the dispute] say that Reyes is always there when the trouble starts and continues," adding, "There seems to be no question on any one's mind that he is one of the ringleaders if not the ringleader behind much of the trouble." No question, but no proof either. To the contrary, as an addendum to the "Partial Report" noted, Tijerina was in Mexico during much of the summer of 1964.[65]

Nevertheless, Sánchez's suspicions explained his incognito presence at the Alianza's second convention that August. To his surprise, he came away favorably impressed. Sánchez learned of the upcoming gathering after seeing large red-and-white posters plastered about Santa Fe inviting land-grant claimants to come to Seth Hall, a high school gymnasium and auditorium in town. "The silence on the part of the heirs which has lasted for 117 years will be shattered at this great convention," they enticed in

Spanish. A concerned Sánchez immediately called the Alianza office in Albuquerque to determine whether the gathering might portend violence. Answering the call, Santiago Tapia y Anaya, an early member and one of Tijerina's strongest supporters, reassured the DA that the Alianza planned a peaceful gathering. In fact, the two-day affair went off without a hitch. It featured music, food, and several guest speakers, including Agustín Cue Cánovas, the historian who came all the way from Mexico City. Dressed in jeans and a work shirt so as not to attract attention, Sánchez had no choice but to credit the Alianza for staging an "orderly" and "well-organized" gathering.[66]

In just one case did Sánchez's hunch regarding Tijerina appear correct: the Alianza leader almost certainly authored a defiant eviction notice sent out by the Corporation of Abiquiú that September. The notice repeated portions of Tijerina's land-grant gospel. Testifying to Tijerina's cross-border work, it also asserted that the land-grant movement enjoyed the support of thousands of peasants and workers in Latin America. Finally, it echoed the sweeping claims contained within the Alianza's constitution. Recipients, it warned, should take only their personal property with them because everything else, including "all machinery, buildings, and all other equipment," was to be left on the premises "as a fraction payment for the use of the land for all these years."[67] Although signed by Corporation of Abiquiú president Amarante Ray Serrano and other corporation members, the September eviction notice was pure Tijerina. In 1964, the most ferocious thing about "King Tiger" was his verbal punch.

Nevertheless in October, Sánchez decided to put the brakes on Tijerina and other land-grant activists through a temporary court injunction. "I do know that they were rooked out of their property many years ago," the district attorney admitted to a reporter at the time. "But it is too late to do anything about it now."[68] Of special concern to Sánchez, corporation members recently had announced that they intended to establish an armed border patrol to keep non-heirs off grant land. Overnight a dozen "No Trespassing" signs appeared, warning outsiders to stay away.[69] Fearing a looming race war, Sánchez in the injunction accused 137 people of engaging in "unlawful acts" and creating "a potential tinderbox" in the state. In an indication of his presumed ringleader status, Reies Tijerina's name appeared at the top of the document alongside those of Corporation of Abiquiú officers. (In contrast, Anselmo Tijerina's name appeared alphabetically amid other names that began with *T*.)[70] Sánchez also reminded the court that a 1956 injunction had already forbade the

Corporation of Abiquiú from making any claims on the Tierra Amarilla grant. Therefore, the actions of members were particularly willful and grievous. In a sweeping ruling that left the corporation "stripped . . . of every vestige of power," Judge Paul Tackett agreed and made the injunction permanent.[71]

The hearing over which Tackett presided before rendering his decision, moreover, clarified the limited room in which any land-grant activist had to maneuver as an American. At one point in the proceedings, a dismayed Tierra Amarilla man pulled out a tattered identification card to show the judge that he had served in the navy during World War II. The gesture was intended to highlight the gap between American democratic ideals and the reality of discrimination: he had served his country as a U.S. citizen but believed he was not being treated fairly. Whipping out his own navy veteran's ID card, Tackett employed the same action to convey an entirely different message. "I have one too," he said, as if to say, "See, we are all Americans; we are all the same." Like many New Mexicans, Tackett sought to promote racial harmony and a version of equality without delving into the matter of land loss at all. "Can't Anglos and Spanish live side by side?" the judge asked the distraught nuevomexicanos gathered before him. In what appeared to be a gesture of consolation, Tackett also blithely affirmed the court as an impartial arbitrator of property rights. "If you can prove in court that the land is yours," he optimistically counseled corporation members, "then the court will uphold your claim."[72] Nuevomexicanos knew better. "The laws are very bad / They have us crucified," went the lines of one song, a corrido, written at the time.[73]

In the end, Tackett's decision probably benefited the Alianza in the sense that disgruntled corporation members migrated to the new land-grant organization. Fortunately for Tijerina, at this point, he gained the support of two academics who shared his critical view.

NEW FRIENDS, OLD DILEMMA

Less than a week after Tackett's decision, Frances L. Swadesh (later Quintana) received a phone call from Reies López Tijerina inviting her to attend an upcoming Alianza gathering as an observer. A curious Swadesh had already heard of the organization. Then a graduate student completing a dissertation at the University of Colorado in anthropology, Swadesh possessed a deep familiarity with the history of Spanish speakers and indigenous people in the area and in central Mexico too. Her dissertation topic, the history of Spanish-speaking settlement on the Ute frontier, had exposed Swadesh to countless land-grant documents. Extensive archival and ethnographic research convinced her to regard land-grant claims sympathetically.

Her own somewhat unusual family and upbringing also may have predisposed her toward the study of other cultures and to identify with the marginalized. The "L." in Frances L. Swadesh stood for León. Her father, Maurice León, had been born in Beirut to Spanish immigrant parents and educated in France before he headed to Wall Street as a lawyer. In the United States, he met and married Frances Juliana Webster Goodrich, who counted among her ancestors a Mayflower passenger and Noah Webster, the lexicographer. Their daughter attended high school in France but had the chance to study indigenous cultures in the United States and in Latin America as a college undergraduate. After graduation, Frances León spent time in Mexico, where she became intimately aware of the poor treatment granted indigenous people south of the border. While in Mexico, she also met Morris Swadesh, an anthropologist, whom she married in 1940. Not until 1958 did she return to graduate school to complete her dissertation.[74]

Swadesh had been carefully contemplating the Alianza cause even before Tijerina called. As she admitted to a senior colleague, Clark Knowlton, the Alianza's constant invocation of the Treaty of Guadalupe Hidalgo probably struck more than a few people as "trying to lock the barn door after the horses have been stolen." Yet Swadesh recalled that in Mexico the "*ley ejido*" likewise had been a dead letter until the 1910 revolution reclaimed the medieval idea of setting aside some landholdings for collective use.[75] Moreover, the Alianza's emphasis on securing for its members' collective use of the natural resources of the land, particularly access to pasture, wood, and water, intrigued her. Given that much of the national forests in the state originally had been "carved out of" grant land in the first place, Swadesh saw no reason why the federal government ought not to "embrace preferential access of Hispanos to the National Forest areas adjacent to their communities."[76]

The more Swadesh found out about the Alianza, moreover, the more she liked. As a result of their initial phone conversation, Swadesh credited Tijerina for largely avoiding the traditional "*envidia* [envy]" that had undercut previous land-grant efforts.[77] As Swadesh knew, heirs from different grants all too often viewed each other as competitors vying for control over a shrinking land base. Debates over selling the land once and for all had also bitterly divided land-grant heirs—to the extent that Tome grant heirs ended one of their meetings with a fistfight.[78] Thus, Swadesh appreciated Tijerina's plea for unity among all land-grant heirs. "I really get the impression that this man is building a true grass-roots movement," Swadesh wrote to Knowlton.[79]

Swadesh's positive impression only increased after meeting Reies and Chris Tijerina in person in November 1964. Although she had been forewarned that the Tijerinas' motives might be "less than pure," meaning that they sought personal financial gain, Swadesh dismissed the accusation. She commented approvingly on how much "homework" the two men had done. "I have been through enough land-grant documents myself to appreciate the breadth and depth of their knowledge," she confided to Knowlton in another letter. For too long, Swadesh maintained, "the historical experience" of land-poor New Mexicans had been "treated with ridicule" by scholars who "never troubled to struggle through the land grant microfilms" and hence produced "ignorant drivel."[80] Based on her own expertise and her favorable impressions, she was persuaded to endorse the Alianza cause.

Soon the person on the receiving end of her commentary, Clark Knowlton, joined her. Like Swadesh, Knowlton tended to view the problems of northern New Mexico through a Latin American lens. As a young man, Knowlton had spent several years in South America, first as a missionary with the Church of Latter-day Saints in Argentina and then as a graduate student conducting research in Brazil. According to Knowlton, growing up Mormon had taught him something about being a minority, while his stays in Latin America introduced him to the intertwined problems of poverty and landlessness.[81] He first arrived in New Mexico in 1958 to teach at Highlands University in Las Vegas. He promptly became enamored with Spanish American village life.[82] To his chagrin, however, Knowlton soon discovered that any research that touched upon the topic of land grants was "virtually tabu."[83] As Knowlton later remembered, both state and campus officials strongly encouraged him to direct his research away from Spanish speakers to avoid "rocking the ethnic boat." In contrast, he noted, Native Americans, whose land claims were much more settled, were considered a much less controversial subject.[84]

The prickly Knowlton rocked away despite (or because of) the advice.[85] Military conquest framed the Spanish American experience as much as the Native American one, he insisted.[86] Asserting that northern New

Mexico operated as "a colonial economy in every sense of the word," Knowlton continued, "If these distressed areas had the good fortune to be located in Africa, Asia, or Latin America, they would be the recipients of foreign aid, peace corps groups, and a concerted effort to resolve their problems."[87] Although he accepted a position at Texas Western University (later the University of Texas, El Paso) in 1962, Knowlton kept in touch with land-grant affairs. Furious about Tackett's decision, which he labeled "perhaps legally correct but morally wrong," Knowlton suggested in a letter that Tackett read an article he had recently completed, "The Causes of Land Loss in New Mexico."[88] After reading the same article, Tijerina sought a meeting with the professor. A careful Knowlton recalled first checking with "contacts in the F.B.I. to ascertain whether Tijerina was a communist." Given assurances that "to the best of their knowledge" Tijerina was not, Knowlton agreed to a meeting in February 1965. The two men immediately hit it off.[89]

Both Swadesh and Knowlton soon emerged among the Alianza's most ardent defenders. In the years to come, they spoke at Alianza conventions, offered expert testimony during trials, drafted reports defending the land-grant movement, and helped raise money when legal costs skyrocketed. Concerned about deeply rooted social and economic inequities in New Mexico, both scholars glimpsed within the Alianza a potential force for positive change. Unlike most government officials, elected politicians, and fellow academics, they viewed land-grant grievances as not only legitimate but also worthy of redress. Although she knew the odds were long, Swadesh favored the redistribution of federal lands that had been appropriated from nuevomexicanos in the first place. She credited Tijerina with raising the topic of treaty violations. Knowlton concurred on both points.[90]

At the same time, the pair also worried that the organization might squander the opportunity before it for lack of a strategic plan. As much as she admired Tijerina, Swadesh also asked him early on what plans he had beyond signing petitions and holding meetings. According to Swadesh, Tijerina responded that he wished to build a land-grant movement that covered the Southwest, a response that left Swadesh wary of what she called an "organizational gap" in the Alianza agenda. Tijerina's grand objectives aside, she wondered, how did members intend to "flex their muscle and organize on a day-to-day basis?"[91] Knowlton shared these concerns. "I feel that if your organization has any weakness, it is that you do not have any intermediate goals that your people can work on right now," he counseled Tijerina in early 1966. “An old friend of mine, an agitator in Argentina, once said, ‘*Hay que agitar, organizar y luchar.*’ You are agitating and you are fighting. Now there remains the problem of organizing.”[92] Both scholars had pinpointed a central weakness of the organization: it had no political plan beyond crafting appeals.

Just a few months before, a *Denver Post* article summarized the dilemma before Tijerina: How to continue mobilizing toward the goal of land-grant justice? On the one hand, the Alianza leader professed a willingness to go slow. “We are not in a hurry. Time is on our side. Each year we grow stronger,” an optimistic Tijerina explained. Yet in the next breath, he admitted, “The people are anxious for us to act.”[93] To address these concerns, Tijerina mentioned the possibility of pursuing litigation. Given the Alianza leader’s repeated denunciation of the courts, this announcement captured a general dearth of ideas as Tijerina pondered the future.

Unwanted in Mexico, Tijerina likewise had difficulty gaining traction in the United States. As much as he tried to present his cause as respectable and moderate, adopting the guise of a good American pursuing his constitutional rights, Tijerina failed to gain a positive reception from any establishment sector. Stuck at a crossroads, Tijerina needed a fresh start, a strategy beyond petition, and an identity beyond Mexican or American. In 1966, he reinvented himself once more.

7

The Indo-Hispano

In early October 1966, the Alianza served "final notice" that "the Descendents, Towns-People, and Owners of the Spanish Land Grants in New Mexico are [taking] over one of the land grants Saturday, October 15th." According to an official "News Bulletin," a motorcade from Albuquerque planned to head north to occupy "the Pueblo San Joaquín del Río de Chama, a town established August 1st, 1806, by Don Carlos IVth, King of the Eastern and Western Indies and Islands and Mainlands of the Ocean-Sea Continent and of the Spains." The announcement referred to the Cañon del Río de Chama land grant, which over time had mostly become U.S. Forest Service property. Members had no choice but to challenge directly this property claim, the bulletin explained, "in view of the fact that the U.S. government has ignored all pleas and petitions relative to the land grants." Underscoring the prior authority of Spanish-era mandates, the announcement concluded with the audacious expectation of law enforcement cooperation. "The Alianza does not expect any difficulty," it read, "but if there is any, the Pueblo-council [the ruling council of the San Joaquín grant] will request the assistance from the State Police and the State Militia."[1]

Swaddled in the presumed glories of the Spanish empire, the planned occupation laid bare the key goal of the organization that Tijerina had founded: to secure for its members what Spanish-speaking settlers had gained through conquest. Inevitably, it also laid bare one of the logistical weaknesses of the organization. As much as Tijerina lamented that Americans had taken the property of nuevomexicanos *after* 1848, he rarely acknowledged that Spanish speakers had encroached upon indigenous holdings long before that date. Recall that Tijerina's land-grant gospel celebrated the Spanish inheritance as both royal and divine. During a research trip to Spain in the spring of 1966, Tijerina reiterated this sense of cultural affiliation. "Our culture is Spanish. We want to speak Spanish. But the Anglos oppress [us] so that this cultural legacy is lost," he explained to a Seville reporter curious about the land-grant cause. According to Tijerina, he looked forward to the day when a people whom he called "Hispanos" would control their own language, their own education, and their own land.[2]

Aware of the Alianza's repeated identification with the Spanish colonial past, scholars understandably have accused the organization of conducting a careless love affair with Spain while maintaining little regard for the "indigenous historical presence" in New Mexico.[3] Yet when it comes to Tijerina, such criticism is only half right. On the one hand, the Alianza leader did promote a rosy view of Spanish-speaking rule. On the other, Tijerina's vision was also racially inclusionary. More so than many of his political contemporaries across the Southwest, Tijerina favored forging coalitions with Native Americans and with African Americans too, a stance that directly challenged an older activist tradition among Mexican Americans. Across the Southwest, Mexican Americans for decades between 1848 and at least World War II had asserted their own racial whiteness in an effort to defy discrimination. In New Mexico, a regional variation of this strategy gave rise by the 1890s to such ethnic identifiers as "Spanish American" and "Hispano." After the American takeover, Spanish speakers who had the most to lose in terms of wealth and political clout invented these terms in order to claim a wholly European—and white—lineage.

In contrast, even before the Alianza was officially founded, Tijerina chose to emphasize what many New Mexican leaders preferred to ignore: centuries of racial mixing between indigenous groups and Spanish-speaking settlers. Toward that end, he invented a new ethnic label by adding the prefix "Indo" to the word "Hispano." In one fell swoop, Tijerina extended the Alianza's claims back in time before the earliest Spanish-speaking settlements. Becoming "Indo-Hispano" also allowed Tijerina to praise the Spanish empire even as he condemned the American one. The first empire had united two populations through the bonds of family and culture, he insisted, while the second had united them only in suffering. Here in embryonic form was Tijerina's response to the charge that Alianza members only sought land that Spanish conquistadores had stolen from the Native Americans in the first place.

The strategy was easy to miss when looking at the public face of the Alianza. Yet just as Tijerina could be both a loyal American and a proud Mexican, when it came to the Spanish empire, he increasingly identified with both the conqueror and the conquered. Against the backdrop of decades and even centuries of navigating racial hierarchies imposed by two sets of conquerors, Tijerina's politics were not only unprecedented but also profoundly liberating for people of Mexican descent of all hues. The term "Indo-Hispano" underscored Tijerina's fervent belief that, tradition be damned, Spanish-speaking New Mexicans shared more in common with nonwhite groups than with white ones. He advanced this insight, and this new identity, to move the land-grant cause from petition to protest.

ESCAPING THE TRAP OF WHITENESS

In March 1953, the residents of Socorro, a small town about an hour's drive south of Albuquerque, declared their independence from the rest of the United States. Certainly, the history of settlement in the area predated any English-speaking town on the continent. In 1598, residents of an indigenous village offered the hungry and thirsty troops of Juan de Oñate provisions, an act of generosity that prompted Oñate to name the town "succor" or "aid." A mission and a garrison soon followed, although both were abandoned in the wake of the Pueblo Revolt of 1680. In 1815, however, a new group of Spanish-speaking colonists resettled the area. In 1875, they launched the necessary legal proceedings to get their land claims recognized by the new American government. It refused to do so. In 1899, citing incomplete and fraudulent documents, the United States limited the Socorro land grant to a small parcel associated with the local church.[4]

Now, in an effort to drum up tourism, town residents rejected U.S. conquest as a done deed. According to town boosters, a hunt through the archives failed to uncover any proof that Socorro had ever been properly incorporated into the United States. Soon a white placard appeared along the main drag through town. It told drivers to pay a twenty-five-cent toll to enter the Free State of Socorro. A dollar more secured Socorro citizenship along with a passport good for a free beer at the local tavern. Edwin Stanton, then the editor of the *Socorro Chieftain*, the sister publication of the paper that he would later operate in Albuquerque, splashed news of these developments on the newspaper's front page. The claim of independence earned the desert town a great deal of publicity, including a tongue-in-cheek spread in *Life* magazine.[5]

Only three people appeared to take the episode seriously. One was a controversial activist for Native American autonomy. The second was a man who claimed to be of Spanish royal blood. The third was Reies López Tijerina. Indeed, in his memoir, Tijerina portrayed editor Stanton as a brave defender of land-grant rights who had been run out of town in fear for his life because of his activism.[6] Evidently Stanton at some point connected Tijerina to the other two men who had voiced support for Socorro independence. Tijerina wrote to both in early 1964. His nearly concurrent appeals to a man who claimed to be a Native American leader and to another who claimed to be a Spanish king challenge earlier interpretations of the Alianza crusade overall that have portrayed it as paying attention to only one side of the family tree.

In fact, Tijerina first wrote to Frank Tom-Pee-Saw, head of a Kansas-based organization known as the League of Nations, Pan-American Indians (or sometimes as the League of North American Indians). The U.S. Bureau of Indian Affairs considered Tom-Pee-Saw a con artist and a fraud because he appeared to be more African American than Indian and because he often requested financial compensation whenever criticizing federal policies that limited tribal autonomy.[7] Yet as historian Steven Crum noted, to be African American did not negate indigenous ancestry. More important, the Bureau of Indian Affairs usually held a low opinion of any activist who championed native rights against federal oversight. During the 1940s and 1950s, Tom-Pee-Saw did just that, even lobbying for Native American representation at the United Nations.[8] Perhaps aware that Socorro's population was still heavily Native American—nearly half of the town's population of 9,000 was "Red Indian," according to news accounts—Tom-Pee-Saw took an interest in the "Free Socorro" episode.[9] In April 1953, he wrote to Stanton to pledge the support of all Native Americans in what he called "this great bid for justice and freedom."[10] Eleven years later, Tijerina reached out to Tom-Pee-Saw. "We too are a people which have been deprived of our constitutional rights," the Alianza leader explained in March 1964. "We are trying to find simpaty and support with other people who are in the same cituation. Please, if you think that we should help each other, ansur our letter. We need good and real friends. Ansur us."[11] Tom-Pee-Saw soon did, inviting the Alianza to join the league as another "Indian group" interested in obtaining lost land.[12]

In May 1964, Tijerina dashed off a letter to Gerald Waynes Barnes (aka Jerry Noll), a Seattle native residing at the Atascadero State Hospital, a facility for mentally ill criminals and those found not guilty by reason of insanity.[13] Noll was there following a conviction for third-degree assault. It was his third stay. Unbeknownst to Tijerina, the Seattle native had started to accrue a criminal record at the age of sixteen: his crimes ranged from bank robbery (with a toy pistol) to assault (with a fork) to check forgery.[14] He had also manifested kingly aspirations early on. In 1954, defendant Barnes claimed to be immune from prosecution because he ruled over the Kingdom of Thulia, an imaginary domain that he described as extending from Kansas all the way to the Oregon coast.[15]

In the years following the "Free Socorro" episode, Noll contacted Edwin Stanton about these royal connections. He first wrote Stanton in 1957, calling himself "His Highness, the Crown Prince and Heir to the Throne of California" and claiming to represent an emperor named Barnesus Quarto Caesar, whose realm included Socorro and, in fact, all of New Mexico.[16] Three years later, Jerry Noll mailed another letter to Stanton asserting that Socorro was part of the Kingdom of the Indies.[17] Finally, in December 1960, Jerry Noll dropped by the offices of the Socorro newspaper in person. This time he claimed to be a lawyer representing Barnesus *Quinto* Caesar and his equally royal sister, Doña Helene Anita de las Indias. He offered that the royal pair stood ready to grant the Socorro independence effort "validity" through their very presence. In addition, Noll complained that President Eisenhower had violated the royal pair's airspace over Brazil during a recent trip to Latin America, thereby risking imperial submarine reprisals from Patagonia. As editor, Stanton evidently did not know what to make of Noll's statements except to consider them highly entertaining front-page news. "The following story is so fantastic that it's almost unbelievable," the newspaperman wrote, but he urged readers to maintain "an open mind," given that Noll seemed to be "a serious young man, [who] did not appear to be having any hallucinations."[18]

Tijerina kept an open mind, entertaining the possibility that Noll and this Barnesus Quinto Emperor were one and the same. The May 1964 letter that the Alianza leader wrote to Noll commenced a lively correspondence between the two men, spurred on by what Tijerina considered Noll's expert historical knowledge and possible royal lineage. "Dear sir, we would like to know if we can communicate with you," Tijerina's first inquiry began. Convinced that Noll had important information to share, Tijerina also asked Noll whether he had any relatives, presumably also royal, whom the Alianza might contact.[19] Not put off by Noll's place of residence, the Alianza leader diligently marked subsequent correspondence from Noll with the words "*El Rey* [the King]."[20] In public, moreover, Tijerina refused to reject Noll's royal claims entirely. "How would I know?" he once responded when pressed whether Noll was really a king. "No, probably not, of course not. I don't know. I liked him," he waffled. What mattered most to Tijerina: Noll "knew a lot about the land grants, even things that I didn't know."[21]

Most scholars have not mentioned the problematic Noll, possibly not knowing what to do about his outlandish claims any more than Stanton did years ago.[22] They have, however, tackled an aspect of the Alianza that Noll, who joined the organization in 1966, claimed to embody—the Spanish colonial past. Scholars have faulted New Mexican land-grant activists in general, and *aliancistas* in particular, for failing to acknowledge, first, the injustices borne by Native Americans during Spanish-speaking rule, and second, the amount of racial mixing that occurred. Referring to the common refrain within memory studies that every act of remembering is also an act of forgetting, Jake Kosek suggested that New Mexican Hispanos in their quest for land had contributed to "uncomfortable silences" about the Spanish treatment of Native Americans and advanced false claims of European "blood purity."[23] Similarly, Lee Bebout argued that Alianza members in New Mexico invariably "privileged Spanish ancestry" to buttress their land claims.[24]

The Alianza leader adopted a subtler approach than such conclusions suggest. When it came to the matter of race, Tijerina never forgot one of his earliest archival discoveries: the Laws of the Indies (specifically law 2, title 1, book 6) decreed "that the Indians be allowed to freely marry, and that no royal order impede them." In authorizing intermarriage between Spanish men and Indian women, and Spanish women and Indian men, the Spanish Crown further ordered that such unions be "protected and accomplished."[25] To Tijerina, this particular law engendered a larger truth: Spanish colonization, however flawed, had given birth to a "new breed."[26] In the spirit of celebration, Tijerina even claimed that the date of the law's enactment, October 19, 1514, marked the birthday of this new people.

Accordingly, in 1962, the Alianza leader traced the origins of all land-grant heirs to "the Spanish conquistadors and colonizers who had mixed [*habían cruzado*] with the aboriginal Americans in these northern territories."[27] Even more telling, he seemed to have retired the word "conquistador" after this usage while keeping the biological connection.[28] Perhaps inspired by the Mexican conquest story of Hernán Cortés and his translator Malintzín, for example, Tijerina in 1965 described nuevomexicanos as a "new people born of a Spaniard and an Indian woman."[29] What to call this "new breed"? Tijerina initially used the term "Hispano-Mexicano-Indio" in Spanish and then "Spanish-Mexican-Indian" in English before finally settling upon "Indo-Hispano" by 1966.[30] In the context of a movement whose aim was to regain lands first secured through conquest, the name change proved strategically useful.

Over the years, Tijerina deployed the history of racial intermixing to deflect criticism and fortify land-grant claims. "Sure, Spain made her mistakes and crimes and whatever you want to call them. But it was not the new breed," he stated in 1967. "Why should we have to pay for the crimes of Spain?"[31] In 1968, the Alianza president offered that Indo-Hispanos "are native children [*hijos*] of the American continent, we are native blood," continuing, "[we] did not come from Europe. . . . We are not foreigners. This is our land."[32] Exhibiting a strong preference for one "parent" over another, Tijerina elaborated: "The Indian was our true mother. Our father, the Spaniard, left us. We decided to stay with our mother, the Indian here in New Mexico."[33] Of course, just a few years before, Tijerina had pronounced Mexico "the mother" of all land-grant claimants in order to blast U.S. colonialism. Recast, the maternal metaphor now served to exempt nuevomexicanos from any responsibility for the negative repercussion of Spanish colonialism.

Instead, Tijerina accentuated the positive by considering the consequences of racial mixing for New Mexico's Spanish-speaking population only. The Alianza leader never mentioned the enslavement of Native Americans or instances of rape. To be fair, the early chroniclers of colonial New Mexico upon whose histories he relied rarely mentioned these crimes either.[34] Dwelling on the more unsavory aspects of Spanish colonial rule like slavery, moreover, hardly served Tijerina's interests.

Presenting the Spanish colonial past as mostly an era of good feelings did. As Tijerina once noted in an "open letter" to the press, colonists initially "faced some hostile tribes," but afterward, "our forefathers learned to live among the Indians for two-hundred and fifty years."[35] In 1964,

Tijerina shared a similar version of the past with a news reporter visiting from Spain. Perhaps inclined toward a favorable assessment of Spanish colonialism in any event, this reporter, after speaking to Tijerina, likewise stressed benevolent assimilation and cultural fusion. "The friendship with the Indians, which at the beginning was very difficult, eventually transformed into a true friendship, even to the point that among the Pueblo Indians that still exist in the state of New Mexico, all but two of the village governors, or chiefs, have a Spanish surname and speak Spanish," Manuel Roglán wrote.[36] The beginning "difficulty," of course, was a near century of brutal treatment that culminated in the Pueblo Revolt of 1680, which violently banished the colonizers from New Mexico for a dozen years.

Nevertheless, Tijerina was right about the extent of racial mixing in New Mexico historically. The "Spanish" conquest always included indigenous people, like the many Tlaxcalans from central Mexico who helped populate early Santa Fe.[37] Most settlers in northern New Mexico originated as mixed-race refugees from earlier frontiers.[38] Yet if Tijerina in acknowledging racial mixing only stated the obvious, he also stated what many Spanish speakers in the region preferred to leave unspoken. Indeed, the more racial mixing that occurred, the more effort some settlers expended to distinguish themselves from the defeated Pueblo Indians and from surrounding indigenous nations on linguistic, religious, and racial grounds. The tendency prevailed even in Rio Arriba, where the majority of settlers traced their arrival to the mid-1700s and the establishment of Abiquiú. Recall that the town was founded by and for *genízaros*, detribalized Native Americans who had been cleaved from their native society through slavery. Whether of Navajo, Apache, or Plains Indian descent, these settlers had entered Spanish-speaking society mostly as ransomed captives. As former slaves, settling on the far frontier offered them a fresh start and a way to escape their lowly and generally despised origins.

Furthermore, Tijerina challenged the politics of whiteness as it operated across *successive* conquests. After 1848, the shift in sovereignty introduced a new racial hierarchy overwhelmingly constructed in black and white, a reflection of the existence of chattel slavery in the United States at the time. Under no circumstances did Spanish-speaking New Mexicans, some of whom owned indigenous slaves, wish to be put in the same "non-white" category as African Americans. The Treaty of Guadalupe Hidalgo, by granting U.S. citizenship at "the appropriate time" to the former citizens of Mexico, offered a small helping hand in this regard. As only white

Americans enjoyed full citizenship rights in 1848, the treaty indirectly recognized the former citizens of Mexico as falling within the most privileged racial category.[39] Spanish-American elites, with the most to lose in terms of wealth, prestige, and political clout, strove to secure that privilege.[40]

They faced serious obstacles. In 1876, the same year that Colorado was admitted to the Union as a state with a population of about 40,000, a *Harper's Weekly* article explained that New Mexico was not fit for statehood despite its far larger population precisely because it lacked white Anglo-Saxon Protestants: "Of the present population of about 110,000 . . . nine-tenths are Mexicans, Indians, 'greasers,' and other non-English-speaking people . . . under the influence of the Roman Church," the article noted.[41] For New Mexicans "the appropriate time" to enjoy full citizenship rights would be a long time coming. Nevertheless, the campaign for statehood helped establish a fragile racial equilibrium in New Mexico. Statehood advocates, Anglo-American and Spanish-surnamed alike, decided that highlighting a glorious conquistador heritage was the best way to convince skeptical congressmen in Washington, D.C., of the superior racial credentials of New Mexico's overwhelmingly suspect population. The statehood campaign also helped popularize the ethnic identifiers "Spanish American" and "Hispano."[42] By alluding to a European origin, both terms signified whiteness.

The result was a "trap of memory and race" according to Charles Montgomery.[43] In New Mexico, all Spanish speakers, no matter the actual color of their skin, technically enjoyed equality as whites. Yet white skin privilege could be narrow indeed when measured against continued land loss and subsequent economic marginalization. Worse, the consistent refusal to acknowledge racial difference made acknowledging racial injustice almost impossible. Now to bring attention to the pervasive inequalities in the state was to risk being dismissed as racially divisive. For that reason, the *Albuquerque Journal* in 1967 blasted the land-grant movement as a "fraudulent effort to read Spanish-Americans out of the white race" and thus as a "reprehensible attempt to divide and exploit."[44] Placing zero value upon whiteness as a goal, Tijerina escaped the trap.

His racial politics set him free to recognize shared interests with Native Americans and African Americans alike. In both cases, Tijerina bucked tradition. As late as 1968, an anthropologist noted that Spanish-speaking residents in Taos, in an attempt to distinguish themselves from their Pueblo Indian neighbors, "point out vehemently that they are the pure and direct descendants of the Spanish Conquistadores."[45] Maintaining that fiction to combat discrimination also strained relations with African Americans. To cite one example: in 1933, a university survey about prejudice sparked enormous outrage statewide among the target population, Spanish Americans, because the survey's questions paralleled those that had been directed at African Americans in previous studies.[46] "The Hispano of New Mexico is a strange creature," admitted a Santa Fe–based newspaper columnist in 1966. "He does not want to admit publicly that he suffers discrimination because then he would have to admit that he is different. But he does not want to be different. He wants to be distinct—culturally distinct as a Hispano but equal."[47]

Unburdened by these constraints, Tijerina began his search for allies even before the founding of the Alianza. In his memoir, Tijerina told of meeting with Pueblo Indian governors in 1960 and with "*mis amigos los apaches*" in Dulce, New Mexico, up in the northwest corner of the state even earlier, in 1957 and 1958.[48] As soon as the Alianza was founded, he also launched a letter-writing campaign. Beyond writing to Tom-Pee-Saw, in August 1963 Tijerina dashed off a letter to Dennis Lovato of the Santa Clara Pueblo. However, he received no response at the time.[49] Nor did he hear back from Bob Burnette, leader of the National Congress of American Indians, a pan-Indian organization founded twenty years before and headquartered in Washington, D.C. In contrast to the controversial Tom-Pee-Saw, Burnette touted impeccable Native American bona fides. He was Lakota Sioux and a member of the Rosebud Reservation. He also apparently had no interest in working with Tijerina.[50]

At some point, Tijerina did cultivate a relationship with members of the Washington-based organization called Hopi House. Hopi House, however, was the creation of several Euro-Americans who had interjected themselves in a long-standing tribal dispute.[51] Otherwise, other than the controversial Tom-Pee-Saw of Kansas, the only Native American who appeared to comment favorably upon the Alianza enterprise early on was an anonymous Pueblo Indian who appeared in the 1964 Roglán report. Identified by neither name nor village, this man expressed solidarity with Alianza members in opposition to Navajos and Mescalero Apaches, who enjoyed sizable reservations. Speaking of the post-1848 era, he insisted, "We, the Indians of the Río Grande, the Pueblo Indians, along with the Spaniards and the Mexicans, we are the ones who suffered the loss of land."[52] Given his singular presence (no other news account mentioned

Pueblo participants), he was no doubt an outlier in his opinion. The native people of New Mexico understandably lacked Tijerina's rose-colored glasses when looking backward at Spanish colonization.

Another obstacle hindered cooperation. While Spanish-speaking settlers had benefited during the Spanish and Mexican eras, some Alianza members suspected that Native Americans had gotten a better deal from the Americans *since* 1848.[53] As recognized dependent domestic nations, Native American groups exerted limited sovereignty on their reservations. Admittedly born of war and misery, a special relationship therefore did exist between native groups and the federal government. In 1946, for example, native groups compelled the formation of the federal Indian Claims Commission to hear unresolved land disputes.[54] The special relationship, moreover, continued to pay dividends to Native Americans into the 1960s. While Alianza members suffered the arbitrary decisions of the U.S. Forest Service, Southern Utes successfully ran their own lumber mill on their own land, while the Jicarilla Apaches, with the help of the Bureau of Land Reclamation, were reseeding acreage for pasture.[55] As Clark Knowlton, one of Tijerina's most steadfast supporters, regretfully noted, Spanish-speaking New Mexicans never "received even the minimal protection given to New Mexico's Indian groups by the federal government."[56] Nevertheless, Tijerina considered Native Americans the Alianza's closest potential allies because both nuevomexicanos and indigenous groups defined self-determination primarily in terms of retaining and regaining land.

The Alianza president also drew significant inspiration from the African American freedom struggle. To him, the passage of the 1964 Civil Rights Act ending segregation offered proof that "justice may be late, but it always arrives." Counseling patience, he assured his followers that their time would come, just as it had for the "pueblo Negro." "For more than one hundred years," he noted, African Americans "had been denied their civil rights but times had changed."[57] In 1965, Tijerina even commented approvingly on the Watts Riots, a massive uprising by African Americans in Los Angeles that cost thirty-four people their lives. Watts, he said, offered a mere "preview" of what northern Mexico might look like if land-grant claimants did not receive a fair hearing. Tijerina's words were so chilling to some New Mexicans that he soon backpedaled, declaring, "I don't want to copy the Negroes."[58]

He certainly wanted African American allies, however, and had for years. In his memoir, Tijerina recounted being intrigued by the Nation of Islam after reading a 1959 *U.S. News and World Report* item about the group. "'Black Cult' Supremacy in the U.S.—How Much a Threat?" the headline queried. The article answered that the menace was real. "Smoldering racial troubles in U.S. cities are being fanned by a cult that has a set a deadline for the extermination of the white race," it read. Tijerina was far more impressed than afraid. Whereas he was still reeling from the collapse of Valle de Paz, from all indications the Nation of Islam had achieved Tijerina's ideal community. Black Muslims owned land, had established separate schools, required women to dress modestly (the article included a picture of veiled women in long white robes), and demanded that members refrain from alcohol and profanity.[59] In another striking similarity from Tijerina's past, Elijah Muhammad claimed to be a prophet of God who preached that the present-day world was coming to an end.[60] Moved to request a visit, Tijerina reported that Muhammad warmly received him and that the two men shared long conversations about how to strengthen black-brown unity.[61]

While in Chicago, Tijerina also made the acquaintance of Alton Davis, a public relations executive who organized a national celebration to mark the 100th anniversary of the Emancipation Proclamation during the summer of 1963. Like Tijerina, Davis, a devout Christian Scientist, was a man of faith. As Davis explained to *Jet* magazine at the time about the celebration, "It was not my idea. It was God's idea. I was just a channel through which he spoke." The two also shared a desire to expose a forgotten history.[62] In September 1963, Davis attended the first Alianza convention in Albuquerque.

At least one Alianza member later wondered what Spanish-speaking New Mexicans had in common with African Americans.[63] The suspicion was telling. Both the priority that Tijerina placed on gaining African American allies and his willingness to reach beyond the civil rights sphere to embrace controversial groups like the Nation of Islam made him a political outlier among most of his fellow ethnics, not only in New Mexico but across the Southwest. For much of the twentieth century, division more than cooperation characterized political relations between African Americans and Mexican Americans. Most mainstream Mexican American civil rights groups initially battled anti-Mexican segregation by insisting upon a white racial identity.[64] Although the post–World War II period witnessed halting efforts by black and brown civil rights activists to work together, Mexican American prejudice toward African Americans, African American ignorance of Mexican Americans, and ongoing competition between the two groups for government attention and resources all hindered efforts at coalition building.[65] The anonymous creators of a poster that showed up on the University of New Mexico campus during the spring of 1966 expressed the divide, melding race and politics in ways that directly refuted Tijerina's inclusive approach. "We true Spanish are white, and we are Catholics. We fight communists," it read. "We don't care for foreigners, Negro or White, to come and lie about our race. The only race problem is the one brought in by dirty communists who try to pass as Spanish to get our land grants."[66] It would have been impossible for locals to miss the Alianza as the poster's target.

Ironically, Tijerina traveled to Spain for the first time that April to investigate more thoroughly what advantages the colonial connection might hold for Alianza members. While there, Tijerina was delighted to learn about the medieval-era *Siete Partidas*, a thirteenth-century compilation of laws that covered a range of topics, including the communal use and ownership of village or pueblo land.[67] Although he might have learned about these laws by visiting the University of New Mexico library in Albuquerque, Tijerina gladly paid to obtain a multivolume set of the *Siete Partidas* and of the Laws of the Indies at a Madrid bookstore.[68] He also submitted his receipts to the Alianza. Increasingly doubtful about their leader's ability to deliver on his promises, Alianza members had begun to keep their leader on a tight financial leash.[69] Arguably even more important than taking the opportunity to conduct research, Tijerina had traveled to Spain in an effort to revitalize a stalled movement. For that reason, the Seville newspaper interview marked another highlight of the visit. It appeared on the pages of *ABC*, a leading publication. After learning all about the land-grant struggle, the reporter, clearly impressed, anointed Tijerina a Martin Luther King Jr. for all Hispanics.[70]

Perhaps inspired by the comparison, Tijerina upon his return decided it was time to take a page directly from the civil rights playbook and conduct a demonstration.

CIVIL RIGHTS, NEW MEXICAN STYLE

Over the Fourth of July weekend 1966, Tijerina and roughly 100 Alianza members commenced a march from Albuquerque to Santa Fe. To beat the summer sun, some carried parasols. Others held handmade signs that read, "We want Justice, not Powdered Milk," "Land of the Free or

Land of Pirates?," and "Public Schools Suppress Truth."[71] The march directly echoed not only civil rights marches across the country but also the march of striking farmworkers in California just a few months before. That march started in Delano, the hometown of Cesar Chavez, with fewer than a hundred people. At stops along the way, however, hundreds and even thousands gathered to show their support and offer accommodations and food. After marching twenty-five days and 340 miles, protesters arrived in the state capital of Sacramento on Easter morning. A triumph of logistics and spectacle, the march directed the nation's attention toward the ongoing grape boycott and made Cesar Chavez one of the most well known Mexican Americans in the country.[72]

Compared to the farmworkers' Easter pilgrimage, the "Spanish American March for Redress of Grievances" was a much more modest affair. Indicative of how regionalized the Mexican American population was, Tijerina and other Alianza members certainly knew of the farmworkers' march, but the two groups in 1966 pursued separate struggles. Not by coincidence did each of the "Four Horsemen of the Chicano Movement" represent a different geographic region: the movement itself represented a deliberate attempt to forge ethnic group unity across many states. And whereas the farmworkers' union benefited from the experience of veteran labor organizers and civil rights activists, the Alianza still operated as a one-man show with a number of loyal followers. Consequently, instead of the numbers of supporters swelling with each stop, the number of participants in the Alianza's first public demonstration dwindled to about thirty-five by noon the first day. That core group continued for three days and seventy miles before finally reaching Santa Fe.[73]

Along the way, Tijerina repeatedly characterized the Alianza's goals as quite limited. Referring to the Treaty of Guadalupe Hidalgo, Tijerina explained, "The Negro asks that they [congressmen] pass new laws. . . . We do not ask [for] new laws. We only ask that they respect the laws that exist." Plus, Tijerina wanted to clarify that he was no political radical. "I'm not socialist, communist, nor red nor pink," the Alianza president stated to reporters on the first day of the march. "I'm just a slave to justice."[74] The Alianza was simply keeping up with the times, he continued. "In our day politicians won't listen unless we come up with some spectacular march or demonstration," Tijerina explained. "We feel we are on the right track now."[75]

Despite those reassurances, the Alianza's first protest march provoked a fierce backlash out of proportion with its modest aims. Along the way,

Alianza members sometimes heard jeers from passing motorists. More seriously, when the demonstrators camped overnight, five bullets flew from the window of a passing car. Fortunately, no one was hurt.[76] The march also drew criticism from fellow nuevomexicanos who objected to Tijerina's rebellious racial politics and from the leading archivist in the state, who targeted Tijerina's historical analysis.

The decision to march that July marked less a dramatic shift toward confrontation, however, than a last-ditch effort to secure White House intervention via petition. Upon arriving in Santa Fe, the grand plan of the marchers was to press New Mexico governor Jack Campbell to ask President Johnson, a fellow Democrat, to intervene in land-grant matters.

Campbell, however, was not interested. Inaugurated just a month before the Alianza's official founding in February 1963, the governor viewed land-grant activism with suspicion. "Follow up on this, it could get serious," Campbell instructed a staffer in his office regarding the flare-up of tensions around Tierra Amarilla in 1964.[77] The following year, the office of the state attorney general in a confidential memo labeled the Alianza "political dynamite" and a "potential danger to the maintenance of order." These conclusions centered on a familiar refrain despite Tijerina's protestations. The organization was "controlled by a person who has been accused [of being] and possibly may be a communist."[78] Echoing that sentiment, a second report urged collecting "sufficient evidence" to support a predetermined conclusion: Tijerina was a "truly dangerous leader capable of moving good people in bad directions."[79] That July the governor's calendar gave him a convenient excuse to avoid *aliancistas*. Exhausted marchers arriving in Santa Fe discovered that Governor Campbell was away at a conference. Defiantly, they camped out to await his return.

Succumbing to the inevitable, Campbell met with Alianza members upon his return a few days later, but his remarks offered little reason for optimism. Campbell patronizingly congratulated those gathered in his office for maintaining cleanliness and order in exercising their First Amendment rights. Although he agreed to forward the Alianza petition to the president, he refused to endorse it. "The only place you can get relief is from Congress," Campbell insisted. "The President can't give you your land back and neither can I." Tijerina immediately shot back that the U.S. president was obliged to uphold the laws of the land, including international treaties.[80] Otherwise, the Alianza leader adopted a strikingly grateful tone. He all but apologized for borrowing the protest tactics of what he obliquely referred to as "other organizations." Alianza members had decided to march only as a "last resort," he admitted. Nearly giddy for the opportunity to meet with Campbell, Tijerina predicted the governor's action would spark "a chain reaction" toward justice.[81] Afterward, a *Denver Post* editorial asserted that Alianza marchers "had a good moral case" and congratulated them for "reopening a fascinating and little-known chapter of Western history."[82]

The woman most familiar with the Spanish and Mexican archives of New Mexico, Dr. Myra Ellen Jenkins, sharply disagreed. With the governor out of town and Alianza members approaching Santa Fe, Campbell's press secretary had asked Jenkins for her assessment of the organization and its claims. Known for her direct, no-nonsense style, Jenkins offered an entirely negative response that reflected her distrust of land-grant activism as much as her familiarity with archival materials. Since 1960, Jenkins had been charged with organizing the chaos of centuries of Spanish-language colonial documents, some on the verge of disintegration.[83] She began by allowing that she had been "mystified" and "perturbed" by the Alianza for several years. Jenkins pointed out that many Spanish land-grant deeds "were falsified or outright forgeries." As she explained in her memo to the governor, "I fear that there are outside influences which are opening this old issue for pecuniary gain. To be blunt, I think that it is a 'con game.'"[84]

Jenkins's condemnation appeared in the press the same day that news of the governor's meeting with Alianza members did. Privately, Jenkins confessed that she would have chosen her words more carefully if she had known that her memo would be made public. Still, she reaffirmed her central message in a longer statement issued a few days later.[85] The time to pursue Spanish and Mexican land-grant claims was over, she maintained. Surveying much of the same history as Tijerina, Jenkins acknowledged that in the nineteenth century, attorneys associated with the Santa Fe Ring, a notorious collusion of legal, business, and political power in New Mexico at the time, had defrauded descendants of land grantees. But individual misdeeds were "scarcely the fault of the United States" and, in any case, did not rise in her estimation to the level of treaty violations.[86] As Jenkins told Thomas B. Catron III, whose grandfather had been one of the leading members of the Santa Fe Ring, "There is nothing . . . in the Treaty of Guadalupe-Hidalgo concerning the guarantee of Spanish Land grants as such."[87] She also defended the adjudication processes that the United States had set up to determine the validity of Spanish- and

Mexican-era land claims. The establishment of the Office of the Surveyor General in 1854 and the Court of Private Land Claims in 1891, she argued, had generously provided a conquered population with not one "but two days in court."[88] Therefore, the question of the land grants already had been addressed more than once through legal means. Whether it had been addressed fairly was apparently beside the point.

Jenkins's stubborn opposition to Alianza land claims stemmed in part from her strong advocacy of Native American ones. From her own research, she knew that despite congressional recognition of Pueblo Indian property rights in 1858, land-grabbers, American and Mexican alike, had trampled native land claims. Regarded as an expert witness, she had testified several times in defense of Pueblo interests before the Indian Claims Commission, that federal agency charged with addressing unresolved land disputes. Consequently, whereas Alianza members admired the amount of federal attention directed at indigenous claims and sought to obtain a similar level of attention, Jenkins emphasized federal neglect—and Spanish-speaking abuse—of native groups. And whereas Tijerina stressed a common experience of conquest between indigenous groups and nuevomexicanos, only native land dispossession concerned Jenkins, and only indigenous claims struck her as worthy of investigation.[89]

Jenkins's harsh assessment stung. As Tijerina and his brothers were from out of state, they certainly fit the outsider description. Her memo lent credence to rumors of financial impropriety that had long swirled around the Alianza leader. Tijerina promptly responded that he was not making a penny from his Alianza leadership and even threatened Jenkins with a $2 million slander suit.[90] Nevertheless, at least three letters soon arrived at the Alianza office that offered some version of "If what Jenkins said was true, then I do not want to be part of this organization."[91] In the wake of Jenkins's allegations, the media routinely portrayed Tijerina "as a mixture of a confidence man, clown, and demagogue," according to one sympathetic observer.[92] Jenkins's comments even prompted an Albuquerque radio editorialist to state conclusively that the Alianza served no other purpose than supporting Reies Tijerina and his family. The proof? "KQEO has been informed that the entire field of the Spanish and Mexican land grants has already been explored and litigated," the commentator declared.[93]

Letters to the editors ridiculed the Alianza as well. These letters facetiously seconded Jenkins's central point: whatever injustice had occurred had happened so long ago that redress was not only impracticable but also inconceivable. In an echo of Tijerina's land-grant gospel, for instance, one writer jokingly traced the chain-of-title to Louisiana backward from the United States to France, then Spain, the Pope, and Jesus Christ, before stopping at God, "who made Louisiana."[94] In a similar vein, a letter to the *Santa Fe New Mexican* issued a rallying cry to "all descendants of Captain Elias Potter, formerly of Trenton, New Jersey," who had been granted land by the British government. "Let us rise, cousins, and demand that the land be returned to us," wrote Barbara Powell, who identified herself as Potter's "great-great-great-great-granddaughter." Poking fun at the Alianza's stance, she continued, "Now I am sure that even though the sale may have been legal, he was cheated, bilked and duped."[95]

Other New Mexicans mocked the Alianza for seeking land that, as far as they could tell, Spanish speakers has stolen in the first place. Did not American Indians hold a "prior claim"? "As part Cherokee Indian, I'd like to protest for our original land grant from God—I've forgotten the exact year—but it was before 1848," stated one letter to the editor that appeared in the *Albuquerque Journal* just after the July march.[96] A few months later, the *Albuquerque Journal* quoted from a telegram that purportedly had arrived at Alianza headquarters. "Spanish king not have legal right give away land we occupy since big ice year 12,382 B.C.," it read. The accompanying signature, "Yashpiyata Chief, Quaua Tribe," poked more fun. A fabricated name of a nonexistent native group, the name, according to an "informed source," meant "young man who shoots at moon."[97]

By far the most scathing critique that Tijerina received in the wake of the July march, however, came from a Spanish-speaking New Mexican who fully agreed with Tijerina's historical analysis but who chided him for daring to emulate the African American civil rights movement. The comments appeared in a Spanish-language column titled "Poco a Poco en la Tierra del Encanto [Bit by Bit in the Land of Enchantment]," which was a regular feature of the *New Mexican*. The unnamed author acknowledged that "the old grants that Spain had given us passed out of the hands of the legitimate heirs and became the property of ambitious, cunning, and crooked men." Still, this writer urged Alianza members to leave the past behind. Trying to obtain redress at this late date was futile and politically potentially catastrophic in that Alianza members had made "disastrous errors" by acting like "blacks from the South." For that reason alone, the columnist contended, the march had elicited overwhelming disapproval, not sympathy, from the majority of Spanish-speaking New Mexicans.

"The Hispanos in New Mexico occupy neither the social nor civil status that blacks hold in the South," this writer intoned. "But every time that a group of Hispanos start to use the Negro tactics, they are clearly asking to be viewed at a similar level." In effect, the author reminded readers that white skin privilege depended upon nuevomexicanos distancing themselves not just from Native Americans but, given the broader U.S. context, even more so from African Americans.[98]

The writer spoke for a class of Spanish-speaking New Mexicans who were uncomfortable with the Alianza's goals and, now more than ever, with the organization's method of achieving them. Three years of promises and three years of unprecedented unity among land-grant heirs had failed to spark any meaningful government intervention. Worse, to these critics, the switch to protest risked a tumble down the racial hierarchy. As one observer recalled, more prosperous and assimilated Spanish-speaking Americans also resented having to explain land-grant history, much less the contours of Tijerina's particular crusade, to Anglo colleagues at work or in social settings.[99] Class interests often divided these critics from those land-poor nuevomexicanos drawn to the Alianza.

The backlash was impressive, given the march's modest goals. Alianza members had been denounced by a fellow nuevomexicano for acting like African Americans. Meanwhile, other New Mexicans chided Alianza members for "playing Indian" by claiming that they too were the victims of conquest.[100] More seriously, anonymous antagonists literally took aim at sleeping demonstrators. Nor did the meeting with the governor prove fruitful; Campbell did forward the Alianza's petition to President Johnson, but the White House once again offered no response. In the end, the most concrete result of the Alianza's switch to protest was public condemnation from the state's leading archivist.[101]

At a strategic dead end, the Alianza leader turned to a Seattle eccentric and ex-con for help.

EL PUEBLO REPÚBLICA DE SAN JOAQUÍN DEL RÍO DE CHAMA

Standing not quite five feet, six inches tall and weighing 188 pounds, Jerry Noll, nearsighted and with a tendency to speak in a soft, whispery voice, appeared every inch the mild-mannered scholar when he addressed the fourth annual Alianza convention in September 1966.[102] Billed as a "historian of international law," he captured the imagination of attendees by recycling the "Free Socorro" idea. As he proposed to those gathered, the land was granted to independent towns, or what he called "municipal corporations." Noll further argued that these entities were the true owners of the land. To reestablish their hereditary rights, he continued, land-grant activists merely needed to "participate in the life of the town."[103] Alianza members enthusiastically endorsed Noll's analysis. Before the convention was over, members announced plans to occupy the Echo Amphitheater picnic area within Carson National Forest, or as the Alianza's press release alternatively defined the same area, El Pueblo República de San Joaquín del Río de Chama.

Tijerina had been contemplating just such a dramatic takeover even before traveling to Seville. "We are going to leave the burden of proof on the government," Tijerina explained to a reporter in April 1966. "There is no other way."[104] Instead of suing to secure property rights, Tijerina suggested, the Alianza would seek to be sued by deliberately trespassing on federal lands. That way the United States would have to assert in court its right to the land when it prosecuted the lawbreakers. Noll's analysis appeared to offer a legal rationale for just that sort of confrontation. He had first outlined this analysis in a congratulatory letter to Tijerina written shortly after the July march. Intrigued, the Alianza leader had heavily underlined some portions of Noll's letter and circled others.[105] "I was very much impress with your letter," Tijerina had replied.[106] He invited Noll to attend the September 1966 convention.

Noll not only accepted Tijerina's invitation but also moved from California to New Mexico to take a room in the Alianza headquarters. He soon entered the inner circle of Alianza advisers. In public, Tijerina once described Noll's position within the organization as "*primus inter pares*," a Latin phrase meaning "first among equals" used to describe the early Roman emperors.[107] Privately, he might have even contemplated marriage between his eldest daughter and Noll in order to launch a new American dynasty. Or so Rose Tijerina recalled years later.[108] Lending credence to that assertion, in 2007 Reies Tijerina maintained that Noll had shown him proof of his family's royal lineage at the National Archives during a visit to Washington, D.C.[109]

To critics, Noll's claims confirmed their opinion that the land-grant crusade was, at best, a laughable endeavor.[110] His make-believe identity, however, only spurred Noll's willingness to assist the land-grant cause. And he struck most Alianza members as a benign and often helpful presence. At the most basic level, Noll's native command of the English language mattered in an organization dominated by members with limited education who had grown up speaking Spanish. Noll, for example, almost certainly authored the Alianza's 1966 pamphlet *The Spanish Land Grant Question Examined*, which neatly summarized the organization's agenda.[111]

Noll also convincingly claimed legal expertise. "He was really smart about legal matters," recalled Juan Valdez, an Alianza member who knew Noll.[112] Like Tijerina, Noll liked to litter his speeches with Latin words and phrases, such as "estoppel," "res judicata," and "stare decisis."[113] If the new arrival never explained exactly what these terms meant, he nevertheless appeared to have mastered the language of the courts that had blocked Alianza members for such a long time. Noll also knew how to construct plausible arguments. In suggesting that the grant land could not be bought or sold any more than Phoenix or Minneapolis could be bought or sold, for example, Noll echoed an 1891 territorial law that had allowed nuevomexicanos to form land-grant corporations. Some land-grant heirs had done so in an attempt to protect their holdings.[114] In his speech before the Alianza convention that September, Noll mined this familiar history to persuade members that these "corporate rights" were within reach.

A familiar history of land dispossession surrounded the town in question. The village of San Joaquín originally sat within the Cañon de Chama land grant. Just as the "News Bulletin" announced, the original grant dated to 1806, when the Spanish government had granted land along the Chama River to Francisco Salazar and his family as well as to the thirty other settler families. Although the town of San Joaquín never flourished, settlers built homes along the canyon formed by the river, a major tributary to the Rio Grande, and pastured their animals along the surrounding high mesas. In 1861, more than 400 people claimed grant land. That year, they petitioned the Surveyor General's Office to confirm their holdings, which they estimated at 184,320 acres. They heard nothing, however, until 1905, when the Court of Private Land Claims declared that the grant consisted of only 1,443 acres of individual tracts along the river. When locals asked about communal land rights, they were directed to that 1896 U.S. Supreme Court decision that deemed land used in common during the Spanish and Mexican eras the property of the U.S. government. Indeed, that same year, President Theodore Roosevelt designated some 300,000 acres of northern New Mexico, including much of the original 1806 grant, national forest. Local residents kept appealing their fate. As late as 1944, Democratic congressman Antonio Fernández appealed to his fellow representatives to convey additional land to the 351 families who remained in the area. Despite every attempt to comply with tortuous adjudication procedures, he pointed out, these "children of the children of the first settlers" could legally lay claim to only "the small patches on which . . . homes and small cultivated pieces were located" while being surrounded by thousands of acres of U.S. Forest Service land.[115]

A generation later, several of those "children of the children of the first settlers" revived the life of the town with dramatic flair. As advertised, on October 15, 1966, as many as 400 *aliancistas* arrived at the Echo Amphitheater, an immense natural hollow in a stunning sandstone cliff. Visitors had long come to picnic and hear their amplified voices. The day of the occupation, protesters brought with them large white sign with the words "Pueblo República San Joaquín del Río de Chama" and "Est. 1806" spray-painted in red.[116] They slapped this stenciled sign directly over the official one that read "Carson National Forest." They also hoisted a blue flag with the republic's name in gold lettering, a standard that women members of the Alianza had sewn in advance of the gathering. In a tactic borrowed from the Corporation of Abiquiú, moreover, several armed males, mostly middle-aged but some significantly younger, donned mail-order badges and patrolled the land in an effort to deter non-Alianza visitors. A chain that suddenly appeared across the entrance of the picnic area sent a similar message. During this first occupation, Alianza members also elected town representatives, including most prominently Mayor José L. Salazar, the great-grandson of the original grantee, Francisco Salazar, and Tijerina himself, who agreed to serve as *procurador*, or city attorney.[117]

The choice of location as well as the decision to break the law placed the Alianza on a deliberate collision course with the U.S. Forest Service. Federal agents, however, never engaged the crowd that weekend. "To tell you the truth," a Forest Service supervisor later explained, "we were unable to contact our attorneys so we left them [the demonstrators] strictly alone."[118] A heavy storm then drove most of the *aliancistas* home before the weekend was over. Undeterred, they decided to try again the following Saturday. In fact, once back in Albuquerque, Tijerina paid a professional processor to serve forester William Hurst, Regional Supervisor for the Southwest, informing him of the rescheduled takeover.

As court testimony later revealed, the Forest Service spent the intervening week busily preparing to contest the Alianza's claim to the land. After meeting with federal attorneys, Hurst was ready when Alianza members crowded his office midweek. Refusing to be served, he instead read aloud a statement addressed to Tijerina. "The property you propose to claim," he declared, "belongs to the United States of America, and I will not, under any condition, allow it to be claimed by any organization or group."[119] Up north, two new stop signs suddenly made an appearance at the entrance to the Echo Amphitheater, as did several posters announcing that the amphitheater was now part of a designated federal recreation area.[120]

The U.S. government, too, seemed eager for a confrontation. Saturday morning, October 22, found additional personnel stationed at the site: three state policemen and half a dozen Forest Service officers. Unlike the previous week, Forest Service rangers insisted upon collecting the entrance fee to the area from all visitors. Normal procedure had operated on the honor system: visitors were expected to be ready to show proof that they had paid in case a ranger asked them during their visit. Now Forest Service officials stood at the Echo Amphitheater entrance ready to stop entering cars and demand payment.[121]

The demonstration quickly veered toward violence. At 11 A.M. a caravan of about forty cars and trucks filled with *aliancistas* drove right past the stop signs, forcing Forest Service employees stationed at the gate to scramble out of the way. When Phil Smith and Walter Taylor of the Forest Service followed the *aliancistas* to collect the fees, an angry crowd quickly encircled them. With local television news cameras rolling, women and children shouted while some men resorted to a show of physical strength. As Smith recalled, "I was pulled, dragged, and pushed, literally, I mean, to [a] picnic table" nearby.[122] Recounting the same moment, Taylor offered, "I felt, very definitely, that I was in big trouble," adding, "I thought I was a dead man."[123] The crowd also momentarily apprehended Chris Zamora, a forester from Albuquerque, until they heard him speak Spanish and decided to let him go.[124] Perhaps because he was not wearing a uniform and thus was mistakenly assumed to be a journalist taking notes, James Evans, a criminal investigator for the U.S. Forest Service, surveyed the scene completely unmolested.[125] Also keeping a close eye was state police captain Martin Vigil.[126]

Asked by the gathered media to explain what was happening, Tijerina said that the two had been arrested "on the town's authority" for the crime of "trespassing on the property of San Joaquín del Río de Chama." Presiding as the town's judge at the picnic table, Noll quickly found Taylor and Smith guilty of that crime as well as the crime of being a public nuisance. Tijerina then jumped on the same table and delivered a speech in Spanish that emphasized the Alianza's claim to the land. Taylor, a Spanish speaker, and Zamora both later testified that Tijerina in his speech upheld Fidel Castro as a heroic example. "Castro has what he has because he has a lot of guts," Tijerina supposedly rallied the crowd. "Castro put the gringos off his island and we can do the same."[127] At some point during the mock trial, Juan Valdez took the occasion to express his anger on behalf of his father, who had died the year before. "[Smith] was always giving my father trouble about our cows and sheep being on the forest [land]," recollected Valdez, who admitted kicking Smith hard in the behind "to get even for everything he'd done to make my father's life so hard."[128] That was the only punishment the trial meted out. Although Noll announced that the rangers' trucks were impounded, Tijerina immediately contradicted him. Noll also ruled that Taylor and Smith were required to serve time and each pay a $500 fine for their crimes but immediately suspended the sentences.[129] Released, Taylor and Smith decided to get back to work and record the license plates of cars parked in the area since none of the drivers had paid the entrance fee.

With tensions already running high, that decision spurred another, even more high-risk confrontation. Once more, angry *aliancistas* started to grab and push the two federal employees and tell them that if they did not leave the area they would be rearrested and thrown in jail. At this point, Taylor, followed closely by Alianza members, went back to his truck to retrieve a gun that he had left in the front seat of his vehicle underneath a jacket. He had brought the weapon to work in violation of his supervisor's orders. As he attempted to retrieve it surreptitiously, it fell to the ground. As Taylor quickly bent down to grab the weapon before any *aliancista* could, Captain Vigil diffused the situation by pointing out that the gun was personal property that belonged to Taylor and not the federal government. Tijerina concurred. Finally, as requested, the Forest Service officials retreated beyond the park entrance. As Taylor described the situation, "I was outside, and they were in."[130] A triumphant Tijerina offered a farewell: "You have done your duty. We have taken charge here. If we have done wrong, you can sue us, but we are in charge here."[131]

That conclusion sent a chill through the New Mexican establishment. Tijerina was guilty of "keeping the pot of racism boiling," charged the *Rio Grande Sun*. For too long, he had duped impoverished New Mexicans through "high-powered oratory" that featured false promises about regaining lost land.[132] "Error Revealed in Alianza Claim" blared another headline, this one from the *Taos News*. The accompanying article recounted the complicated history of the Cañon de Chama grant from

1861 to 1905 to reach what the paper considered an irrefutable conclusion: the Alianza's claims were unfounded because the U.S. Supreme Court had already decided the matter.[133] Myra Jenkins soon joined this particular chorus, dismissing the entire episode as "historical nonsense." Jenkins pointed out that no independent republic ever existed under the Spanish Crown and that the original land-grant papers had gone missing, in any event. Consequently, she noted, anyone's best guess placed the location of the town of San Joaquín, which had been long abandoned, some six miles to the west of the Echo Amphitheater.[134]

Such details hardly mattered to exhilarated Alianza members, who felt that they had finally turned the tables on their opponents. In a corrido written to commemorate the Echo Amphitheater protest, for example, Pedro Padilla, the lyricist, heralded not only Tijerina's leadership but also the bravery of the many other participants: "Death is preferable than being held captives," proclaimed the corrido's lyrics, which specifically praised "*la* Hispana" as ready to take her vengeance.[135] Uvaldo Velasquez, who hailed from the northern village of Youngsville on the Piedra Lumbre grant, similarly remembered the Echo Amphitheater occupation as a moment of hope and pride. "When we were at Echo Park in 1966, everyone was confident that we were going to win [our land back]," he recalled years later. Velasquez, who was born in 1919, recalled how, against a lifetime of shabby treatment that he had experienced as a nuevomexicano, the protest reigned as a moment when *aliancistas* took a stand without being "afraid of any guard or any Anglo or anything."[136] For his part, Juan Valdez imbued the mock trial in particular with tremendous significance: "I know it sounds ridiculous now but it was serious business back then."[137] That the word "republic" never appeared in any land-grant documents was beside the point. Its use captured the themes of autonomy and independence that Alianza members were eager to convey. For many protesters, the occupation marked an unprecedented attempt to express their collective frustration at the federal government, which they viewed as both an oppressive landlord and nasty squatter.

For five days, Alianza members controlled the Echo Amphitheater and surrounding areas, about 500 acres in total.[138] The occupation brought together Albuquerque-based members along with those from such nearby northern New Mexico villages as Cebolla, Gallina, and Canjilón, in some cases for the first time. Setting up camp, the demonstrators stayed overnight and cooked their meals there. In the mornings, the smell of campfire coffee filled the amphitheater. Just like the weekend before, men, carrying hunting rifles and pistols and deputized by Tijerina to serve the town, patrolled the area. The patrols at least twice forbade curious Anglos from entering the picnic spot. To the dismay of police officials watching from outside, teenage boys were among those participating in these armed patrols. When the press asked about the wisdom of youth carrying guns, a nonchalant Tijerina responded, "Our boys are in Vietnam and they are here."[139] Dreaming big, he also announced plans to build a jail, a town hall, and, just as he had hoped to do in Valle de Paz, a school for children who had joined the protest. "They can learn more here in two or three days than they can learn in school in 20 years," Tijerina boasted to reporters about the children. "The only thing they learn in school is that they have no right to the land."[140]

An act of political theater that openly challenged the legitimacy of U.S. rule in New Mexico, the Echo Amphitheater occupation put the land-grant struggle before the New Mexican public in a manner almost impossible to ignore. In the past, Tierra Amarilla land-grant activists had "performed their property rights." The Echo Amphitheater occupation built upon these early efforts. Unleashing the collective frustration of Alianza members, the occupation also epitomized Tijerina's willingness to adopt and adapt the strategies of the African American freedom struggle for Alianza use. Many civil rights protests aimed to capture the gaze of the viewer. Think of college students being bathed in ketchup, sugar, and mustard for daring to sit at a "whites only" lunch counter in Greensboro, North Carolina. Or consider the image of children being attacked by police dogs in Birmingham, Alabama. These incidents too demanded the attention of the public, politicians, and media. As a land occupation, the Echo Amphitheater protest also directly foreshadowed the Native American occupation of Alcatraz that began in 1969 and lasted for two years or even the Second Battle of Wounded Knee that occurred in 1973. In fact, only afterward did the Alianza finally gain some Native American allies.

The Echo Amphitheater occupation prompted admiration across the border in Arizona with Hopi Indians, a Pueblo people who remained outside the reach of the Spanish empire after 1680. Even then, Tijerina found friends not among tribal council members but among a group of outsiders who called themselves "traditionalists." After the Echo Amphitheater occupation, he, Noll, and other Alianza members accepted an invitation to visit the breakaway village of Hotevilla, which had been a hotbed of traditional activism since its founding in 1906. While there, Tijerina met with Oswald Fredericks, also known as White Bear. Soon afterward,

Fredericks wrote to the Alianza asking for a copy of the Treaty of Guadalupe Hidalgo, translated into English. "If you do this, I will be the happiest man in Ariz.," he wrote.[141] Also requesting a copy of the map of the Mexican Republic circa 1847, Fredericks was apparently interested in exploring to what extent the provisions of the Treaty of Guadalupe Hidalgo might advance Hopi land claims. Tijerina was only too happy to help, sending a copy of the treaty five days later and, because he could not find a copy of any map, forwarding explicit directions on how to acquire one. In closing, Tijerina, clearly foregrounding the "Indo" portion of Indo-Hispano, approximated a Native American farewell: "Walk in the ways of the Great Spirit, and may he bless you and your people in their work."[142]

Perhaps more surprising, Noll likewise exchanged friendly letters with a Hotevilla traditionalist named Thomas Banyacya. An anticolonialist like Tijerina, Banyacya completely rejected cooperation with U.S. institutions. During World War II, Banyacya spent seven years in jail after refusing to recognize American sovereignty and register for the draft.[143] Now this Hopi leader wished to convey his approval of the Alianza's turn toward protest. In December 1966, Banyacya shared with Noll that many elders admired "the courage and truthfulness and sincerity of the President Reies López Tijerina and all those who stood by him during his march to Santa Fe and the takeover of your land grant within the Forest Area controlled by the U.S. Forest Department." Banyacya was also glad to hear that members of the San Juan Pueblo had joined the Alianza, a comment that suggested that Tijerina had made some headway with indigenous New Mexicans too. The would-be king, in turn, had no problem recognizing the claims of Banyacya's "Hopi Independent Nation."[144] As much as Noll's participation had pushed the Alianza protest in a Spanish—or at least a regally flamboyant—direction, as evinced by the original "News Bulletin" announcing the Echo Amphitheater takeover, the switch from petition to protest also made clear to at least some potential allies what Tijerina had been saying all along: that nuevomexicanos, like Native Americans, had suffered conquest.

As Tijerina had hoped, the Echo occupation also provoked a federal reaction. Four days after the Saturday mock trial, Judge H. Vearle Payne of the U.S. District Court issued an injunction evicting all Alianza members from the Echo Amphitheater and furthermore forbidding their return "except as ordinary citizens obedient to and in compliance with all laws of the State of New Mexico and the United States."[145] Although Chris Tijerina had promised that Alianza members intended to occupy the amphitheater "indefinitely" and his brother had dreamed big, by then the number of protesters had dwindled to about thirty. They left without incident except for one young hothead, Baltazar Martínez of Canjilón, who was taken to jail after a shooting incident in which someone fired a rifle at a passing car.[146] In addition, and more important to Tijerina, U.S. attorney John Quinn filed criminal charges against the Alianza leader, his brother Cristóbal, Noll, and two others, Ezekial Dominguez and Alfonso Chavez. Quinn accused each of these men with assaulting two forest rangers and with "conversion" of Forest Service property, namely depriving the Forest Service of its use of the two trucks during the protest.[147]

The pending criminal charges invigorated Tijerina. At the start of the occupation, the Alianza leader had neatly summarized its purpose in a single word: "publicity."[148] Tijerina happily noted that everyone associated with the Alianza "feels just great" following the arrests.[149] "We got what we wanted—a criminal case against the Alianza," he enthused. "The U.S. is now going to have to prove we were trespassing on government property and to do that they have to prove the land is theirs." With more than a hint of smugness, he added, "If I didn't think we could win [in court], I would never have gone along with the idea of taking possession of the forest."[150] Yet this positive appraisal overlooked the fact that, although five Alianza members stood accused of multiple violations of federal law, none had been charged with trespassing. In other words, the Alianza was still in no position to force the United States to prove its ownership of the land.

As an Indo-Hispano, Tijerina had challenged ossified racial and class hierarchies, forged new alliances, and orchestrated a takeover of property claimed by the federal government. If he could not prove that his efforts were making a difference, neither was Tijerina willing to abandon them. To the contrary, an emboldened Tijerina announced Alianza plans to take over the entire city of Albuquerque before the year was over. "We just want our land back . . . it is as simple as that," he stated. "If they don't hand back what rightly belongs to us, we will have to take it."[151]

Soon he tried, with a pistol in his hand.

8

The Gunslinger

The violence of June 5, 1967, transformed the "unthinkable" into the "thinkable."[1] Caught by police just a few days later, Tijerina proudly proclaimed the events of the day a "terrific success" precisely because the sheer drama of the shoot-out and subsequent manhunt had splashed the land-grant movement across the pages of the nation's newspapers.[2] During the 1960s, Black Power activists threatened to achieve their aims "by any means necessary," but few actually picked up a gun and fired. Alianza members did. The violence that day represented a rare instance in U.S. history when militant words became militant actions and caused actual injury. Reporters from across the country descended upon the region. They immediately elevated Tijerina from the leader of a land-grant group to a leader of "his people." Indeed, Tijerina's quick ascension as one of the "Four Horsemen of the Chicano Movement," the uppermost pantheon of Mexican American leaders during the 1960s, rested almost entirely upon this moment of violence. In all these ways, the assault upon the Tierra Amarilla Courthouse accomplished what the Alianza president had failed to achieve despite years of effort: introduce a national audience to the long saga of land-grant injustice.

Yet years later, Juan Valdez, the first Alianza member to enter the courthouse, strenuously objected to the word "raid" to describe what transpired that day. Also popularized by reporters, the word implied a military-style maneuver, a quick attack launched during war. As far as Valdez was concerned, the intent that day was much nobler than the word "raid" conveyed. It fell within the realm of constitutional conduct. "We weren't a bunch of revolutionaries like Alfonso Sánchez wanted everyone to believe—we were a group of land-grant heirs trying to get the government's attention," Valdez insisted. "All we wanted was a chance to explain how the government had mistreated our people and taken millions of acres from land grants our families had lived on for generations."[3] The same intent, of course, had guided Alianza members in their occupation of the Echo Amphitheater the previous fall.

The period from fall 1966 to late spring 1967 saw hope give way to frustration and then a rapid ratcheting up of tensions between land-grant activists and law officials. In the immediate aftermath of the Echo Amphitheater occupation, emboldened Alianza members pressed their case with renewed vigor in Washington, D.C., and Santa Fe. Yet the absence of real progress drove activists to contemplate bigger and better occupations. By mid-May, talk of armed liberation, reports of some ammunition purchases, and, finally, the capture of some rudimentary maps prompted a law enforcement crackdown on the organization. Convinced that Alianza members sought to create "a new Cuba in the North"—that is, launch a communist revolution in the northern portion of the state—District Attorney Alfonso Sánchez moved to quash the organization.[4] Infuriated Alianza members decided to arrest Sánchez for the crime of trampling on their First Amendment rights.

To New Mexicans sympathetic to the land-grant cause, and to a growing number of Tijerina admirers outside the state, the raid therefore signified a glorious moment of well-deserved retribution. From this perspective, Tijerina as leader of the Alianza displayed manly bravado. He played the role of avenging hero, a fighter for justice against the forces of discrimination and land dispossession. Through sheer daring, he and other Alianza members finally disrupted the ability of institutionalized power to dismiss the land-grant movement as misguided and their claims as absurd. The image of Tijerina and his band of rebels catapulted the Alianza's message right past generations of accumulated naysayers.

Lost amid the celebration of the raid as an archetype of resistance, however, was any understanding of the confrontation as many participants themselves experienced it: as a mostly bungled affair. In the words of Juan Valdez, the planned arrest of Sánchez turned into "*un desmadre*," a complete mess.[5] Less heroic than skittish, Tijerina decided to hide his face that day and waited for others to enter the building first. Upon his advice, participants carried weapons to force Sánchez's compliance, but they ended up shooting fellow nuevomexicanos. As it turned out, moreover, Sánchez was not even in the building. Nor did anyone think of what came next. With the exception of Tijerina, Alianza members who stormed the courthouse were left alone to navigate criminal charges, legal costs, and a great deal of uncertainty about their eventual fate.

In contrast, the events that day positioned Tijerina—having earned fame as a fearless gunslinger—to enter the stratosphere of 1960s protest politics.

THE COMING CONFLICT

In February 1967, a lengthy "Manifesto" appeared in the "Legal Notices" section of the *Albuquerque Journal*, right next to the classified ads. Using the royal "we," a man named Don Barné claimed as his personal possession all of New Mexico, as well as the Philippines, Oregon, Cuba, Patagonia, Louisiana, the Hawaiian Islands, and, finally, Thulia, the make-believe kingdom that Gerald Wayne Barnes had first claimed in 1954. Don Barné warned that he could no longer tolerate the United States trampling upon his sovereign rights. A military conflict loomed. "We shall commence to liberate our kingdoms, realms and dominions, and if the aggressors shed one drop of blood of any of our soldiers during the progress of this liberation campaign, a state of war shall exist," the manifesto pledged. "We shall not take prisoners of war, but shall take only war criminals and traitors, and try these war criminals and traitors by a military tribunal and execute them."[6]

From the Alianza's office the next day, a suddenly shy Jerry Noll feigned bewilderment as to the authorship of this ominous document.[7] He had advanced similar challenges to American sovereignty, however, ever since the occupation of the Echo Amphitheater in October 1966. In the months that followed, Alianza members sent a barrage of letters, inquiries, and press releases to Washington, D.C., and to news organizations, pressing for land-grant independence. Some of these documents invoked the authority of the "governor" of various "pueblos" or "villas," while others displayed the official seal of the San Joaquín Republic. One letter warned that land-grant heirs had the right to defend themselves from invasion.

Another contested the validity of presidential decrees that had created the national forests in the first place.[8] Although each bore either Tijerina's signature or that of another *aliancista*, the uniformly florid and exceptionally dense and legalistic prose pinpointed the would-be king as the missives' likely author.

These extravagant claims infused rebellious new energy into the cause. In January 1967, for example, a "Hidalgo and Caballero de las Indias" who claimed to be the "Proctor of the Pueblo República San Joaquín del Río de Chama" took a trip to the nation's capital. There, Don Tijerina attempted to present his "mission credentials" to the Department of State.[9] He failed. As the State Department had warned in advance of the trip, "the United States does not recognize the Pueblo República de San Joaquín del Río de Chama."[10] The Department of Justice and the Department of the Interior issued similar rejections.[11] With Noll as his scribe, Tijerina continued to send written inquiries. In March 1967, the Alianza leader evidently wrote to President Lyndon Johnson, asking whether he had "any objections to the various Spanish Pueblos exercising all of their rights . . . under the laws of the Kingdoms of the Indies." The reply failed to satisfy. A subsequent broadside scolded the president for his "highly unresponsive, evasive and unnecessarily threatening" response.[12]

Tijerina had more luck in Santa Fe with the new Republican governor, David Cargo, who had made it a point to court nuevomexicano votes. "[Tijerina] said he wanted to know if I had any objection to him taking over New Mexico," Cargo explained. "I told him to come up and talk about it."[13] During his long-shot campaign the previous fall, Cargo had been the only person running for governor who had accepted an invitation to attend the fourth Alianza convention in September 1966. Just thirty-seven at the time, and running against a more established Democratic candidate, Cargo also earned the nickname "Lonesome Dave" because of his relentless travels across the state. Married to a twenty-five-year-old woman with historic ties to the Atrisco grant, Ida Jo Cargo, née Anaya, Cargo also campaigned knowing something about land-grant matters. While he journeyed from one nuevomexicano village to another along dirt roads that resembled glorified cow paths, his wife joined the Alianza for the same reason: to secure nuevomexicano electoral support. Unbeknownst to Cargo, some Alianza members convinced his wife that a six-dollar, six-month membership stood to benefit her husband politically.[14]

Cargo also hoped his election might benefit nuevomexicanos, whom he saw as nursing legitimate grievances that deserved redress. "I can sympathize with the people involved," he stated about the Alianza's protests. "These people are very, very poor."[15] Instead of attempting to untangle a long history of land dispossession, however, Cargo concentrated instead on maximizing economic relief. He lobbied Washington, D.C., for more federal spending on schools and job programs up north.[16] He also hired a California-based consultant group to investigate the socioeconomic conditions confronting northern New Mexicans and to devise a plan of action.[17] Finally, he tried to tackle the problem of reduced grazing rights by arranging a series of meetings between U.S. Forest Service officials and angry nuevomexicanos.[18] Those meetings fell flat, but Cargo still hoped, in the words of one of his advisers, to channel Alianza activity "along a reasonable and law-abiding course."[19]

Cargo's cultivation of Alianza goodwill extended to Alianza members who made threats. Just a few days before at a protest rally in Albuquerque, Tijerina had issued what he called the "last human warning" before Alianza members began to arrest and punish the invaders upon their land.[20] When some 100 members crammed into the governor's office on April 21, 1967, Tijerina explained what his odd phrasing meant: "We are only human," he told the governor, and thus their patience had limits. "We can't stop these people from burning down houses," Tijerina added.[21] Nonplussed, Cargo agreed to run interference between the Alianza and officials in Washington, D.C. He also invited members to drop by an open house at the executive mansion the following week. An impatient Baltazar Martínez, a young Alianza member from Canjilón, wanted more. "We want action!" he yelled. "Put that guy on a committee!" Cargo quipped back.[22]

Tijerina evidently wanted action, too. According to Peter Nabokov, then a reporter for the *Santa Fe New Mexican*, a month before meeting the governor, Tijerina had written to Rodolfo "Corky" Gonzales, founder of a Denver-based Mexican American advocacy group called the Crusade for Justice, inviting him to participate in a forthcoming plot by members of the Alianza: "to take possession of San Joaquin del Rio de Chama once and for all" sometime around June 3. In this letter, Tijerina shared that a group of followers that he called the "Sons of San Joaquín" had demonstrated unprecedented zeal and ardor ever since the Echo Amphitheater occupation. Ready to take advantage of this moment, Tijerina envisioned staging a formal "*toma*," that is, a reenactment of the formal ceremony of possession that had accompanied the granting of a piece of land during both the Spanish and Mexican periods, as one way of directing their enthusiasm.[23] The plan was hardly a secret. "We are going to push it," a gleeful Tijerina had announced following the Echo Amphitheater occupation. "We'll push harder and harder until they arrest somebody."[24] In a similar vein, Tijerina nonchalantly had reminded the press directly after meeting with the governor that land-grant activists outnumbered Forest Service personnel in the area surrounding the Echo Amphitheater. With that numerical advantage, they could "just take over" at any time they desired to do so.[25]

Tijerina nonetheless wished "to push it" short of landing in jail. A ceremonial *toma* was not an armed invasion. In mid-May, moreover, Tijerina attended a meeting in Tierra Amarilla during which words prevailed over more risky actions. The 500 activists in attendance declared the Tierra Amarilla land grant, just like the San Joaquín one, free and sovereign. They also formed a town council that former Corporation of Abiquiú members happily populated. As to the future, Tijerina insisted, "We will of course try to enforce certain rights." In undertaking this action, he did note one clear exception: "We don't have to step on so-called forest government property."[26] Still facing federal charges from the occupation of Echo Amphitheater, the Alianza leader had every reason to avoid another direct confrontation with federal authorities.

Not everyone agreed with Tijerina's restraint. The day after the meeting in Cargo's office, two Alianza members forcibly tried to stop two Forest Service employees from constructing a fence on the Cibola National Forest, south of Albuquerque.[27] In their eagerness to reclaim the land, anonymous others struck out at private landholders that spring, cutting fences and burning haystacks. In one of the worst incidents, suspected arsonists destroyed a barn and about 2,000 bales of hay on the property of Bill Mundy, a longtime foe of land-grant activists.[28] Raymond Spill, another large landowner who lived within the historic boundaries of the Tierra Amarilla grant, returned home from vacation to discover that someone had shot his parked 1960 Cadillac with a high-powered rifle.[29] Although plenty of suspicion fell upon discontented Alianza members, police had difficulty making arrests for the actions of these vandals. As District Attorney Alfonso Sánchez conceded, law enforcement lacked evidence.[30]

Jerry Noll, the would-be king, sought more than anonymous acts of vandalism. He favored armed insurrection. In May 1967, he crafted a letter to Tijerina that raised the possibility that a number of other Alianza members did too while expressing frustration that Tijerina apparently did not. Instead, Noll dismissed Tijerina's tough talk of a looming conflict as "another one of your publicity stunts." With considerable insight, he also labeled Tijerina an "egoist" who enjoyed seeing his name in print. Yet beyond tough talk, Noll contended, the Alianza leader had demonstrated a "reluctance to commence the liberation of your country." Making an oblique reference to "summer activities," Noll complained that Tijerina had not "put out one dime towards being well-prepared" and had failed to buy the necessary "equipment." Perhaps Noll meant guns and dynamite, given his conviction that the people "wanted blood and land."[31]

If Tijerina was not paying attention, U.S. attorney John Quinn certainly was. Quinn was in charge of prosecuting five Alianza members for charges stemming from the Echo Amphitheater occupation, a group that included Reies López Tijerina, his brother Chris, and Noll. After the manifesto's publication, Quinn asked the court to evaluate Noll's mental competency to stand trial that April.[32] Quinn also quickly pressed charges against the two Alianza members who had tried to prevent the work of Forest Rangers in the Cibola National Forest. Judge Vearle Payne, however, found Quinn too hasty. He dismissed the charges, concerned that these two men may not have even known about the federal court order forbidding Alianza members from occupying national forest land.[33]

This setback, however, provided a pretext for Quinn to take even more aggressive action against the Alianza: he sought a court order compelling Tijerina to turn over the Alianza's membership list. That way, Quinn argued, the court could inform all members about any standing orders. The list also provided Quinn a means to investigate the finances of the group and to determine whether anyone whom he suspected of criminal activity was actually an Alianza member. With the fires and fence cuttings forming an increasingly ominous backdrop to the Alianza's already militant marches and manifestos, Judge Payne granted Quinn's request on May 19. Tijerina had just five days to turn over the membership rolls or risk contempt of court charges.[34]

Tijerina refused to cooperate. Police officials looked hard, but they did not even locate Tijerina until May 24 in Tierra Amarilla. Accompanied by a television film crew interested in the land-grant cause, Tijerina had clearly prepared a moment of defiance. Upon being served, he produced a letter stating that he had resigned as leader of the Alianza at the beginning of the month. Therefore, he insisted, he could not be prevailed to turn over the list.[35] Two days later, Tijerina announced the formation of a new organization called La Confederación de Pueblos Libres, or what he translated as the Confederation of Free City States.[36] This new group did not have individual members but only member land grants, thus rendering Payne's order moot, or so Tijerina argued. To the press, he defended his uncooperative stance as necessary to protect members from discrimination on the part of employers who opposed the land-grant movement.[37]

Tijerina had another reason for keeping the size and, implicitly, the strength of the Alianza a secret. The alternative meant exposing his penchant for exaggeration. Whereas Tijerina liked to speak of 30,000 members, for instance, that number magnified the Alianza's membership rolls probably by a factor of ten. Similarly, Tijerina often boasted that the organization stood poised to launch a massive lawsuit aimed at recouping millions of acres across the Southwest. In truth, based upon dues collected, the organization lacked the deep pockets necessary for any sort of protracted legal fight. This fiscal reality only enhanced the appeal of a low-cost, high-profile protest as one of the few options available to Alianza members eager to effect change.

"No longer the president, but sounding like one," in the words of one reporter, on May 28 Tijerina finally detailed his plans for a "showdown action." He announced a national meeting of the new confederation to occur in Coyote, New Mexico, on June 3, the same date that Tijerina originally had set aside to occupy the San Joaquín land grant "for once and for all."[38] Although Tijerina announced plans to take over 600,000 acres, the switch in location obscured a careful move on his part. Coyote sat on private land, meaning the declared takeover avoided a direct confrontation with federal authorities. Tijerina seemed less concerned about embarking upon a collision course with local police. The land-grant leader boasted that attendees intended to set up ports of entry on roads throughout the area and to issue visas to "outsiders." He also warned that all non-nuevomexicano residents in the area might face taxation on the part of grant authorities.[39]

According to multiple police reports, Tijerina's announcement coincided with some highly suspicious activities on the part of some Alianza members. On May 27, the FBI disclosed that one member had peppered a fellow employee at Carco Air Service in Albuquerque with questions about how to acquire rifles and machine guns. The coworker also received a phone call from an Alianza official named "Chris," presumably Chris Tijerina, Reies's brother, who wanted to purchase ammunition and antipersonnel grenades. Invited to attend a June 3 "picnic," the gun collector contacted the police instead.[40] On May 30, state police recounted that Felix Martínez, son of longtime Tierra Amarilla activists Juan and Fernanda Martínez, had purchased large quantities of ammunition at an Albuquerque sporting goods store along with gas masks and some rifles.[41] That same day, warning signs appeared in and around the town of Chama in Rio Arriba County. Issued in the name of "Don Geraldo Nol, Governor," some informed residents that "all improvements and chattel property" situated on "these premises" were about to be impounded by the Pueblo República de San Joaquín del Río de Chama.[42] Pamphlets appeared in mailboxes that read, "U.S.A. is trespassing in New Mexico."[43] Most worrisome, a smaller group of committed activists within the Alianza who called themselves "Los Comancheros" apparently had decided that the time had come to shed blood. At least that is what a state police officer reported after overhearing Alianza members in Hernandez, New Mexico, where the organization had opened a second office and where police labeled an old metal structure next door a "barracks."[44]

District Attorney Sánchez collected troubling information as well. Police officers in the field told him that Alianza plotters openly shared their hope that Mexico might be drawn into the fray on the side of the land-grant cause. On a lighter note, Sánchez received a call from a Tierra Amarilla housewife complaining that her husband, a higher-up in the Alianza organization, had stopped working in the expectation that the Tierra Amarilla grant soon would be returned to its rightful owners.[45] Sánchez swiftly concluded that the best way to maintain the peace was to grind the Alianza to a halt.

Sánchez first aimed to shut down the Coyote meeting by jailing as many activists as possible in advance of the gathering.[46] The strategy abandoned the judicial presumption of innocence and ignored standard police procedure. Just days before, State police chief Joe Black had reminded the press of that fact. Although state police stood ready to halt any attempt on the part of Tijerina's supporters to block highways, he said, "there's no move we can make until they make their move."[47] Stymied, Sánchez on May 31 brainstormed with federal and local police officials, including Black. The solution, they agreed, was to arrest land-grant activists for reasons unrelated to the upcoming meeting or possible brewing plot. Toward that end, they devised a long list of potential charges that encompassed both minor infractions and major crimes, ranging from motor vehicle violations to obstructing justice, from vagrancy to assault and battery.[48]

That same day, moreover, Sánchez consulted with U.S. attorney Quinn to determine if he could file any additional charges against top-level activists in connection to the Echo Amphitheater protest the previous fall. The answer was yes.[49] Whereas Quinn sought to prosecute federal crimes, such as assaulting a forest ranger, Sánchez on June 1 charged Reies Tijerina, his brother Chris, Noll, and the two others previously charged Alianza members with violating state law. Specifically, they were accused of killing deer and cattle in order to feed the crowd that weekend. In addition, Sánchez charged all five men of conspiring to take property belonging to the U.S. government. Under the sweeping provisions of a 1953 New Mexico anti-riot law, Quinn stated that attendance at any Alianza meeting became potential grounds for arrest under the assumption that these gatherings had provided the occasion for members to plot the violent takeover of the state.[50] Such conspiracy laws made planning to commit a crime itself a crime and were thus useful means to tamp down dissent. To Sánchez, moreover, the short-term benefit mattered as much as any long-term conviction. If Tijerina and other top land-grant activists spent the weekend in jail waiting to post bail, then they would not be in Coyote.

In his memoir, Sánchez vigorously defended his actions in the days before the courthouse raid as motivated by concern for fellow nuevomexicanos. In this respect, he sounded a lot like Tijerina acting on behalf of "his people." Before drawing up any warrants, Sánchez wrote, he and his staff carefully reviewed all that they knew to help gauge "the seriousness of the Tijerina threat." They concluded that the combined criminal records of Reies, Anselmo, and Margarito Tijerina offered plenty of proof of a familial propensity toward violence. Portraying the land-grant leader as a Svengali-like figure preying upon an impressionable population, Sánchez worried about the sway of the Alianza leader's words. "My past personal knowledge of Reies and his preaching power of persuasion, of God and Blood and Land, convinced me that I must act now—before June 3—or many people would be hurt," Sánchez wrote. Switching to all capital letters to convey the enormity of his incredulity, the district attorney continued, "IN FACT THE PEOPLE BELIEVE HIM AND HIS CONVICTIONS THAT THE LAND IS THERE'S TO TAKE" and that "NOBODY HAS JURISDICTION OVER THEM." Ultimately, according to the district attorney, only his swift action stood between Tijerina supporters and disaster.[51]

Revealing a slim streak of jealousy and a broad sense of paternalism, Sánchez sought to characterize Tijerina's appeal as inexplicable and incomprehensible. As a corollary, any militant actions on the part of nuevomexicanos were likewise devoid of reason or sense. "Reies is a one-man show" who had gained his fame by promising the impossible, Sánchez pronounced in his memoir. "Even if [Alianza members] are right, they must use the courts to decide the issue!" he insisted. "Two wrongs don't make a right." Sánchez therefore wondered why land-poor Spanish speakers had listened to Tijerina instead of to him, asking plaintively, "Why do I fail to convince heirs of [the] grant?"[52] Despite his professed bewilderment, the district attorney knew the answer to that question even as he posed it. In an admission that closely echoed his thoughts when he sought an injunction to shut down the Corporation of Abiquiú in 1964, he acknowledged that the courts had offered "no remedy" to aggrieved Spanish speakers over the years. Demanding that land-grant activists go through the courts to achieve justice therefore constituted the greatest farce of all. "Tijerina thrives on that," Sánchez admitted.[53] Unable to resolve that problem, the district attorney concentrated on the crisis at hand. He pushed for law enforcement to set up roadblocks on all roads leading to Coyote and to pass out leaflets warning of the possible infractions of criminal law.[54]

Police soon found evidence of a rudimentary military-style operation in the offing. On the night of Friday, June 2, state police pulled over Felix Martínez as he drove toward Coyote. They found that he was carrying a loaded automatic revolver. Inside the car trunk, they discovered eight gas masks, a high-powered rifle with telescopic sight, a walkie-talkie, and a sleeping bag. That same evening, a state police officer arrested Chris Tijerina as he was driving in the town of Hernandez, just outside of Española. He carried a loaded pistol, and in the trunk of his car, law enforcement found what the court order had sought: the Alianza membership rolls recorded on hundreds of index cards stored in metal trays. Each card contained the name and contact information of an Alianza member, including, to the surprise of Governor Cargo, the name of his wife. In addition, the trunk yielded financial information in the form of ten receipt books that tallied dues paid in 1965 and 1966.[55]

More disturbingly, police also found several hand-drawn maps that hinted at future battle plans. Consisting of a few pencil lines, the maps crudely depicted a roughly fifty-square mile region surrounding the Abiquiú reservoir. With different sections labeled "Phase 1," "Phase 2," and "Phase 3" in one case and "Face 1," "Face 2, and "Face 3" in another, the maps featured brief commands, such as "Women and children activate to the East Side," "Heavy Defense Stays in Position," and "Take Over." In addition, one map noted three key targets. Labeled "No. 1 Choice" was Ghost Ranch, the former home of artist Georgia O'Keeffe, which had been held by the Presbyterian Church since 1955. In another map, a tiny rectangle represented a future prison, while other markings noted multiple lines of defense. Officers also found a chart of a basic command structure running from the president to generals to foot soldiers.[56]

Two books in the trunk piqued further suspicion: William Shirer's *The Rise and Fall of the Third Reich* and Che Guevara's *Guerrilla Warfare*.[57] Especially in light of Reies Tijerina's later comments about Jewish people, the presence of Shirer's book is particularly intriguing. Was he sharing an incipient anti-Semitism with his brother, or trying to understand what regime gave rise to the horrors of Holocaust? Answering that question is impossible. But at the time, the second tome concerned Sánchez more. As far as the district attorney was concerned, the seized material conclusively proved that the Alianza's calls to establish a city-state in reality masked an attempt to build a "new Cuba in the North." Years later, Reies Tijerina insisted that whatever plans Felix Martínez and Chris Tijerina had been hatching prior to the Coyote meeting, they acted without his knowledge.[58]

Sent to the Santa Fe jail, Chris Tijerina and Martínez soon had company. Executing Sánchez's original plan to round up as many people as possible, between Friday night and early Saturday morning state police arrested nine more Alianza members, including Alfonso Chavez, fifty, who already was facing federal charges for his participation in the Echo Amphitheater occupation. Other warrants targeted former members of the Corporation of Abiquiú. To the surprise of Samuel Benavidez, fifty-nine, of Chama, state police grabbed him when he opened the door to his store on Friday night. Although an Alianza member, Benavidez had not been at the Echo Amphitheater protest, nor, he maintained, had he planned to attend the Coyote gathering. Yet in keeping with the district attorney's plan, the Chama carpenter, complaining bitterly that he was not allowed a phone call until Sunday night, did not make bail until Monday.[59] Also arrested were Cruz Aguilar, forty-three, Nicholas López, fifty-two, José Martínez, seventy, Juan Martínez, fifty-eight, Ubaldo C. Martínez, fifty-two, and Juan I. Valdez, sixty-six, all of whom had been named in the 1964 court injunction forbidding corporation members from engaging in any unlawful action on the Tierra Amarilla grant.[60] Each arrest stood as a testament to the dedication of these men, who must have been aware of their legal jeopardy. Finally, the roundup concluded with the arrest of two more Tijerina brothers. On Saturday morning, police picked up Anselmo at the Hernandez office and booked him on a concealed weapons charge.

Meanwhile, Ramón was stopped at a roadblock. Upon his arrest, Ramón asserted that Reies, the only Tijerina brother not located by this point, had gone into hiding to escape an assassination plot.[61]

Labeling the situation "extremely explosive and volatile," Governor Cargo in Santa Fe feared that Sánchez's roundup might inflame tensions instead of tamping them down.[62] He agreed with Sánchez that prudence demanded canceling the Coyote meeting. As a precautionary measure, Cargo also placed a National Guard unit on stand-by Friday evening.[63] But he clearly preferred persuasion to violent coercion. While Sánchez defended his tough stance, declaring at one point that Alianza members "had been coddled too much," Cargo went to visit arrested activists in the Santa Fe jail that Friday night.[64] Cargo later recalled stressing the importance of peaceful protest. On Saturday morning Cargo also met in his office with three longtime Alianza members, Santiago Tapia y Anaya, Eddie Chavez, and F. M. Cassaus, the Alianza member whom Cargo blamed for enrolling his wife in the Alianza. They drove up from Albuquerque at the governor's request. Afterward, a relieved Cargo took to the airwaves to make an important announcement: the showdown had been postponed. "We will have a peaceful meeting at some other time and some other place," the governor broadcast. "The leadership of the Alianza urges you to go home."[65]

The New Mexican press, overwhelmingly anti-Tijerina, gloated. "Meeting in Coyote Was a Big Bust," blared one headline.[66] "Tijerina Force Loses Steam," chortled another. "A ballyhooed 'showdown,'" the accompanying article reported with glee, "fell flat."[67] While Reies Tijerina had promised thousands in attendance, an overestimation to be sure, only 100 or so activists showed up in Coyote that morning despite the radio announcements and roadblocks. Outnumbered by press and police in attendance, they disbanded after waiting in vain for Tijerina to arrive. At least one press report credited the governor's intercessions for the day's peaceful conclusion, but most proclaimed Sánchez the hero of the day. Rumor had it that a few stalwarts had planned to use dynamite to bring down the cliffs along Highway 84 near Ghost Ranch, an act that would have blocked all traffic coming from Santa Fe.[68] Police also heard talk of imminent attacks farther afield, upon a U.S. Forest Service office in Canjilón or upon a state fish hatchery in Parkview.[69] Thus, the district attorney's "quick action" had averted a "potential tragedy."[70] "He had guts," a state criminal investigator agreed, referring to Sánchez's decision to take swift action in advance of the meeting. A vindicated Sánchez returned the compliment. "I can't say how proud I am of the state police," the district attorney gushed to news reporters on Sunday.[71]

Yet the reaction of disappointed land-grant heirs sounded a note of caution. Until the very last moment, the few who gathered in Coyote held out the hope that Tijerina might make at least a brief appearance, perhaps swooping down by helicopter despite all the warnings to stay away. They denounced Sánchez for overreacting to a mere "picnic." "It made us mad," one man stated. "How could he throw us into jail when we weren't going to do anything against the law, only go to a barbecue? Besides my wife had been cooking all the night before," he said.[72] José Madril, a decorated veteran from the Korean War, agreed. "We are here peacefully," he insisted. "The ones who have confused this issue are the State Police. They are armed. We are not."[73] Leaving the governor's office earlier that day, Cassaus, although nearly seventy, likewise warned that matters were less settled than his fellow Republican Cargo had suggested. Trouble might still arise if land-grant activists felt provoked. "If they want a revolution, we are ready," Cassaus warned police.[74]

According to Reies Tijerina, the cancellation of the Coyote meeting directly led to the courthouse raid. Sánchez's success in shutting down their meeting sparked tremendous anger among Alianza members. "The people were furious, like never before," he stated at the time. In the face of official repression, land-grant activists sought another way to regain the upper hand.[75]

THE RAID REVERBERATES

Rose Tijerina had every intention of heading to Coyote with her brothers David and Danny and her father-approved fiancé, Fabian Duran, when at the last minute she heard that plans had changed. Her father wanted everyone to regroup at Tobias Leyba's ranch in Canjilón instead. "So we get to Canjilón and I notice that my father is being all secretive with the men," she recalled. "They go into this room, where they keep alfalfa for the animals . . . and I thought, 'Something is going on in there.'" A short while later, the men exited. As instructed by her father, Rose Tijerina hopped into the cab of a truck along with Juan Valdez and Fabian Duran. Others, including her brothers, climbed into the back of the truck, where they hid beneath a tarp. Sharing the cab with Valdez and Duran on the road to Tierra Amarilla, about twenty miles to the north, Rose remembered that both looked pale and scared. To lighten the tension, she recalled, Fabian started singing a popular song from the 1940s, "Traigo mi 45 [I'm carrying my 45 (caliber pistol)]," whose lyrics poked fun at the fragility of life: "Why speak of fear, boys, if we are born to die?"[76]

As the only woman in the group, Rose Tijerina was also the only raider not to carry a gun. The violence of that day nevertheless remained her most vivid memory, prompting a great deal of anguish. When recounting the events, she spoke of feeling tremendous fear and deep sorrow at the harm that the raiders inflicted. She remembered hearing the shot that hit Nick Saiz as she was descending the courthouse steps to retrieve the other raiders. "I thought it was a policeman [who had fired]," she recalled. "I thought I was going to get one [a bullet] in the back." Rose also recalled that her older brother, David, tried to protect her. He told her to stay in the truck and then, when she decided she was too scared to be alone, to hide in a broom closet. "If I have to die I want to die with you guys," she remembered insisting. Relenting, David ordered her to stick right behind him. From that vantage point, Rose remembered seeing the blood on the stairwell wall where Undersheriff Dan Rivera had leaned his cracked skull and hearing state police officer Nick Saiz's groans of pain. In addition, she recalled going outside and seeing the raiders firing upon two police cars as they approached the courthouse. "Everyone starting shooting at the tires, you know, the ground," she said (although those on the receiving end experienced shattered windows). "You could see all the rocks flying and stuff."[77]

Yet even as she shared her recollections, Rose Tijerina cautioned that memories about the courthouse raid frequently collided because everyone was seeking to maximize their role. "You know those guys up north?" she asked, referring to the men who raided the courthouse. "Everyone is fighting for credit and glory and 'I did more' and 'I did this' and 'I did this.'" In fact, Rose Tijerina's memories imperfectly align with those of other participants.[78] Yet they suggest a major divide that buffeted the movement in the immediate aftermath of the raid. For many it exemplified righteous fury in action: it was a moment of glory and source of pride. Yet others in New Mexico—from family members to the governor—drew the line at violence. Law enforcement did too. Although the raid made Tijerina a hero to some, its meaning was deeply contested in New Mexico from the start.

Some of the strongest objections came from the women closest to the participants. In the years after the raid, Rose Tijerina expressed her regret many times over concerning the outbreak of violence. At the time, however, she did what her father told her to do. Her mother, Mary Escobar, also expressed surprise and dismay at the turn of the events. Then living in Denver, she heard through radio reports that her ex-husband had endangered the lives of three of their children without her knowledge, much less consent.[79] She wept at her daughter's court hearing following the raid.[80] Both of these women had contributed mightily to the land-grant cause, but they disagreed with this course of action. In the tiny hamlet of Canjilón, Mary Leyba, the wife of Tobias Leyba, took a similar stance. She too supported the land-grant cause through her labor. Countless times her husband showed up with the Alianza leader and his entourage at dinnertime with the whole crew expecting to be fed, she recalled. Mary Leyba also remembered feeding them without complaint. But even years later, she drew the line at going outside the law to achieve justice.[81]

Conversely, others praised the raid precisely because it provided an occasion for men to regain their honor and status. In northern New Mexico, the inexorable loss of land had seriously compromised the ability of men in the area to provide for their families. As both long-term and short-term provocations demanded a response, the raid stood as a bold act in defense of tradition, including of traditional gender roles. Tellingly, women played no role in planning the raid. Many, like Rose Tijerina and her mother, were left in the dark.[82]

Competing views of the raid played out in the Alianza stronghold of Canjilón, the hamlet that five men later arrested on raid charges called home. This town attracted a steady stream of tourists who came to fish and hunt along the continental divide. For locals, however, neither the beautiful mountaintop scenery nor the well-stocked lakes compensated for what they had lost. Entirely surrounded by national forest, Canjilón, population 500, technically fell within the boundaries of no particular land grant but was populated by people whose families a generation or two before had been displaced from their original homesteads.

In Canjilón, family ties reinforced political ones. Alianza stalwarts included not only Juan Valdez but his younger brother Tony. Although Tony too had traveled to Tierra Amarilla on June 5, he had stayed outside the courthouse. So did Moises Morales. He had acted as a scout, visiting the courthouse in advance of the showdown to let the other men know the number of policemen there. Finally, Tobias Leyba and Baltazar Martínez also hailed from Canjilón. Not only were the Valdez brothers and Morales second cousins, but Leyba was Martínez's uncle. They nursed the same grievances. Each of these men had felt the sting of the Forest Service policy of unilaterally reducing grazing permits. All five knew what it meant to grow up poor, drop out of school to earn money, and struggle to make a living after that.[83] All resented becoming, as the title of Juan Valdez's memoir lamented, "trespassers on our own land." As Tobias Leyba once sarcastically noted, "My cow, she almost got arrested . . . because she walked over [a] line to eat some grass."[84]

A true Tijerina fan, Leyba not only had offered his home as a place to regroup after the canceled Coyote meeting but, before the raid, had actively encouraged his neighbors to join the group. On June 5, having experienced the adrenaline of confrontation at the courthouse, Leyba was not yet done venting his rage. Racing back with Juan Valdez from Tierra Amarilla, the pair passed the U.S. Forest Service office that stood at the entrance to Canjilón. As Juan Valdez recalled, Leyba tried to grab the steering wheel and direct the car toward the Forest Service building so that they could storm it too. Valdez, however, thought the better part of wisdom was to keep driving. The two men ended up at Leyba's house along with several other raiders. Having risked violence but not prepared for its repercussions, the men had no plan in mind other than to take to the hills to escape the long arm of the law.[85]

That is when Mary Leyba put her foot down. Born in Fruita, Colorado, to a farmworker family, Mary had married Tobias at the age of seventeen, when he was already a twenty-six-year-old widower with four children. By the time of the raid, she was the mother of a dozen more children and pregnant with her youngest. Accustomed to feeding a lot of people at every meal, she just fed a few more whenever a hungry Tijerina and his supporters appeared. In a variation on that pattern, late in the afternoon on June 5, Mary recalled, a group of men rushed through her kitchen grabbing as much food as they could, including some tortillas that she had just made. Leyba pulled her husband aside. "All I told him was, 'I ask nothing for myself. But think of the children,'" she recalled. Bowing to his wife's wishes, Tobias Leyba stayed as others hurried away.[86]

Despite his mother's intervention, Baltazar Martínez, just twenty-two, fled. He and a fellow raider, Baltazar Apodaca, his senior by fifty years, had left the courthouse with two hostages, Larry Calloway, the UPI news reporter, and Deputy Sheriff Pete Jaramillo. They bound Calloway's wrists with electrical cords and used Jaramillo's own handcuffs on him. Ignoring the deputy's protests, they then drove away in Jaramillo's GTO, a 1960s muscle car. Martínez raced toward Canjilón at speeds of eighty miles an hour with the state police in close pursuit. He reached his destination but drove the car into the soft shoulder of the road, where it got stuck. Surrounded by police, each of the Baltazars used a hostage as a human shield to try to make their escape. Calloway, who had worked his hands free of the electrical cords during the ride, took advantage of a moment when Apodaca had slipped in the mud to push the barrel of his gun toward the ground and away from him. As he ran away, Calloway heard Apodaca fire two shots at him before police officers tackled the older man to the ground. They could not get close to Martínez, however, who had a pistol pointing at Jaramillo's neck.[87]

As he contemplated his next move, Martínez saw his mother, Aurelia, "walking in a gruff toward us," meaning directly between him and the officers. According to her son's recollection, Aurelia was scolding the police.[88] Jaramillo recalled that she was scolding her son. In either case, she risked her own safety to protect their lives. A few minutes later, after Baltazar managed to commandeer another car, he literally took both his mother and the deputy along for the ride as he drove toward the mountains. Jaramillo later testified that Aurelia Martínez argued fiercely with her son as he drove the car about five miles into the mountains. She alternatively begged him to give himself up and not to kill Jaramillo.[89] Fortunately for Jaramillo, his captor granted the latter request. Stopping the car, Baltazar took Jaramillo at gunpoint into the woods with him. But when the older man could not keep pace with the younger one, especially with his hands cuffed, and he stumbled to the ground, Martínez ran away on foot alone.[90]

His mother regretted her inability to sway events more. According to Peter Nabokov, one of the first journalists on the scene, he overheard Baltazar's mother, whom he described as frail and "birdlike," muttering to herself in Spanish, "When they are young, you can look after them, but when they are old, they follow their own path." In this case, her son's path led the sixty-three-year-old woman directly into a sheep pen on the Leyba property along with about forty others.[91]

There, Alianza members experienced firsthand the way that anger ricocheted from raiders to police officials and back to those activists gathered in Canjilón. After the Coyote cancellation, entire families had shown up at the Leyba ranch with food and supplies for a daylong gathering. After the shoot-out at the courthouse, some of the fleeing raiders joined them, including Rose Tijerina. As she recalled, her father told her to stay there and not to worry, that she would face no repercussions from the raid because she was young and a woman. But Reies Tijerina was wrong. Within the hour, police officials swept through the village. "They were really angry because we made them look bad," Rose surmised years later, recalling how one officer furiously shouted at the group, "Nobody gets away with shooting a policeman. Nobody. Do you understand? Nobody!"[92] As a cold rain began to fall, officers gathered everyone against the protective roof of an outdoor shed before turning the Leyba sheep pen into an impromptu holding cell. Two more hours passed before law officers carted off more than a dozen people in paddy wagons to the Santa Fe jail, including Rose Tijerina, Fabian Duran, Tobias Leyba, and Patsy Tijerina, Reies's wife. The couple's baby daughter, Isabel, was sent to foster care. Everyone else remained in the sheep pen under armed guard as the day turned into night.[93]

For the next twenty-four hours, police kept Alianza members in the open in the sheep pen, hoping other members might try to break them out and be caught as well. With access to just one outdoor privy, food supplies running low, and the night chilly and damp, the plight of the detained attracted the attention of reporters arriving in Canjilón later that afternoon. They wondered on what grounds law enforcement were detaining Tijerina supporters, as none had been formally charged with a crime. Held overnight by gun-wielding officers, the group finally received some army C rations the next morning before being released in the late afternoon of June 6. Major General John Pershing Jolly, commander of the National Guard troops called to the scene, was unapologetic about the involuntary incarceration. Convinced that the group deserved what they got, he dismissed their constitutional rights. "Let's don't get involved in civil liberties," he told reporters. "None of them has complained."[94]

Meanwhile, New Mexico officials had other matters on their mind: coordinating the largest manhunt in the state's history. Officials sought to stop Tijerina and his followers at all costs. Under the mistaken impression that tempers had cooled as of June 3, Governor Cargo had flown to Michigan, his home state, to attend a series of Republican functions, leaving Lieutenant Governor E. Lee Francis in charge. "Jumbled communications" contributed to the sense of crisis.[95] Had Tijerina fled with as many as 150 men?[96] Was another raid imminent? Did the "rebels" have access to a large cache of automatic rifles and possibly dynamite? From Michigan, Cargo first heard, erroneously, that a judge had been killed and

The armed assault on the Río Arriba County Courthouse on June 5, 1967, prompted a massive manhunt for Reies López Tijerina and other Alianza participants that featured hundreds of National Guardsmen, helicopters, and planes. Here, a National Guard tank shares the road with a New Mexican farmer on horseback and a foal. (Associated Press photograph)

the district attorney taken hostage.[97] Fearing the worse, Francis opted to call out the National Guard and its heavy equipment. By early evening, an estimated 450 men, two tanks, and a low-flying plane had all been sent to Rio Arriba County to scour a 2,500-square-mile search area. State police officers, deputy sheriffs from two counties, forest rangers, and FBI agents joined the hunt across the rugged terrain. Some searched on foot, others on horseback. In addition, a helicopter, carrying two men armed with submachine guns, scanned the area from the skies. The searchers were granted permission to shoot if necessary.[98]

Six wanted men nonetheless slipped away. Refusing to take the "bait," they walked right past the sheep pen that afternoon and past the fires of National Guard troops later that night. The six were Reies Tijerina; his eldest son, David; Juan Valdez; Moises Morales; Gerónimo Borunda, whom his friends often called "el Indio"; and Jerry Noll. Out of shape, Noll soon fell behind the pace set by Morales and Valdez, who knew the terrain. Reluctantly, the group left Noll behind; police picked him up the next day wandering in the hills about ten miles from Canjilón, looking scruffy and exhausted and still carrying Mary Leyba's tortillas.[99]

Walking in the wilderness of the high desert that first night, the rest of Tijerina's party nearly plunged over a cliff they had not seen in the dark. They also quickly realized that they had brought food but no water. Sitting in the cold and damp and too frightened to start a fire for fear that they might betray their location, they debated where they might go. Mexico, after deporting Tijerina a few years earlier, hardly seemed an option. Juan Valdez briefly pondered how he might reach Cuba but also worried about leaving behind his pregnant wife and three children. (The following day, his wife, Rosina, gave birth to their fourth child without knowing where her husband was.)

As the group continued, Valdez narrowly escaped drowning as he crossed the Chama River, still chilly and swollen with melted snow in early June. Despite this mishap, he and the others slowly made their way to Youngsville, about thirty-six miles southwest of Canjilón, where Uvaldo Velasquez, an Alianza member, lived. He welcomed his surprise visitors with food and shelter. Exhausted, they mostly felt a sense of relief to have evaded capture. Finding out that Saiz had not died compounded Valdez's relief. He was not a killer.[100]

But New Mexicans stunned by the violence concluded that the raiders were dangerous criminals threatening the social order. "The word is revolution," insisted the *Albuquerque Tribune* in a June 6 editorial that praised the massive militarized response.[101] The usually more sympathetic *Santa Fe New Mexican* sounded equally alarmed, denouncing the raid as a "vicious act of open insurrection" and Tijerina a "fanatic fomenter of civil unrest" and a "false prophet" who had led others "down a road to personal disaster."[102] District Attorney Sánchez echoed that view. Speaking before a largely nuevomexicano audience a few days after the raid, at the state convention of the American GI Forum, the district attorney faulted the land-grant leader for offering outsized promises that "duped and misled . . . our people."[103] Sánchez quickly filed multiple felony charges against the suspected raiders, ranging from conspiracy to assault and battery to two counts of first-degree kidnapping, a capital offense in New Mexico.[104] Taking no chances, Judge James Scarborough opened proceedings against some of the captured defendants later that week with an antique pistol prominently holstered to his hip.[105]

A dismayed Governor Cargo likewise condemned the raid as an unacceptable episode of aggression. "We'll see to it that these people are prosecuted, that's for damn sure," he told journalists upon arriving from Michigan. "Everyone involved at the courthouse committed a felony. If one person dies, they are all guilty."[106] After having met with Alianza officials several times and having extracted, or at least he thought, a promise to wait patiently for another meeting, the governor clearly felt deceived by Tijerina. "I made it specifically clear that I would tolerate no violence. I told [Tijerina] that if we had any violence up there I was going to prosecute him," Cargo reminded the press. "We're dealing with a person who is a little mentally unbalanced, there's no question about it," he pronounced.[107]

Still, Cargo also believed that the lieutenant governor and police officials had overreacted in his absence and managed to make matters worse. Eager to return the state to normal as fast as possible, he pulled all National Guard troops out of Rio Arriba County starting at 9 A.M. Wednesday following the Monday afternoon raid.[108] In addition, he sought intermediaries who might be able to contact Tijerina in hiding. "It's not a matter of coddling them, it's a matter of resolving this thing," he insisted.[109] The next day, however, even Cargo was ready to meet the land-grant leader mano a mano after receiving a threatening press release issued in Tijerina's name. Almost certainly written by a combative Jerry Noll the weekend before, the press release offered some chilling advice: "The officers and agents of the U.S. Government and the State Administration should realize that their families are in a vulnerable position."[110] Cargo snapped back. "If he wants to come to my house, let him. He has threatened my family," he said of the fugitive Tijerina. "I'll meet him in my front yard and he won't get a chance to explain."[111] But aside from that outburst of manly bravado, the governor quickly shifted his energies to soothing relations between activists and state officials.

This approach incensed District Attorney Sánchez. The raid pushed the simmering feud between the men to the boiling point as each blamed the other for contributing to the outbreak of violence and for reacting inappropriately afterward. Sánchez accused the governor of "holding hands" with radical extremists; Cargo countered that Sánchez's heavy-handed methods amounted to "sheer stupidity" that further riled already angry people.[112] Ironically, their intense recriminations overshadowed how similarly the two men viewed the raid. Not only did both denounce it as an intolerable episode of violence, but they also viewed Tijerina as fundamentally misguided. According to both men, anyone who inspired people into believing that they could reclaim lost land was misleading a vulnerable population. Tijerina had fooled his followers, in Sánchez's view, or was downright crazy, according to Cargo. Tijerina deserved such negative categorization, moreover, precisely because, they both agreed, the land-grant movement itself was futile.

Speaking for establishment Spanish Americans, Democratic senator Edmund Delgado of Santa Fe concurred. Using his ethnicity as a trump card, Delgado condemned not only the raid but also Cargo. By deigning to meet with Alianza members, he said, the governor had "dignified the status of this organization," which in Delgado's estimation was a big mistake. Neither Tijerina nor the Alianza deserved respect. Instead, Delgado assured the press that Tijerina and his followers were engaged in a fruitless endeavor. "Those of us who have been around here a long time and who are from old Spanish families would have made claims on that land long ago if we had thought there were any legitimate claims," he insisted.[113] Delgado was not alone. According to at least one news source, Spanish Americans interviewed on the streets in Santa Fe, Española, Albuquerque, and Las Vegas, New Mexico, were quick to label Tijerina and his followers "crackpots," "nuts," and "ignorant."[114] The raid, however, zoomed right past such dismissive sentiments and stuffy blowhards as Senator Delgado to focus national attention on years of accumulated grievances.

Alianza members praised the raid as righteous justice in motion and took advantage of the opportunity it provided to school the press. "They call us communists for trying to get the land back," Felix Martínez complained to reporters, even though, he explained, "the land was stolen from these people." Martínez also sought to convey that the true value of the land belied simple economic calculations. "The land is the mother of the people here. Without land, they are nothing," he insisted. "They are not educated. They cannot go out and get a job. Most of them don't want to, because the land is more important to them than just a piece of property. Without the land, there is nothing."[115] For his part, Chris Tijerina spun a lengthy metaphor to underscore why the loss of land cut so deep. As he explained later that summer, a man who faced continual land encroachment saw both his economic livelihood and his status within the family threatened: "Listen, let's say you have a house and you are doing okay. You have your furniture, your things around you, your way of living. Then somebody comes into your house, and maybe he has a paper from the court and maybe he has a gun or maybe he is just too smart for you, I don't know, but pretty soon he starts moving things around and telling you what to do and your wife what to do and before you know it you're out on the porch looking in." A man relegated to the metaphorical porch could still make a living, enjoy the view, and even go fishing, Chris Tijerina admitted, until someone "comes out on the porch and starts telling you how to live there too." And what about the man's wife? Maybe she kept peering through the windows to look with envy inside her former house, Chris Tijerina offered. Or worse, she started listening to those outsiders about what she should do. In either case, she undermined her husband's authority. Eventually, he concluded, proud New Mexican men had had enough.[116]

Professor Clark Knowlton sympathized with this point of view. In the immediate wake of the raid, when the attention of most of the state was focused upon capturing the fugitive raiders, Knowlton suggested again that the federal government purchase acreage as it became "available on the market and then give it to Spanish-American villagers." Only by addressing the inexorable process of land loss could the state alleviate the "tremendous feeling of injustice" that many Spanish Americans harbored. That point of view had persuaded many land-grant activists, including Tijerina, to give Knowlton a certain level of trust. Cognizant of that fact, officials from the New Mexican Office of Economic Opportunity officials flew Knowlton in from El Paso to help find the fugitive leader.[117]

With Knowlton's help, state anti-poverty workers soon got hold of people who got hold of other people who got hold of Tijerina. As a result, and much to the chagrin of police officials who continued to hunt unsuccessfully for the land-grant leader, reporter Peter Nabokov interviewed Tijerina the evening of June 7 from his hiding place in Youngsville. To Nabokov's great surprise, Tijerina began his address "with a calm historical recapitulation of the land-grant issue." Only after the reporter nudged him to concentrate on the raid itself did Tijerina begin to elaborate about the anger surrounding the cancellation of the Coyote meeting. He expressed "no regrets" for the violence.[118] He also declined to turn himself in. The land-grant leader was not apprehended until the early morning hours of Saturday, June 10. Police picked him up along with his eldest son, David, and Uvaldo Velasquez near Bernalillo, just north of Albuquerque. Law enforcement had received a tip from a gas station attendant who had seen Tijerina in Velasquez's car at a previous stop.[119]

Still, Tijerina had plenty of reason to take heart. A testament to his

After the courthouse raid, Tijerina managed to elude authorities for nearly five days. Here he stands behind chain-link fencing at the Santa Fe State Penitentiary following his arrest in the early morning of June 10, 1967. (Ray Cary photographer, *Albuquerque Journal* photograph)

popularity among some of the most marginalized sectors of New Mexican society, upon arriving in the Santa Fe jail he heard a round of cheers from other inmates: "Viva Tijerina!"[120] In a matter of days, a new celebratory corrido was making the rounds in northern New Mexico. Composed by Tijerina's longtime friend Juan Roybal, the "Corrido de Rio Arriba" praised those "Hispano Americanos" whose "hearts did not tremble" in the face of injustice. According to the song, on June 5, 1967, brave men met "to reclaim their rights" and to "answer the violence" imposed upon them. As the song's Tijerina warns, "One of these days, I will get even."[121]

Yet the song lyrics belied the sense of doubt or regret that some participants experienced. Even though the men who had gathered in Tobias Leyba's shed shared a determination to arrest Sánchez, they had debated exactly how to proceed. As Juan Valdez recalled, Reies Tijerina wanted everyone to cover their faces, a suggestion that offended Valdez. "I asked . . . why should we wear masks—we were land-grant heirs, not a bunch of robbers," he wrote. "I asked [Tijerina] what we had to be ashamed of."[122] In the end, only Tijerina covered his face with a handkerchief that afternoon. Yet, as Valdez recollected, the Alianza leader won a more important point: he convinced everyone to carry a weapon. Listening to Tijerina's assurances that the raid would be peaceful, Valdez later insisted, ranked among the biggest mistakes of his life. "But I don't blame him," Valdez continued about Tijerina. "After all, I was old enough to know better than to go to the courthouse with a pistol." Again, stressing his own culpability, Valdez elaborated, "Every time I think about [Nick] Saiz—about what happened—how he has suffered . . . I want to spin around and kick myself in the ass."[123] As Valdez recalled, the task of entering the building fell to him because no one volunteered for that job, not even the Alianza president. Valdez, fearful of getting shot and knowing that his wife was about to give birth, did not wish to be the first one inside the courthouse either. After someone put forward his name, however, everyone else apparently latched onto it as a good choice. "It happened so fast I did not have a chance to say no," Valdez later related.[124]

Spur-of-the-moment decisions characterized the raid. Years later, Baltazar Martínez explained that he and Baltazar Apodaca never heard Tijerina's order to clear out. Suddenly aware that they had been left behind, they improvised the taking of hostages in order to ensure their escape.[125] Martínez also improvised in deciding to show the captives to his aunt in Tierra Amarilla before leaving town. Fernanda Martínez (Felix's mother) stood as proof that not all women opposed the use of violence. Her succinct advice regarding the fate of the hostages: "Hang them." Upon hearing those words, Calloway, the kidnapped reporter, recalled the warning a professor friend had shared with him just before he moved to northern New Mexico: "Remember you are going to a conquered land. And you are the invader."[126]

At the same time, the raid reverberated with an odd dissonance that defied such a neat divide. It encompassed both destructive acts of violence and moments of courtly behavior. Baltazar Martínez, whom observers described as "the *loco*," the wild or crazy one, among the participants that day, was the master of both. Before leaving the Tierra Amarilla area, Martínez eagerly fired upon unmanned police cars and ransacked the contents of their trunks for weapons. Yet the young man was no ordinary thief. Discovering Jaramillo's car needed gas on the way to Canjilón, the armed Martínez could have demanded a fill-up at the gas station. Instead, without money himself, he coolly took $20 out of Calloway's wallet and then returned the change.[127] His comrade in arms, Apodaca, fired at Calloway twice yet fondly remembered the reporter "as a very nice" man who "told the police not to bother me."[128] For his part, Juan Valdez, after shooting Saiz, then directed the loading of the injured lawman into an ambulance. He also intervened when another raider threatened to finish off the wounded officer as he lay on the ground.[129]

Although the raiders hoped to arrest a single man, Sánchez, they ended up confronting other nuevomexicanos, including land-grant heirs, with whom they held no particular quarrel. In Rio Arriba County, where law enforcement and county government jobs offered some of the most secure wages around, the raiders knew most of the workers in the courthouse, and courthouse employees knew the raiders. County Clerk Cipriano Padilla, for example, recognized his longtime friend Tobias Leyba among the raiders. "Cómo estás?" he instinctively asked even as he saw a handgun pointed at him.[130] For his part, Eulogio Salazar, who was shot twice, had signed an Alianza petition eight years before. In fact, many nuevomexicanos sympathized with the Alianza's aims and with its reading of history but rejected violence as a tactic. That group included the injured Saiz. As he later told a reporter, "I think that these people lost their lands by not being educated and that the U.S. government should have recognized that these lands were given these people just the way Indians were given their reservations," adding, "The overall goal . . . I can identify with, but not with the way they went about it."[131]

As for the absent Sánchez, fortune smiled on him that day. After his planned arrest, the raiders intended to put Sánchez in a small shed and, as one raider put it, "leave him there for a couple hours to sweat it out and then we would let him go."[132] Given how high emotions were running, however, Sánchez may have faced a more perilous fate. While a fugitive, Tijerina suggested that his followers had also considering moving Sánchez from place to place until the DA died.[133]

Others may have planned a more immediate end. Although in utero during the courthouse raid, Alex Leyba, the youngest child of Maria and Tobias Leyba, disclosed that he had grown up watching the slow decay of a rope that dangled from a tall, sturdy branch of a nearby tree. According to family lore, he said, that rope was meant to serve as a noose for DA Sánchez.[134]

The fact is, the men who took up arms that day gave little thought to the long-term consequences of their actions. Seen as fearless gunslingers by friends and foes alike, they mostly wanted to bring attention to the land-grant issue. Ironically, as much as Tijerina liked to be in control, and as much as he received credit for the raid later, events spun out of control as the raiders made a series of impromptu decisions that fortunately cost no lives.

In the short term, the raiders did spend time behind bars. Among those taken into custody, only Patsy Tijerina was swiftly released; no charges were filed against her.[135] Law enforcement apprehended most suspects quickly at home. Juan Valdez and Moises Morales both turned themselves in a few days after Tijerina.[136] The last one to surrender, almost exactly one month later, was a young Baltazar Martínez. He had spent the intervening weeks in and around the Canjilón area, often visiting his mother's house for supplies. After Governor Cargo personally posted a $500 reward for information leading to Martínez's whereabouts, his mother collected the money with her son's cooperation.[137] In a surreal twist, Martínez then used the money to pay for his wedding to Juan Valdez's sister and invited the governor. Cargo declined to attend.[138]

Denied bail at Sánchez's urging, those facing charges stemming from the raid spent weeks, and in Valdez's case months, in jail as they awaited trial. Although police in the immediate aftermath of the raid rounded up twenty suspects, the state soon reduced the number of defendants to ten plus Reies López Tijerina. These men faced charges that ranged from first-degree kidnapping, a capital offense, to assault to false imprisonment. The multiple charges and multiple defendants made the legal process slow and unwieldy. For men trying to support their families, it was also extremely costly. One Alianza appeal pointed out that, combined, those facing criminal prosecution were fathers to 113 children.[139] Despite such requests for donations, raid participants complained that they never received any financial assistance for their legal problems, whereas Tijerina presumably did. The injustice prompted some to break from Tijerina permanently.[140]

In the end, however, only Tijerina faced prison time. In November 1968, Baltazar Apodaca was ruled incompetent to stand trial.[141] During the summer of 1969, Baltazar Martínez and Juan Valdez both had their day in court. Martínez was found innocent by reason of insanity. Valdez was found guilty of assault with intent to injure and maim.[142] Shortly before Valdez was about to enter prison in the spring of 1973, however, Governor Bruce King (Cargo's successor) issued him a full pardon.[143] After spending close to $20,000 to prosecute three raid defendants, the state decided against prosecuting the rest.[144]

Recalling those years, Rosina Valdez, Juan's wife, offered bitter memories of her husband's deep involvement in the Alianza. "We suffered a lot," she said in an understatement. She never fully understood, as she put it, "the anger that [Valdez] carried in his heart." Declining to join the Alianza herself, she knew in the days before the courthouse raid that her husband "was up to something, but I didn't know what." Nor did she ask.[145] Instead, she tried to exert her influence more subtly by taking advantage of the time that she spent helping her husband improve his reading skills. Initially, Juan Valdez recalled, he and his wife together would read the newspaper, which was filled with stories about the Alianza and which allowed him to keep up with events. But after the raid, he recalled, his wife handed him the Bible instead. When he asked why, his wife only laughed and told him that maybe he needed to learn other lessons besides just how to read.[146]

The repercussions of the raid continued to reverberate far beyond the homes of the individual participants, however. As an ethnic leader and a gunslinger, Tijerina hit the big time in the wake of the raid. He grabbed the opportunity to widen his sphere of influence. The Alianza leader had always argued that he, as leader of the land-grant movement, spoke on behalf of all Mexican Americans. Now, the raid became a springboard for him to speak to the nation as a whole about race, discrimination, and poverty more broadly. While other land-grant activists waited for meaningful change on the ground in New Mexico, Tijerina's crusade went national.

9

The Chicano

On May 2, 1968, about 600 people gathered to hear Coretta Scott King launch a nationwide anti-poverty campaign from the Memphis motel balcony where her husband had been killed the month before. The Poor People's Campaign called for Americans from across the country to start marching toward Washington, D.C., where they would gather on the National Mall and live in an impromptu shantytown called Resurrection City in order to dramatize the plight of the poor. At the conclusion of the widow's remarks, the gathered crowd turned into a procession and started marching. Three people stood at the front: Ralph Abernathy, the new head of the Southern Christian Leadership Conference (SCLC) in the wake of King's death; Linda Aranaydo, a young Native American activist; and Reies López Tijerina.[1]

For all its haphazardness, the June 1967 courthouse raid placed Tijerina firmly in the mix of 1960s politics. The Alianza president not only met Martin Luther King Jr. several times before his assassination but also shared the stage with numerous Black Power advocates. Indeed, Tijerina fit the profile of a 1960s race radical surprisingly well. Whether a Valle de Paz or a República de San Joaquín, his version of an ideal society always had been one removed from white-majority control. In storming the courthouse, Tijerina had also demonstrated unparalleled—and unprecedented—militancy during an era known for it. Not until 1969 did

Red Power activists occupy Alcatraz. Not until 1973 did Native Americans exchange gunfire with federal agents at the Second Battle of Wounded Knee. "While we're talking revolution, this cat is making it," a Black Power activist admiringly noted about Tijerina shortly after the raid.[2] "A Mexican Malcolm X," cheered *The Movement*, an alternative publication out of San Francisco.[3] Events in New Mexico captured the attention of a handful of liberal politicians too. But in the months that followed, Tijerina concluded that moderation had permanently ceded ground to militancy. "The death of Dr. King was the end of the peaceful approach and non-violence," Tijerina explained to a newspaper reporter days after King's assassination. "His role was great and very important, but now his followers and the whole world will believe this government cannot be changed without being destroyed totally."[4]

That uncompromising attitude, coupled with his daring tactics, earned Tijerina recognition as a new kind of ethnic leader, one of four recognized "horsemen" of the Chicano movement. The word "Chicano" itself indicated the movement's break with traditional Mexican American politics. Most commonly understood as a shorthand version of "*mexicano*," the word "Chicano" had been popular among some Mexican Americans for much of the twentieth century, but as an in-group term. Now it became a point of public pride. Likewise, the Chicano movement shifted political action to the public sphere. Marches and sit-ins replaced an earlier generation's emphasis on lawsuits and loyalty to the United States. Within this broad and multifaceted movement for equal rights, economic progress, and cultural recognition, Cesar Chavez concentrated on union politics, Corky Gonzales primarily on youth and urban woes, and José Angel Gutiérrez on how to wrench power electorally from the two-party system. Tijerina meanwhile introduced an entire generation to the long presence of Spanish-speaking people in the present-day Southwest, providing inspirational fodder to young Mexican Americans across the country as they reimagined their place in U.S. society. Although personally he preferred the ethnic identifier Indo-Hispano, Tijerina's exploits received constant coverage in Chicano movement publications.

Yet even as Tijerina easily slipped into this new role of Chicano movement hero, he clung to his fundamental view of the world and of his place in it. "To be radical is to grasp matters at their root," Marx once wrote. "But for man the root is man himself."[5] For Tijerina, that meant a radical politics rooted in his religious beliefs rather than in Marx's humanism. Tijerina's interpretation of the Bible guided his interactions with potential coalition partners. More than ever, he had reason to believe that he had been divinely appointed to lead a special crusade. These tendencies, however, undermined his grand political visions. At the moment of his greatest fame, the Alianza leader pushed away potential friends and alienated former allies. He never managed to navigate the gulf between being an orator preaching onstage and being an organizer working with others.

For all these reasons, as a Chicano, Tijerina rode triumphant for only two years.

BLACK AND BROWN, TOGETHER AND APART

In late August 1967, Tijerina spotted Martin Luther King Jr. at the airport in Chicago. King was just leaving the conference that Tijerina had arrived to attend, the National Conference on New Politics, a gathering of some 2,000 Left-leaning activists looking for alternatives to establishment politics. Starry-eyed, Tijerina after receiving his invitation could not contain his amazement at the company he was about to keep. "They have reserved a seat with me right there on the platform with Martin Luther King and the others!" he gushed.[6] The presence of King at the airport, however, punctured that expectation. Nonetheless, Tijerina recollected making the best of the opportunity. Rushing over to speak with the civil rights leader, he wrote in his memoir, "I suggested to him a coalition between the brown people and the black people. And the Indians and the poor whites. And he said it was high time."[7] In fact, although Tijerina surmised that he planted the seed that became the Poor People's Campaign, King had broached the topic with fellow members of the SCLC earlier that month.[8]

The brief cordial interchange between the two men at the airport nonetheless highlighted the potential for unity that the Chicago gathering was designed to foster. Attendees were deeply dissatisfied with the "old politics" as represented by the administration of President Lyndon B. Johnson.[9] Although the Civil Rights Act in 1964 had ended de jure segregation and the Voting Rights Act in 1965 had removed legal barriers to the franchise, these victories came only after civil rights activists had been beaten, bombed, and even killed, experiences that prompted many to question the goal of integration as well as the sanctity of the ballot. Similarly, continued U.S. military intervention in Southeast Asia despite massive peace protests had disheartened antiwar activists. Summarizing the range and depth of discontent at the New Politics conference, Martin Luther King Jr. in his speech before the gathering had stressed the need to fight not one but "three evils," namely, "the sickness of racism, excessive materialism, and militarism."[10] Notably, on each count, Tijerina had every right to declare, "*¡Presente!*"

Despite the uniqueness of his own political journey, the Alianza leader arrived in Chicago deeply in sync with the priorities that King outlined. As a preacher, Tijerina had railed against consumer society and rejected Cold War priorities as misguided. As a land-grant leader, he had blasted discrimination as one of the legacies of conquest. His anticolonial analysis, in turn, directly contributed to his opposition toward the war in Vietnam. Speaking before a crowd of nuevomexicanos just a few months before in Albuquerque, Tijerina had thundered, "They are sending your children to die in Vietnam and won't give you a decent living here. They have attempted to destroy your culture, now they want you to destroy another culture. They are not satisfied with having stolen all the land from us here, they send your boys to a bloody death so that they can take more land away from the poor people over there."[11]

Tijerina's participation in the courthouse raid alone, however, secured his invitation. Conference organizers knew little about Tijerina beyond this one incident. Julian Bond, a veteran civil rights activist and one of the main organizers of the New Politics conference, was not even sure if Tijerina spoke English. Committed to coalition building, Bond asked Maria Varela, one of two Latinas in SNCC (the Student Nonviolent Coordinating Committee), a civil rights organization that Bond had helped found, if she might attend the conference too and help Tijerina navigate what might be unfamiliar surroundings. The child of a Mexican immigrant father and an Irish American mother, Varela acquiesced to this request, even though she described her Spanish as "lousy."[12]

As both she and Bond discovered, Tijerina needed little assistance in making his presence known. "The black man is marching in the streets," Tijerina told the New Politics crowd upon his arrival. "You think we should sit down and relax?"[13] While in Chicago, Tijerina focused his attention on gaining more clout for the fifty or so Spanish-speaking attendees. The conference location in Chicago, which boasted a significant Mexican American and Puerto Rican population, guaranteed that representatives from both groups were there. Yet none had been involved in the conference planning, they complained. Quickly emerging as a leader of this group, Tijerina also discovered that even the most basic facts about Mexican Americans, and about other Spanish-speaking people in the country, remained a mystery to most other activists. At least one African American organizer of the New Politics conference admitted as much. "I didn't know there were six million of them," he noted, implicitly suggesting that such a large population merited more attention.[14] Tijerina was also surprised to discover that some African Americans considered him white.[15] He took the opportunity to offer some enlightenment. "The situation of the Mexicans and Puerto Ricans is similar to that of the Negro people, but it is not the same. We have to fight for the right to speak our language. Even the demand of the Puerto Rican for [island] independence is different from the Mexicans' demands," he patiently explained. "But we must unite . . . with the Negro, the Indian and the 'good Anglos' to improve our condition."[16]

That message of unity appealed to Varela, who, although not needed as a translator, spent time with Tijerina during the conference learning about the land-grant movement. Only twenty-seven, she already boasted a long activist career that took her from a Catholic social justice organization called Young Christian Students to SNCC.[17] As a SNCC staff member, she fully supported the organization's embrace of Black Power by 1966, which she later defined as "black people taking leadership to change their communities." While on the staff, Varela taught herself photography in order to document black empowerment frame by frame. She also spearheaded a literacy program that featured educational materials focused on the African American experience.[18] In May 1966, when a minority of SNCC members at a conference in upstate New York, mostly newcomers and troublemakers in Varela's recollection, voted—at 2 A.M.—to expel all whites from the organization, Varela did not consider the vote legitimate. Nor did she consider herself white. Admittedly, some people associated with SNCC did, however, a phenomenon that ran counter to Varela's more inclusive vision of racial justice.[19] "The same racism that brutalizes your people brutalizes our people," she wrote a friend and colleague after he ranked fighting black oppression a top priority at the New Politics conference.[20]

Impressed with parallels between the plight of land-poor New Mexicans and land-poor African Americans in the South, a week later Varela dashed off a letter to "Señor Tijerina" to address how to let more African Americans know about the land-grant movement. She suggested that an article about the Alianza appear in a forthcoming national SNCC newsletter. Ideally, Varela wrote, this article would point out that both Mexican Americans and African Americans did not own the land they worked and that both groups had been targets of racial violence. Varela also suggested that Tijerina mention his meeting with Elijah Muhammad back in 1962. She signed off with the words "*su hermana*," indicating that she saw herself as a sister in struggle to Tijerina.[21] Although the formal Alianza reply suggested a relationship more akin to parent and child—"I am so glad to know that you are a true fighter and a very brave girl," the letter began—it included an invitation that Varela come visit Albuquerque and "spend some time among your people."[22] Already contemplating her next move after SNCC, Varela did just that.

Yet Tijerina's commitment to coalition building was far more conditional than Varela's. After literally chasing King down in the airport, for example, he put a stunning qualification upon King's participation and the participation of other black people at an upcoming Alianza convention. "Of course, we are only going to admit Negroes when Martin Luther King speaks," Tijerina insisted. "Following that speech, they [African Americans] have to get out because the convention belongs to our *raza*," ("*raza*" being another word for Mexican American).[23] This forecast failed on both counts. King never came, and no African American who did was ever asked to leave. Still, Tijerina's comment cast any alliance with African Americans as a matter of expediency at best. African Americans and "his people" stood to benefit from "moral support and a mutual push" toward justice, Tijerina conceded. That is why he had renewed his acquaintance with Elijah Muhammad while in Chicago, he explained. Otherwise, "I don't care about their ideas or their cause."[24]

This utilitarian stance directly clashed with Tijerina's impressive efforts before the courthouse raid to cultivate African American allies, efforts that had secured the presence of Alton Davis at the first Alianza convention and that had prompted him to seek a meeting with Elijah Muhammad in the first place. What changed? At first glance, very little. Tijerina still recognized a common enemy in white oppression. He certainly still recognized the benefit of tapping into a level of political influence that far surpassed anything that he could muster. Encapsulating these differences, by 1967 Martin Luther King Jr., as the most famous civil rights leader in the country, had met with three U.S. presidents, whereas Tijerina had never met one. Such disproportionate power, however, also prompted a post-raid Tijerina to worry that the movement he led might become a subsidiary of the larger and more established African American freedom struggle. He was not alone in nursing such concerns.[25] In addition, Tijerina still confronted substantial prejudice on the part of some Alianza members. "Negroes were brought to this country as slaves and have no land here, so they have absolutely no business in the Alianza," one Alianza member later complained.[26] Consequently, a post-raid Tijerina constantly weighed the advantages of working with African Americans against competing reasons to keep his distance.

His Bible-based beliefs directly informed his calculations. In early October 1967, Tijerina gave a speech at St. John's College in Santa Fe that outlined his conception of race as a fundamental category of allegiance. Speaking before a mostly sympathetic Anglo-American crowd curious about land-grant matters, Tijerina compared Indo-Hispanos, his "new breed," to an old "breed," the ancient Hebrews. Metaphorically, the first group was a naive child compared to the latter, Tijerina explained, and Spanish Americans were less sophisticated than Anglos, who, relatively speaking, were young adults. Extending the analogy, the Alianza leader went so far as to assign theoretical ages to each group: if the Spanish American was like a child of four and a half, then the Anglo was twenty-five and "the Jew" sixty. He then proposed that only a "well-developed" race could have masterminded so much land thievery, which led him to announce that Thomas B. Catron, leader of the Santa Fe Ring, "was a Jew."[27] That Catron had attended services at Holy Faith Episcopal Church in Santa Fe was entirely beside the point.[28] Tijerina wished to convey that the Jewish people, as an ancient "breed," were particularly wily.

Although some observers at the time generously hypothesized that Tijerina's awkward command of the English language led him to misspeak, the St. John speech accurately portrayed Tijerina's views.[29] He tended to divide the world's population into distinct "breeds," endlessly jockeying for power across centuries and continents. In 1967, Tijerina responded to criticism of the speech by sharing his conviction that the wandering Jew, embittered after being kicked out of Spain, decided to collude with the aggressive Anglo in New Mexico.[30] The blatant anti-Semitism that Tijerina manifested later in life clearly built on these earlier ideas and biases. (In 2007, Tijerina reprised a similar argument when he tried to convince me that the Jewish people sought global domination. Kicked out of Israel in 70 CE, and then kicked out of Spain in 1492, he explained, they were looking for revenge.)[31]

Tijerina regularly quoted Isaiah 13:14 to support his analysis. According to the passage from the Old Testament, during the last days, the Lord will show his rage, and then "shall every man turn to his own people and flee every one to his own land." No less than when he was a preacher or a prophet, Tijerina remained fixated on God's relationship with humankind as mediated through the land. Just as blacks already had their own continent, by which he presumably meant Africa, Tijerina told the Santa Fe crowd that the Southwest was home to Indo-Hispanos.[32] The comment implied that African Americans might one day return to a place that few of them had ever been. When paired with Isaiah 13:14, it also hinted at a foreboding future. The book of Isaiah promised salvation but only after a time of great tribulation and destruction, a woeful scenario that made division among groups inevitable, as the verse captured. To Tijerina, moreover, this pending doomsday made achieving unity within each group (*la unión de un pueblo*) all the more important. As early as March 1966, Tijerina had posited different "ages" for racial groups while also predicting the breakdown of humanity at world's end.[33] On occasion, Tijerina promoted the flip side of this thinking by suggesting that Indo-Hispanos might serve as peacemakers between blacks and whites.[34] In either case, however, he theorized race as a fundamental and unchanging source of division.

Nevertheless, scholars understandably have pointed to the Alianza convention that took place just three weeks later as a moment of unprecedented unity among 1960s activists and as evidence of Tijerina's interest in building coalitions.[35] In October 1967, Tijerina warmly welcomed about twenty-five African American from across the country as well as a smattering of Native American activists to the fifth Alianza convention in Albuquerque. Thanks in part to Varela's behind-the-scenes efforts, five high-ranking SNCC staff members came from the Deep South to attend the gathering.[36] Hailing all the way from Mississippi, a dashiki-clad Ralph Featherstone of SNCC led the crowd in a rousing chant of "*Poder negro* [Black Power]!" He also held up a sign that read, "Che is alive and hiding in Tierra Amarilla," a reference to the Latin American revolutionary slain in Bolivia earlier that month. For his part, Maulana Karenga (a Swahili name that replaced his original moniker, Ronald McKinley Everett), the founder of the Los Angeles–based Black Power group US (as in "us vs. them"), delivered his speech entirely in Spanish, a gesture that gave weight to his message about a common sense of purpose. "Somos juntos. Somos hombres de color. Tenemos una nueva misión [We are together. We are men of color. We have a new mission]," Karenga proclaimed. Karenga and other US members headed an African American entourage from Southern California that included a young Angela Davis.[37] When Tijerina's Hopi ally

Building on early efforts to forge strong relationships with Native Americans, Tijerina spent time with Thomas Banyacya, a Hopi leader, at the fifth Alianza conference in October 1967. Banyacya wore a concha belt that reflected native craftwork. Tijerina tried, perhaps less successfully, to capture ethnic authenticity in his choice of clothing too. (Center for Southwest Research, University of New Mexico, Albuquerque)

Thomas Banyacya took the stage, he condemned the Bureau of Indian Affairs. In another gesture of unity, a Hopi elder who accompanied Banyacya sprinkled sacred cornmeal as a blessing for all.[38]

At the convention, Tijerina embraced the message of solidarity as well as the theme of ethnic pride. After asking his fellow Alianza members to don traditional ethnic garb, Tijerina showed up on the second day of the convention wearing a ruffled white shirt, bright waist sash, and flared black pants with a satiny ribbon running along each side. If the flamboyant result appeared more evocative of a Latin dancer than a rural nuevomexicano, the attempt fit the times. Tijerina's clothing was meant to complement Featherstone's African dashiki and the Native American turquoise jewelry that Banyayca wore. In each case, the nod to ethnic culture indicated an understanding that many 1960s power advocates shared, whether they sought black, yellow, brown, or red power, namely, that reclaiming cultural pride and dignity was the first strike against white oppression. Swept up in the moment, Tijerina praised his guests as "brothers fighting the same enemy" and denounced Anglo-Americans as "murderers, thieves, and devils." The choice of the last word was particularly instructive. "God has given us a sacred fight that we must carry on," Tijerina announced. "We are going to make history."[39]

A veritable who's who of Chicano movement participants endorsed this call to arms. Tijerina's guests at the convention also included about twenty-five Mexican American activists from across the Southwest. Each spoke admiringly of the Alianza leader and the forces of change he represented. From Texas, José Angel Gutiérrez vowed to help take back the land by force if necessary.[40] Gutiérrez had recently helped found the Mexican American Youth Organization, a student group that embraced a plan for "revolution" in the southern portion of the state.[41] Corky Gonzales likewise spoke of imminent revolution, one "sparked by the Tierra Amarilla raid."[42] He had already famously declared that Chicanos would "rather die in Tierra Amarilla than in Vietnam."[43] For his part, Bert Corona of California, who had started labor organizing in the 1930s, spoke from the vantage point of experience. He viewed the moment as ripe with political possibility. "The cause of Tierra Amarilla is the cause of our people," Corona told the crowd. "We must take advantage of this and organize our young people."[44]

Fittingly, the gathering concluded with a group of male leaders signing a pact of "Peace, Harmony, and Mutual Assistance." Tijerina likely organized it: no women were invited to this closing ceremony.[45] The Alianza leader, moreover, almost assuredly drafted the document. In a direct echo of the Treaty of Guadalupe Hidalgo, the pact gathered signatures "in the Name of God Almighty." The document also invoked "the Divine Law of the GOD of JUSTICE" and predicted "the holy JUDGMENT of GOD against the United States." In addition, the pact captured Tijerina's long-standing preoccupation with the end times. "In case a nuclear war should erupt upon this earth," the pact read, the signers "SOLEMNLY promise to assist each other."[46] The pact seemed a perfect culmination to a gathering that had brought so many different people together.

Yet appearances could be deceiving. The pact actually favored the narrowest realm of cooperation. It endorsed coming to each other's aid only once and under the most extraordinary circumstances, the aforementioned nuclear war.[47] Signatories vowed "to respect the Faith, [and] the CULTURE of each other" and "not to make false propaganda of any kind against each other, either by SPEECH or by WRITING." They also promised to keep the lines of communication open. But there was no commitment to ongoing collective action. "We signed that treaty but that was for the future, to assure that we would be at peace with those people," Tijerina clarified. Because few Native Americans attended the conference, "those people" referred primarily to African Americans. Regarding the present, he continued, "I'm not sure it is wise to be tied up with them."[48]

The statement accurately captured Tijerina's doubts about allying with African Americans in the wake of the raid. However much he was willing to work together with African Americans in the present moment, Tijerina always worried what the future might hold. Like the hardest-nosed diplomat, he assumed that peace and harmony with other groups depended upon first securing the safety and protection of his own people.

Perhaps that is why, in contrast to all these constant calibrations, an easy rapport characterized Tijerina's relations with Chicano activists—at least initially.

THE TRIUMPHANT HORSEMAN

Just one week after the Alianza's October convention, Tijerina traveled to El Paso to join Chicanos and Chicanas protesting a set of federal hearings on the status of Mexican Americans. Hosted by a new White House group called the Inter-agency Committee on Mexican American Affairs, the hearings marked an attempt by the Johnson administration to get ahead of burgeoning ethnic group discontent nationally. The hearing provided a forum for 1,000 experts and activists to present their concerns to federal officials regarding different aspects of Mexican American life, from educational opportunities to job prospects to housing conditions.[49] The head of the Inter-agency Committee, Vicente Ximenes, avoided inviting anyone too controversial or confrontational. Years before, as a high-ranking American GI Forum member, Ximenes had sent fifty dollars on behalf of the forum to a young Alfonso Sánchez to support his land-grant investigations.[50] Sympathy for the land-grant movement then, however, did not extend to the Alianza leader now. The nation's best-known Mexican American militant did not make the invite list.

Nevertheless, the plight of New Mexicans featured prominently in the official testimony. Speaking just a few months after the raid, several attendees exuded sympathy. They agreed that a receding land base was threatening centuries-old cultural traditions such as wood carving and wool weaving.[51] Another invitee complained that the Spanish language was devalued in New Mexico.[52] Echoing Alianza grievances, still another directly targeted an imperious U.S. Forest Service. "It is not uncommon for the native population to see the forest ranger in his olive drab uniform as an American occupational trooper guarding the spoils of the Mexican-American war," offered one labor advocate.[53] For his part, Professor Clark Knowlton essentially channeled Tijerina by once more suggesting land redistribution as a solution to unrest in New Mexico. Lands that had already passed into private ownership were probably gone forever, he admitted, but why not distribute national forest property to impoverished northern New Mexicans?[54]

While that suggestion went nowhere fast, the federal hearings overall showcased a revolution in governmental attitudes. For the first time, officials openly acknowledged the complaints of land-grant activists. To be sure, Secretary of Agriculture Orville Freeman's acknowledgment first reduced nuevomexicanos to a series of cultural inadequacies. "There is pathetic poverty, great ignorance, unfortunately, emotional unreasonableness too, but the Forest Service, I am sure, is big enough and tolerant enough to live with that and to help people who need help," Freeman stated.[55] Nonetheless, the next day's headlines noted the shift: "Farm Chief Backs Views of the Spanish."[56] In his closing remarks to the hearings, Vice President Hubert Humphrey bestowed unprecedented legitimacy on the land-grant cause. The Mexican American suffered "historic injustices because his forefathers were driven from their Spanish and Mexican land grants," Humphrey stated. "Yet most of these same people have been American citizens for generations—many of them since well before the Humphreys arrived from Scotland."[57] Before the hearings ended, two Democrats, Senator Robert F. Kennedy of Massachusetts and Congressman Thomas G. Morris of New Mexico, independently made preliminary inquiries about the possibility of conducting an investigation into land-grant matters.[58] As the hearings in El Paso evinced, the courthouse raid forced at least some government leaders to pay attention to land-grant matters.

Tijerina's fellow protesters in El Paso were paying attention too. They drew up a plan of political priorities that specifically called for "the strong enforcement" of the Treaty of Guadalupe Hidalgo. Like their counterparts at the New Politics conference, these Mexican Americans, who either had refused to attend the formal federal hearings or had not been invited in the first place, were deeply frustrated with the pace of social change.

The "Plan de la Raza Unida" stood as a transitional document between the old style of ethnic politics that had emphasized working within the system and the more confrontational politics of the Chicano movement. Thus, the plan professed respect for "constitutional democracy" but also warned that "the time of subjugation, exploitation and abuse of human rights of La Raza in the United States is hereby ended forever."[59] In general, signers were moving toward what Ignacio García argued was the defining characteristic of the Chicano movement: a rejection of an earlier generation's "liberal agenda" that had emphasized education, patriotism, and a faith in government reform.[60] By that measure alone, Tijerina made a terrific Chicano. As leader of the Alianza, he had routinely criticized public schooling, condemned U.S. foreign policy, and rejected the War on Poverty, Johnson's liberal crowning achievement, as a poor substitute for the land loss that really ailed nuevomexicanos.

Nevertheless, since the Chicano movement's heyday, some scholars have emphasized how Tijerina and his politics diverged from the mainstream of the movement overall. He was middle-aged in a movement dominated by youth. He dared to take pride in a Spanish inheritance, whereas movement participants sought to recapture an indigenous past. Most important, neither his narrow focus on land grants nor his preacher past had much to do with the dominant cultural nationalist thrust of the movement, the argument goes.[61] Specifically, as cultural nationalists, Chicano movement participants hoped to foster cultural pride and ethnic unity as the first steps to obtaining political liberation. They questioned the cost of assimilation and sought to recapture their own history. A closer look at Tijerina's life, however, shows just how neatly his activism reverberated with these priorities. Even before he led the Alianza, he had dreamed of living apart from the white world. He had promoted the use of the Spanish language and taken pride in his Mexican heritage. As noted, he had advocated "la unión" of his people. He had mined Spanish and Mexican history on behalf of land-grant justice.

That history, moreover, greatly mattered to many young Chicanos and Chicanas questioning their place in U.S. society. For them, the courthouse raid sparked a moment of profound revelation. By publicizing the land-grant cause and, therefore, the long presence of Spanish-speaking people in the United States, the courthouse raid presented them with a radical shift in perspective, an entirely new way of seeing themselves, even if they lacked ties to a land grant. Tijerina's actions made them aware of a history that they had never seen in any textbook. As Salomón Baldenegro, from

Tucson, Arizona, recalled, "My generation . . . grew up in the 1950s and early 1960s, when American society viewed Americans of Mexican descent as foreigners and there was a concerted campaign by society, particularly the schools, to make us feel inferior and treat us as interlopers in our own land." But Tijerina, he contended, changed all that. "By documenting and publicizing the land-grant issue and the dynamics surrounding it, Reies brought home the point, and emphatically so . . . that we are not interlopers or foreigners."[62] The excitement and emotion guaranteed that news of the raid traveled "like wildfire in the (Chicano) movement," recalled Moctezuma Esparza, snapping his fingers. "We heard it like that!"[63]

The raid, moreover, exemplified Tijerina's willingness to risk his life for what he believed. Within this cultural nationalist movement, it ranked unparalleled as a display of manly courage. Not coincidentally, a central movement trope celebrated an idealized *familia*, that is, one headed by a strong male father figure.[64] Notwithstanding troubles in his own family, a broader public could see Tijerina exemplify the role of patriarch. The violence of the courthouse raid also distinguished him from the pacifist Cesar Chavez. After the farmworkers' grape strike commenced in 1965, "*la huelga* [the strike]" metamorphized into "*la causa*," a point of pride and protest for many Mexican Americans, whether they came from farmworker families or not. Yet other Chicano movement activists defended the right to self-protection. "How can one guarantee complete non-violence when one lives in a completely VIOLENT country?" asked one Chicana activist. "With the violence committed against Raza, I cannot stand by and relinquish my right to violence when I may see my neighbors and friends beaten."[65] Accordingly, a series of corridos praised Tijerina's bravery for leading an assault on the courthouse. In movement circles, he earned comparison to two generals of the Mexican Revolution, Pancho Villa and Emiliano Zapata, who had defended the rights of the poor. The controversial Villa had also led an armed invasion of New Mexico in 1916.[66]

Tijerina's fiery oratory added to his popularity. He expressed the anger and frustration that many Chicano movement participants felt toward majority society. During the early years of the Alianza, Tijerina had carefully cloaked his most incendiary comments in Spanish. After the raid, however, he no longer bothered to take even this small step to hide his sharp critique of Anglo-American society. More confrontational than ever, he started to use the term "self-proclaimed angels" to refer derogatively to white people in general. Here he borrowed from a story about a sixth-century pope. Supposedly Pope Gregory I had been struck by the fair complexions of a group of blond slaves from the British Isles, all tribal Angles (an ethnic group whose later merger with the Saxons gave rise to the term Anglo-Saxon). These Angles, he supposedly said, looked like angels.[67] In Tijerina's version, however, the angelic status was a profound lie, for Anglos were not angels at all but devils who promoted the evils of racism and discrimination. Trying out another insulting metaphor, during the fifth Alianza convention, Tijerina had compared U.S. district judge Howard C. Bratton to a vampire who was "using the law to drink blood and humiliate our race." In response, Bratton slapped a contempt of court charge on Tijerina and, for good measure, on Jerry Noll too, for violating his order to refrain from speaking in public about their upcoming federal trial.[68]

Tijerina's tremendous popularity helped him weather a series of setbacks that soon followed. First, in November 1967, Tijerina, Noll, and two other Alianza members stood trial in Bratton's court on multiple charges stemming from their participation in the Echo Amphitheater occupation the year before. The trial took place in Las Cruces, in the southern part of the state and far from the Alianza's main base of support.[69] Sidestepping even the best efforts of his own lawyer to direct his comments, a defiant Tijerina tried mightily on the witness stand to make the trial a referendum on land-grant injustice.[70] But Judge Bratton was having none of it. The question of land rights fell outside the purview of the proceedings, he instructed the jury. "We are not trying any land titles, like whether the Treaty of Guadalupe Hidalgo applies to the Echo Amphitheater campground area," he insisted.[71]

Not surprisingly, in light of the location, the judge's instruction, and the evidence presented, which included television film footage of the confrontation between alianciastas and forest rangers, the jury found all five defendants guilty of felony assault and of converting a federal vehicle for private use.[72] That December, Tijerina received a two-year prison term, while Gerald Wayne Barnes, aka Jerry Noll, in light of his past criminal history, received a three-year sentence. The other men received much lighter sentences of between sixty days and six months.[73] Given that the accused faced between three to twenty-six years behind bars and thousands of dollars in fines, the outcome could have been a lot worse. Nevertheless, a displeased Tijerina announced, "If it's tried again, I'm going to direct it."[74] He remained out on bond as he appealed the conviction, ready to resume his triumphant ride.

Instead, Tijerina became a murder suspect in the new year. On January 3, 1968, law enforcement discovered the car of Eulogio Salazar, the Rio Arriba County Courthouse jailer, about six miles from his Tierra Amarilla home. It had been driven off the road and about forty feet down a snowy embankment. Inside, they found Salazar's body beaten so badly that the jailer's face was not recognizable. Later the coroner's office estimated that he had received as many as twenty-four separate blows.[75] As Salazar had positively identified Tijerina as the man who shot him in the jaw during the courthouse raid, suspicion immediately rested on the Alianza leader and other courthouse raid participants. Adding to a possible motive, Salazar, along with state police officer Nick Saiz, who also had been shot during the courthouse raid, had recently filed a civil suit against Tijerina.[76]

Suspicion was so strong that the day after the murder, district court judge Joe Angel revoked the bond of twenty people who were facing charges for their participation in the raid, including Tijerina and his two eldest children, David and Rose.[77] Criticism rained down in two languages. Even if the Alianza was not directly involved in this crime, wrote one editorial pundit in English, it had "nurtured hate such as never existed before in Rio Arriba County" and thus was indirectly to blame.[78] Similarly, in his Spanish-language column that appeared in the *Santa Fe News*, Pedro Ribera Ortega dredged up the words "savage," "barbarous," and "horrifying" to implicate the cowardly "*tijerinistas*" in Salazar's death. "Will there be more killings before we finish with this matter of *tierra y mercedes* [land and grants]?" he ominously asked.[79] Calling Salazar's death "terrorism," Governor David Cargo agreed that the mass revocation of bond was the right approach.[80]

Tijerina's second extended jail stay awaiting charges—the first had occurred after he had been caught following the raid—dramatically fueled his sense of outrage at American society in general. Citing the absence of any evidence linking them to the murder of Salazar, Judge Angel released the majority of those taken into custody after the jailer's death within a matter of days. The judge, however, decided to keep Tijerina and three other high-profile Alianza members (Tobias Leyba, Juan Valdez, and Baltazar Apodaca) behind bars until he concluded a preliminary hearing on all the courthouse raid charges a month later. In early February 1968, Judge Angel delivered a favorable ruling against nine of the accused, dropping all charges. For eleven more, he reduced the charges of kidnapping to the lesser crime of false imprisonment. After sitting in jail for more than a month, Tijerina hardly considered the good news worth the wait.[81] "God speaks through his prophets," he warned in an essay that he crafted while behind bars. It again quoted Isaiah 13:14 about the last days and returning to one's homeland. What the passage portended for the present, he argued, was that Indo-Hispanos should stay away from the "bad Anglo" who did not want them to remember that the land belonged to them. But that was not all. The culture of the Anglo, he fumed, "has rebelled against God and it will be destroyed."[82] Month's end provided another reason to be angry. Tijerina and Noll were both found guilty of the previous fall's contempt of court charge and ordered to spend thirty days in jail and pay a $500 fine. Once again, Tijerina immediately appealed.[83]

Remarkably, neither Tijerina's multiple convictions nor Salazar's unsolved murder damaged Tijerina's reputation as a movement hero. To the contrary, after witnessing Tijerina in action in Albuquerque and then again in El Paso, Bert Corona of California decided that the Alianza leader was a "serious political actor," although perhaps one taken aback with the responsibility of leading a social movement after being suddenly thrust into the political spotlight.[84] Corona decided to lend a hand. During the Echo Amphitheater trial, the veteran organizer dashed off a series of press releases asserting that prosecuting the land-grant leader for his righteous protest was itself a crime. In January 1968, as Tijerina suffered under the weight of suspicion regarding Salazar's death, Corona sent out a mass letter to fellow Californians on behalf of the Alianza, comparing the land struggle in New Mexico to recent events in L.A.'s Chavez Ravine, where a vibrant Mexican barrio had been razed to make way for a new Dodgers stadium.[85] Tapping into a lifetime of organizing contacts, Corona also asked his activist friends across the country to write telegrams in defense of Tijerina too. They did.[86] As soon as Judge Angel ordered Tijerina's release from jail on reduced raid charges, Corona arranged for Tijerina to tour California.

There Tijerina was warmly welcomed as a conquering hero. On a shoestring budget, the Alianza leader spoke at community centers, churches, and even private garages, anywhere a crowd of twenty to thirty people might gather. Even though very few Californians could boast any connection to a local land grant, Tijerina's message that people of Mexican descent had every right to belong in the United States found an enthusiastic audience, Corona remembered. Whether urban residents or from farmworker families, he recalled, audience members often ended up

After the courthouse raid, Tijerina was invited to speak at many student conferences throughout the Southwest, including this Mexican American symposium at the University of California, Los Angeles, in February 1968. The sweat on his brow, his emphatic hand gesture, and his expressive features all demonstrate the intensity of his oratory. (Photo by Devra A. Weber; courtesy of La Raza Collection, Chicano Studies Research Center, UCLA)

donating to the Alianza cause.[87] The tour reaped Tijerina another financial benefit: free legal advice. During Tijerina's visit, Corona introduced the Alianza leader to Beverly Axelrod, a San Francisco attorney best known for representing members of the Oakland-based Black Panthers, including the Panthers' founder Huey Newton. (One of the most iconic images of the beret-clad Huey Newton showed him sitting in a wicker chair holding a shotgun and a spear. The chair belonged to Axelrod, who took the picture.) Tijerina must have made a favorable impression upon Axelrod too. She soon moved to New Mexico to provide the cash-strapped Alianza leader counsel at no charge.[88]

In the meantime, Tijerina happily shared the stage with black militants at two giant "Free Huey" rallies held in February 1968, one in Northern California, the other in Southern California. Newton was then behind bars, accused of shooting Oakland police officer John Frey. In Los Angeles, the speakers' list featured Karenga of US, Black Panthers cofounder

(top) Cristóbal, Reies, and Anselmo Tijerina during a press conference at California State University, Los Angeles, in February 1968. Tijerina relied heavily upon family members to run the Alianza, including these two brothers. Behind them are two unidentified bodyguards. (Photo by William J. Warren, © 1968)

(bottom) Tijerina speaking at a "Free Huey" rally, referring to Black Panther leader Huey Newton, in DeFremery Park, Oakland, California, in August 1968. In the photo, he is framed by two unidentified Black Panther members acting as security; behind them, some unidentified Brown Beret members are doing the same. (Bob Fitch Photography Archive, Department of Special Collections, Stanford University Libraries)

Bobby Seale, and Stokely Carmichael and H. Rap Brown, both of SNCC. Speaking at the city's Memorial Sports Arena, a venue with nearly 17,000 seats, Tijerina's only complaint regarded the schedule, which granted him just ten minutes to speak.[89] During these precious minutes, however, Tijerina found time to refer to Isaiah 13:14, if somewhat obliquely. "The last war on earth," he stated, "will be decided on color and race." Otherwise, he vented his anger toward the "white man." Referring to himself in the third person, Tijerina accused this enemy of "poisoning the minds of the public and saying that Tijerina is a violent man, Tijerina is advocating revolution, that Tijerina is breeding poison, [and] hatred among races." Ironically, Tijerina then endorsed violence, at least for self-defense. "Oh, I don't hate the white man. No, of course not," the Alianza leader cooed. "All I'm going to do if I'm sleeping and he breaks down my door, I'm going to shoot him between the eyes and I'm going to keep on sleeping."[90]

That militant rhetoric only enhanced Tijerina's reputation among many on the left. In March 1968, Tijerina returned to California and attended the founding convention of the Peace and Freedom Party, a third-party effort holding its founding convention in the San Francisco Bay area town of Richmond. The diverse group of party adherents included Black Panthers and antiwar leftists. Again, Tijerina found a warm welcome. Convention attendees even contemplated nominating Tijerina as the party's vice-presidential candidate on a national ticket headed by Dick Gregory, an African American activist and comedian. The convention disbanded before rendering any formal decision, but Tijerina's name continued to pop up in party circles as a potential nominee as late as August 1968.[91]

Only Cesar Chavez kept his distance. A few months before, as Tijerina awaited sentencing in the Echo Amphitheater case, Chavez had dropped by a regular Alianza meeting in Albuquerque one Saturday evening in a surprise show of support. He had even declared that, if he lived in New Mexico, he would be an Alianza member too.[92] Yet in March 1968, when Chavez ended a historic twenty-five-day fast in Delano, California, he broke bread with Robert F. Kennedy by his side and Tijerina somewhere in the crowd. Observers speculated whether the decision to keep the hot-tempered Tijerina at arm's length rested with Chavez, who courted Democratic politicians, or Kennedy, running for president.[93] In either case, a *New York Times* journalist commented approvingly that the "sad-eyed, gentle, and introspective" Chavez was "totally unlike" the volatile land-grant leader.[94]

Tijerina listened intently to Martin Luther King Jr. speak in Atlanta, Georgia, during an early planning meeting of the Poor People's Campaign in March 1968. The following month King was shot dead, a tragedy that Tijerina argued marked the end of political moderation as an effective means of change. (Associated Press photograph)

No matter. Tijerina had bigger fish to fry. Also in March 1968, he received a telegram from Martin Luther King Jr. inviting him as someone whose "leadership is known and well recognized" to join other select representatives of "different racial, religious, and ethnic groups" in Atlanta on March 14. There, they were to commence "joint thinking" on the contours of an emerging anti-poverty campaign.[95] Awed by the opportunity and by his own inclusion, Tijerina put any warnings inspired by Isaiah 13:14 on hold. Instead, he counseled his fellow Mexican Americans invitees to be grateful. "It was born in his heart and we must NOT question that," he cautioned about King and his plans.[96]

Soon, however, Tijerina was questioning, criticizing, demanding, and, in all respects, showing himself to be a very uncooperative Chicano.

In early June 1968, at the height of the Poor People's Campaign in Washington, D.C., Tijerina and a group of followers attempted to meet with U.S. secretary of state Dean Rusk. "If any government agency were to escape the wrath of the Poor People's Campaign, the State Department would seem to have been the likeliest candidate," noted a reporter with the *Washington Evening Star*, that era's evening rival to the *Washington Post*, for it would "take a particular genius to blame domestic poverty on the diplomats in Foggy Bottom," a nickname for the State Department resulting from its location in a formerly swampy area of the city. The reporter continued, "Genius or not, Reies López Tijerina has done just that. And if his legal case against the department is a bit shaky, his passionate cry for justice might at least tweak the national conscience. . . . Put as simply as possible, Tijerina's claim is that the government welshed on the 1848 treaty with Mexico. . . . If the government would recognize the old Mexican grants of common land to the pueblos, or villages in what is now New Mexico, Tijerina says, the poverty of Spanish-Americans would be substantially relieved."[97] At the end of the day, after lengthy debates over the size or constituency of the visiting delegation, no meeting between Secretary Dean Rusk and Tijerina ever occurred.[98]

Beneath the broad umbrella of the Poor People's Campaign, Tijerina and other land-grant activists nevertheless had gained the opportunity to press their case in the nation's capital. Alianza stalwarts traveling to D.C. made the most of the opportunity by expertly showcasing the cause and highlighting its unique characteristics. "We are a proud people who do not want welfare. We can churn our own butter given enough elbow room," Cleofas Vigil explained to a newspaper reporter. "[But] the big companies and the federal government are taking our land away from us and fencing us in like a concentration camp," Vigil insisted. Another Alianza stalwart, Ralph Durán, captured just how long land-poor New Mexicans had been waiting for justice. "Since I was a kid, my grandfather used to tell me that we were robbed of our land by the U.S. government," he told the press. "I was always looking for a way to come back to Washington and get it back."[99]

The Poor People's Campaign sought to bring together millions of Americans of all backgrounds: "Negroes, whites, Mexicans, Puerto Ricans, [and] Indians," according to the campaign's statement of purpose.[100] In one respect, the campaign marked the natural evolution of a successful

At the head of a march during the 1968 Poor People's Campaign in Washington, D.C., in 1968, Tijerina carried a sign announcing the primacy that treaty rights have according to the U.S. Constitution. Other signs charged land theft. While in Washington, Tijerina also began to claim that the Treaty of Guadalupe Hidalgo was a defective document. (Maria Varela Photography)

civil rights movement. After all, what good did it do to end segregation in restaurants if the poor lacked enough money to buy food at all?[101] Yet in an effort to address Mexican American and Native American concerns specifically, the Poor People's Campaign also listed among its central goals "access to land" along with "a meaningful job" and an "adequate income."[102] In addition, King's successor as head of the SCLC, Ralph Abernathy, asked Tijerina, who had been among a handful of Mexican Americans to attend King's funeral in Atlanta, to assume a leadership role within the anti-poverty campaign.[103] Abernathy's invitation explained Tijerina's presence when Coretta Scott King launched the official start of the Poor People's Campaign in Memphis the following month.[104]

Tijerina and the land-grant movement immediately benefited from the relationship. Invited to attend a critical planning meeting in D.C. in late April 1968, he found himself behind bars instead. Unhappy after Judge Angel had reduced the most serious kidnapping charges against Tijerina and other raid defendants, DA Alfonso Sánchez had convened a new grand jury that issued a new set of kidnapping charges that prompted Tijerina's rearrest.[105] The Poor People's Campaign rushed to Tijerina's defense. The Alianza leader had been "subject to a pattern of intimidation and persecution," its national office declared. Campaign participants helped post a $20,500 bond for Tijerina to secure his release from jail four days later.[106] In the interim, SCLC organizers also worked closely with Chicano representatives who made it to D.C. When asked about the Treaty of Guadalupe Hidalgo, for example, an SCLC organizer turned the floor over to Maria Varela, who had attended the meeting in Tijerina's stead, so that she could teach the gathering about land and cultural rights.[107] This critical interchange explained why "access to land" ranked so high among the campaign's priorities.

Kickoff events in Albuquerque similarly brimmed with promise. More than a thousand people filled the city's Civic Auditorium for a rally one evening that featured the SCLC's Abernathy and Wallace "Mad Bear" Anderson, a Tuscarora Indian from the state of New York who had been pressing for indigenous sovereignty and land claims since the 1950s. In the spirit of interracial solidarity, Abernathy warmly addressed Anderson as his "red brother" and then Tijerina, who was also onstage, as his "yellow brother." "Brown," Tijerina whispered in polite correction.[108] The next day, all "ages, faiths, [and] races mingled" at a peaceful march that again drew about a thousand people. Along with New Mexicans of all backgrounds, the events welcomed activists from Los Angeles, El Paso, and Phoenix who had converged on Albuquerque before heading out to Denver, Kansas City, St. Louis, and, ultimately, Washington, D.C., the route of the Southwestern contingent of the Poor People's Campaign.[109] An elated Tijerina compared the diverse gathering to "a beautiful bouquet."[110]

The moment of solidarity soon faded, however. Under the best of circumstances, organizational lapses and differences of opinions were bound to plague such a broad coalition. Campaign plans called for participants to coordinate their journeys from different regions of the country before converging at the National Mall in D.C., the site of Resurrection City. Even before leaving Albuquerque, Tijerina griped that the SCLC had provided funding for only two buses, whereas New Mexicans needed three.[111] Although technically part of the campaign's executive steering committee, Tijerina also complained that he often did not know when or whether that committee had met. "They do not consult us," the Alianza leader stated about SCLC members.[112] Others shared this criticism. At a massive rally in Kansas City on the way to D.C., an angry Corky Gonza-

Four of Tijerina's eldest children attended the Poor People's Campaign with him. Huddled against the rain and damp, they are (*left to right*) Daniel, sixteen; Rachel, fifteen; Reies López Tijerina; David (also known as Reies Hugh), twenty; and Rose, nineteen. Each met Tijerina's expectations to work on behalf of the Alianza. (Photograph courtesy of Rose Tijerina, gift to the Center for Southwest Research, University of New Mexico, Albuquerque)

les discovered to his dismay that not one of seventeen speaker spots had been assigned to a Mexican American. Native Americans and poor whites voiced similar concerns about being sidelined within a campaign dominated by African Americans.[113]

Relations continued to deteriorate when the groups reached the nation's capital. After torrential rains turned Resurrection City into a mud pit, members of Denver's Crusade for Justice found alternative accommodations at Hawthorne School, a private school about two miles away from the National Mall.[114] Soon Hawthorne School became home to most Mexican American and American Indian campaign participants. This outcome displeased SCLC organizers, who wanted to see Chicano movement activists at the main encampment to send a signal of unity to the press.[115] Newspapers instead emphasized conflict. At the end of May, after hearing Tijerina complain that "black militants have taken over and nobody else gets a chance to talk," African American activists countered that his comments amounted to "just a lot of junk."[116] Two days later, African Americans and Mexican Americans traded obscenities and almost came to blows at a misnamed "unity rally."[117] As far as Hosea Williams, a longtime King associate and SCLC member was concerned, Chicanos were receiving more than their fair share of press attention.[118] The high-handed manner of some SCLC folks had already aggrieved fellow activists in the civil rights movement. Now, in D.C., rumors flew that SCLC members referred to white and brown activists in attendance as "children" or, in the case of Mexican Americans, not as "brown brothers" but as "*little* brown brothers."[119]

Official attempts to foster brown-black solidarity failed to impress Tijerina. During the campaign, African American activists joined Native American protests at the U.S. Supreme Court and Indo-Hispano gatherings in front of the State Department.[120] When Tijerina led a delegation to the Mexican Embassy to request that Mexico submit land-grant grievances to the United Nations, Abernathy personally accompanied him.[121] In addition, "black representatives of the Poor People of the United States" issued a statement fully endorsing Tijerina's trip to the State Department.[122] Nevertheless, Tijerina kept a long list of perceived slights. He not only pushed the SCLC to fund the New Mexican campaign more generously, which it probably needed to do, but also noted with concern, for example, that security staff at Resurrection City had access to two-way radios and to donations of new clothing while those gathered at Hawthorne School had access to neither. He exaggeratedly accused the SCLC of sitting on "millions."[123]

In the meantime, Tijerina enjoyed what privileges he could accrue. Although the regular menu at the school featured rice and beans, Tijerina routinely ate steak while staying at nicer accommodations. With some key exceptions, the admiration of Chicano movement participants toward him had been based on knowing him from afar, either from reading about the courthouse raid or possibly from hearing him speak onstage. Now witnessing Tijerina up close for days on end, at least one activist complained that he acted like a *rey*, a king protecting his royal authority and prerogative.[124]

Others found the Alianza leader's insatiable desire for attention during the campaign unseemly. "The greatest duel under the sun, Tijerina vs. Rusk," predicted one flyer announcing that short-circuited visit to the State Department.[125] Both the allusion to the cinematic Wild West and the casting of Tijerina as the hero of the piece were hard to miss. Another flyer sent out in advance of the first anniversary of the courthouse raid invited attendees to come to a celebration honoring the "June 5th Revolution." Both flyers literally profiled Tijerina, the first by featuring an extra-large drawing of his face taken from the side, the second by including a flattering headshot from the same angle.[126] Mocking Tijerina's radar-like ability to be where the cameras were, youthful members of the Crusade for Justice nicknamed him "TV-rina."[127] Tijerina meanwhile defended his privilege. As he insisted to an interviewer in mid-June, he alone led the Southwest contingent to the Poor People's Campaign. The position was *not* shared between himself and Corky Gonzales.[128]

While a concerned Gonzales kept his growing doubts about Tijerina's autocratic behavior within "the family," meaning he did not speak about them to non-Chicanos, he was not alone.[129] One disaffected welfare advocate from New Mexico openly theorized to the press that "an extremely emotional" Reies was gunning for Abernathy's position.[130] Although the public airing of such criticism distressed Varela, she too decided to break with Tijerina during the campaign.[131] The fate of fellow activists who had been arrested during a protest did not seem to concern him, she noted.[132] Years later, she traced Tijerina's desire to be the center of attention to an inherent weakness in his political skill set. In an interview during the 1990s, she explained what she meant by comparing Tijerina and Gonzales. "Personality-wise, Corky understood the working of the politics. He was skilled in that. Reies was so single-minded around his issues that I think it was difficult for him to swim in that atmosphere [of the Poor People's Campaign]. Reies was not an organizer. He was a leader. Corky was a person who could both organize and lead," Varela stated.[133] Or as she later elaborated in an interview with Gordon Mantler, for Tijerina "any media attention was one more brick in the wall or stepping stones to build power. That's what he thought his job was." She added, "He was a preacher. And preachers need an audience."[134]

Tijerina might have countered that he needed to fulfill his God-given destiny. While similar accusations regarding food, accommodations, and leadership plagued SCLC higher-ups, in acting like a *rey*, Tijerina was also living up to the promise embedded in his name, *el Rey de los Reyes*, the King of Kings, Jesus Christ himself. More than ever before, he had reason to believe that he acted with God-sanctioned authority. Consider that following the courthouse raid, he had received an extraordinary amount of attention. The movement that he led had been granted unprecedented legitimacy. At the Poor People's Campaign, he then reached the highest pinnacle of power yet in terms of his ability to command a national audience. Although the evidence is more suggestive than conclusive, Tijerina even may have come to believe that the day of divine justice was at hand. His speech at a "Solidarity Day" rally, which concluded the Poor People's Campaign, hinted that was the case. In front of an estimated crowd of 40,000 people, Tijerina returned to his prophet past by alluding to the Beatitudes, in which Jesus proclaimed that the meek would inherit the earth (*la tierra* in Spanish, the land), to announce a moment of final confrontation. "This government . . . has openly declared war on God and his meek people," Tijerina declared, before issuing a rallying cry. "Let us pursue JUSTICE and PEACE. Let us sacrifice our lives for the Kingdom of JUSTICE and RIGHTEOUSNESS."[135] The same speech, moreover, made clear that when that kingdom arrived, Tijerina expected Native Americans to be standing alongside Mexican Americans.

As the Alianza leader often noted, in contrast to African Americans, Native Americans and Mexican Americans shared a similar colonial status vis-à-vis the United States. Consequently, when Tijerina complained during the campaign that demands for "jobs, jobs, jobs" filled the newspapers but the media "doesn't mention land; it doesn't mention treaties," he was both demanding more attention and articulating what he perceived as a fundamental political divide.[136] In his memoir, Tijerina highlighted this exact distinction. Whereas Indo-Hispanos sought land and cultural rights as protected by treaty, he wrote, African Americans essentially sought governmental aid in the form of "more jobs, more and better education, and better public assistance."[137] To Tijerina, both Native Americans and Mexican Americans, as similar "breeds," fell within the privileged category of inheritors of the earth. Just as clearly, as far as Tijerina was concerned, African Americans did not. To the contrary, if Tijerina suspected that the kingdom of justice drew near, then, in accord with Isaiah 13:14, he had every reason to see his alliance of convenience with African Americans coming to an end.

Conversely, Tijerina went out of his way to forge friendly relations with Native Americans. During the Poor People's Campaign, for instance, Hank Adams, a Native American activist, invited Tijerina to participate in a demonstration in front of the U.S. Supreme Court to protest a recent decision that had undermined indigenous fishing rights. In soliciting Tijerina's participation, Adams also asked that the land-grant leader help maintain a "central focus on . . . Indian issues" and a "controlled situation on non-Indian speakers." Essentially, Adams was requesting that Tijerina show up but keep quiet.[138] Remarkably, "TV-rina" complied. The next day about 500 Mexican Americans joined 100 Native American activists who smoked ceremonial pipes and beat drums on the steps of the U.S. Supreme Court. As planned, Native Americans and their demands occupied the center of attention throughout the demonstration. Although Tijerina later joined a delegation that was invited inside the building, per Adams's request he stayed in the background.[139] His profession of solidarity that day explained why: "We support our Indian brothers at all times, in all places, and under all conditions, when it is a matter of their treaty rights[,] for their fight and our fight are one and the same."[140]

Drawing closer to Native Americans still, Tijerina while in Washington, D.C., also offered a new twist on his own family's past. Forget those landed Tejanos, as he once described his ancestors; the Alianza leader now emphasized that he was the descendant of an Indian princess from the Tejas (Texas) Indian tribe. She had married a Spaniard who in an act of rebellion against his parents adopted the tribal name as his own surname but tacked on a Spanish ending. Over generations, Tijerina suggested, the composite Teja-rina became Tejerina, which became Tijerina.[141] In fact, the etymology of the surname "Tijerina" is almost certainly derived from *tijeras*, or "scissors" in Spanish, an origin that makes it akin to the English "tailor." Nevertheless, the Alianza leader stood by his latest reinvention, confiding to a reporter after his return to Albuquerque that he was "mostly Indian."[142]

As such, Tijerina suddenly had little use for the Treaty of Guadalupe Hidalgo, long the centerpiece of the Alianza crusade. Early on during the Poor People's Campaign, Tijerina mentioned the peace treaty in the usual way, as proof that the United States had promised to protect landholdings.[143] By mid-June, however, he was referring to the "so-called" treaty. A list of Alianza demands to the State Department that month encompassed the ambivalence. The organization called for "for an impartial committee [to] investigate the validity of the treaty of Guadalupe-Hidalgo" while also labeling the treaty a "defective document."[144] Later Alianza documents flatly declared the treaty "a fraud" and "invalid."[145] The change of tune stemmed from an obscure detail regarding the signing of the document. Somewhere along the way, Tijerina discovered that President James K. Polk had tried to recall Nicholas Trist, the U.S. envoy to the peace negotiations, on the grounds that Trist was being overly generous to Mexico. Aware of his boss's displeasure, Trist signed the treaty anyway.[146] In either case, Alianza members saw a bright side. If the United States thought the treaty valid, then it needed to prove it by honoring its property protections. Better yet, if the treaty was invalid, then the north of

Mexico had never been ceded to the United States and Indo-Hispano land claims reigned supreme.

In the midst of it all, Tijerina's mercurial nature was on full display. During the course of the Poor People's Campaign, he worked closely with African American activists and castigated them. He supported the Treaty of Guadalupe Hidalgo and rejected it. After calling both Spain and Mexico his "mother," Tijerina decided that he was actually more "Indo" than "Hispano." By the end of the campaign, the Alianza president even offered contradictory evaluations about the anti-poverty effort overall. He blasted it as a "shameful, hypocritical" effort that "betrayed" and "mocked" the poor and then, a few days later, ranked it as "the greatest experience" of his life precisely because it represented a new era of justice for all.[147]

Despite Tijerina's talent for changing his mind with whiplashing rapidity, one constant remained: he unwaveringly interpreted 1960s militancy through his long-held notions of God's justice and his own role in advancing it. From all appearances, by the conclusion of the Poor People's Campaign, Tijerina looked forward to the last days and to the fulfillment of Isaiah 13:14. To get there, moreover, he was willing to acknowledge that the kingdom of justice encompassed more than land-grant concerns. "Tijerina's vision has expanded beyond land-grants . . . to include civil, political and cultural rights," one Alianza appeal for donations announced. Without apology, the appeal further explained that the land-grant struggle was now subsumed within a greater "movement for minority militancy."[148]

Apparently unaware that his stature as a Chicano leader had diminished quickly during the Poor People's Campaign, Tijerina anticipated leading this broader movement. But almost nothing went according to plan. In his own memoir, Bert Corona, Tijerina's California ally, rehearsed a litany of woes that Tijerina confronted as a result of his activism: "He was persecuted, threatened, and harassed. His every move was watched. And his family was watched. He couldn't make a decent living." Finally, Corona noted, "He was indicted, sentenced, and sent to jail."[149]

In yielding to this fate, one more role remained for Tijerina: martyr.

10

The Martyr

Presiding judge Paul Larrazolo warned him to stop making speeches. Reies López Tijerina kept on talking.

Finally standing trial in November 1968 on charges stemming from the courthouse raid, Tijerina, acting as his own defense attorney, took every opportunity to emphasize the persecution he was experiencing for his cause. "The newspapers are crucifying a man in this land of the free," he insisted during jury selection.[1] Once the trial began, Tijerina hammered home his innocence to an Albuquerque jury. Faced with the charges of kidnapping, assault on a jail, and false imprisonment of a hostage, he insisted that true guilt rested with DA Alfonso Sánchez, who had tried to quash the Alianza over the years and especially in the days preceding the courthouse raid.

Tijerina emphasized that Alianza members had acted within their constitutional rights. "Do you know that citizens of the United States could arrest an officer if they believed they had a grievance against [him]?" Tijerina queried one state police officer whose car had been greeted with gunfire when he drove up to the courthouse that afternoon. "No," admitted the officer. Tijerina then posed another question that, like the first, mattered more than the answer it solicited: "Isn't it possible that these people pushed to the brink of desperation had to teach you a lesson, teach you what you were not taught by your superiors?" Judge Larrazolo promptly declared the second question improper, but Tijerina already had schooled the officer—and the jury—on the right of citizens to make an arrest.[2]

Tijerina also distanced himself from any wrongdoing. Only one person who had suffered bodily injury on June 5, 1967, identified Tijerina as the guilty party, but, as Tijerina pointed out, that person had been struck from behind. How could he even have seen the culprit? Tijerina additionally solicited helpful testimony from two other witnesses. Up on the stand, Sheriff Benny Naranjo swore under oath that he did not see the Alianza leader hit anyone or shoot anyone. Undersheriff Dan Rivera, who had been hit on the head and then directed at gunpoint to release prisoners from the jail, testified that he never heard Tijerina order anyone to touch him, much less beat him. "Then as far as you know, I am not to blame for your injuries?" Tijerina inquired. "I don't blame you for anything, sir," Rivera responded.[3]

Tijerina then wrapped up the trial with a bravura closing performance that impressed a reporter with the usually hypercritical *Albuquerque Journal*: "The flamboyant and articulate Tijerina, largely self-educated, delivered an emotional 60-minute summation, his eyes blazing and flashing, arms slashing the air, and fingers snapping. He did not direct his remarks solely to the jury but frequently spoke out into the packed spectator section and to the counsel table where the state's attorneys sat."[4] Four hours later, the jury of four Spanish Americans, seven Anglo Americans, and one African American returned a verdict of "not guilty" on all three charges before them. Jurors had entered deliberations with instructions from Larrazolo about what constituted a citizen's arrest. Afterward, they declared that the prosecutors had failed to prove their case that the Alianza leader was directly responsible for any of the violence. They credited Tijerina for sowing doubt on that point. "That guy has a fantastic mind and he did an unbelievable job for not being an attorney," one juror later explained.[5]

Still, Tijerina's description of himself during the trial as a persecuted man also proved apt. As much as the courthouse raid had gained him admirers, his activism also had provoked a ferocious backlash. Almost as soon as he returned to Albuquerque from Washington, D.C., Tijerina announced plans to run for governor of New Mexico. Technically an extension of the Poor People's Campaign, the campaign also served as a way for Tijerina to strike back at his many adversaries in the media and elsewhere. As early as September 1968, for example, one New Mexican gleefully awaited Tijerina's crushing defeat at the poll because, he argued, most Spanish Americans "want no part of his impractical and violence-tinged publicity-seeking shenanigans."[6] In fact, in what he perceived as still more persecution, Tijerina was ruled off the ballot before the November election.

The courtroom victory thus stood as a bittersweet triumph for a man whose fortunes quickly soured in the months that followed. Already the object of scathing media commentary, Tijerina also faced anonymous acts of violence and intensified police surveillance. Of course, overcoming adversity had long ranked among Tijerina's top talents, as manifested by his chameleon-like reinvention whenever circumstances threatened his vision of justice. A new identity always moved to the foreground as soon as an old one proved ineffective. In this way, Tijerina remained a man on a mission, even as he continually refined and redefined his ultimate goal, be it saving souls, establishing a desert paradise, seeking land-grant redress, or leading a broader political revolution. His denouement, however, followed a different script. Whereas Tijerina struggled to succeed as a prophet, or to be taken seriously as an American, martyrdom fit him perfectly.

THE BACKLASH

"Reies Tijerina: The Communist Plot to Grab the Southwest," blared an October 1967 headline that appeared in *American Opinion*, the national journal of the ultraconservative John Birch Society.[7] Founded in 1958 to expose traitors within the U.S. government, Birchers during the 1960s attacked the African American civil rights movement as a communist conspiracy to destroy freedom in the United States.[8] Applying the same thesis to Tijerina and the Alianza, author Alan Stang warned in this article that the courthouse raid was not the work of a "few isolated nuts" but part of a greater conspiracy supported by the Communist Party to carve a separate nation within the American Southwest. Stang's description of Tijerina as a "Marxist," a "guerrilla leader" like Cuba's Fidel Castro, and a "terrorist" found a receptive audience among conservative New Mexicans. A promotional tour included three stops in the state. Some 400 people came to see the writer in Albuquerque alone.[9] Stang went on to write two more damning articles about the Alianza leader for *American Opinion*.[10]

Closer to home, what little sympathy media outlets in New Mexico had expressed before the courthouse raid for Tijerina and the Alianza evaporated rapidly afterward. The *Albuquerque Journal*, the largest-circulation newspaper in New Mexico, led the state's anti-Tijerina media brigade. Inclined to dismiss the Alianza's claims as "phony," in the wake of the raid the newspaper provided a forum for Tijerina's critics, most prominently Senator Joseph Montoya, who in December 1967, in an unprovoked diatribe, denounced Tijerina as a liar, fraud, and failure. Not only did Montoya's criticism earn front-page, above-the-fold coverage in the *Journal*, but the newspaper also ran an editorial that chided the senator for not speaking out sooner.[11] A month later, the newspaper faulted Tijerina and his supporters for the brutal murder of Eulogio Salazar.[12] After reports circulated that Tijerina might play a prominent role in the Poor People's Campaign, a *Journal* editorial flatly denounced the Alianza president as "the wrong choice."[13] Not surprisingly, the newspaper likewise had little good to say about Tijerina's gubernatorial bid.[14]

Officially, the idea behind the People's Constitutional Party (PCP) was to continue the work of the Poor People's Campaign. Toward that end, the party platform advanced an agenda designed to appeal to almost every kind of left-of-center and youth voter in the state. Planks called for lowering the voting age to eighteen, legalizing marijuana, and protecting "the rights of hippies."[15] Given the Alianza president's own social conservatism, chances are that new friends from the Poor People's Campaign drafted the party platform. A separate bilingual list of party priorities that called for respecting God and upholding moral principles sounded more like the Alianza leader.[16] True to Tijerina's pronouncement that he now wished to effect broader social change, neither document mentioned the matter of the mercedes. "Is the Alianza only interested in land grants?" queried an information sheet distributed during the campaign. The answer: "Not at all."[17]

Unofficially, Tijerina viewed his run for governor as a moment to seek retribution against his enemies and address his critics. "Isn't he an unscrupulous demagogue who rides around in a white Cadillac?" one press release rhetorically asked about Tijerina before offering evidence to the contrary.[18] Tired of constant accusations that he was fleecing vulnerable nuevomexicanos, candidate Tijerina vowed to donate all but $1,500 of his gubernatorial salary to charity.[19] Still a murder suspect in some quarters, he likewise promised a $100,000 reward for information that would solve the murder of Eulogio Salazar.[20] Furthermore, he announced plans to file lawsuits against two long-standing antagonists, the school system in Albuquerque and the local press. First, Tijerina filed suit against the New Mexico State Board of Education and the Albuquerque school board for discriminating against Indo-Hispano children, particularly his own. "My daughter was kicked out of school in Albuquerque because she was trying to protest a ban against speaking Spanish," the Alianza president explained, referring to Rachel Tijerina's involvement in a school protest in April 1968.[21] The injustice galled Tijerina, who had long faulted schools for erasing the Indo-Hispano past. The second point of litigation involved filing antitrust claims against the *Albuquerque Journal*, the biggest newspaper in the state, and its afternoon counterpart, the *Albuquerque Tribune*, on the grounds that the newsrooms produced nearly identical content, none of which accurately covered Indo-Hispano matters.[22] Personally, Tijerina hoped to rein in Bob Brown, the *Journal* editor.[23]

In pursuing this two-point plan, Tijerina relied upon a new legal adviser, Bill Higgs, a civil rights attorney whom he had met at the Poor People's Campaign. A native of Mississippi and a Harvard Law School graduate, Higgs had defended James Meredith and other African Americans trying to integrate the University of Mississippi in 1962. The following year, Higgs fled the state after being tried and found guilty in absentia on a morals charge, police-speak for engaging in homosexual activity.[24] Whether or not Tijerina knew about these accusations, he valued Higgs, who soon moved to New Mexico, acting for all intents and purposes as a replacement for the extradited Jerry Noll, now back in the state of Washington.[25] At the first Alianza meeting upon his return from D.C., Tijerina introduced Higgs as "*el abogado de ora* [*ahora*]," literally, the lawyer of now.[26] Beverly Axelrod's role faded in comparison.[27] Legal obstacles, however, soon stymied Tijerina's "two-point plan of litigation."[28]

They likewise derailed his plans to run for governor. During the fall of 1968, New Mexican secretary of state Ernestine Evans declared almost the entire slate of PCP candidates unfit to run. Evans ruled Tijerina off the ballot first. As a convicted felon following the guilty verdict in the Echo Amphitheater trial, she pointed out, the Alianza president was ineligible to hold elected office in New Mexico.[29] Evans then declared the PCP candidate for lieutenant governor likewise ineligible because his candidacy was paired at the top of the ticket with the now defunct candidacy of Tijerina. In short order, Evans also pronounced the party's candidate for state attorney general insufficiently "learned in the law"; disqualified a PCP congressional candidate for living in one district while running to represent another; and decided yet another candidate for Congress had failed to meet state residency requirements. According to the secretary of state, still other PCP candidates had missed various certification deadlines.[30]

Although the quick formation of the party, and its quicker recruitment of candidates, left PCP office seekers vulnerable to these sorts of technical objections, party advocates detected an anti-Tijerina bias. They were correct. Evans maintained she was simply following the letter of the law, but she was also following the advice of New Mexico attorney general Boston Witt, the top lawman in the state and a fierce Tijerina antagonist.[31] The previous year, he had released a massive report that slammed state employees who purportedly had helped the land-grant leader in the wake of the courthouse raid. Filled mostly with innuendo, the sheer size of the report—some fifteen inches thick and weighing five pounds—nonetheless impressed.[32] Eventually the New Mexico Supreme Court decided that Evans (and Witt) had gone too far. Just ten days before the election, the court, in an indirect rebuke, reversed five of the secretary of state's eight rulings that had disqualified PCP candidates. Tijerina, however, stayed off the ballot. The court rejected Tijerina's plea that he should be allowed to run for governor while he was appealing his convictions. The court also rejected his argument that he should be allowed to run because, if elected, he could pardon himself![33] Nevertheless, after party members rallied at the last minute to find a new crop of candidates, Tijerina brashly predicted that this substitute PCP ticket would gain 20,000 votes, enough to serve as a powerful swing bloc in the state.[34]

He was wrong. Historically, third-party efforts have struggled to gain much traction against the two more established political parties. In announcing his candidacy, Tijerina realized that he was "taking a chance on a miracle" in terms of actually winning office.[35] Still, the official results showed that the party not only failed to attract new voters but also failed to make a strong showing where the Alianza had some of its deepest roots. Tijerina had long boasted of an Alianza membership that numbered in the thousands, if not tens of thousands. That November, the top of the PCP ticket received just 1,800 votes statewide. In contrast, New Mexico governor David Cargo won reelection with 153,000 votes. Even more telling, Cargo received 1,984 votes in Rio Arriba County alone, while his Democratic challenger, Fabian Chavez, carried the county with 2,538 votes.[36]

The November 1968 defeat was intensely personal. Even when ruled off the ballot, Tijerina remained the head of the party and its best-known spokesman. To one former Tijerina fan, that was precisely the problem.

In December 1968, following his successful self-defense on courthouse raid charges, Reies Tijerina, Bill Higgs (a lawyer working for the Alianza), and Reies's daughter Rose leave the Alianza headquarters to attend a Christmas party. The main Alianza office also served as the headquarters for the People's Constitutional Party and as a meeting place for Los Caballeros de las Indias, a group within the Alianza. (Getty Images)

He charged that a campaign that had begun as a political vehicle for the poor had devolved into an exercise in "feeding Reies' ego." Or as he put it, "The caudillo emerged over the organizer. The messiah over the prophet. The man over the movement."[37]

Yet Tijerina had only the briefest window to contemplate the magnitude of his defeat. Exactly one week later, the trial on the courthouse raid charges opened. In an attempt to streamline a process that involved nine defendants facing 600 different counts of wrongdoing, Judge Paul Larrazolo had severed Tijerina's case from the rest in advance of the trial.[38] The judge also requested that the state limit the upcoming trial to just three of the most serious charges facing Tijerina—kidnapping, assault upon a jail, and false imprisonment—pushing back the rest of the charges to a later date.[39] In another let's-get-down-to-business move, the judge rejected Tijerina's request that he be allowed five months to prepare to conduct his own defense, offering him thirty minutes instead.[40]

Tijerina's ability to secure a "not guilty" verdict under these circumstances thrilled his supporters. For months he had purported to lead a broader revolution; the trial brought him home politically to the arena of his greatest expertise. Heading out of court that day alongside her husband, a relieved Patsy Tijerina called the December verdict "the best Christmas present."[41]

Other New Mexicans were more appalled at the verdict than pleased. The *Santa Fe New Mexican* blamed the court for allowing "the self-proclaimed 'King Tiger' to use the trial as a sounding board for his baseless land grant claims and for demagogic tirades."[42] Before the week was out, James Thompson, the new incoming Rio Arriba County district attorney who had defeated Alfonso Sánchez in an election that fall, announced that he intended to bring Tijerina to trial on the remaining raid charges as soon as possible.[43] That stance no doubt pleased an unnamed woman who interrupted the Alianza leader's victorious exit from the courthouse. "We will get you yet, Tijerina!" she shouted.[44]

UNDER ATTACK/UNDER SURVEILLANCE

On April 17, 1968, a man blew off his right hand in a dynamite explosion that occurred immediately outside the Albuquerque offices of the Alianza. Police discovered the suspect's injury and identity after a high-speed chase through town ended in a crash. Rushed to the hospital, William "Tiny" Fellion refused to talk to law enforcement.[45] State police, however, already knew him. According to a March 1968 New Mexico State Police report, Fellion, a former deputy sheriff and federal marshal, had recently boasted to state police that he was a "demolition expert" and a "paid assassin for the right price" who was willing "to kill Tijerina and his followers free of charge" because he had "no use for that type of people." Astonishingly, instead of moving to protect Tijerina, investigator Robert Gilliland, the author of the report, advised his superiors that he would keep the lines of communication open to see what "further information" Fellion might provide.[46] Five months later, a municipal court judge found Fellion guilty of the crime of reckless driving and sentenced him to sixteen hours' community service.[47]

Both the attack and the lackadaisical law enforcement response fit part of a broader pattern of persecution that plagued Tijerina throughout 1968 and into 1969. Preoccupied with the danger that the Alianza leader and his henchmen presumably posed, state and federal law officers did nothing to counter the danger that Tijerina and other Alianza members actually faced. In October 1968, for example, anonymous individuals threw rocks through the windows of the Alianza's main office in Albuquerque.[48] During the courthouse raid trial, unknown assailants fired guns at the Alianza office and shattered the front window.[49] Aside from Fellion, however, no culprits were ever found, despite intense law enforcement scrutiny of the Alianza.

The anonymous acts of terrorism dramatically ratcheted up after Tijerina's courtroom victory. Just a few days after the acquittal, an explosion occurred at the home of his ex-wife, Mary Escobar, who lived with several of their older children. In January 1969, a bomb exploded just outside a metal garage door at the Alianza's headquarters, frightening Patsy Tijerina and her young children, who still called the headquarters home, as well as others at the office at the time. The blast blew apart one wooden door, broke several windows, and dented a garage door.[50] In February 1969, just hours after Tijerina announced that he intended to open an Indo-Hispano Studies Institute on a ranch owned by Jenny and Craig Vincent—two supporters in San Cristobal, New Mexico—a fire utterly destroyed a building on the ranch. The four-alarm blaze was particularly suspicious because electricity at the ranch was shut off at the time.[51]

The worst violence occurred in mid-March 1969. During an Alianza meeting with about fifty people in attendance, an explosion occurred that left Vice President Santiago Tapia y Anaya's car "a mangled pile of metal," dented and damaged two other cars belonging to Alianza members, and shattered the windows of surrounding buildings. The blast packed such a punch that a car seat from one automobile landed half a block away. Roughly ninety minutes later, a stick of dynamite exploded in front of the home of Thomas Gallegos while he was attending the Alianza meeting. The blast destroyed the home's front door and its garage door too. Like Tapia y Anaya, Gallegos was a high-ranking Alianza member. City police at the scene promised to contact bomb experts at the nearby Sandia army base for help in finding those responsible for the two explosions. They also sent pieces of Tapia y Anaya's car to the FBI for analysis.[52]

The FBI, however, viewed the Alianza as the problem. Its director, J. Edgar Hoover, had been concerned about Tijerina's politics since 1964. The courthouse raid prompted renewed alarm about the Alianza leader and additional surveillance. Working undercover, bureau agents concluded that Tijerina posed a danger as a master manipulator of the uneducated masses.[53] In the words of the agent who attended the October 1967 Alianza convention, "Extreme care should be taken with Reies

Tijerina especially if he can assemble a crowd of Mexican Americans of lower economic and scholastic achievement. He can easily turn a crowd like this into a violent, riotous crowd. He has the ability to make wild and unfounded statements and get crowds who don't know any better to go along with him. He has an uncanny ability to express himself verbally in Spanish. There is not a great deal of depth to what he says but nevertheless he can get crowds to listen to him. He speaks with an evangelical fervor and is also able to feel out his crowds very well."[54] After hearing Tijerina speak in El Paso, another FBI agent compared the Alianza leader to Mussolini and Hitler.[55]

By February 1968, the FBI decided that Tijerina merited inclusion in the bureau's "Rabble Rouser Index." That designation made Tijerina another kind of target. As defined by Hoover, the index tallied "individuals of national prominence" who had "demonstrated by their actions and speeches that they have a propensity for fomenting racial disorder."[56] Tijerina's elevation to the highest echelon of troublemakers meant that he shared the same subversive category as the Black Panthers and other 1960s radicals. The FBI routinely unleashed counterintelligence operations against indexed individuals that ranged from besmirching their reputations to disrupting their activities to destroying their organizations.[57] What Tijerina or any of his associates did not merit, according to the FBI, was any assistance as the victims of violence. Following the January 1969 explosion at the Alianza's headquarters, the local FBI field office decided against any involvement in solving the case. As a letter to FBI director Hoover explained, "Because of [the] controversial nature of the organization and the pending prosecution in state court of several of its members, it is recommended that no investigation should be conducted."[58] The explanation made no sense except as a ranking of FBI priorities: when it came to such a "controversial" organization, protecting members mattered less than prosecuting them.

With many nuevomexicano officers on the payroll, New Mexico State Police were in an even better position to get close to Tijerina. Like the FBI, state police had been surveilling Tijerina for years.[59] These efforts, too, drastically intensified after June 5, 1967. Confident that the Alianza leader was "an avowed racist and militant," investigators trolled through Tijerina's past. They interviewed former Bible school classmates and disenchanted *aliancistas*. They traveled to Mexico to speak to acquaintances there. They paid informants, but state police officers went undercover too. During the fall of 1967, for example, two younger state police officers posed as students of New Mexico's Highlands University to secure an interview with Mary Escobar.[60] Undercover agents also attended the wedding of the highest-ranking War on Poverty official in the state because they suspected him of being too close to Tijerina.[61] While keeping an eye on the October 1967 Alianza convention, still another undercover state investigator found himself the object of recruitment. After all, one middle-aged member told him, the organization needed an infusion of young people.[62] Finally, one informant gained Tijerina's confidence to such an extent that the Alianza leader asked him to spy on his daughter Rose while she attended a dance with a young man whom Tijerina did not trust.[63]

Such ignorance did not last. In his memoir, Tijerina complained of the toll that constant surveillance took on the organization. "During the year 1967 and 1968, the police tormented [us] daily. . . . The Alianza was plagued with spies paid for by the police who watched every step that Reies made. They wanted to find flaws. They did not let us rest. It was a campaign of terror."[64] Even before the Alianza had made a public splash, Tijerina had sensed a conspiracy at work to keep nuevomexicanos poor and vulnerable. His early writings had constantly referred to "a sinister panorama," "organized crime," and "secret plans."[65] The constant scrutiny likely aggravated this tendency to see himself as the victim of such plots.

As surveillance continued, state police chief Joe Black maintained that the Alianza got what it deserved. After receiving a complaint in July 1969, Black testily replied, "If it were not for certain outside members of the Alianza, who are constantly stirring up trouble in Rio Arriba County, the New Mexico State Police would not find it necessary to keep them under constant surveillance. They have brought this upon themselves."[66] Infiltrators reported that certain Alianza members had accrued a cache of weapons and dynamite up north.[67] They also repeated more outlandish scenarios, including, for instance, that Anselmo Tijerina during the Poor People's Campaign planned to stay behind and "import 60 Cuban trained guerillas [*sic*]" to cause havoc in Albuquerque. Notably, considering the strained relations all around, one infiltrator boasted of having sown discord between members of the New Mexican delegation while in Washington, D.C.[68]

Another man publicly claimed years later to have been an agent provocateur within the Alianza. According to Tim Chapa, he began gathering information for the state police before the courthouse raid, but his role later shifted from surveillance to sabotage with the benefit of FBI counterintelligence training. Although federal and state police mostly operated on separate tracks when it came to keeping tabs on the Alianza, on occasion they cooperated. Chapa claimed he engaged in illegal activities that ranged from cutting fences and burning haystacks to trying to frame both Reies's brother Chris Tijerina by giving him a stolen car and Reies's son David (Reies Hugh) by providing him with a stolen check. According to Chapa, however, he proved a disappointment to law enforcement because he never got any dirt on Tijerina. Instead of behaving like a dangerous criminal, the Alianza president struck him as quite personable: "I could walk up to him anytime and talk to him. He was a friendly guy. He would greet everyone like a politician."[69]

Determining the veracity of Chapa's story is difficult. On the one hand, his oral history interview described several of the misfortunes that afflicted the Alianza in late 1968 and into 1969 from the perspective of a low-level informant—that is, from someone with only partial knowledge of who and what was being attacked.[70] On the other, his name first entered the public record in connection with the deaths of two Chicano activists.[71] Over the years, his story changed according to where suspicion fell.[72] Nor were law enforcement inclined to offer independent confirmation. About the possibility of Chapa being an informant, one New Mexican officer said, "It's not something we would discuss anyway."[73] For its part, the FBI did release thousands of pages about the Alianza as a result of Freedom of Information Act requests that Tijerina submitted in the 1970s and 1980s. Before doing so, it also blacked out large sections of text for two main reasons: national security and to protect the identity of informants.[74]

In the end, all of this surveillance never yielded a single arrest when it came to the bomb blasts and shootings directed at the Alianza. Nor did such intense law enforcement scrutiny ever uncover proof of further wrongdoing on Tijerina's part. Indeed, the lack of evidence prompted a desperate Hoover to forward a copy of an *American Opinion* attack on Tijerina to the FBI office in Albuquerque to use as a resource in an upcoming report.[75] As far as Chapa goes, his story, especially when placed against the mountain of state police reports and FBI briefs compiled on Tijerina over the years, at the very least suggests that the extent of law enforcement antipathy toward Tijerina has yet to be fully revealed.

On May 6, 1969, an NBC news program called *First Tuesday* broadcast a special segment on Reies López Tijerina and his followers. Upon hearing of the plans, Alianza members looked forward to seeing their cause receive prime-time national coverage. Imagine their surprise when the program labeled Tijerina the state's "most hated man" and the Alianza a product of "years of isolation and in-breeding." The segment began by linking Tijerina to the Penitentes, the religious brotherhood whose members had first schooled Tijerina about land-grant matters. "Religion and violence is in the blood of New Mexico," the voice-over by Tom Pettit, an award-winning journalist, intoned. "It's the home of the cult which practices self-flagellation on Good Fridays. They no longer crucify one of their own, but the worship of death remains a deep emotion in the remote mountain villages of New Mexico."[76]

The courthouse raid, the program asserted, stemmed from precisely this sort of inexplicable lust for bloodletting and violence. Just like "in the old days" when one Penitente received the honor of being crucified, the prospect of danger and death thrilled Alianza members. In one scene, a young man described dying in defense of his culture as a "beautiful" and "exciting" possibility.[77]

The rest of the program emphasized just how far apart the land-grant crusade stood from the American mainstream and the modern world. The program turned to the Pablo Valdez family, who lived in the tiny village of La Ensenada (where Tijerina had lived during the winter of 1959). The family of eleven shared a three-room house that lacked indoor plumbing, central heating, and a telephone. The family could not afford milk or meat. Successive generations of Valdez children learned English in school as a second language. Particularly revealing to Pettit, family members "see the outside world on a $28 television set on one channel," apparently the only one that received any signal. Here, it seems, was the real answer to the mystery of land-grant activism circa 1969. With few "channels" to the outside world, northern New Mexico remained backward and isolated, making it "fertile country for Tijerina."[78]

The Alianza leader received the toughest treatment. The opening voice-over professed agnosticism. Viewers needed to decide for themselves; was the Alianza leader a "mountebank, a mystic, or just a man who . . . for his own needs . . . must seek martyrdom? We don't pretend to know." Yet like the segment's title, the bulk of the program actually tilted heavily against the Alianza leader. Although a few supporters spoke highly of Tijerina, viewers heard critics describe him as a "foreigner," a "communist," a "charlatan," a "publicity hound," and an "opportunist." According to *First Tuesday*, evidently struggling with Spanish names, Tijerina also was a suspect in the murder of jailer *Julio* Salazar. Finally, the program captured the Alianza leader giving a rousing and disturbing speech. "The rape of the culture and language of a people is a greater crime than the rape of a two-year-old child," he proclaimed in his thickly accented English, which he no doubt employed for the benefit of television viewers. Tijerina then followed that cringe-inducing image with a religious metaphor that excused all the crimes associated with the courthouse raid. "We believe in Jesus Christ who used a whip . . . to drive . . . the false preachers out of the temple," Tijerina expounded jubilantly. "That's all we did in the courthouse of Tierra Amarilla. We just used a little whip."[79]

The irony was sharp. For more than ten years, Tijerina had sought to bring the Alianza's message to the broader public. The program reduced him to a fool, a fanatic. Yet Tijerina did not beckon bullets to fly through the Alianza office or welcome the explosives that blew up in that office as well as the homes and cars of people who knew him. Despite the segment's title, the news program spent very little time elaborating upon this pattern of violence directed at him. It did include Tijerina commenting that he expected to be assassinated. But without context, the comment served as further proof of an irrational death wish on Tijerina's part.

In a greater irony, in the weeks following the broadcast, Tijerina did move toward desperate and self-destructive protest. As the second anniversary of the courthouse raid approached, the *First Tuesday* broadcast represented a new way to draw attention to the Alianza cause and perhaps make a fresh start. Tijerina urgently needed one. Despite the services of William Kunstler, one the era's most well known radical attorneys, in April 1969 the 10th U.S. District Court of Appeals upheld Tijerina's conviction in the Echo Amphitheater case.[80] Tijerina's only hope to stay out of federal prison now rested on a long-shot appeal to the U.S. Supreme Court.

In the past, Tijerina's standard modus operandi had been to scale up confrontation whenever he needed to recharge the movement. By that standard, the Alianza's first protest following the broadcast was both innocuous and somewhat desperate. On May 17, 1969, Tijerina led a parade to mark the 429th anniversary of the Spanish language in New Mexico. The explorer Francisco Vázquez de Coronado and his troops had first marched through the region that long ago. Still, the arbitrary anniversary date of 429 years suggested that Tijerina was looking for something, perhaps anything, to inspire a demonstration and gain attention.[81] Equally important, the parade indicated an increasing gap between Tijerina and the mainstream of the Chicano movement. At a time when many Chicano movement participants were celebrating their mestizo heritage, the parade promoted an uncritical celebration of the Spanish colonial past. Just a few months before, Tijerina had written a letter to the "Excellentisimo Generalísimo Francisco Franco" asking the fascist dictator of Spain to take pity on his country's "orphan children" and embrace the land-grant cause.[82] Considering Tijerina's prior inclination to rave about Cuba's Castro, that move too carried a whiff of desperation.

Thanks to the Presbyterian Church and *Albuquerque Journal* editor Bob Brown, who happened to be a Presbyterian, Tijerina soon found a new protest occasion. In March 1968, church officials had invited him to appear at a national gathering in New York City. He had seized the opportunity to contest the church's ownership of the famous Ghost Ranch near Abiquiú where Georgia O'Keeffe, the artist, once lived. The ranch sat within the historic boundaries of the Piedra Lumbre grant and adjacent to the San Joaquín del Río de Chama grant, which had been the focus of so much Alianza attention.[83] In May 1968, after learning a bit about land-grant history, church officials decided to return a 20,000-acre parcel to "a recognized Spanish American organization," a description that sounded an awful lot like the Alianza.[84]

Brown then intervened to make sure the money went elsewhere. He appeared on the pages of the *Journal* opposing Tijerina as a possible recipient. While the Alianza leader had illuminated an injustice that had been "festering for years," read a statement that Brown and other church members from New Mexico authored, "it has not been demonstrated that he has any substantial following in New Mexico." Church officials also clarified that they always intended to work with local residents, not Tijerina. A $50,000 church grant to support land-grant efforts was never intended for the Alianza, either.[85] In response, on June 1, 1969, Tijerina and an estimated 100 Alianza members confronted a group of 100 Presbyterians as they gathered for a church synod at Ghost Ranch. Tijerina insisted that the church negotiate any return of lands with "legitimate" representatives, namely them. "We're looking for justice and you will answer to Christ," Tijerina insisted. "I'm like Christ . . . a tiger against criminals and a lamb to the innocent and poor."[86]

According to Peter Nabokov, the *Santa Fe New Mexican* reporter who closely followed Tijerina's exploits both before and after the courthouse raid, the Ghost Ranch clash initiated the "most manic and ultimately most disastrous week of [Tijerina's] career."[87] Just two days after he confronted Presbyterian Church officials, Tijerina flew to Washington, D.C., with every intention of conducting a citizen's arrest of Warren Burger, then a nominee for chief justice of the U.S. Supreme Court. Tijerina planned to make the arrest during Burger's confirmation hearings on the grounds that Burger had participated in "a conspiracy to violate civil rights of [the] poor and minorit[ies]." Tijerina, however, never got into the closed-door sessions. Nor did he confront Burger outside the hearing room. The nominee left through a back door while the gathered news media heard Tijerina's complaints in a public hallway. But they also heard Republican senator Everett M. Dirksen, the minority leader from Illinois, deem Tijerina's plans "perfectly stupid."[88] An inspector with the U.S. Capitol Police concurred, saying about Tijerina, "He sounds like some kind of nut, doesn't he?"[89]

Tijerina and his closest followers continued the tactic of trying to make citizen's arrests after returning to New Mexico. On June 7, they voted to arrest Governor David Cargo on the ground that he had backed the refusal of the Presbyterian Church to work with the Alianza. Cargo considered the threat grave enough that he promptly left a public gathering and was whisked away to an undisclosed location. Foiled on that front, Alianza members decided as citizens to arrest the head of Los Alamos National Laboratory for "constructing techniques of mass destruction." During World War II, physicists secretly had built the atomic bomb at Los Alamos, an achievement that Tijerina had opposed then. Now with about forty Alianza members dispersed in fifteen different vehicles, Tijerina haphazardly revisited his opposition. Tijerina did not even know who the lab director was until a public relations official for the lab offered Norris Bradbury's name. The same official, however, refused to provide Bradbury's address or even confirm his whereabouts, leaving Tijerina and his companions to find a public telephone booth and look up Bradbury's address themselves. Without a map, they roamed the streets of Los Alamos for about twenty minutes until some local teens pointed out the director's house. They then knocked on the door and rang the doorbell, but no one ever answered. With Los Alamos police watching but not interfering, Tijerina finally placed the arrest "warrant" in the mailbox.[90]

Patsy Tijerina, Reies's second wife, waiting in the car at a gas station after burning a Santa Fe National Forest sign in a protest to commemorate the second anniversary of the courthouse raid in June 1969. Later that morning she burned another national forest sign. While her husband did not directly partake in either burning, the subsequent clash between him and law enforcement that day nearly saw those guns in the front seat of the car fired. (Mark Bralley Photography)

The joke almost turned deadly the next day when Patsy Tijerina, Reies's twenty-one-year-old wife, announced that she intended to burn U.S. Forest Service property. First, she set fire to a $900 Santa Fe National Forest sign in Gallina. Although it was highly doubtful that Patsy conceived of the protest entirely on her own, she set the sign on fire without her husband's direct help in order to indicate, as she announced in advance, her personal commitment to the land-grant cause. According to one observer, Tijerina stayed at least forty feet away. After the couple drove away, however, Tijerina helped fill up plastic bottles at a gasoline station while Patsy waited in the car. Patsy then used the gasoline to burn down another Forest Service sign at the Coyote Ranger Station about twelve miles down the road. During this second sign burning, law enforcement officials, including New Mexico State Police officer Robert Gilliland and James Evans, a Forest Service investigator, arrived on the scene. Evans immediately tried to arrest the Tijerinas for destruction of government property. Reies Tijerina, in turn, announced that he intended to conduct a citizen's arrest of

Evans, who snapped back that an arrested citizen could not make a citizen's arrest. The entire exchange might have been comical if it had not involved guns. Instead of cooperating with Evans, Tijerina turned toward his car, where a rifle lay across the front seat. The moment that he reached for a weapon, Tijerina swiftly found a carbine, a shotgun, and a pistol all cocked and aimed at his head, courtesy of the surrounding law officers. "Drop it Reies, or I'll kill you," Evans told Tijerina.[91]

Miraculously, everyone emerged physically unscathed that afternoon, including three-year-old Isabel Tijerina, the daughter of Patsy and Reies, who might have been caught in the crossfire as she was in the car at the time.[92] Tijerina, however, paid a high price. A free man pending his appeal of his Echo Amphitheater conviction, he immediately faced a bond revocation hearing that showcased the level of official animus directed at him. Testifying at the hearing, New Mexico State Police officer Robert Gilliland responded clearly when asked by a defense lawyer whether he hated the Alianza leader: "Yes, I do." Yet Gilliland also maintained that he lacked any desire to shoot Tijerina because such an action would play into Tijerina's hands. "That is just what he would like," he said. "He would like the glory of being a martyr."[93] After hearing from several law enforcement officers, Judge Howard C. Bratton revoked Tijerina's bond.

Remanded to federal custody, the Alianza leader thus sat behind bars while he awaited trial for charges related to the sign-burning incident and news regarding his pending appeals. Before the month was out, a U.S. District Court let his contempt of court conviction stand.[94] In late September 1969, an Albuquerque jury found him guilty of two counts of aiding and abetting in the destruction of U.S. government property and one count of assault against James Evans that day.[95] A federal judge sentenced him to three years.[96] The following month, the U.S. Supreme Court let stand all the convictions stemming from the Alianza's occupation of the Echo Amphitheater in October 1966.[97] At this point, the two-year sentence that Judge Bratton had imposed on Tijerina the year before also became effective. Serving these sentences concurrently, with some time off for good behavior and for time served, Tijerina stayed in federal prison until July 26, 1971.[98]

The experience elicited a range of emotions from Tijerina as he struggled to make sense of life behind bars. At first, he insisted that he valued the opportunity to rest, read, and reflect.[99] In August 1969, however, Tijerina crafted an angry letter that, after publication in a Chicano movement newspaper, circulated widely. In this letter, he accused Evans, the Forest

Service investigator, of attempted assassination that June. Tijerina also vigorously defended his reputation. "My only crime is demanding the respect and protection of our property, which has been confiscated illegally by the federal government."[100] That October, Tijerina adopted a more conciliatory approach. The same day that the U.S. Supreme Court rejected his appeal, Tijerina, not yet aware of the decision, issued another letter that mostly enumerated the same legal texts that he had long relied upon to buttress land claims. As scholar Josue David Cisneros noted, Tijerina now aimed to inform rather than condemn.[101]

Yet Tijerina's embrace of martyrdom united the two letters. "I write to you as one of the clearest victims of the madness and racism in the heart of present-day politicians," he lamented in the first letter. At the same time, Tijerina voiced optimism that his suffering might rejuvenate the land-grant movement.[102] In the second letter, Tijerina clung to the role of martyr for this precise reason. "For the land, culture, and inheritance of my people, I am willing to suffer . . . imprisonment," he wrote, conveying a sense of deep contentment at his plight.[103] In either case, he looked forward to a new reign of justice built upon his sacrifice.[105]

Accumulated legal defeats interfered with these grand hopes and all but ended Tijerina's glory days on the national stage. In addition to the federal convictions, in November 1969 an Albuquerque jury found Tijerina guilty of intent to maim and false imprisonment during a state trial on the second set of raid charges.[105]

Unaware of what the future might hold, Tijerina closed the year 1969 the perfect martyr. He had not only suffered for his cause, but he had sought out and welcomed that suffering.

Epilogue

In a dingy apartment just a stone's throw from the Mexican border in El Paso, Texas, I sat down to talk to Reies López Tijerina in April 2010. As much as political adversaries had accused him of squeezing money from gullible followers through the years, Tijerina's activism clearly never made him rich. The apartment consisted only of a tiny kitchen and a slightly larger room that featured a coffee table stacked high with books and papers, an old-style television, a double bed, and, wedged between the side of the bed and the door to the bathroom, another small table where Tijerina and I sat across from each other. The close quarters no doubt helped Tijerina navigate his surroundings. At eighty-three, the once vigorous leader suffered from a weak heart and diabetes. He appeared bloated and frail. Often tethered to an oxygen tank, Tijerina found it taxing to walk even the shortest distances. His mane of white hair showed the passing of years, too. Clean-cut and clean-shaven during what he once called his "prime looking period," the bearded Tijerina now wore his hair long and slicked back in a style that minimized trips to the barber. Only Tijerina's eyebrows remained almost jet black. They framed eyes, moreover, that were as piercing as ever. Unchanged too was Tijerina's forceful blend of ego and conviction. After I explained to him that I was writing a history of the Alianza Federal de Mercedes, Tijerina immediately leaned forward, looked at me square in the eye, and insisted, "But Lorena, I *was* the Alianza."[1]

He had a point. Brilliant, charismatic, and deeply disconcerting, Tijerina ran the Alianza as his personal fiefdom. As observers subsequently noted, the organization seemed to have little structure beyond his own dictates. Guided by a sense of God-granted destiny and emotionally and financially supported by family members, Tijerina managed to harness a long history of land-grant activism and transform it into his personal crusade. While the powers-that-be throughout the 1960s dismissed his ideas about conquest and land usurpation as dangerous, subversive, or just plain preposterous, his critical look backward at the repercussions of the U.S.-Mexican War slowly became more acceptable. Within a generation, Tijerina's anticolonial analysis had emerged as the conventional wisdom that academics adopted and that politicians parroted.

Still, Tijerina and the broader land-grant movement were never one and the same. They only overlapped temporarily. Tijerina admitted as much at the fortieth anniversary of the courthouse raid in 2007 when, seated before a gathered crowd, he complained that history had placed him in too narrow an interpretative box. In another snapshot of his mercurial nature, he offered a summation of his career that directly contradicted his later assertion to me in 2010. "The public is so backward, so retarded in terms of my activities. . . . A lot of people like to keep thinking Reies is the Alianza, Reies is the land-grant, blah, blah, blah. They are wrong."[2] Yet this statement too revealed an important truth. With few key exceptions—courthouse raid anniversaries being one of them—the man and the movement largely went their separate ways in the decades that followed. Their intersection, however, reverberated with significance for both.

THE MAN

Mental illness likely contributed to Tijerina's declining fortunes. Upon entering federal custody in mid-June 1969, Tijerina was first sent to La Tuna, a federal prison outside of El Paso, a location that facilitated both his attendance at various legal proceedings and visits from friends and family.[3] In early 1970, however, federal authorities transferred Tijerina to the Medical Center for Federal Prisoners in Springfield, Missouri, 800 miles away from Albuquerque, a distance that guaranteed fewer visitors. While at Springfield, Tijerina underwent minor throat surgery. Yet possible psychiatric ailments concerned doctors more. Norman A. Carlson, director of the Springfield facility, explained to Tijerina's eldest son that his father had been transferred for "careful medical and emotional evaluation."[4] A staff report further described Tijerina as "a sincere man who believes in his cause with which he is obsessed" and determined that he belonged "in an intensive psychiatric ward" because of a "tentative diagnosis of personality disorder of a schizoid type."[5] In September 1970, physicians associated with the prison's neuropsychiatric department offered an official "diagnosis of schizophrenia, chronic, with intermittent periods of persecutory and grandiose thought."[6]

Tijerina rejected the diagnosis. Upon his release, he complained that he had suffered poor medical care, including receiving medicine for "crazy people" instead of genuine relief for his painful throat.[7]

Barred as a condition of his parole from holding any Alianza office or engaging in political protest, Tijerina on the day of his release announced a newish crusade. Harking back to his old proposition that Indo-Hispanos might serve as potential peacemakers between blacks and whites, he announced his intention to promote international brotherhood.[8] For the next several years, in the interest of "world harmony," Tijerina spearheaded annual "brotherhood awareness" conferences, the main theme connoting the exact opposite of "violent revolution."[9] In a testament to Tijerina's continuing ability to reinvent himself, local businessmen, the Albuquerque chief of police, and some of the state's top politicians all endorsed these gatherings.[10] So did such out-of-town celebrities as Dennis Hopper, the Hollywood actor, and boxing champion Muhammad Ali.[11] At the height of his brotherhood awareness campaign, Tijerina even scored an invitation to appear on NBC's *Today* morning show.[12]

Of course, land-grant matters still mattered to Tijerina. The broad concept of brotherhood awareness neatly left room for the real business of recovering land rights. "After this brotherhood awareness jubilee," he confided to one Native American ally and conference invitee, "then we can talk about the rights that our people have under the treaties."[13] Behind his parole officer's back, Tijerina also continued to exert influence within the Alianza. That fact became public knowledge when the organization's official president, Santiago Tapia y Anaya, accused Tijerina of trying to execute an illegal power grab.[14] The moment his probation ended, moreover,

Tijerina resumed the organization's top spot.[15] During the early 1970s, Tijerina also took trips to Mexico to seek support for the land-grant movement and finally met two Mexican presidents.[16] He tried and failed to launch a new Alianza-type organization among Tejanos.[17]

Yet Tijerina never regained his former position of influence. According to his own account, continued persecution was to blame. In October 1971, Tijerina upstaged all the other speakers at a national Hispanic conference in Washington, D.C., when he made the stunning accusation that ten men, including one New Mexico State Police officer, had sexually assaulted his wife while he was in prison.[18] After conducting a lengthy investigation, the New Mexico Office of the Attorney General released a report that dismissed any allegation that Patsy had been raped as "patently spurious and unfounded."[19] Tijerina immediately rejected the report as "a political document" designed to hide the "greatest scandal."[20]

Reies Tijerina's recollections of threats from the outside world had support from other family members, however. In 1972, according to both Rose Tijerina and her father, Rose was picked up by a group of men who—in an apparent reference to Reies's allegations concerning his wife—promised to show her what rape really was. Rose told of managing to escape only by jumping from a moving vehicle as it slowed to turn a corner.[21] And in the most clearly documented case, New Mexico State Police officer Albert Vega sexually assaulted the youngest son of Reies Tijerina and Mary Escobar, Noe, who was just fourteen at the time. Vega pled guilty, but as Noe was a minor, his involvement as a victim only came to light in 1974, when his family filed civil suit against the officer.[22]

To Reies Tijerina, the suffering of his wife and children fit a broader pattern of persecution directed at him because of his unrelenting commitment to justice. "My wife was violated by police. My daughter Rose was kidnapped by police. My son Noe was kidnapped and raped by police. My home and office were bombed four times," he later noted. "And why all this terror? To cover up the ruthless raping of our municipalities that were created under the governments of Spain and Mexico."[23]

Years later, Noe, who was just nine at the time of the courthouse raid, added that growing up Tijerina meant having to deal with constant abuse and teasing during his high school years.[24] Citing the harassment of his children, Reies Tijerina decided to educate all four of his youngest children at home and within his political orbit.[25] In 1973, he named his tenth and last child "Danitha," Hebrew, he said, for "God is my judge."[26] Nevertheless, he still had to answer to secular authorities. The next year, Tijerina spent another six months in state prison for his 1969 conviction on raid charges, his final incarceration.[27]

Upon his release, Tijerina retreated to his home in Coyote to study, reflect, and defend his reputation. He approved of a Mexican-made movie, released in 1976, based upon his exploits.[28] It was also then that he compiled his lengthy biography, *Mi Lucha por la Tierra*, calling out his enemies by name and emphasizing his close relationship with Eulogio Salazar, the murdered jailer.[29] Not until 1977 did the New Mexico attorney general's office issue a report that officially cleared Tijerina of any wrongdoing in connection to Salazar's death.[30] In the years that followed, Tijerina developed other interests, which included solving the problems of "warring tribes" within the Middle East, numerology, and genealogy. For a short while in the 1980s, Tijerina insisted that his name was actually spelled Tixerina.[31] Eventually, the former Alianza president concluded that he was an Israelite, an identity that he asserted was distinct from being Jewish. He used this identity to fend off mounting accusations that he had become virulently anti-Semitic.[32] In 1993, in what must have struck him as further evidence of persecution, his Coyote home burned to the ground in a possible case of arson.[33] Tijerina moved to Mexico shortly afterward, and there, after divorcing Patsy, he remarried a Mexican national named Esperanza Garcia Valladares.[34]

Even as his interests expanded, Tijerina's desire for compliance among his family, friends, and followers remained. Many of his writings after the Alianza's heyday lamented the end of patriarchy. "They have taken away from the father all his rights, honor, and place within the family," he complained in 1974.[35] More than ever, to disagree with Tijerina was to risk being seen as his enemy, as someone who had joined the web of persecution that bedeviled him. "My father is the kind of man that will say if you speak out and not to his agreement, 'You're an enemy of the cause,'" recalled Noe Tijerina.[36] The Alianza hobbled through the 1970s with a dwindling number of members, all hyper-loyal to the organization's founder.[37] The land-grant group then faded into obscurity. To a large extent, so did Tijerina.

After his release from federal prison in 1971, Tijerina was invited to attend the first, and only, Raza Unida Party national convention in El Paso in 1972. The two men beside him, José Angel Gutiérrez, wearing glasses, and Rodolfo "Corky" Gonzales, battled over who would become party chairman, with Gutiérrez winning. Despite his center position in the picture, Tijerina was never in the running. (Center for Southwest Research, University of New Mexico, Albuquerque)

THE MOVEMENT

The deepest irony about Tijerina's story is that although he increasingly inhabited the political sidelines, his ideas spread far and wide. That duality characterized his post-prison relationship with land-grant activists and Chicano movement participants alike. In the early 1970s, Chicano student groups inundated Tijerina with invitations to speak, expecting to hear from a hero and a militant.[38] But his softer talk of brotherhood awareness disappointed. Few Chicano activists wished to heed his advice to "temper their revolutionary spirit."[39] Respect for his past achievements gained Tijerina an invitation to the first—and only—national La Raza Unida Party conference in El Paso in 1972. In an iconic photo from the convention, Tijerina stands between José Angel Gutiérrez of Texas and Corky Gonzales of Colorado, all three men clasping their hands together, arms raised in victory. Despite Tijerina's position in the photo, the contest for party leadership had occurred between the other two men, bypassing him entirely. Tijerina no longer played a central role in the movement. By

1972, "the claws and the fangs of El Tigre were gone," recalled one convention attendee.[40] Among those put off by Tijerina's mellower tone, unsubstantiated rumors began to circulate that the former Alianza leader had undergone a lobotomy in Springfield.[41]

By then, however, Tijerina's ideas about conquest, culture, indigeneity, and the injustice of land theft had already entered the Chicano movement mainstream. They all appeared in the premier organizing document of the Chicano movement, *El Plan Espiritual de Aztlán*. Corky Gonzales and others wrote this action blueprint during a youth conference that the Crusade for Justice hosted in Denver in March 1969. The word "Aztlán" itself referred to the ancient homelands of the Aztecs. For most Chicano movement participants, however, the term mattered less as actual territory than as a means of asserting a radical notion of belonging based on the long history of indigenous and mestizo people in the hemisphere. "In a spirit of a new people that is conscious not only of its proud heritage but also of the brutal gringo invasion of our territories" the document opened, before asserting an ancestral claim to the land. With a nod to the farmworkers' struggle too, the preamble asserted, "Aztlán belongs to those who plant the seeds, water the fields, and gather the crops and not to the foreign Europeans." As an indigenous people, moreover, Chicanos refused to "recognize capricious frontiers on the bronze continent." Perhaps most telling of all, the preamble defined the Chicano struggle as one against "the foreigner '*gabacho*' [a slang term meaning American or "whitey"] who exploits our riches and destroys our culture."[42]

Moved by the spirit present in Denver, Alianza members in October 1969, while their leader sat in jail, endorsed the establishment of an independent nation somewhere in the U.S. Southwest to be called La República de Aztlán.[43] The following year, attendees at the second Chicano Youth Liberation Conference in Denver proclaimed the then-imprisoned Tijerina the "First National Hero of Aztlán."[44]

Surprising many who had accused him of seeking just that sort of separatism, an angry Tijerina resigned. "My motto is justice but not independence or revolution," he insisted, reverting to the role of the good American as his judicial fate hung in the balance.[45] A cranky Tijerina also decided he did not like the word "Aztlán," which he equated with Aztec imperialism. He also did not like the word "Chicano," which he now denounced as a made-up word reeking of assimilation, and he really did not like Chicano movement participants refusing to do what he said.[46] "Estos niños no saben nada [These children don't know anything]," Tijerina supposedly huffed about younger activists who would not follow his lead.[47]

Yet these momentary disputes faded in importance compared with Tijerina's contribution to Chicano movement and land-grant politics. It was no coincidence that a premier Chicano movement publication, *El Grito del Norte*, called northern New Mexico home. Founded by Beverly Axelrod, once Tijerina's lawyer, and Elizabeth "Betita" Martínez, a New York City editor (and the other Latina in SNNC), and staffed by Alianza veterans and supporters, the newspaper gained fame for its blend of local politics alongside national and international concerns.[48]

In northern New Mexico, land-grant activists acknowledged, sometimes grudgingly, that the Alianza had reinvigorated the pursuit of land-grant justice. They also moved on.[49] In 1969, a group that included Anselmo Tijerina, Valentina Valdez, and Maria Varela founded an agricultural cooperative to meet the needs of local farmers and hungry families. Members "just wanted to show people what we could do with the land if it was returned," explained Valdez.[50] This initial effort rapidly expanded to include a law office, a graphic arts workshop, and perhaps most important of all at a time when the closest doctor practiced seventy-six miles away, a medical clinic.[51] Other activists, including Moises Morales, who as a young Alianza member had acted as a scout on the day of the raid, challenged the entrenched political machine of Emilio Naranjo (Sheriff Benny Naranjo's father) as members of the Raza Unida Party. Direct protest continued too. Most dramatically, during the late 1980s, a dispute between a development cooperation and a Tierra Amarilla man named Amador Flores over 500 acres that Flores claimed as his own, as had his father and grandfather before him, led to a fourteen-month armed standoff. Pedro Archuleta, a veteran of the Alianza, and of the Raza Unida Party, played a leading role in establishing a bunker and an impressive system of defense.[52]

A broader solution to obtaining land-grant redress, however, required congressional intervention. During the 1970s, the amount of effort on that front stood as testament to how deeply the ideas that Tijerina helped popularize, and that had once seemed so transgressive and dangerous, had found widespread acceptance. In response to Alianza activism, as early as March 1969 Representative Henry B. González of San Antonio proposed a congressional investigation into land-grant claims. Tijerina had pressed for exactly this sort of investigation since 1964, when he met with González for the first time. The congressman's proposal, however, aimed to quiet false expectations among some "undereducated" folks—in other words, to tamp down Tijerina's influence.[53] In 1971, two black congressmen, Augustus F. Hawkins of Los Angeles and Ron Dellums of Oakland, both Democrats, proved much more sympathetic, proposing legislation to enforce the Treaty of Guadalupe Hidalgo.[54] Then, in what amounted to previously unimaginable support for Tijerina's long-term dream, in 1974 both the New Mexico House and Senate unanimously passed a resolution urging the federal government to adjudicate common lands claimed by Indo-Hispano people using the model of the Federal Indian Claims Commission.[55] That vote finally prompted Senator Joseph Montoya to back federal legislation to settle land-grant claims.[56]

Although these efforts stalled, the ideas behind them endured. In 1998, for example, Republican representative Bill Redmond of New Mexico, hoping to court nuevomexicano voters, introduced a bill "to establish a presidential commission to determine the validity of certain land claims arising out of the Treaty of Guadalupe-Hidalgo," which passed the U.S. House of Representatives 223 to 187.[57] That achievement merits notice. Despite the great successes of the civil rights movement, Congress never voted on a bill for reparations to the descendants of African American slaves. To gauge community interest regarding the proposed legislation, members of the New Mexican congressional delegation held hearings in Española, New Mexico, that September. A generation before, officials had taken the stance that no injustice had been committed, and even if it had, nothing could be done about it now. As New Mexico senator Clinton P. Anderson, like Montoya a Democrat, had laconically maintained in 1968, events "nearly 100 years ago" had established "a pretty permanent title."[58] In sharp contrast, in his opening remarks at the federal hearings in Española, New Mexico, Senator Pete Domenici labeled the proposed legislation the "first step in addressing the longstanding unfairness that has blemished the conscience of New Mexico's history." He noted the problems that land-grant claimants had confronted, from "an unfamiliar legal system" to "very hostile government officials." The question then was "where do we go from here," Domenici asserted. "If we choose wisely, it is an opportunity to reverse a heritage of ill will."[59]

Ultimately, the U.S. government chose foolishly. After any attempt to pass meaningful legislation regarding land grants became hopelessly entangled in congressional budget talks, New Mexican land-grant activists increasingly centered their hopes on a U.S. General Accounting Office report. Released in 2004, the report concluded that the United States had properly met all of its responsibilities under the treaty. In what seemed like some sort of painful flashback to the earliest days of Alianza organizing, however, the report mostly outlined U.S. adjudication proceedings and mentioned significant court rulings without delving into the inherent fairness of these proceedings and rulings at all.[60] New Mexicans dedicated to the land-grant cause pushed back. Now a respected elder, Juan Valdez, who had entered the courthouse first on June 5, 1967, "smelled a skunk." To him, the report aimed to bury problems, not resolve them.[61] The New Mexico Land Grant Forum, the latest statewide land-grant group, charged the report with "fairly serious flaws" of interpretation.[62] Malcolm Ebright, a lawyer turned historian who in the wake of the Alianza made studying land grants his life's work, declared the report a "slap in the face" to all land-grant heirs.[63]

The pushback highlighted one of the most significant accomplishments of Tijerina and the Alianza: the land-grant movement during the 1960s punched through the "shroud of silence" regarding land-stealing in New Mexico. Recall that Alianza ally Professor Clark Knowlton, arriving in New Mexico in 1958, had been advised to direct his research interest elsewhere to avoid "rocking the ethnic boat."[64] As Carolyn Zeleny observed in her 1944 Yale dissertation, "local custom forbade the overt mention of tensions and conflicts between the two ethnic groups [Spanish Americans and Anglo-Americans] in the interests of maintaining a front of harmonious relations." Twenty years later, moreover, custom prevailed. The University of New Mexico refused to publish Zeleny's work, thinking "it unwise to sponsor a book on such a delicate subject."[65] Under these circumstances, some argued that forgetting offered the best way forward. In the wake of the raid, Governor David Cargo advised an infusion of federal dollars for schools and job programs in northern New Mexico with exactly this aim in mind. "We have got to do all of these other things so that they will forget what happened a long time ago," Cargo testified before Congress. "It is the only way you can do it."[66]

Refusing to forget, Tijerina and other Alianza activists inspired scholars to take a second and then a third look at land-grant history. An early indication of a shift in thinking occurred in December 1971, when the New Mexico State Planning Office released the blandly named *Land Title Study*. Officially, the study merely sought to consider ways to quiet land titles in New Mexico ostensibly for the purpose of spurring economic development in the state. Under that mandate, however, the report recognized the legitimacy of the land-grant cause. It pointed out that out of nearly 35 million acres claimed by the former citizens of Mexico in New Mexico, the U.S. Court of Private Land Claims confirmed less than 2 million acres, that is, less than 6 percent of the total property claimed.[67] Senator Domenici directly quoted this figure in his 1998 testimony.

Intrigued, academics and independent scholars began to explore the parameters and permutations of this injustice. Ebright ranked among the first and most prolific. In 1979, he founded the Center for Land Grant Studies, which nearly four decades later still operates as a central clearinghouse for land grant matters. In 1980, he published a sixty-six-page essay on the Tierra Amarilla land grant in which he denounced a history of "chicanery."[68] That same year, Roxanne Dunbar-Ortiz published *Roots of Resistance*, which examined land tenure in New Mexico since 1680 while also making the case for Native-Hispano solidarity. Dunbar-Ortiz estimated that within fifty years after conquest, Spanish speakers had been deprived of as much as 80 percent of their landholdings.[69] An avalanche of studies followed. Those that examined Spanish-speaking village life in New Mexico tended to highlight both the cultural richness of the area and the history of diminishing land and water rights.[70] The new literature captured a striking change over time. In 1973, Victor Westphall, an expert on land policy in the state, wrote a largely complimentary biography of Thomas Benton Catron, the lawyer and politician who in the late 1800s became the largest landowner in New Mexico as a member of the Santa Fe Ring. Ten years later, however, Westphall weighed in heavily in favor of land-grant rights. "The Congress of the United States has been constantly and infamously remiss in implementing the obligations incurred as a signatory of the Treaty of Guadalupe Hidalgo," he concluded. Redress, he admitted, would require "heroic measures" because of so much "government bureaucracy favoring private interests," but "it can be done."[71]

The afterlife of Tijerina's ideas also found a home in the new field of Chicano and Chicana history. Before the 1960s, with few exceptions, Mexican Americans appeared in the academic literature primarily as sociological problems to be solved rather than as legitimate historical subjects. In the same way that the fields of women's history and women's studies arose in response to the women's movement of the 1960s and 1970s, this field arose as a response to the Chicano movement. Scholars placed conquest at the center of its story. In 1971, for example, Juan Gómez-Quiñones wrote one of the first articles that attempted to define an overarching "paradigm" for this emerging field; an emphasis on conquest topped the list of eight factors to consider.[72] Similarly, the title of Rodolfo Acuña's

Reies López Tijerina in 2007 at a fortieth anniversary commemoration of the courthouse raid. He was speaking in the remains of his home in Coyote that had been destroyed by arson in 1993. About two dozen people gathered to hear him address the evils of cosmetics and the numerological significance of Franklin D. Roosevelt's name, as well as the Alianza's accomplishments. Behind him was a mural depicting a younger version of himself. (Eddie Moore photographer, *Albuquerque Journal* photograph)

1972 overview of Mexican American history, *Occupied America: The Chicano's Struggle toward Liberation*, pounded home the significance of war and conquest, as did his chapter titles. "Legacy of Hate: The Conquest of the Southwest" read one; "Land Grab in New Mexico" read another.[73] The field soon produced pathbreaking monographs that made clear that New Mexicans were hardly unique in dealing with the repercussions of war and subsequent land dispossession.[74] Later works examined the implications of conquest for women in particular.[75]

Finally, the social movements of the 1960s influenced the emergence of what scholars called the New Western History, which took into greater account race, class, and gender. In 1987, Patricia Nelson Limerick published *The Legacy of Conquest: The Unbroken Past of the American West*, an influential survey among historians that marked the dawn of the New

Western History. When it came to the U.S.-Mexican War, that meant looking at the conflict from a Tijerina-like perspective. "It takes only a modest effort of imagination to see America's grand venture in continental Manifest Destiny as it looked to Mexico: a shameless land grab and an attack on Mexican sovereignty," she wrote, before detailing how arriving Americans pried the land from the former citizens of Mexico.[76] Under the more recent rubric of "U.S. settler colonialism," scholars routinely pair the land struggle in New Mexico with places as far away—but as deeply affected by U.S. imperialism—as Hawaii and Puerto Rico.[77] In seeing these commonalities, Tijerina had them beat by more than a generation.[78]

INCONVENIENT TRUTHS

The Tijerina story prompts a mediation on the historical process as much as it tells the story of a man and a movement. Indirectly, his life experiences raise a series of questions: How do Americans understand their contested past? How does a nation decide what merits inclusion in the historical record and what does not? At a time when the Vietnam War raged and Americans were beginning to question the justification and purpose of a military intervention 10,000 miles away, the 1967 courthouse raid exposed the deep roots of U.S. imperialism on the North American continent. In the early twenty-first century, as the immigration debates roar on and "Mexicans" have once again been typecast as consisting of law-breaking and dangerous foreigners, the raid performs another equally important function: it serves as a reminder that the history of Spanish-speaking settlement in what is now called the American Southwest predates the founding of the United States.

The Tijerina story's repeated intersections with sexual violence, religious extremism, and mental illness, moreover, tests the historian's craft by destabilizing what counts as evidence. Take the allegations of sexual abuse. As much as feminists during the 1960s pronounced that the personal was political, a question posed by one of my senior colleagues early on haunted me: "What does incest have to do with the land grants?" he asked.[79] To answer that question, I needed to grapple with the inherently contested "he said/she said" nature of the accusations and then sift through colliding memories for significance. I also needed to reject the implicit assumption built into my colleague's question, namely that to incorporate this "open secret" into any Tijerina tale detracted from more important matters. But as a historian wanting to understand this man and this movement, I could not look away.

This book instead centers experiences of abuse. The stories of Mary Escobar and Rose Tijerina expose how the control of women and their sexuality lay at the root of Tijerina's leadership style and his beliefs about how society should be organized. Although women and gender historians have paid attention to the topic of sexual abuse, biographers of male political leaders rarely do, much less do they consider sexual violence as *central* to understanding the politics of these male leaders. In daring to ask Tijerina about allegations of abuse in 2010, I not only worked toward a new way of understanding a male movement leader but also transgressed his still-strong gender norms. "Your education comes from the university," he yelled at me during our interview. "But my knowledge comes from God."[80]

Tijerina's faith undergirded his views of women as much it undergirded his politics. Yet it also provided another scholarly challenge. By definition, faith lies beyond that which can be proved. Furthermore, Tijerina's religious beliefs appeared to provide the most abundant evidence of his "weirdo" status. Throw together his constant desire to detect God's hand in human history, his visits with angels, and his secret life as a prophet, and here was a man seemingly out of step with contemporary society, a modern-day Menocchio.[81] Upon closer inspection, however, some of even the most fantastical elements of his faith were held in common with his Pentecostal or former Pentecostal brethren caught up in the religious revival that swept across the country after World War II. In 2005, Rudy V. Busto attributed the failure of scholars to delve into Tijerina's religious background to their loyalty to a cultural nationalist heroic narrative that then dominated Chicano movement history.[82] In my own research, however, another explanation arose: the sheer difficulty of making political sense of Tijerina's all-encompassing "religious vision." To rephrase my colleague's question, "What does *Hallará Fé* have to do with the land grants?" The difficulty of discernment only increased once Tijerina was out of the pulpit and restricted his religious pronouncements to passing references to biblical passages and familiar metaphors of justice and salvation. In the end, however, Tijerina's religious faith was the kaleidoscope containing all of his shifting views.

Considering seriously the matter of religious beliefs placed Tijerina in a comparative context that rendered him less a singular, inexplicable figure. From Joan of Arc to Jim Jones of the People's Temple, the juncture between faith and dreams of political liberation is common enough.[83]

Martin Luther King Jr. traced his courage to continue with the Montgomery bus boycott in the face of death threats and bombings to one night when, sitting down for a cup of coffee at his kitchen table, he heard the encouraging voice of Jesus.[84] Rigoberta Menchú and her fellow Mayan villagers confronting brutal repression in the 1960s and 1970s in Guatemala took comfort and encouragement from the story of Old Testament figures fighting against the oppression of their people.[85] Closer to home, during the late nineteenth century, the Ghost Dance leader Wovoka inspired others with messianic visions.[86]

My accepting the centrality of Tijerina's religious beliefs, however, also meant pondering at what point faith crosses over into fanaticism and even mental illness. The topic is a tender one because so many of his opponents were quick to label Tijerina insane for daring to dream of land-grant justice at all. Against that backdrop, Tijerina's repeated tendency to compare himself to Jesus Christ stood out to me, as a historian and not a medical clinician, as most illuminating in terms of understanding Tijerina's motivation. Recall the Alianza office mural described in this book's introduction that showed three figures, "the Negro, the Indian, and the Hispano," bound together in a quest to reach justice. The mural contained two other revealing details. One was a snake, aka Satan, that impeded the three by wrapping its body around them. The other was a secretary bird, the official avian symbol of the Alianza, swooping down from the upper right-hand corner of the mural to attack and kill the snake. Now remember that Tijerina understood via his 1956 super-dream that his role was secretary. And in Christian theology, Christ sits at the right hand of God the Father. The not-so-secret message of the mural: Tijerina was savior to all.[87] Throughout his life, that foundational assumption fed a massive and uncompromising ego.

His powerful personality played out on the page. Writing this work required seizing control of the narrative from Tijerina. Regardless of whether he was correctly diagnosed as mentally ill, to fully comprehend Tijerina demanded that I move beyond what he had always recounted about his past in his own handwriting over and over again and in countless interviews. It also demanded that I make sense of a worldview unlike any that I had ever encountered, a worldview that excused cruel behavior yet provided incredible historical insights, a worldview that featured super-dreams but was grounded in the bitter reality of poverty and injustice. Ultimately, it was the sum total of this difficult material, as it appeared in neatly indexed archival folders and in less neatly contained memories, that provided the answers to what made Tijerina tick.

During my 2010 visit with him, Tijerina asked me to obtain a copy for him of a 2002 ruling by the Colorado Supreme Court. After twenty-one years of litigation, in a victory for Sangre de Cristo land-grant activists, the court affirmed their right to access the mountain range over the objections of the owners, the sons of Jack Taylor, that Colorado lumberman who once had beaten men he deemed trespassers on his property. Against a long tradition of favoring individual property rights, the landmark ruling finally placed the courts on the side of land-grant activists. Inspired by this decision, Tijerina spoke during our meeting of seeking a similar sort of victory in the case of the San Joaquín grant. He envisioned launching one enormous lawsuit against all those who had wronged him, and his family, and all land-grant heirs. Like so many of his dreams, this idea seemed impossible to obtain.

Yet absent such outrageous aspirations, such a ferocious sense of destiny, and such an unswaying conviction in the righteousness of his anticolonial crusade, how else would this man, in all his imperfections, have managed to rewrite our understanding of American empire?

Acknowledgments

Two of my favorite words in English are "grace" and "faith." In this book, I aimed to weave together storytelling and significance. If I have succeeded, it is because so many people had faith in me and because so many others, some of whom I knew only casually, if at all, graced me with their time and wisdom.

My first thanks go to Mary Escobar, Rose Tijerina, and Rachel Tijerina for trusting me with their memories. I also want to acknowledge other members of the Tijerina family, some of whom I met and some of whom I never did. In writing this story, I was always cognizant that I was writing about someone's husband, father, or grandfather. If he were still alive, I would thank Tijerina himself for sharing two days with me. As that is not possible, I will thank his widow, Esperanza.

Next, I am grateful to the two anonymous readers for the University of North Carolina Press (who I later found out were Matt Garcia and Felipe Hinojosa) for the tremendous care with which they read an earlier draft of this book. Both provided comments that helped me strengthen the book's coherence and thematic richness overall. Devra Weber, Roxanne Dunbar-Ortiz, and Lorena Márquez also read the entire manuscript in draft form to my great benefit. For her part, Maria Varela read a "rawer" version of this book and took the time to make some critical interventions. My dear friend Enriqueta Vasquez read the same material early on while repeatedly opening her home in San Cristobal, New Mexico, to me.

Without the help of several nuevomexicanos, I could not have written this book. Gloria Maes literally opened doors for me. Moises Morales spent a day with me in Canjilón years ago and introduced me to Alex Leyba and to Alex's mother, Mary Leyba, who introduced me to Juan Valdez, who introduced me to his wife, Rosina, and to his brother Tony. Sociologists speak of "snowballing" in terms of recruiting interviewees, but the truth is that Canjilón is a tiny village without a hotel or even a McDonald's nearby, as Mary Leyba once pointed out. So she fed and housed me overnight twice.

At the University of New Mexico in Albuquerque, I owe my deepest debt to David Correia, whom I met at a fortieth anniversary celebration of the courthouse raid and with whom I was still swapping ideas at a fiftieth! A quick glance at this book's endnotes reveals how much his scholarship meant to me; I value his friendship just as much. I'm likewise grateful to Alyosha Goldstein, also in American studies at the University of New Mexico, for inviting me to participate in the pathbreaking volume that he conceived of and edited, *Formations of United States Colonialism*. In addition, I wish to recognize Federico Reade for the amount of work that he poured into his master's and doctoral theses at the University of New Mexico. Federico's work focused on corridos to tell the story of Tijerina and other Alianza members from a fresh point of view.

For help in the archival hunt, I'm indebted to the tremendous staff at the Center for Southwest Research, including Beth Silbergleit, Nancy Brown-Martinez, Samuel Sisneros, and Rose Díaz, who led the effort to obtain and organize the Tijerina papers, as well as Jacobo Baca, who worked on the Tijerina collection as a graduate student. I would also like to thank the staff at the New Mexico State Records Center and Archives in Santa Fe, including the same Samuel Sisneros, who worked there when I first launched this project, and Estevan Rael-Gálvez, who was then state historian. The state archives also awarded me a small grant to fund research in New Mexico. Finally, for providing a second home so that I could spend days and even weeks at the archives, and for their good company too, I'm grateful to my cousins Ralph and Natalie Figueroa of Albuquerque.

Colleagues and friends from across the country played a role in supporting and encouraging this work, especially Vicki Ruiz, May Fu, Beth Castle, Pedro Castillo, Eric Avila, David Montejano, Christine Marin, John Van Ness, Gabriela Arredondo, Ben Johnson, Lisa Chavez, Valerie Mendoza, Rudy Busto, Laurie Coyle, Jose Alamillo, Frank Barajas, Dennis Downey, Simon Trujillo, Mark Rudd, and Lloyd Barber. Ernesto Vigil, Dionne Espinoza, and Lucy Grace Barber read versions of early chapters. In addition, I would like to thank those three scholars who years ago taught me at Cornell: Walter LaFeber, Debra Castillo, and Tom Holloway. I drew upon every bit of their training to complete this book.

Colleagues at the University of California, Davis, supported this work in many ways. First, Andrés Reséndez read material that never made the cut into this book and enhanced some material that did. Louis Warren invited me to participate in a western history/borderlands seminar held with Stanford and UC Davis folks; from there emerged chapter 7. UC Davis faculty and graduate students saw pieces of this work in two different departmental seminars. I especially appreciated comments by Ali Anooshahr, Edward Dickinson, and Victoria Langland. Sudipta Sen was good for hallway conversations about Marx and theory. And I am grateful to sociologist Fred Block for reminding me that a little theory can go a long way! Diane Wolfe in the same sociology department was an excellent mentor. Also at UC Davis, the now-defunct Chicana/Latina Research Center secured funding for a writing retreat in Southern California that provided me the opportunity to confront the difficulty of some of this material. I especially wish to recognize UCLA's Alicia Gaspar de Alba for leading that writing workshop. More recently, not only did the Davis Humanities Institute provide a quarter's break from teaching, but the 2018 cohort, particularly my history department colleague Cecilia Tsu, helped me sharpen the introduction.

Also at UC Davis, Ellen Hartigan-O'Connor and A. Katie Stirling-Harris played a special role in reviewing some of my earliest work and encouraging me to keep on going.

Baki Tezcan and Corrie Decker also read and critiqued a chapter. David Biale, Kathy Stuart, Daniel Stoltzenberg, and John Smolenski, my third-floor hallmates, and Kyu Kim, one floor above, all contributed to making this book better. So did Clarence Walker; he retired but he will always have a designated chair in my office.

UC Davis introduced me to a group of graduate students who have acted as my sounding board many times over. A sincere thanks go to Andrew Higgins, Diana Johnson, Yesika Ordaz, Marco Rosales, Genesis Lara, Griselda Jarquín, Ashley Serpa-Flack, Mary Mendoza, Melanie Peinado, Vanessa Madrigal-Lauchland, and Brenda Medina-Hernández, *que descanse en paz*. In a special category is Melissa Moreno, whom I first met when she was a Chicana/Latina Dissertation Fellow at UC Davis.

Years ago, during a minor health crisis, I received an invitation to eat lunch with a group of fellow professors, Susan Mann, Joan Cadden, Beverly Bossler, and Cathy Kudlick. We decided then that we need not wait for bad news to share a meal. Their wisdom suffuses this book. Susan taught me to write first and then figure out the analysis; Joan pointed out that simply dismissing someone as crazy hardly suffices as historical argument; Beverly reassured me that charges of sexual abuse belonged in this book; and Cathy always reminded me that a commitment to social justice and scholarship can be one and the same. Warm thanks go to this lovely circle.

I have been blessed with still more brilliant and generous friends. Dan Ringer-Barwick gave sage advice, which ranged from comma placement to the overall structure of the book; Rachel Jean-Baptiste and Lisa G. Materson, two Davis colleagues, offered on-the-mark questions, helpful insights, and a big-picture perspective and pushed, cajoled, encouraged, and demanded until I wrote the best book that I could. Between April and September 2018, Rebecca Brown spent over a hundred hours of her life formatting this book (and reorganizing all my computer files along the way), thus helping push me over the finish line.

I so enjoyed working with Mark Simpson-Vos and Jessica Newman at the University of North Carolina Press. Jessica was endlessly patient as I navigated the business of photo acquisitions and permissions. A great editor, Mark understood the bigger themes at play while reviewing every page with care.

Finally, I wish to thank an extended circle of family and friends for their support in my finishing, to share its informal title, "that damn book." The circle starts with the sister-of-my-heart, Julia Aguirre. She understood probably more than anyone the importance of putting this book behind me. Finally, Julia! It also includes Nicoletta Gherardi and Fernando Sannibale, who as my Roman *famiglia* have provided good food and good company for years. Neighbors Charles and Nina Smith and Ellen Goldstein and Jack Holleman made me feel like I was living next-door to my own personal cheering section. In terms of providing constant backup for me and my family, Elizabeth Pérez has proven herself special beyond measure. As researching this book required dealing with people as well as with documents, I want to acknowledge my parents, Celia and Armando (who passed away in 2017) Oropeza, for teaching me so much about how to move forward in this world. I'm also deeply fortunate to enjoy the love and support of my aunt Herminia Sepúlveda and my mother-in-law, Catherine Byrd. Special thanks go to my brothers and their spouses, Mark and Deb Oropeza and Bob and Marcie Oropeza, and to my brother Alex, who provided wise words on more than one occasion.

During the course of writing this book, I saw my two boys, Armando James and Juan-Miguel Alejandro, grow into generous and caring young men. Thank you, *mijos*, for loving me even though that computer was never far away. Finally, no one has had more faith in me than Mr. John Byrd. He has graced my life for more than thirty years and made it better every day.

Notes

ABBREVIATIONS

AJ	*Albuquerque Journal*
AT	*Albuquerque Tribune*
RLT Papers	Reies López Tijerina Papers, Center for Southwest Research, University of New Mexico, Albuquerque
RLT Vertical File	Reies López Tijerina Vertical File, Center for Southwest Research, University of New Mexico, Albuquerque
SFNM	*Santa Fe New Mexican*

INTRODUCTION

1. A series of newspaper articles to commemorate raid anniversaries in 1977, 1987, and 1997 provided many of the details here. The articles are in the RLT Vertical File. Within this file, *¡Salsa!*, the monthly supplement to the *Rio Grande Sun*, devoted its entire May 28, 1987, edition to remembering the raid. See "Wounded Officer Went for Gun" in that issue for the encounter between Valdez and Saiz that day. The most detailed printed account of the raid appears in Richard Gardner, *¡Grito!*, but he provided no citations.

2. Quoted in Scarborough, *Trespassers on Our Own Land*, 132.

3. Susan Landon, "Courthouse Raid Remains Vivid Memory," *AJ*, June 5, 1987, RLT Vertical File.

4. "Raid Surprised County Workers" and "Murdered Jailer's Family in Pain," both in *¡Salsa!* The *Rio Grande Sun* on November 17, 1977, also published the entire transcript of Salazar's raid testimony; the transcript is also in the RLT Vertical File. Tijerina always maintained that he did not fire at Salazar. See "Tijerina Explains Raid," *¡Salsa!*

5. "County Workers" and "Chama Woman, Seeing-Eye Dog, Ready to Fight," both in *¡Salsa!*

6. "Tijerina Explains Raid."

7. While Rivera always identified Juan Valdez (whom Rivera had known since he was a young man) as his assailant, both Valdez and Tijerina maintained that it was Ventura Chavez who hit Rivera. Chavez's grandson Simón Ventura Trujillo concurred. In a con-

versation on April 7, 2016, Trujillo said that his grandfather always ended his recollections about his participation in the courthouse raid with the words, "And then I hit the jailer." Although Rivera was not technically the jailer, he had keys to open the jail and, after he was struck, freed two people upon the orders of his assailants. According to his grandson, Ventura Chavez also provided a reason for striking Rivera that echoed Tijerina's account: bullets flying from the jury room through the closed jury door.

8. "Hostage Reporter Tells Story," *¡Salsa!* See also Calloway, "June 5, 1967."

9. Gardner, *¡Grito!*, 5.

10. "Wounded Officer Went for Gun"; "County Workers"; "Tijerina Explains Raid."

11. "In the Courtroom," *¡Salsa!*

12. According to the Internet Movie Database (IMDb), Leone's *Fistful of Dollars* was released in the United States in January 1967, and *For a Few Dollars More* was released in the United States in May 1967 (see http://www.imdb.com/title/tt0058461/?ref_=nv_sr_1, accessed March 24, 2018). (These Italian "westerns," in turn, borrowed from the work of Japanese filmmaker Akira Kurosawa.) According to IMDb, *Bonanza* ran from 1959 to 1973 and *Gunsmoke* from 1955 to 1975. According to the PBS website for its series *Pioneers of Television* (http://www.pbs.org/wnet/pioneers-of-television/pioneering-programs/westerns/, accessed April 7, 2018), TV westerns were one of the most popular post–World War II genres, with thirty different shows sharing airtime in 1959 alone.

13. "Mensaje a todos los herederos," radio script, n.d., KLOS, box 1, folder 1, RLT Papers.

14. "La Voz de la Justicia," radio script, April 23, 1965, KABQ, box 1, folder 36, RLT Papers.

15. Bell Blawis, *Tijerina and the Land Grants*.

16. Nabokov, *Tijerina and the Courthouse Raid*.

17. Gardner, *¡Grito!*

18. Also see Jenkinson, *Tijerina*.

19. For a summary of the state of academic literature on Mexican Americans circa 1969 and a sharp critique, see Romano-V, "Anthropology and Sociology of Mexican Americans."

20. Rendón, *Chicano Manifesto*, 140.

21. Meier and Rivera, *Chicanos*.

22. Tijerina, *They Called Me "King Tiger,"* xvi. José Angel Gutiérrez did not mention gunfire between Black Panthers and police officials.

23. Tijerina, the Ohtli announcement explained, became "internationally famous for leading an armed raid on the Tierra Amarilla Courthouse in 1967." C. Gonzalez, "Reies López Tijerina."

24. In the words of Thomas Hietala, "U.S. leaders in the 1840s eschewed colonialism and militarism. They intended to transform acquisitions into states equal in status to those already in the Union." Although in his *Manifest Design* Hietala was among the first to encourage historians to recognize 1848 as a turning point in American empire on par with 1898, he drew this statehood distinction in "Expansionism and Imperialism."

25. See, for example, Montoya, *Translating Property*, 5; and Gómez, *Manifest Destinies*, 7. Underscoring just how self-evident the concept had become, Kosek's *Understories* repeatedly mentioned "colonialism" in New Mexico in passing; see pp. 14, 20, 33, 138, 147, 175, 179, 231, and 240.

26. Carmichael and Hamilton's *Black Power*; Barrera, Muñoz, and Ornelas, "Barrio as an Internal Colony."

27. Schroeder, *Mr. Polk's War*; Greenberg, *Wicked War*. Greenberg's title borrowed from Ulysses S. Grant's summary of the conflict.

28. Knowlton, "Spanish and Mexican Land Grants: A Key to the Past," a 1989 conference paper, in Clark S. Knowlton Vertical File.

29. A classic example was Limerick's *Legacy of Conquest*.

30. J. Wilson, "Not-Quite National Holiday." Between 2008 and 2015, works on Chavez included Pitti, "Chicano Cold Warriors"; Ganz, *Why David Sometimes Wins*; Shaw, *Beyond the Fields*; Matthew Garcia, *From the Jaws of Victory*; Pawel, *Crusades of Cesar Chavez*; and Orosco, *Cesar Chavez and the Common Sense of Nonviolence*.

31. Tijerina made no appearance in two of the leading surveys of that era's protest, Farber's *Age of Great Dreams* and Isserman and Kazin's *America Divided*. Nor did he appear in Farber's anthology *The Sixties*. White did mention Tijerina briefly in his survey of U.S. Western history, *It's Your Misfortune and None of My Own*, 596.

32. A federal officer was shot and killed during the raid, Kosek wrote, but actually no one was killed; see *Understories*, 11. T. Anderson, in *Movement and the Sixties*, 305, asserted that Alianza members developed their movement largely in Tijerina's absence, while the opposite was true: in Tijerina's absence, the Alianza fell apart.

33. Some examples of a broader, integrated approach include Araiza, *To March for Others*; Mantler, *Power to the Poor*; and Wu, *Radicals on the Road*.

34. Love, "La Raza," 283.

35. Gitlin, *The Sixties*, showcased the declension narrative. The declension narrative also came through the titles of two standard works that were both reprinted: O'Neill, *Coming Apart*, and Matusow, *The Unraveling of America*.

36. Joseph made this point in *Waiting 'til the Midnight Hour*. Joseph's book also contested the sharp divide between the civil rights movement and black power activism. In terms of the Black Panthers, the declension narrative stressed how men within the organization mistreated women. For a more nuanced view, see Spencer, *Revolution Has Come*.

37. Bebout, in *Mythohistorical Interventions*, 82–104, spoke of the broad appeal of the "bandido/ revolutionary trope" and the political work done by it.

38. Jenkinson, *Tijerina*, 7.

39. "Reies López Tijerina ¿Héroe or Malhechor?," *El Hispano*, August 29, 1967, clipping in box 59, folder "Land Grants-Miscellaneous," David F. Cargo Papers, New Mexico State Records Center and Archives, Santa Fe. The Cargo Papers were only partially processed.

40. With thanks to Lori A. Flores. Commenting on Tijerina's religious extremism, she noted years ago at a writing workshop that, relative to other leaders, Tijerina had gained a reputation as "the weirdo of the Chicano movement." The description stuck with me.

41. Reies López Tijerina oral history interview.

42. The only exception was a collection of oral history interviews compiled by Gutiérrez, Meléndez, and Noyola, *Chicanas in Charge*, which featured information gained from a joint interview with Mary Escobar and Rose Tijerina.

43. Chávez, *My Penitente Land*, 57, 59.

44. Busto's *King Tiger* first highlighted the role of religion in Tijerina's life. Also see Gutiérrez, "Religious Origins."

45. Both shall remain anonymous.

46. Pete Herrera, "Tijerina is Moses to Hopeful Mexican-Americans," *El Paso Herald Post*, August 7, 1968.

CHAPTER 1

1. Reies López Tijerina oral history interview. Tijerina recalled that Anselmo drove a car for the first time that day. In that case, given the six-year age difference between the brothers, Reies Tijerina was probably closer to six when he had this experience.

2. Gardner, *¡Grito!*, 32. A lively and even sensationalistic writer who liked to wax lyrically about "la raza," Gardner apparently conducted interviews, clearly gathered information from newspapers, and also culled liberally from one of the first books on this topic, Nabokov's *Tijerina and the Courthouse Raid*. In Nabokov's book, the Jesus dream appeared on page 195. Nabokov was a reporter with the *Santa Fe New Mexican* during the 1960s and interviewed Tijerina many times.

3. The interviewer was Busto, *King Tiger*. The quotation, along Tijerina's recollection that he was pulling the wagon, appeared on page 37.

4. Certificate of Baptism, box 53, folder 43, RLT Papers. Correspondence from the Alianza issued under his name was invariable signed "Reies López Tijerina." During the 1950s, however, Tijerina sent letters to his then wife Mary Escobar signed "Rey" or "R. L. Tijerina." An affidavit obtained thirty years later likewise noted the birth of a boy child named "Reyes," not "Reies." As for his parents, see a portion of a handwritten autobiography that begins, "I was born in the State of Texas on Sept. 21, 1926." On page 2, Tijerina wrote, "Even my father and mother, they could hurdly read and write in Spanish, much less in English," box 53, folder 43, RLT Papers.

5. Additional examples of Tijerina's tendency to review his life can be found in box 53, folders 43, 45, and 46, as well as in box 54, folders 1, 3, 8–10, and 17, all in RLT Papers. As these autobiographical sketches appear in no particular order, and as the page numbers frequently repeat, I have done my best to identify them below.

6. The original quotation mistakenly transcribed the name of one town as Forestville; Gardner, *¡Grito!*, 36. A similar quotation, with the same mistake, appeared in Nabokov, *Tijerina and the Courthouse Raid*, 194.

7. Handwritten reminiscences all from box 53, folder 43, RLT Papers, including "El Rancho de Stevens," "Memorias que siguen conmigo" (Memories that stay with me), sheet that begins, "I loved to play," and sheet that begins "1931–1936, Estos años los pasó mi padre rodando a un rancho a otro" (My father spent these years traveling from one ranch to another). The quotation about garbage can delicacies starts another sheet of handwritten recollections. For similar stories of Tijerina's youth, see Nabokov, *Tijerina and the Courthouse Raid*, 193–96; Gardner, *¡Grito!*, 30–33, 36–37; and Busto, *King Tiger*, 35–39.

8. For Erlinda's experiences giving birth, see handwritten recollection that begins "El Rancho del John Mathas" and "Memorias que siguen conmigo," which also mentions snake-catching, as does another typed sheet, signed by Wilfredo Sedillo, all in box 53, folder 43, RLT Papers.

9. See "El Rancho de Stevens" for calluses; and Nabokov, *Tijerina and the Courthouse Raid*, 195, for slashed thigh. For amputated toes, see handwritten notes that begin on a sheet of paper with typed numeral 6 at top, box 53, folder 43, RLT Papers.

10. Second page of recollection that begins, "I was born in the state of Texas in Sept. 21, 1926," box 53, folder 43, RLT Papers. Tijerina revisited the topic again in "El Rancho de John Mathas."

11. "Memorias que siguen conmigo"; as well as Busto, *King Tiger*, 38; Nabokov, *Tijerina and the Courthouse Raid*, 195; and Gardner, *¡Grito!*, 32.

12. Handwritten recollection with bright red numeral 3 circled at top of first page, box 53, folder 43, RLT Papers; see also Gardner, *!Grito!*, 36.

13. "El Rancho del John Mathas."

14. See partially typed recollection, numeral 7 at top, in box 53, folder 43, RLT Papers.

15. First quotation about planting seeds part of a handwritten recollection dated September 20, 1974, box 54, folder 10, RLT Papers. Other quotation appeared in "El Rancho del John Mathas."

16. Handwritten recollection, page beginning "mention of our poverty," box 53, folder 43, RLT Papers. For more about Mexican migration to Michigan, see Valdés, *Al Norte*, 8–29 and 45–46.

17. Report cards, box 53, folder 43, RLT Papers. Folder 43 also holds Tijerina's many musings on the topic of his schooling; see several pages of the handwritten collection that begins with a bright red numeral 3 circled at top of first page, box 53, folder 43, RLT Papers.

18. Blanton, "From Intellectual Deficiency to Cultural Deficiency."

19. Handwritten recollection, page beginning, "the teacher spank my brother," in box 53, folder 43, RLT Papers.

20. Balderrama and Rodríguez, *Decade of Betrayal*.

21. McKay, "Federal Deportation Campaign in Texas."

22. Busto, *King Tiger*, 38.

23. Handwritten recollection, year 1936 at top, in box 53, folder 43, RLT Papers.

24. Montejano, *Anglos and Mexicans*, 113.

25. Zamora, *World of the Mexican Worker*, 32.

26. The term comes from Montejano, *Anglos and Mexicans*, 34. Also see Hernández, *Migra!*, 19–20, for more about the pivotal role played by the Texas Rangers in ensuring Anglo-American supremacy.

27. Johnson, *Revolution in Texas*, 120.

28. "Protecting Mexicans in the United States," *New York Times*, November 18, 1922.

29. Alexander, *Crusade for Conformity*.

30. Neil Foley made the case for Texas being as much a part of the South as the Southwest in *White Scourge*.

31. Hillerman, *Great Taos Bank Robbery*, 117.

32. Gardner, *¡Grito!*, 33, 35–36; Nabokov, *Tijerina and the Courthouse Raid*, 196.

33. Eleventh page of handwritten recollection that starts with bright red numeral 3 circled at top of first page, box 53, folder 43, RLT Papers.

34. Handwritten recollection, numeral 8 at top of page, box 53, folder 43, RLT Papers. Also see Nabokov, *Tijerina and the Courthouse Raid*, 197.

35. Ninth page of handwritten recollection that starts with bright red numeral 3 circled at top of first page, box 53, folder 43, RLT Papers.

36. Handwritten recollection, numerals 4, 5, and 6 at top of the respective pages, box 53, folder 43, RLT Papers.

37. Handwritten recollection, numerals 4, 5, and 6 at top of the respective pages.

38. Much thanks to Felipe Hinojosa for this insight.

39. Gardner, *¡Grito!*, 37.

40. I am grateful to Jacobo Baca for pointing out an alternative translation for *justicia*.

41. Busto, *King Tiger*, 36.

42. Savage, *Spirit Bade Me Go*, 25.

43. The Assemblies of God preference for baptism by immersion versus sprinkling meant that converts from other denominations often underwent a second "water baptism"; see Blumhofer, *Restoring the Faith*, 226. Another possibility: Tijerina might have been baptized within a branch of Pentecostalism that rejected any baptism (including Catholic) made "in the name of the Father, the Son and the Holy Spirit." The "Oneness" branch of Pentecostalism recognized baptism in the name of Christ Jesus only. See Ramírez, *Migrating Faith*, 42. For Tijerina's musings about his religious reawakening, see handwritten recollection, numerals 7–10 at top margin of successive pages, box 53, folder 43, RLT Papers.

44. In 2003, for example, only 21 percent of Mexican Americans identified as Protestant. Yet of this minority, some 64 percent specifically identified as Pentecostal. See Gastón Espinosa, "Brown Moses," 288.

45. Blumhofer, *Restoring the Faith*, 56–62; Sánchez Walsh, *Latino Pentecostal Identity*, 17.

46. As late as 1941, for example, church officials lamented that "cigarette-smoking, liquor-drinking, theater-going parents" were ruining the next generation. See "Home Builders, Let's Have More of Them," *Pentecostal Evangel*, August 16, 1941, 12.

47. Busto, *King Tiger*, 84.

48. Ramírez, *Migrating Faith*, 8, 11, 27, 34, 38, 40, 112.

49. Busto, *King Tiger*, 39, 79, 82–83, 91–92.

50. Savage, *Spirit Bade Me Go*, 52, 60.

51. "Libro de la Vida de Reies," handwritten recollection with repeating page numbers. This quote comes from a page numbered 9 that begins, "my father," box 53, folder 43, RLT Papers.

52. "Libro de la Vida de Reies," page numbered 13.

53. "Libro de la Vida de Reies," page numbered 7 that begins, "difficult for me."

54. "Libro de la Vida de Reies," page numbered 3 that begins, "all wars."

55. "Libro de la Vida de Reies," page numbered 10 that begins, "I would raise questions."

56. "Libro de la Vida de Reies," page numbered 12.

57. Latin American Bible Institute document signed A. O. Martinez, box 1, folder 18, Alfonso Sánchez Papers, Center for Southwest Research, University of New Mexico, Albuquerque.

58. Handwritten recollection, page with circled numeral 4 at top that begins, "a wonderful brave of justice," box 53, folder 43, RLT Papers.

59. Handwritten recollection, page with numeral 11 at top that begins, "So my grade marks," box 53, folder 43, RLT Papers.

60. Nabokov, *Tijerina and the Courthouse Raid*, 199; Gardner, *¡Grito!*, 38–39.

61. Tijerina mentioned Margarito's enlistment on a handwritten sheet with the

numeral 2 at top that begins, "I left for home on May 1944," and mentioned Anselmo joining Margarito in the service on a handwritten sheet with the numeral 7 at top that begins, "the more I longed," both in box 53, folder 43, RLT Papers. Without citation, Gardner wrote that the U.S. Navy and U.S. Army alike rejected Anselmo on the grounds of insufficient education. Gardner, *¡Grito!*, 41. However, his daughter Ofelia Theresa Tijerina Laughlin asserted in a conversation with me that her father served in the U.S. Navy, a claim confirmed by Anselmo Tijerina's 1987 burial at Santa Fe National Cemetery.

62. Handwritten recollection with bright red numeral 3 circled at top of first page, box 53, folder 43, RLT Papers. I date this lengthy reminiscence to the 1970s because it includes the term "Indo-Hispano," an ethnic label that Tijerina adopted in the 1960s. Not until the decade was over did he have the time to sit down and start reviewing his life.

63. Reies López Tijerina oral history interview.

64. D. Wilson, *Armageddon Now!*, 74–76, 94. See also Gannon and Horton, *Shifting Romance with Israel*. Gannon led Jewish conversion efforts for the Assemblies of God for over forty years. In the text, which lacks pagination, he documented a "new intensity to American Jewish Missions" during the immediate postwar era. Also see Boyer, *When Time Shall Be No More*, 219–21.

65. Marks, "Our Debt to Israel," *Pentecostal Evangel*, August 26, 1941, 3.

66. Handwritten recollection with numeral 5 at top that begins, "when I was already cold dead," box 53, folder 43, RLT Papers. Yavenditti cited an 85 percent approval rate on August 26, 1945, in "American People and the Use of Atomic Bombs," 225.

67. Divorce decree, March 22, 1963, box 54, folder 32, RLT Papers; Mary Escobar oral history interview. In addition to conducting this oral history interview in 2006, I also spoke with her during a car conversation in 2006 and conducted a follow-up conversation in 2013.

68. Escobar oral history interview; Bell Blawis, *Tijerina and the Land Grants*, 22.

69. Handwritten recollection, sheet with numeral 9 at top that begins, "my father to send me," box 53, folder 43, RLT Papers. Tijerina identified Escobar as the Maria in this story and in an oral history interview with Rose Díaz, a New Mexican historian and the archivist in charge of the processing of his papers, which he donated in 1999 to the Center for Southwest Research at the University of New Mexico. The oral history begins at the back of the massive finding aid published in 2005 and available at the Center for Southwest Research.

70. Escobar oral history interview.

71. Busto, *King Tiger*, 41.

72. Reies López Tijerina oral history interview.

73. Escobar oral history interview.

74. Gardner, *¡Grito!*, 39, for "illumination" and "struggle with my conscience." Also see sheet of paper marked with numeral 12 that begins, "my name ringing from coast to coast," as well as pages that follow, marked 13 and 14, all in box 53, folder 43, RLT Papers.

75. The list of milestones *(pilares)* can be found in box 54, folder 10, RLT Papers.

76. Gardner, *¡Grito!*, 39. Also "El Libro de la Vida de Reies," box 53, folder 43, 13–15, RLT Papers.

77. "El Libro de la Vida de Reies," 14–15.

78. Gardner, *¡Grito!*, 39.

79. Busto, *King Tiger*, 95.

80. Nabokov, *Tijerina and the Courthouse Raid*, 199.

81. Savage, *Spirit Bade Me Go*, 68.

82. Part of a recollection that begins, "I learned that human values," box 53, folder 45, RLT Papers; Savage, *Spirit Bade Me Go*, 36–40. See also Busto, *King Tiger*, 111.

83. Tijerina noted visits in 1945, 1951, and 1952 in his published memoir *Mi Lucha*, 32, and mentioned more about the 1945 visit during a phone conversation with me in 2007; also see Gardner, *¡Grito!*, 44. For the significance of the date of Rose's birth, see a handwritten recollection, circled numeral 1 at top of page, box 53, folder 43, RLT Papers.

84. Handwritten recollection, circled numerals 9 through 11 at top of respective pages, box 54, folder 1, RLT Papers. Also see Gardner, *¡Grito!*, 44; and Nabokov, *Tijerina and the Courthouse Raid*, 201.

85. Handwritten recollection, "Summer—1949, The man from Cuero, Texas," pages numbered 1–11 at top, box 54, folder 1, RLT Papers. See also Gardner, *¡Grito!*, 43.

86. Handwritten recollection, list of milestones box 54, folder 10, RLT Papers.

87. Gardner, *¡Grito!*, 40.

88. Escobar oral history interview.

89. Escobar oral history interview.

90. Escobar oral history interview.

91. Gardner, *¡Grito!*, 96.

92. Escobar oral history interview. Reies López Tijerina likewise recalled Rose becoming extremely ill in Kansas City, handwritten memoir, June 13, 1975, box 53, folder 45, RLT Papers.

93. Handwritten recollection, circled numeral 14 at top of page, box 54, folder 1; also see document marked "Junio 13, 1975," and another handwritten recollection, numbered 4, both in box 53, folder 45, all in RLT Papers.

94. Nabokov, *Tijerina and the Courthouse Raid*, 200.

95. Nabokov, 200.

96. Handwritten recollection, circled numeral 14 at top of page, box 54, folder 1, RLT Papers.

97. Handwritten recollection, circled numerals 12 and 13 at top of successive pages, box 54, folder 1, RLT Papers.

98. Handwritten recollection, numeral 49 at top right-hand side of page, box 53, folder 43, RLT Papers.

99. Handwritten recollection, circled numeral 6 at top of page, box 54, folder 1, RLT Papers.

100. Handwritten recollection, circled numeral 2 at top of page followed by quotation, box 53, folder 43, RLT Papers.

101. As quoted in Busto, *King Tiger*, 96.

102. Rachel Tijerina oral history interview.

103. Rose Tijerina oral history interview.

104. Handwritten recollection, numerals 2 and 3 at top of respective pages, box 53, folder 43, RLT Papers.

105. Rose Tijerina oral history interview.

106. Rose Tijerina oral history interview.

107. Rose and Rachel Tijerina oral history interviews.

108. Reies López Tijerina oral history interview.

109. Rachel Tijerina oral history interview.

110. Savage, *Spirit Bade Me Go*, 90, 109.

111. Gardner, *¡Grito!*, 44.

112. Busto, *King Tiger*, 44.

113. Handwritten recollection with bright red numeral 3 circled at top of first page, box 53, folder 43, RLT Papers.

114. Busto, *King Tiger*, 44.

115. Nabokov, *Tijerina and the Courthouse Raid*, 199.

116. Gardner, *¡Grito!*, 44.

117. Ramírez focused on "heterodox" Pentecostalism in *Migrating Faith*.

118. See second page of a handwritten recollection dated June 12, 1975, box 53, folder 45, RLT Papers.

119. Busto, *King Tiger*, 43.

120. Busto, 92.

121. Gardner, *¡Grito!*, 39.

122. Gutiérrez described Tijerina's preaching as a "social gospel" in "Religious Origins," 299.

123. Busto, *King Tiger*, made a similar point about the cost of reproducing these sermons in print, 97.

124. Reyes López Tijerina, *¿Hallará Fé en la Tierra?*, 70. A complete copy of the booklet can be found in box 54, folder 2, RLT Papers.

125. Tijerina, 51, 91.

126. Tijerina, 49.

127. Just once in 119 pages did he allude to it. "It is very certain that no one is saved by good works [alone]," Tijerina, 98.

128. Tijerina, 110.

129. Tijerina wrote admiringly, and correctly, that George Washington and Socrates had rejected salaries. He also looked askance at teachers accepting them. Tijerina, 14, 16, 34, 93.

130. Tijerina, 38–40.

131. Tijerina, 19.

132. Tijerina, 81–82.

133. Tijerina, 4.

134. Tijerina, 86.

135. Tijerina, 69.

136. Tijerina, 14, 46.

137. Tijerina, 81.

138. Tijerina, 113.

139. Tijerina, 88.

140. Tijerina, 88, 11.

141. Tijerina, 64. My translation differed slightly from Busto's in *King Tiger*, 103.

142. Marty, *Modern American Religion*. For brief synopses of the role of religion during the Cold War, see Kirby, "The Cold War and American Religion"; and Allit, "Religion and Politics since 1945."

143. See chart on p. 50 in Roozen and Hadaway, *Church and Denominational Growth*.

144. Blumhofer, *Restoring the Faith*, 204–10. See also Riss, "Latter Rain Movement."

145. Harrell, *Oral Roberts*. Also see a special section of the *Tulsa World*, "Oral Roberts, 1918–2009, Legacy," December 20, 2009.

146. Peale, *Power of Positive Thinking*; Lane, *Surge of Piety*; Bowler, *Blessed*, 55.

147. Bowler, *Blessed*, 64–65; Harrell, *Oral Roberts*, 461.

148. Herzog, *Spiritual-Industrial Complex*.

149. Aikman, "How Billy Graham Killed Communism with Kindness."

150. Blumhofer, *Restoring the Faith*, 145–49, 195.

151. Gardner, *¡Grito!*, 256.

152. Tijerina, *Hallará Fé*, 64.

153. Tijerina, 64.

154. Tijerina, 110.

155. Tijerina's questioning of Cold War divisions, his opposition to the Korean War, and his support of Puerto Rican *independistas* are all mentioned on page three of a handwritten recollection that begins, "I learned that human values," box 53, folder 45, RLT Papers.

156. Tijerina, *Hallará Fé*, 119.

157. Kirk, "Letters from Moscow," 46–47, 192–202.

158. Tijerina, *Hallará Fé*, 66.

159. Rose Tijerina oral history interview.

160. Gutiérrez, "Religious Origins," 299.

161. For rising standard of living, see R. García, *Rise of the Mexican American Middle Class*, 313.

162. Tijerina, *Hallará Fé*, 36.

163. Tijerina, 56.

164. Tijerina, 87.

165. The exact number of families varied across different sources, although Busto in *King Tiger* determined nine as mostly likely, 116. In *Mi Lucha*, 27, Tijerina listed eight names. In another account, he listed nine, page with "Biog" and "1956" at the top, box 43, folder 45, RLT Papers.

166. Gardner, *¡Grito!*, 44.

CHAPTER 2

1. Gardner, *¡Grito!*, 45.

2. Tijerina, *Mi Lucha*, 27.

3. Rose Tijerina oral history interview.

4. Tijerina, *Mi Lucha*, 27, 28.

5. Escobar oral history interview; Reies López Tijerina oral history interview. Also see Tijerina, *Mi Lucha*, 27.

6. Reies López Tijerina oral history interview.

7. Handwritten recollection, list of milestones (*pilares*), box 54, folder 10, RLT Papers.

8. Reies López Tijerina oral history interview.

9. Reies López Tijerina oral history interview. Other renditions of this dream appear in his memoir, *Mi Lucha*, 30–32; and in Busto, *King Tiger*, 122–23.

10. Busto, *King Tiger*, 124; Nabokov, *Tijerina and the Courthouse Raid*, 204; Gardner, *¡Grito!*, 84.

11. Kino, *Historic Memoir of Pimería Alta*, 127.

12. U.S. Bureau of the Census, "Number of Inhabitants, Arizona, 1950," p. 8, table 6.

13. Tijerina, *Mi Lucha*, 27.

14. Gardner, *¡Grito!*, 45.

15. Serna letter to Tijerina, dated November 9, 1962, box 48, folder 2, RLT Papers.

16. Serna letter to Tijerina.

17. Tijerina bemoaned that "racial egoism, sectarian egoism, and national egoism" all interfered with God's work, *Hallará Fé*, 19.

18. Pitzer, *America's Communal Utopias*. Chapter 2 is about the Shakers, chapter 5 about the Church of Latter-day Saints.

19. Walker, "'Banner Is Unfurled,'" 75.

20. Blumhofer, *Restoring the Faith*, 72–73.

21. Lemke-Santangelo, *Daughters of Aquarius*.

22. Busto noted these parallels first. See *King Tiger*, 115, and "'In the Outer Boundaries,'" 68.

23. M. Weber, *Economy and Society*, 440–41, 445. Espinosa similarly invoked Weber in regard to another Latino Pentecostalist, Francisco Olazábal, who was forty years older than Tijerina. There is no evidence the two men ever crossed paths. See Gastón Espinosa, "El Azteca."

24. Serna letter to Tijerina, dated January 31, 1961, box 48, folder 2, RLT Papers.

25. Rachel Tijerina, conversation with author. Rachel was visiting her mother when I dropped by her mother's house in February 2013.

26. Escobar oral history interview.

27. The 2017 documentary film *Adios Amor* focused on Maria Moreno's life in the early 1960s, when she played a key role in organizing California farmworkers. By then, she had had a dozen children. The film's director, Laurie Coyle, shared with me an excerpt of her 2015 interview with Lillian DeLaTorre, Moreno's eldest daughter. Also see correspondence in box 41, folder 39, and letters from Serna, box 48, folder 2, RLT Papers.

28. Tijerina, *Mi Lucha*, 38.

29. Escobar oral history interview; Tijerina, *Mi Lucha*, 29. Perhaps because this crime involved a juvenile, I did not find any mention of it in local papers.

30. "Tracing Tijerina," *Casa Grande (Ariz.) Dispatch*, September 4, 1968.

31. Tijerina, *Mi Lucha*, 37.

32. Tijerina, 28. About Randolph, see LeSeur, *Not All Okies Are White*.

33. Letter to the editor, *Casa Grande Dispatch*, January 31, 1952.

34. For more on the program in Arizona and elsewhere, see Cohen, *Braceros*; and Mitchell, *They Saved the Crops*.

35. Tijerina, *Mi Lucha*, 41.

36. Tijerina, 29–30.

37. Escobar oral history interview.

38. "Tracing Tijerina," *Casa Grande Dispatch*, September 4, 1968; "Reyes Court Trial

Opens Today," *Casa Grande Dispatch*, November 13, 1968. Tijerina's association with the Casa Grande area prompted these retrospective articles.

39. Rose Tijerina oral history interview.

40. Reies López Tijerina oral history interview.

41. Escobar oral history interview.

42. Escobar oral history interview.

43. Escobar oral history interview.

44. Escobar oral history interview. In her interview with Laurie Coyle, Lillian DeLaTorre mentioned the heat and rattlesnakes too. Also see Tijerina, *Mi Lucha*, 27, 28.

45. Tijerina, *Mi Lucha*, 28.

46. Tijerina, 32.

47. Tijerina, 32.

48. For more information on the Penitentes, see Weigle, *Brothers of Light*; and Carroll, *Penitente Brotherhood*.

49. Tijerina, *Mi Lucha*, 33.

50. Tijerina, 33.

51. Tijerina, 32–34.

52. Tijerina, 35.

53. Tijerina, 34.

54. Tijerina, 35.

55. Busto, *King Tiger*, 151.

56. The text of the treaty can be found on multiple websites as well as in Griswold del Castillo, *Treaty of Guadalupe Hidalgo*, 189–90.

57. Tijerina later shared this insight in his speeches. See sheet labeled "1964 file," and "Para todo Heredero a quien concierna los intereses que cubre el Tratado de Guadalupe Hidalgo," June 12, 1963, both in box 1, folder 1, RLT Papers.

58. Tijerina, *Mi Lucha*, 34.

59. Wolfe, "Settler Colonialism," 308.

60. Tijerina, *Mi Lucha*, 73.

61. Tijerina, 36.

62. Tijerina, 37.

63. Nabokov, *Tijerina and the Courthouse Raid*, 197.

64. The assumption that "racial inferiors" were prone to criminal behavior was widespread. See Chávez-García, *States of Delinquency*.

65. Seven pages of Margarito Tijerina's prison records from Indiana can be found in box 1, folder 18, Sánchez Papers. Also see "Court's Finding of Fact and Conclusions of the Law," January 31, 1967, box 41, folder 17, RLT Papers.

66. Tijerina, *Mi Lucha*, 38.

67. "*Unos friazos feos*," Escobar oral history interview.

68. Tijerina, *Mi Lucha*, 39.

69. Tijerina, 39–40.

70. Escobar oral history interview. Michael L. Trujillo, a Trujillo descendant and American studies professor at the University of New Mexico, confirmed her recollection.

71. Tijerina, *Mi Lucha*, 40.

72. Tijerina, 39.

73. Tijerina, 39. In his memoir, Tijerina maintained that the pair had encountered a

frozen deer carcass but did not want to let the families know that they were about to eat scavenged meat, so the two men claimed to have killed the deer. According to Rose Tijerina and Mary Escobar, the two men did kill the animal; Escobar oral history interview. Rose Tijerina commented about killing a deer during my interview with her mother.

74. Gardner, *¡Grito!*, 30. Although Gardner mistakenly dated the initial appearance of Tijerina in New Mexico to 1958, a recent oral history interview by Lloyd D. Barba corroborated a portion of Gardner's account. While recruiting in Salinas for Valle de Paz residents, Tijerina preached that men and women alike ought to wear long tunics like Jesus did, and men, again like Jesus, ought to wear beards, according to Manuel Perez, who headed the congregation that Tijerina visited. See Barba, "California's Cross," 194.

75. Rose Tijerina, email to author, September 12, 2012; Escobar conversation with author, February 6, 2013.

76. Tijerina, *Hallará Fé*, 67.

77. Gardner, *¡Grito!*, 33, 46.

78. "Offense Report" and "Supplementary Offense Report," Pinal County Sheriff's Department, box 2, Folder 24, Nabokov Papers. Tijerina referred to "Zebedeo Martínez" in *Mi Lucha*. A list of stolen items also appeared in "Tracing Tijerina," *Casa Grande Dispatch*, September 4, 1968.

79. FBI rap sheet on Tijerina, box 1, folder labeled "Mug Shots," Attorney General Collection, Eloy Blea Papers, New Mexico State Records Center and Archives, Santa Fe. As with the Cargo Papers, the Blea Papers were only partially processed. The FBI was called in because the items were federal property.

80. Pinal County Jail sheet signed upon release by Sevedeo Martínez, box 1, folder labeled "Mug Shots," Blea Papers.

81. Tijerina, *Mi Lucha*, 41.

82. Tijerina, 41; Gardner, *¡Grito!*, 46; James H. Green, Casa Grande chief of police, to Alfonso Sánchez, Río Arriba County district attorney, August 18, 1964, box 2, folder 24, Peter Nabokov Papers, Center for Southwest Research, University of New Mexico, Albuquerque.

83. "Soap-Slick Jail Breaker Foiled in Pinal County," *Tucson Daily Citizen*, July 8, 1957.

84. "Offense Report," Pinal County Sheriff's Department, July 7, 1957, box 58, folder "Alianza: Correspondence with Law Enforcement Agencies," Cargo Papers.

85. Tijerina, *Mi Lucha*, 41.

86. Escobar oral history interview.

87. Escobar oral history interview.

88. Tijerina, *Mi Lucha*, 42.

89. Tijerina, 42.

90. Pinal County sheriff Coy K. DeArman to Alfonso Sánchez, Río Arriba County district attorney, August 10, 1964, box 2, folder 24, Nabokov Papers.

91. Rose Tijerina oral history interview. She added that she remembered the depopulation of Valle de Paz so well because she had had nowhere else to stay except with this couple.

92. Escobar oral history interview; Rose Tijerina commented during it.

93. Marez's approval of Tijerina's flight can be found in a police intelligence report on Tijerina, n.d., box 1, folder "Mug Shots," Blea Papers.

94. Tijerina, *Mi Lucha*, 44–45.

95. Western Union telegram, July 15, 1961, in box 48, folder 2, RLT Papers.

96. Serna letter to Tijerina dated November 9, 1962, in box 48, folder 2, RLT Papers.

97. Serna letter to Tijerina dated January 15, 1963. In another letter, dated April 2, 1961, Serna mentioned keeping track of a .38-caliber pistol, a weapon that might have aided a robbery. Both letters in box 48, folder 2, RLT Papers.

98. Letter from Serna to Tijerina, who apparently mistakenly scrawled "1967" in the top margin, box 48, folder 2, RLT Papers. The content of the letter and the accompanying envelope date the missive to January 1963.

99. Letter from Serna to Tijerina, "1967" scrawled in the top margin.

100. DeLaTorre interview by Laurie Coyle (see note 28 above).

101. Coyle, *Adios Amor.*

102. Ramírez, *Migrating Faith*, 16, 38–39, 75.

103. Ramírez, 77–78. The allegations of sexual abuse appeared primarily in press reports. See, for example, Mary Beth Sheridan, "A Growing Faith," *Los Angeles Times*, March 10, 1998. Fortuny-Loret de Mola wrote extensively about the church in English and Spanish in the early 2000s. For starters, see "La Luz del Mundo Church."

104. Weyermann, *Answer Them Nothing.*

105. Reies López Tijerina oral history interview.

106. Reies López Tijerina oral history interview.

107. Escobar oral history interview: "Es muy mentiroso, Reies. Mentiroso [Reies is a really big liar. A big liar]."

108. Nabokov, *Tijerina and the Courthouse Raid*, 202; "Jet Plane Crashes, Disintegrates near Toltec; Pilot Lands Safely," *Casa Grande Dispatch*, May 24, 1956.

109. Specifically, Tijerina mentioned Sheriff Lorance White and FBI agent Don Pelton instead of Lawrence White and Dan Pelton. Tijerina, *Mi Lucha*, 30.

110. "Reyes Tijerina Court Trial Opens Today," *Casa Grande Dispatch*, November 13, 1968.

CHAPTER 3

1. Trillin, "Cloud on the Title," 125. More details culled from local newspapers can be found in Johnston's self-published *Taylor Ranch War*, especially chapter 5. A retired newspaper reporter, Johnston maintained that no academic or popular press would publish his work because he was sympathetic to Taylor. See also N. Gonzales, "Yo Soy Loco," especially the introduction, for the clash between Taylor and the locals.

2. N. Gonzales, "Yo Soy Loco," 1–2.

3. New Mexico Office of the State Historian, "One Land, Many Hands: The Story of the Sangre De Cristo Land Grant."

4. Trillin, "Cloud on the Title," 122.

5. Trillin, 122.

6. Pat Smith, "A Mountain of Trouble," *Raleigh (N.C.) News Observer*, December 15, 1974.

7. Tijerina, *Mi Lucha*, 112.

8. "Nosotros los herederos que antes teníamos riquezas," box 1, folder 1, RLT Papers.

9. To borrow a phrase from Cuban independence hero José Martí.

10. Tijerina, *Mi Lucha*, 46; Gardner, *¡Grito!*, 78.

11. Dunbar-Ortiz, *Roots of Resistance*, 84.

12. Tijerina, *Mi Lucha*, 44, 45, 49, 51; also see Simón Serna letters to Tijerina in which he mentions sending small sums of money to Tijerina, box 48, folder 2, RLT Papers.

13. Escobar oral history interview; Tijerina, *Mi Lucha*, 44–45.

14. Tijerina, *Mi Lucha*, 45, 49.

15. Gardner, *¡Grito!*, 86. Gardner wrote down this quote as if Fernanda Martínez spoke a pidgin English, which I have not reproduced.

16. The words are Maria Varela's in an email to author, August 20, 2017. Also see Correia, "Who is Reies López Tijerina?"

17. Tijerina, *Mi Lucha*, 81.

18. For a general history of New Mexico, see Sánchez and Spude, *New Mexico*. The literature on early settlement, warfare, and slavery is vast. See Frank, *From Settler to Citizen*; Brooks, *Captive and Cousins*; Blackhawk, *Violence over the Land*; DeLay, *War of a Thousand Deserts*; and Gutiérrez, *When Jesus Came*. For a new interpretation of the 1680 revolt and a broader discussion of indigenous slavery, see Reséndez, *Other Slavery*.

19. Martínez, petition, 1832, in Ebright, *Tierra Amarilla Land Grant*, 32–33.

20. Correia, "Hijuelas of Tierra Amarilla."

21. Julian, "Land-Stealing in New Mexico"; Urias, "Tierra Amarilla Grant," 2. Correia's *Properties of Violence* also focuses on the Tierra Amarilla grant. For the fate of two other grants, see Correia, "Making Destiny Manifest." Ebright, *Land Grants and Lawsuits*, investigated the history of nine more grants. In chapter 12 of *Enchantment and Exploitation*, deBuys traced the history of Las Trampas grant. Also see Montoya, *Translating Property*.

22. Ebright, *Tierra Amarilla Land Grant*, 8, 22.

23. Correia, *Properties of Violence*, 105, 116–17. Correia's chapter 3 provided the fullest history of the Corporation of Abiquiú to date.

24. Gardner, *¡Grito!*, 49. Family reminiscences appeared as part of an online memorial to Bill Mundy following his death at the age of ninety-one in 2009. See Jim Mundy, "Rocks and Pine Stumps."

25. News clipping, "Call on Governor to Act on Suspected RA Arson," box 34, folder "Alianza: News Clippings," Cargo Papers. Gardner similarly noted that Mundy owned 25,000 acres by 1960; Gardner, *¡Grito!*, 90.

26. I determined Martínez's birthplace and date by bringing together his World War I registration card and looking under his father's name, Ricardo Martínez, in the 1900 U.S. Census. Both of these sources were made available via ancestry.com, accessed August 30, 2016.

27. Correia, *Properties of Violence*, 113.

28. Mundy, "Rocks and Pine Stumps."

29. Gardner, *¡Grito!*, 77.

30. Rose Tijerina oral history interview.

31. As is my custom, after interviewing Tijerina in 2010, I offered to take him and his wife, Esperanza, out to dinner. He accepted and then named a restaurant. I kept hearing "Billie Jean." He was saying "Village Inn."

32. Consecutive handwritten pages with circled numerals 4, 5, and 6 at top of the respective pages, box 53, folder 43, RLT Papers. Tijerina's use of the term "Indo-

Hispano" to describe the Mexican people he met suggests that he was writing sometime after the Alianza's founding, probably during the 1970s.

33. Tijerina, *Mi Lucha*, 47, 49.

34. Tijerina, 43, 48.

35. Tijerina, 50–52; Escobar oral history interview; Rose Tijerina oral history interview.

36. Griswold del Castillo, *Treaty of Guadalupe Hidalgo*, 114–27; Avila and Santoni, "Historiography of the Mexican-American War," 301–4.

37. Cue Cánovas, *Los Estados Unidos y el México Olvidado*. Based upon the publication date of 1970 for this book, Griswold del Castillo suggested that 1960s social protest influenced Cue Cánovas, but Cue Cánovas appeared to favorably endorse the Alianza's agenda much earlier than that. In 1963, "Mexicans in the United States," an article that purported to summarize Cue Cánovas's views regarding the Treaty of Guadalupe Hidalgo, appeared in a newspaper widely read by land-grant activists with Tijerina's fulsome endorsement. Even more intriguing, the article replicated a document that Tijerina had written in 1959. Given that Tijerina was just starting his land-grant studies, the coincidence raises the possibility that Tijerina wrote the 1959 document with Cue Cánovas's help. See *Albuquerque News Chieftain*, September 6, 1963. For its antecedent, see press release dated January 17, 1959, box 1, folder 1, RLT Papers.

38. In addition to the *Chieftain* article mentioned above, Cue Cánovas's name appears in early Alianza paperwork; see box 59, folder 66, RLT Papers. The Mexican historian also attended the second Alianza convention in 1964; see convention program, box 1, folder 19, RLT Papers.

39. Tijerina, *Mi Lucha*, 57. More about Luna and the Frente can be found in box 31, folders 11–13, RLT Papers.

40. Spanish translation of a September 9, 1959, UPI article detailing the meeting in box 57, folder 27, RLT Papers; Tijerina, *Mi Lucha*, 57.

41. Press release dated January 17, 1959, box 1, folder 1, RLT Papers. This is the press release that was reprinted in the *Albuquerque News Chieftain* in 1963.

42. Press release dated January 17, 1959. As Johnson, *Revolution in Texas*, pointed out, probably thousands of ethnic Mexicans did die at the hands of law enforcement during the 1910s.

43. Press release dated January 17, 1959, RLT Papers.

44. Press release dated January 17, 1959.

45. Tijerina, *Mi Lucha*, 32; for more on Lombardo Toledano, see Coerver, Pasztor, and Buffington, *Mexico*, 110–11.

46. "You now want to be justified in front of your friends, saying that Cárdenas is your friend, that Vallejo is with you," angry letter written by former follower Simón Serna, scrawled "1967" in the top margin but dating from January 1963 according to the content and postmark, box 48, folder 2, RLT Papers. For more on Vallejo and his times, see Robert F. Alegre, *Railroad Radicals in Cold War Mexico: Gender, Class, and Memory*. See also a news clipping from August 19, 1964, edition of *Política*, box 2, folder 14, RLT Papers. Jacinto López was mentioned only in passing in several books on development and agrarian rights. See, for example, Ochoa, *Feeding Mexico*, 159.

47. Tijerina dated the trip to May 1950. Handwritten recollection, circled numeral 5 at top of page, box 53, folder 43, RLT Papers.

48. As quoted in Bell Blawis, *Tijerina and the Land Grants*, 33.

49. Tijerina, *Mi Lucha*, 87, 96.

50. Slim documentation on this organization can be found in box 49, folder 15, RLT Papers.

51. Güemes, "En busca de la méxicanidad," especially 93–96, 99, 106, and 116–17. Tijerina mentioned meeting with a Comité de Anáhuac representative in Tijerina, *Mi Lucha*, 35. Also see box 49, folder 16, RLT Papers.

52. Reséndez, *Changing National Identities*.

53. Tijerina, *Mi Lucha*, 53.

54. Corporación de Abiquiú to the Frente Mexicano Pro Derechos Humanos, August 1, 1959, box 46, folder 22, RLT Papers.

55. Cruz Trujillo letter to R. López T, August 4, 1959, box 46, folder 22, RLT Papers.

56. Tijerina, *Mi Lucha*, 55.

57. Douglas E. Kneeland, "New Mexico Is Tense as Rebel Faces Court Today," *New York Times*, June 22, 1967.

58. Martin Waldron, "Insurrection in Our Own New Mexico," *New York Times*, June 11, 1967.

59. Lopez, "Minority Groups in New Mexico," 18.

60. U.S. Department of Labor, "One Hundred Years of Consumer Spending."

61. Lopez, "Minority Groups in New Mexico," 21, 24.

62. George W. Grayson, "Tijerina: The Evolution of a Primitive Rebel," *Commonweal* clipping dated July 28, 1968, box 50, folder 24, RLT Papers; Kneeland, "New Mexico Is Tense as Rebel Faces Court Today."

63. Peter Nabokov, "The Mother Is a Memory," *SFNM*, February 4, 1968.

64. Letter to Sr. Dwight Eisenhower, December 12, 1959, box 46, folder 22, RLT Papers.

65. Lopez, "Minority Groups in New Mexico," 18.

66. That was the complaint of Alfonso Sánchez, the future Río Arriba district attorney who was then a young lawyer hired by the Corporation of Abiquiú. He asserted that, as plaintiffs, corporation members wanted to fight for all their lost land-grant rights versus securing their right to the seventy acres only. Sánchez to José C. Martínez, September 20, 1958, box 1, folder 15, Sánchez Papers.

67. Tijerina claimed authorship of the letter in *Mi Lucha*, 60. The letter mentioned the depopulation of La Ensenada at a time when he was living there and detailed the work that he had done in Mexico.

68. Letter to Sr. Dwight Eisenhower, December 12, 1959, box 46, folder 22, RLT Papers.

69. Tijerina, *Mi Lucha*, 59.

70. For a summary of the case and its significance, see Correia, *Properties of Violence*, 120–22.

71. Tórrez and Trapp, *Rio Arriba*, chapter 9.

72. Mundy, "Rocks and Pine Stumps."

73. Gardner, *¡Grito!*, 91.

74. "Tensions Mounting as RA Ranches Razed," *SFNM*, May 10, 1960.

75. "Partial Report on Tierra Amarilla Dispute," n.d., but probably 1964, box 1, folder 17, Sánchez Papers.

76. See Sánchez's notes, arrest record signed by Freddie Martínez, and "Judgment and Sentence" against Anselmo Tijerina, all in box 1, folder 18, Sánchez Papers.

77. During the author's phone conversation with Tijerina, he said he had once cut fences on Mundy's property.

78. Tijerina, *Mi Lucha*, 63–64.

79. Only the second half of this letter appears in the archives, box 41, folder 39, RLT Papers.

80. Letter from José María Martínez to Adolfo López Mateos, Secretaría de Relaciones Exteriores de México, Archivo Genaro Estrada, Mexico City, classification number: 111-2984-2.

81. Reies López Tijerina oral history interview.

82. Gregorita Aguilar conversation with author. Her low opinion of Tijerina then contrasted greatly with her high opinion of him decades before. In 1968, Frances Swadesh described Gregorita and her husband, Cruz, as "passionate 'tigers' and no wonder" because each had experienced land dispossession in their lifetimes. See Swadesh Field Diary, box 5, folder 12, Frances León Quintana Papers, Center for Southwest Research, University of New Mexico, Albuquerque.

83. Tijerina to "*Amada Esposa*" (Mary Escobar), April 14, 1960, box 54, folder 32, RLT Papers.

84. Lic. Alfonso de Rosenweig Diaz Jr. to José María Martínez, Secretaría de Relaciones Exteriores de México, Archivo Genaro Estrada, classification number: 111-2984-2.

85. "Clamor de Pueblo Olvidado," April 9, 1962, box 47, folder 23, RLT Papers.

86. This news clipping and others can be found in box 59, folder 80, RLT Papers. In his memoir, Tijerina mistakenly dated the press conference to 1961.

87. Tórrez, "New Mexico State Archives Groundbreaking."

88. New Mexico Commission of Public Records, "Research Resources."

89. Tijerina to Gustavo Díaz Ordaz, February 8, 1964, box 47, folder 23. Also see similar letters from Tijerina, same dates, to Adolfo López Mateos, box 47, folder 24, and to Luis Echevarría, box 47, folder 25, all in RLT Papers.

90. "Programa de la Alianza Federal de Mercedes," January 28, 1964, box 31, folder 12, RLT Papers.

91. Handwritten itinerary, box 53, folder 45, RLT Papers.

92. Nabokov interview with Fernanda Martínez, box 8, folder "Transcripts for Tapes," Nabokov Papers. The transcripts identify the interviewee as an unnamed Tierra Amarilla woman and land grantee, but the information provided in the interview revealed her to be Fernanda Martínez.

93. Tijerina to Escobar, May 2, 1962, box 54, folder 32, RLT Papers. Pedro Ribera, a Spanish-language columnist, recalled Tijerina making the same pledge of nonviolence the first time the two met, probably in the early 1960s. See Ribera's column, "Entre Nosotros," *Santa Fe News*, June 15, 1967, news clipping in box 80, folder 12, Myra Ellen Jenkins Collected Papers, Center of Southwest Studies, Fort Lewis College, Colo.

94. Sánchez, *Forgotten People*, 12.

95. Mary Escobar mentioned that Tijerina having owned a copy of the book; see undated letter that begins, "Reies: Tengo gusto de saber de ustedes," box 54, folder 32, RLT Papers.

96. Mario García, *Mexican Americans*, 253.

97. Blanton, *George I. Sánchez*, 37.

98. As quoted in Mario García, *Mexican Americans*, 256. Chapter 10 of the book was devoted to Sánchez's political thinking.

99. Statement on Alianza letterhead, "Agosto 3, 1962," box 1, folder 1, RLT Papers.

100. "Agosto 3, 1962"; Tijerina, *Mi Lucha*, 95.

101. "Agosto 3, 1962."

102. "Para todo Heredero a quien concierna los intereses que cubre el Tratado de Guadalupe Hidalgo," June 12, 1963, box 1, folder 1, RLT Papers.

103. Meeting minutes, February 15 and 22, 1964, box 1, folder 16, RLT Papers. Also see Eddie Chavez letter to Tijerina, April 3, 1963, box 41, folder 38, RLT Papers.

CHAPTER 4

1. Tijerina, *Mi Lucha*, 101.

2. Rose Tijerina oral history interview. Rose Tijerina also alleged sexual abuse by her father in an oral history that appeared in Gutiérrez, Meléndez, and Noyola, *Chicanas in Charge*, 57–69.

3. Escobar oral history interview.

4. Reies López Tijerina oral history interview.

5. Herman, *Father-Daughter Incest*, 46–49, 81, 71, 219, 301.

6. Rachel Tijerina oral history interview.

7. Rose Tijerina comments during Escobar oral history interview.

8. Herman, *Trauma and Recovery*, 100, 103, 105.

9. Letter dated September 26, 1967, to "Querido Papisito," box 55, folder 6, RLT Papers.

10. Rachel Tijerina oral history interview.

11. Tijerina, *Mi Lucha*, 78.

12. Escobar oral history interview. Escobar shared her recollections of her work at the hospital not on tape but in a conversation in November 2006 as we drove across town from her home to Rose's, passing the hospital where Escobar used to work.

13. Tijerina, *Mi Lucha*, 60.

14. Escobar oral history interview.

15. Escobar oral history interview.

16. Author's phone inquiry to her cousin Dr. Mary Figueroa, a family practice medical doctor.

17. Rose Tijerina oral history interview.

18. Escobar oral history interview. Also see Alice Mata letter to Mary Escobar, dated March 1961: "Did they fix you so you can't have anymore? I hope so for your sake. . . . You have more than you can handle," box 54, folder 32, RLT Papers.

19. Escobar oral history interview.

20. Escobar oral history interview.

21. Rose Tijerina speaking during Escobar oral history interview.

22. Escobar oral history interview.

23. Escobar oral history interview.

24. Escobar oral history interview.

25. Escobar to Tijerina, dated 1962 at the top in Tijerina's handwriting, box 54, folder

32, RLT Papers. Given that the letter's contents include a reference to Rose in Mexico City, it may be from 1963. Rose Tijerina recalled that she took her first trip with her father that year.

26. Escobar to Tijerina, typed letter, n.d., box 54, folder 34, RLT Papers. The letter's contents suggest that it dates from 1964.

27. Escobar oral history interview.

28. Gardner, *¡Grito!*, 96.

29. Escobar to Tijerina, n.d., letter begins, "Reies: Tengo gusto de saber de ustedes," box 54, folder 32, RLT Papers. Thanks to David Montejano for suggesting the possible reference to God in the sentence.

30. For the multiple ways that women operated politically despite societally imposed gender constraints in post–World War II America, see Meyerowitz, *Not June Cleaver*.

31. Tijerina to Escobar, April 14, 1960, box 54, folder 32, RLT Papers.

32. Tijerina to Escobar, n.d., letter begins, "María, hoy llegaré de Vera Cruz," box 54, folder 32, RLT Papers.

33. Tijerina to "*Amada Esposa*" (Mary Escobar), April 14, 1960, box 54, folder 32, RLT Papers.

34. Tijerina to Escobar, May 7, 1962, box 54, folder 32, RLT Papers.

35. Tijerina to Escobar, n.d., letter begins, "María, que esta carta te haye con salud," box 54, folder 32, RLT Papers.

36. Tijerina to Escobar, "Julio [?] 1963," box 54, folder 32, RLT Papers. Tijerina recalled the name of the film during his oral history interview.

37. I compiled the list of tasks from information mentioned in the letters above.

38. Early minutes can be found in box 1, folder 16, RLT Papers.

39. Escobar oral history interview.

40. Rose Tijerina oral history interview.

41. Della Rossa, "Tijerina and the Alianza," unpublished manuscript, box 51, folder 34, RLT Papers. Quote appears on p. 75.

42. Tijerina, *Mi Lucha*, 78.

43. Tijerina, 53.

44. Tijerina, 97.

45. Tijerina, 77.

46. Tijerina, 78.

47. Tijerina, 94.

48. Tijerina, 52, 60, 61.

49. Rose Tijerina oral history interview.

50. Tijerina, *Mi Lucha*, 61.

51. Tijerina, 66–67.

52. Tijerina, 105.

53. Rose Tijerina oral history interview.

54. Rose Tijerina oral history interview. According to psychologists, silence, or the "freeze" response, is another method that children employ to cope with abuse. Cozolino, *Neuroscience of Human Relationships*, 21.

55. Rose Tijerina oral history interview.

56. Gardner, *¡Grito!*, 3.

57. Calloway, "June 5, 1967."

58. Rachel Tijerina oral history interview.

59. As is confirmed by a quick glance at Alianza correspondence found in boxes 42 and 43, RLT Papers.

60. Rose Tijerina oral history interview.

61. Rose Tijerina oral history interview.

62. Escobar oral history interview.

63. George W. Grayson, "Tijerina: The Evolution of a Primitive Rebel," *Commonweal* clipping dated July 28, 1968, box 50, folder 24, RLT Papers.

64. Tijerina, *Mi Lucha*, 115.

65. "Albuquerque Public Schools, Report from Guidance," box 55, folder 1, RLT Papers.

66. Grayson, "Tijerina: The Evolution of a Primitive Rebel."

67. Tijerina, *Mi Lucha*, 117.

68. See a series of letters Tijerina wrote to Patsy in April 1966 from Seville, box 55, folder 1, RLT Papers.

69. Reies López Tijerina oral history interview. Specifically, Reies Tijerina said that Patsy threatened suicide if he did not marry her.

70. Rose Tijerina oral history interview.

71. Rachel Tijerina oral history interview.

72. Oral history protocol frowns upon interviewing anyone who is not able to fully comprehend the interview process. Arguably, to speak about someone in the absence of such an interview is also ethically questionable. Faced with this dilemma, I have done my best to parse for political and historical significance.

73. Reies López Tijerina oral history interview.

74. 1963 Constitution, box 1, folder 2, RLT Papers; "Land Grant Chief Renamed," *Albuquerque News Chieftain*, September 27, 1963, clipping, box 1, folder "Alianza Federal de Mercedes," Blea Papers.

75. 1963 Constitution, RLT Papers.

76. Julian Rains to Boston E. Witt, investigative report, November 21, 1967, box 2, folder "Investigative Reports," Blea Papers.

77. Tijerina, *Mi Lucha*, 86. Only the name "Reies López Tijerina" appeared on more Alianza documents than that of Cristóbal Tijerina. In return, Rose Tijerina remembered that Reies Tijerina and Mary Escobar opened up their two-bedroom rental to Chris Tijerina and his family. The experience of eleven children and four adults living together in such a small space apparently also took a toll on the Escobar-Tijerina union. Rose Tijerina oral history interview.

78. Anselmo Tijerina to Reies Tijerina, April 13, 1961, box 54, folder 30, RLT Papers.

79. "Tijerina's brother assumes leadership of Alianza," *SFNM*, October 27, 1969.

80. Margarito Tijerina to Juan Martínez, January 27, 1961, box 54, folder 29, RLT Papers.

81. Margarito Tijerina to "Roy López," May 17, 1961, box 54, folder 29, RLT Papers.

82. See "Perjury Charge Filed," news clipping, box 60, folder 4, RLT Papers; and "Brother of Land-Grant Leader Sentenced," *Clovis (N.Mex.) News Journal*, August 4, 1966, and "Habitual Criminal Charged," *AT*, dated August 31, 1966, news clippings, both in box 60, folder 6, RLT Papers. Also see Gardner, *¡Grito!*, 118.

83. Frances Swadesh Quintana provided the most detailed account of this crime

and the subsequent trial, as well as the most critical examination of the evidence used to convict Margarito Tijerina. See her "Legal Harassment and Unequal Justice in New Mexico," box 2, folder 20, Nabokov Papers.

84. Alfonso Sánchez made this contention in his memoir, box 1, folder 6, Sánchez Papers.

85. Swadesh, "Legal Harassment and Unequal Justice in New Mexico," Nabokov Papers.

86. Escobar mentioned her childcare role during her February 2013 conversation with me.

87. See letters contained within box 55, folders 5 and 7, RLT Papers, which show David acting in his father's stead while the elder Tijerina was in prison. Oral history interviews with either son were impossible: Daniel died in a car accident in 1974, while David (Reies Hugh) died at the relatively young age of fifty-three, according to his obituary in *AJ*, November 15, 2000.

88. Rose Tijerina comments during Escobar oral history interview.

89. R.H. Tijerina to Reies López Tijerina, August 17, 1970, box 55, folder 5, RLT Papers.

90. Tijerina, *Mi Lucha*, 213, 215; news clippings about the Supreme Court confrontation appear in box 60, folder 8. Also see Mantler, *Power to the Poor*, 154.

91. Tijerina, *Mi Lucha*, 135.

92. "Suspended Students Ask 'Equal Rights,'" *AJ*, April 26, 1968; more news clippings about the school strike appear in box 61, folder 6, RLT Papers. The list of demands appears in box 55, folder 8, RLT Papers.

93. Rachel Tijerina comments during Reies López Tijerina oral history interview.

94. I interviewed Reies López Tijerina in 2010 at his daughter Rachel's house, during which she offered occasional comments. Three years later, I had a conversation with her mother, Mary Escobar; once again, Rachel offered occasional comments. On February 6, 2013, she told me that she and her father were no longer close because her father had become angry with her after she was unable to provide him a ride.

95. Confidential report by Wilfred Garcia and Julian Raines, October 18, 1967, box 1, folder "Investigators Reports," Blea Papers.

96. Wilfred Garcia, "Summary of Information on Reies Tijerina and the Alianza de Mercedes," box 1, folder "Wilfred Garcia," Blea Papers.

97. Nigel S. Hey, "Heirs to Land Grants Meet This Week to Plan Strategy," *North Valley News* (Albuquerque), August 27, 1964, clipping in box 1, folder 1, RLT Papers.

98. Garcia, "Summary of Information on Reies Tijerina and the Alianza de Mercedes," Blea Papers.

99. Reies Tijerina to Chris Tijerina, n.d., box 54, folder 27, RLT Papers.

100. Chris Tijerina reply to Reies Tijerina, n.d., box 54, folder 27, RLT Papers.

101. Minutes, November 2, 1963, in Escobar's handwriting, box 1, folder 13, RLT Papers.

102. 1963 Constitution, RLT Papers.

103. By-laws, November 8, 1963, box 1, folder 3, RLT Papers.

104. "Jamás en la historia de Nuevo Mexico," radio script, box 1, folder 36, RLT Papers.

105. "La Voz de la Justicia," radio script, April 23, 1965, KABQ, box 1, folder 36, RLT Papers.

106. 1963 meeting minutes for attendance, box 1, folder 13; for Los Caballeros, box 31, folder 17; for the Mesa Cósmica, box 1, folder 7, all RLT Papers.

CHAPTER 5

1. Tijerina, *Mi Lucha*, 76, 98.

2. Sale receipt, box 1, folder 6, RLT Papers.

3. The University of New Mexico's Zimmerman Library has the entire run of the *Albuquerque News Chieftain* on microfilm.

4. "Para todo Heredero a quien concierna los intereses que cubre el Tratado de Guadalupe Hidalgo," June 12, 1963, box 1, folder 1, RLT Papers.

5. Nabokov, *Tijerina and the Courthouse Raid*, 212.

6. As a review of the newspaper revealed.

7. Program announcement, box 2, folder 19, Nabokov Papers.

8. "La Alianza Informa" column of October 2, 1965, mentioned television broadcasts starting Saturday afternoons in November on Channel 4. Box 7, untitled folder, Blea Papers.

9. Juan Valdez oral history interview.

10. "La Voz de la Justicia," radio script, April 21, 1965, KABQ, box 1, folder 36, and handwritten letter, July 7, 1965, box 1, folder 1, both RLT Papers.

11. "Otra vez desde Albuquerque," box 1, folder 1, RLT Papers.

12. "La Alianza de las Mercedes," February 15, 1963, box 2, folder 6, RLT Papers, for fourteen grants. Also see meeting minutes for February 2, 1963, box 1, folder 13, RLT Papers.

13. Estimate of 800 attendees found in "Land Grants Chief Renamed," *Albuquerque News Chieftain*, September 27, 1963, clipping in box 1, folder "Alianza Federal de Mercedes," Blea Papers.

14. Although later membership estimates vary greatly, the estimate of "at least 3,000" was achieved by counting names on membership lists, boxes 5–15, RLT Papers. A January 1965 list showed 130 grants represented by the Alianza, box 1, folder 9, RLT Papers.

15. First mention of 6,000 appears in Nigel S. Hey, "Heirs to Land Grants Meet This Week to Plan Strategy," *North Valley News* (Albuquerque), August 27, 1964, clipping in box 1, folder 1, RLT Papers.

16. The 1960 U.S. Census estimated that the "Spanish-surnamed population" of New Mexico numbered 269,122. See "Nativity, Parentage, and Country of Origin of White Persons of Spanish Surname by Sex, for Five Southwestern States," table 1, p. 2. A factor of 10 is conservative. A 1964 injunction against the Corporation of Abiquiú, one of the most active organizations, listed just 137 names. And presumably law enforcement was trying to cast as wide a net as possible. "Petition," box 1, folder 17, Sánchez Papers.

17. "Spanish Land Grant Heirs to Meet Here," *Albuquerque News Chieftain*, September 20, 1963, clipping in box 1, one of several folders marked "Alianza Federal de Mercedes," Blea Papers.

18. Rose Tijerina phone conversation.

19. See, for example, "La Alianza Federal de Mercedes Informa," September 17, 1963,

and "El radio y los periódicos día a día nos están diciendo," March 25, 1964, both in box 1, folder 1, RLT Papers.

20. Author's observations based upon photographs and filmed footage of Tijerina including a 1969 news profile, "The Most Hated Man in New Mexico," directed by Walter Miller, which appeared in 1969 as part of the NBC News program *First Tuesday*. A complete transcript of the show is available in box 1, folder 1, Reies López Tijerina News Reports Collection, Kenneth Spencer Research Library, University of Kansas Libraries.

21. Nabokov, *Tijerina and the Courthouse Raid*, 212.

22. Gardner, *¡Grito!*, 92.

23. "Violación del Tratado de Guadalupe Hidalgo," box 1, folder 1, RLT Papers.

24. Typewritten address dated July 2, 1962, box 41, folder 39, RLT Papers.

25. "To all the heirs of the Spanish land grants," box 1, folder 1, RLT Papers.

26. 1963 Constitution, box 1, folder 2, RLT Papers.

27. "Para todo Heredero a quien concierna los intereses que cubre el Tratado de Guadalupe Hidalgo," June 12, 1963, box 1, folder 1, RLT Papers.

28. Thanks to A. Katie Stirling-Harris, a scholar of early modern Spain, for pointing out the richness and rootedness of this language.

29. "Pues siempre se llevó a cabo la junta en Cuba, N.Mex.," box 1, folder 1, RLT Papers. The speech then informed a newspaper column, "La Alianza Federal de Mercedes Informa," November 15, 1963, box 60, folder 11, RLT Papers.

30. Simmons, *Last Conquistador*, 65.

31. D. Weber, *Spanish Frontier in North America*, 89–91.

32. United States v. Sandoval, 167 U.S. 278 (1897).

33. "Cuando el Presidente Theodore Roosevelt," n.d., box 1, folder 36, RLT Papers.

34. "Cuando el Presidente Theodore Roosevelt."

35. Membership appeal signed by José A. Lucero, dated 1963–64, box 2, folder 1, RLT Papers.

36. "Origen de las Mercedes Protegidas," "1963 file," box 46, folder 4, RLT Papers.

37. "Mensaje a Todos Los Herederos," box 1, folder 1, RLT Papers.

38. Rose Tijerina phone conversation.

39. Tijerina, *Mi Lucha*, 59.

40. Gardner, *¡Grito!*, 255–56.

41. As quoted in Busto, *King Tiger*, 192.

42. Tijerina always referred to the 1493 bull as the *Bula Noverint Universi*.

43. Brown, *1494*, 3.

44. "Mensaje a Todos Los Herederos," RLT Papers.

45. "Cuando el Presidente Theodore Roosevelt," RLT Papers.

46. "Ya se aproxima la Segunda Real Convención," n.d. but 1964, and "Copiada el día 24 de marzo de 1964," both box 1, folder 1, RLT Papers. Tijerina may also have been influenced by a land-grant lawyer who as early as 1938 had argued that Mexican colonization laws granted land in perpetuity, Correia, *Properties of Violence*, 92.

47. "Pues siempre se llevó a cabo la junta en Cuba, N.Mex.," box 1, folder 1; "Con todo respeto nos dirijimos a los dos gobiernos," June 13, 1963, box 1, folder 1; and "La Alianza de las Mercedes," February 15, 1963, box 2, folder 6, all RLT Papers.

48. "Estimado y digno Heredero," dated 1963, box 1, folder 1, RLT Papers.

49. "Ya se aproxima la Segunda Real Convención," RLT Papers.

50. 1963 Constitution, RLT Papers.

51. "Mensaje a Todos Los Herederos," RLT Papers.

52. "Para todo Heredero a quien concierna los intereses que cubre el Tratado de Guadalupe Hidalgo," RLT Papers.

53. "En los tiempos que vivimos," dated "1964 File," box 1, folder 1, RLT Papers.

54. "Las Leyes de las Indias—Unico Derecho Para los Herederos," box 1, folder 1, RLT Papers.

55. "Para todo Heredero a quien concierna los intereses que cubre el Tratado de Guadalupe Hidalgo," RLT Papers.

56. "En los tiempos que vivimos," RLT Papers.

57. The text of the treaty can be found on multiple websites as well as in Griswold del Castillo, *Treaty of Guadalupe Hidalgo*, 189–90. For his discussion of the deleted and edited articles, see 46–48.

58. Griswold del Castillo, 54.

59. See, for example, "The Treaty of Guadalupe Hidalgo of Feb. 2, 1848 left the United States with a land problem," handwritten notes, n.d., box 1, folder 1, RLT Papers; and "Estas Son Nuestras Demandas al Gobierno Federal," n.d. but probably 1965 as well, both box 46, folder 4, RLT Papers.

60. See, for example, "Hermano Heredero y Miembro de la Alianza Federal de Mercedes," April 1966, box 1, folder 1, RLT Papers.

61. Larson, *New Mexico's Quest for Statehood*, 274.

62. The nearly 40 percent estimate is from the Pew Research Center; see Krosgstad and Lopez.

63. Lozano, *American Language*, traces the limits of the bilingual promise in New Mexico.

64. "Violación del Tratado de Guadalupe Hidalgo," RLT Papers.

65. "En los tiempos que vivimos," RLT Papers.

66. About the destruction of the archives, see Tijerina, *Mi Lucha*, 58–59, 84. Tijerina also condemned Pile in an interview with KPFA radio station in Berkeley, California. The transcript was reprinted in Rosales, *Testimonio*, 308–20. Robert J. Tórrez, former state historian of New Mexico, produced a succinct summation of the destruction of the archives during Pile's tenure; see his online essay "New Mexico State Archives Groundbreaking."

67. See "Lo Que El Pueblo Heredero Debe Saber de las Cortes de Nuevo Mexico," which condemned Pile and Catron both, box 46, folder 4, RLT Papers.

68. "Kansas City Bookseller Files Historical Documents Brief," *SFNM*, May 17, 1961.

69. "Violación del Tratado de Guadalupe Hidalgo," RLT Papers, featured such a request.

70. "Nosotros los herederos que antes teníamos riquezas" and "Después de la real convención" named names, both in box 1, folder 1, RLT Papers.

71. "Land Areas of the National Forest Service."

72. United States v. Sandoval, 1897.

73. Tally from David Correia. See his "Future of the Commons."

74. "Violación del Tratado de Guadalupe Hidalgo," RLT Papers.

75. Kaufman, *The Forest Ranger*, 75.

76. "Nosotros los Herederos que antes teníamos riqueza," RLT Papers.

77. "Desde el hospital de San Jose," handwritten note, July 5, 1965, box 1, folder 1, RLT Papers.

78. 1963 Constitution, RLT Papers.

79. "Con todo respeto que demanda la Ley," dated 1965, box 2, folder 1, RLT Papers.

80. G. Gonzalez, "Racial Intelligence Testing."

81. As quoted in Correia, *Properties of Violence*, 174. Also see Correia, "From Agropastoralism to Sustained Yield Forestry," 32, 36–38; and Pulido, "Ecological Legitimacy."

82. Thanks to David Montejano for telling me about the research of Clyde Kluckhohn and Florence Rockwood Kluckhohn; with Fred Strodtbeck, Florence Rockwood Kluckhohn wrote *Variations in Value Orientations*. For a critical view of "cultural determinism," see Vaca, "Mexican American in the Social Sciences."

83. "Nosotros los herederos que antes teníamos riqueza," RLT papers; "Jamás en la historia de Nuevo Mexico," RLT Papers; "La Voz de la Justicia," radio script, April 21, 1965, KABQ, box 1, folder 36, RLT Papers.

84. "Marzo 25, 1964, Albuquerque, Nuevo Mexico," box 1, folder 1, RLT Papers.

85. "La Voz de la Justicia," April 23, 1965, RLT Papers.

86. "Mensaje a Todos Los Herederos."

87. Speech dated May 19, 1964, box 1, folder 1, RLT Papers.

88. Hobsbawm, *Primitive Rebels*.

89. Wallace, "Revitalization Movements."

90. Jelin, *State Repression*, 33. In the original Spanish, Jelin preferred "*emprendedor*" to "*empresario*" to distance her term "memory entrepreneur" from the notion of lucrative gain; see Jelin, *Los Trabajos de la Memoria*, 48.

91. "Entre las promesas," n.d. but probably 1963, box 46, folder 4, RLT Papers.

92. Handwritten statement, February 19, 1965, box 1, folder 1, RLT Papers.

93. "El radio y los periódicos día a día nos están diciendo," RLT Papers.

94. "Violación del Tratado de Guadalupe Hidalgo," RLT Papers.

95. "En los tiempos que vivimos," RLT Papers.

96. "Todos los Profetas," July 9, 1962, box 41, folder 39, RLT Papers.

97. "Confesiones Personales," May 7, 1965, box 1, folder 36, RLT Papers.

98. "Confesiones Personales."

99. Gregorita Aguilar and Cruz Aguilar conversations.

100. Ebright, *Land Grants and Lawsuits*, 8.

101. Nostrand, *El Cerrito*, 176.

102. Ebright, *Tierra Amarilla Land Grant*, x–xi. William deBuys, in contrast, drew a distinction between indigenous and nuevomexicano views: "To the Hispanos of New Mexico, the land was not a sacred thing as it was for the Pueblos, but it was still not altogether inanimate. It was the mother and protector of their traditional subsistence pastoralism," *Enchantment and Exploitation*, 9.

103. New Mexico Office of the State Historian, "Land of Enchantment—1935."

104. Tórrez, "Spanish and Mexican Land Grants."

105. Ebright, *Land Grants and Lawsuits*, 23.

106. Frank, *From Settler to Citizen*.

107. I am borrowing the phrase from Hayden, *Power of Place*. Similarly, in Glassberg's *Sense of History*, a sense of place and a sense of history are often intertwined. In

thinking about the significance of place and space, I was influenced by S. Rodríguez, *Acequia*; Tuan's *Space and Place*; and the introduction to *Power and Place in the North American West*, edited by Findlay and White. The editors quote the work of D. W. Meinig, who described space as being "some kind of location and ensemble of features. Such things are human creations in the sense of perceptions, a mental imposition of order, a parcelization of the earth's surface, a transformation of space—an abstraction—into something more specific and limited." As Findlay and White noted, "constructing space through an 'imposition' of order entails asserting some sort of control over the environment as well as over other people with different ideas about the same physical space; in other words, the exercise of power," x.

108. S. Rodríguez, *Acequia*, 92–93.

109. S. Rodríguez, 92–93.

110. Steele, *Alabados of New Mexico*, 303. Steele noted that this particular alabado has thirty-seven different versions. Yet another appeared in Wallis, *En Divina Luz*, 21.

111. Encinias, "Iratéo," 86, 104–7.

112. González, *Spanish-Americans*, 99.

113. Waters, *Book of the Hopi*, 37–38.

114. González, *Spanish-Americans*, 99.

115. Tijerina, *Mi Lucha*, 58.

116. Juan Valdez oral history interview.

117. Juan Valdez showed me these letters during our 2007 oral history interview.

118. Scarborough, *Trespassers on Our Own Land*, x. Scarborough wrote the book based upon his oral history interviews with Juan Valdez.

119. Juan Valdez oral history interview.

120. "Otra vez desde Albuquerque," RLT Papers.

121. "La Voz de la Justicia," April 23, 1965, RLT Papers.

122. Valentina Valdez oral history interview.

123. Lewis, *Elmer Gantry*.

124. Nabokov, *Tijerina and the Courthouse Raid*, 213.

125. Río Arriba district attorney Alfonso Sánchez among them. See his notes, box 1, folder 10, Sánchez Papers.

126. The observation was made by Maria Varela in an email to author, August 20, 2017.

127. Tijerina, *Mi Lucha*, 98.

128. Confidential report by Wilfred Garcia and Julian Raines, November 23, 1967, folder "Investigative Reports," Blea Papers.

129. Chris Tijerina to Reies López Tijerina, April 15, 1964, box 54, folder 27, RLT Papers.

130. "Otra vez desde Albuquerque" and "El radio y los periódicos día a día nos están diciendo," RLT Papers.

131. "Otra vez desde Albuquerque," RLT Papers.

132. "La Voz de la Justicia," April 21, 1965, RLT Papers.

133. Handwritten letter, February 19, 1965, box 1, folder 1, RLT Papers.

134. Reies López Tijerina to Chris Tijerina, handwritten letter dated June 25, 1965, box 54, folder 27, RLT Papers.

135. Handwritten letter dated July 5, 1965, box 1, folder 1, RLT Papers.

136. Confidential report by Wilfred Garcia and Julian Raines, October 18, 1967, box 1, folder "Investigators Reports," Blea Papers.

137. Hey, "Heirs to Land Grants Meet This Week to Plan Strategy," RLT Papers.

CHAPTER 6

1. Tijerina, *Mi Lucha*, 105–10; *Política* clipping, dated August 1, 1964, box 2, folder 14, RLT Papers; *El Fronterizo, Ciudad Juárez* daily newspaper, July 15, 1964, as quoted by FBI document dated July 20, 1964, box 2, folder 6, RLT Papers; memo to José Gorostiza, Secretario de Relaciones Exteriores, from Luis Echeverría, Subsecretario de Gobernación, dated August 11, 1964, Secretaría de Relaciones Exteriores de México, Archivo Genaro Estrada, Mexico City, classification number: IV-2984-2.

2. "Reies López Tijerina y el Movimiento de la Alianza Federal de las Mercedes," n.d., p. 39, box 2131, 1964–1983, Fondo [Collection]: Gobernación, Dirección General de Seguridad, Investigaciones Políticas y Sociales, Archivo General de la Nación, Mexico City.

3. In passing during one of our many conversations, Mary Escobar mentioned losing her car this way. Tijerina to Dirreción de Registro Federal de Automobiles, July 25, 1965, box 41, folder 44, RLT Papers.

4. Tijerina letter to Gongorio Hernández, box 41, folder 42, RLT Papers.

5. Tijerina, *Mi Lucha*, 111.

6. February 2, 1963, minutes, box 1, folder 16, RLT Papers.

7. Petition for a court injunction, filed by Alfonso Sánchez, box 1, folder 17, Sánchez Papers.

8. Nigel S. Hey, "Heirs to Land Grants Meet This Week to Plan Strategy," *North Valley News* (Albuquerque), August 27, 1964, clipping in box 1, folder 1, RLT Papers.

9.*Man of La Mancha*, based on Miguel Cervantes's *Don Quixote*, opened on Broadway in 1965, won the Tony for best musical that year, and ran until 1971. "The Impossible Dream" became a popular song from the show.

10. "Ya pasaron dos semanas desde el día qué asesinaron a nuestro, John F. Kennedy," box 1, folder 1, RLT Papers.

11. "Ya pasaron dos semanas desde el día qué asesinaron a nuestro, John F. Kennedy."

12. Elizabeth "Betita" Martínez made this point in an oral history interview by the author. Also see her article "View from New Mexico." Also see letter written by E. Dicho (the name is a pun for "*He dicho*" meaning "I have spoken") to Gov. David Cargo, June 13, 1966, box 59, folder "Alianza Citizens' Letters 1," Cargo Papers. The letter writer complains that the Forest Service had expropriated his land in a "Castro-like fashion."

13. Gardner, *¡Grito!*, 112.

14. Julian Rains to Boston E. Witt, investigative report, November 21, 1967, box 2, folder "Investigative Reports," Blea Papers.

15. "La JUSTICIA ha nacido . . . ," n.d., box 1, folder 1, RLT Papers.

16. By-laws, box 1, folder 3, RLT Papers.

17. "Biography of Senator Montoya," box 37, folder 77, Joseph M. Montoya Papers, Center for Southwest Research, University of New Mexico, Albuquerque; and "Montoya, Joseph Manuel," an official biography offered by the History, Art and Archives website of the U.S. House of Representatives.

18. Hey, "Heirs to Land Grants Meet This Week to Plan Strategy," RLT Papers.

19. See, for example, Montoya to Prax Rivera, June 8, 1964; and Montoya to Reies López Tijerina, April 18, 1965, and June 15, 1965, all in box 47, folder 26, RLT Papers.

20. Montoya to Miguel Flores, March 1, 1965, box 47, folder 26, RLT Papers.

21. Minutes, "sábado [the month was January] 18, 1964," box 1, folder 16, RLT Papers.

22. "Pues siempre se llevó a cabo la junta en Cuba, N.Mex.," box 1, folder 1, RLT Papers.

23. "Conversación por teléfono con el congresista Henry González," n.d. but before November 1963, box 1, folder 1, RLT Papers.

24. Department of Justice to Tijerina, April 5, 1963, box 41, folder 40, RLT Papers.

25. Tijerina to Steward [*sic*] Udall, February 15, 1964, box 48, folder 29, RLT Papers.

26. Robert Mangan, Department of the Interior, to Tijerina, March 2, 1964, box 48, folder 29, RLT Papers.

27. Handwritten letter to "Cris, Anaya, y Eddie," April 16, 1964, box 54, folder 27, RLT Papers.

28. Tijerina, *Mi Lucha*, 101; "La Alianza de las Mercedes," February 15, 1963, box 2, folder 6, RLT Papers.

29. Reies López Tijerina to Chris Tijerina, n.d., box 54, folder 27, RLT Papers.

30. "Jamás en la historia de Nuevo Mexico," box 1, folder 36, RLT Papers.

31. Rowan, "Minority Nobody Knows."

32. The 1960 U.S. Census estimated that the "Spanish-surnamed population" of New Mexico numbered 269,122. See "Nativity, Parentage, and Country of Origin of White Persons of Spanish Surname by Sex, for Five Southwestern States," table 1, p. 2.

33. Sandoval, *One of Our Fifty Is Missing*.

34. Five million mentioned in "Con todo respeto nos dirijimos a los dos gobiernos," June 13, 1963, box 1, folder 1, RLT Papers; "La Alianza Federal de Las Mercedes publica," March 19, 1963, stated "Diez Millones de Latinos," box 1, folder 1, RLT Papers.

35. Dugger, "Segregation Filibuster of 1957."

36. See "González, Henry B.," an official biography offered by the History, Art and Archives website of the U.S. House of Representatives.

37. "Jamás en la historia de Nuevo Mexico," radio script, box 1, folder 36, RLT Papers.

38. Letters can be found in box 49, folder 29, RLT Papers.

39. The Charter of the United Nations; see http://www.un.org/en/charter-united-nations/, accessed July 15, 2015.

40. C. Anderson, *Eyes Off the Prize*.

41. 1963 Constitution, box 1, folder 2, RLT Papers.

42. Hand-drawn bond, box 1, folder 8, RLT Papers.

43. Reies López Tijerina to Johnson, November 4, 1964, and January 12, 1965, both in box 47, folder 19, RLT Papers.

44. Chris Tijerina to Johnson, September 10, 1965, box 47, folder 19, RLT Papers.

45. Chief, Lands Adjudication Section, to Tijerina, December 1, 1964, box 48, folder 29, RLT Papers.

46. Turner, *Frontier in American History*. See also Lamar, *Far Southwest*. Against this trend, Edward Spicer, an anthropologist, published his award-winning *Cycles of Conquest* in 1962, but the book examined the repercussions of Spanish, Mexican, and Anglo rule for Native Americans only.

47. Immerman, *Empire for Liberty*, 5.

48. Bemis, *Diplomatic History of the United States*, 216.

49. Montoya to Arthur Candelaria, August 16, 1965, box 47, folder 27, RLT Papers.

50. "Entre las promesas," n.d. but probably 1963, box 46, folder 4, RLT Papers.

51. Gutiérrez, "Chicanos and Mexicanos under Surveillance."

52. Correia, "'Rousers of the Rabble,'" 570–71.

53. Tijerina, *Mi Lucha*, 104.

54. Correia, "'Rousers of the Rabble,'" 570–71.

55. Correia, 570–71.

56. See two sets of notes, both dated "10/8/63"; one appears in box 1, folder 17, the other, with additional notes, in box 1, folder 18, Sánchez Papers.

57. Sánchez oral history interview. In addition, when he was interviewed for the 1996 documentary *Chicano!: A History of the Mexican American Civil Rights Movement* (NLCC Educational Media, PBS), Sánchez made almost exactly the same comments about being the one to stop Tijerina.

58. Sánchez oral history interview.

59. Sánchez to José C. Martínez, September 20, 1958, box 1, folder 15, Sánchez Papers.

60. Gilbert Espinosa, "New Mexico Land Grants," 9–10.

61. Kenneth A. Heron to FBI, August 18, 1964, box 1, folder 17, Sánchez Papers.

62. Correia, *Properties of Violence*, 126. Additional complaints of a Chama land and cattle company show up in box 1, folder 17, Sánchez Papers.

63. Correia, *Properties of Violence*, 86–87; Sánchez notes, box 1, folder 17, Sánchez Papers.

64. Goldstein, *Poverty in Common*, 101–2.

65. "Partial Report on Tierra Amarilla Dispute," n.d., box 1, folder 17, Sánchez Papers.

66. Sánchez's recollection of the event, the notes he took at the time, and the conference agenda and poster all are in box 1, folder 18, Sánchez Papers.

67. Eviction notice, box 46, folder 22, RLT Papers. Another version of this eviction notice that refers to the Protocol of Querétaro can be found in box 2, folder 5, Nabokov Papers.

68. Pearl Holmquist, "D.A. to Seek Injunction in TA Land Grant Dispute," *Rio Grande Sun*, October 1, 1964, news clipping in box 1, folder 5, Sánchez Papers.

69. Pearl Holmquist, "Grant Appeals to U.S. Authorities," *Rio Grande Sun*, October 22, 1964, news clipping in box 60, folder 2, RLT Papers.

70. "Petition," box 1, folder 17, Sánchez Papers.

71. Doyle Akers, "Judge Strips Abiquiu Power," *SFNM*, October 18, 1964, news clipping in box 1, folder 5, Sánchez Papers.

72. Akers, "Judge Strips Abiquiu Power."

73. In Spanish:

> Y las leyes están muy malas
> Nos tienen crucificados . . .
> A ustedes les pertenece
> Les viene por herencia.

Federico A. Reade collected and transcribed this corrido in his doctoral dissertation, "La Voz del Pueblo," 307. The corrido's author is Miguel Aguilar.

74. See a short biography of Frances Swadesh Quintana compiled by the New Mexico Office of the State Historian. More details about her education and research can be found in the finding aid that accompanies the Frances León Quintana Papers, Center for Southwest Research. Quintana's résumé and a short personal essay, "Past Is Present: How I Got from There to Here," are in box 1, folder 2, Quintana Papers.

75. Swadesh to Knowlton, September 28, 1964, box 5, folder 15, Quintana Papers.

76. Swadesh to Knowlton, "10/24," probably October 1964, box 5, folder 15, Quintana Papers.

77. Swadesh to Knowlton, "10/24."

78. "Fist Fight Interrupts Tome Land Grant Co. Meet," and "Disorder, Colorful Language Highlight Tome Grant Meeting," news clippings, box 60, folder 4, RLT Papers.

79. Swadesh to Knowlton, "10/24," Quintana Papers.

80. Swadesh to Knowlton, "11/8/64," box 5, folder 15, Quintana Papers.

81. "Mormon" here refers to a broader cultural experience and not specifically to the Church of Jesus Christ of Latter-day Saints, which in 2018 asked that "Mormon Church" or "the Mormons" not be used as a substitute for its official name. Thanks to Charlotte Terry for helping me navigate the subsequent scholarly debate over terminology.

82. Details of Knowlton's life including his missionary and graduate student experience are recounted in his online autobiography.

83. Clark S. Knowlton, "Spanish and Mexican Land Grants: A Key to the Past," a 1989 conference paper, in Knowlton Vertical File.

84. Clark S. Knowlton, "Spanish American Protest Movements in Northern New Mexico," n.d., Knowlton Vertical File.

85. I chose the description "prickly" after reading his letters to colleagues, editors, and students.

86. Knowlton to *Harper's Magazine*, May 27, 1963, box 7, folder 1, Clark S. Knowlton Collection, New Mexico State Records Center and Archives, Santa Fe.

87. As quoted in Goldstein, *Poverty in Common*, 91–92.

88. Knowlton to Tackett, October 21, 1964, box 5, folder 10, Knowlton Collection.

89. Knowlton recounted that meeting in chapter 13 of his online autobiography.

90. Knowlton, "Spanish and Mexican Land Grants."

91. Swadesh to Knowlton, August 1, 1965, box 6, folder 8, Knowlton Collection.

92. Knowlton to Tijerina, January 26, 1966, box 7, folder 1, Knowlton Collection.

93. "New Mexico Group Plans to Reopen Litigation on Land Grants," *Denver Post*, November 1, 1965, clipping in box 2, folder 20, Nabokov Papers.

CHAPTER 7

1. "News Bulletin-Release," n.d., box 2, folder 1, RLT Papers.

2. *ABC* interview, May 1, 1966, box 42, folder 3, RLT Papers.

3. Bebout, *Hero Making*, 113.

4. Bowden, "Socorro Grant."

5. "Secession of Socorro." Also see Harden, "Free State of Socorro."

6. Tijerina, *Mi Lucha*, 99.

7. For a negative view of Tom-Pee-Saw, aka Frank W. Kirk, see Metcalf, *Termination's Legacy*, 126–29.

8. Crum, "Almost Invisible."

9. Socorro's declaration attracted attention as far away as Australia; see "This American Would be King," *Sydney Herald*, August 10, 1953, for "Red Indian."

10. Tom-Pee-Saw to Stanton, April 30, 1953, box 47, folder 4, RLT Papers.

11. Tijerina to Tom-Pee-Saw March 24, 1964, box 47, folder 4, RLT Papers.

12. Frank Tom-Pee-Saw to Tijerina, April 9, 1964, box 47, folder 4, RLT Papers.

13. Tijerina to Gerald Barnes c/o the Atascadero State Hospital, May 27, 1964, box 33, folder 16, RLT Papers.

14. The arrest record of Barnes/Noll can be found in box 7, folder "Gerald Barnes a.k.a. King of the Indies," Blea Papers.

15. Noll's story earned him entry into the web-based Museum of Hoaxes. The website included facsimiles of newspaper clippings from 1954 and 1944 that detail his claims and early troubles with the law.

16. Noll to Stanton, dated 1957, box 33, folder 16, RLT Papers.

17. Noll to Stanton, November 21, 1960, box 33, folder 16, RLT Papers.

18. "Alleged Heir of Spanish King May Try to Prove He Owns 'Socorro Free State,'" *El Defensor Chieftain* (Socorro, N.Mex.), December 22, 1960; John McMillion, "New Mexico Still Hearing Fairy Tales," *AJ*, February 26, 1968.

19. Tijerina to Gerald Barnes, May 27, 1964, box 33, folder 16, RLT Papers.

20. See documents in box 33, folder 16, RLT Papers.

21. Gardner, *¡Grito!*, 126.

22. He is the unnamed "town's judge," for example, in Oropeza, "Heart of Chicano History."

23. Kosek, *Understories*, 60, 179.

24. Bebout, *Mythohistorical Interventions*, 113.

25. Busto, *King Tiger*, 239n42, contains an English translation of the law.

26. "Demands of the Indo-Hispano People," 1966, box 1, folder 1, RLT Papers.

27. "Pueblos Quemados por Yanquis," n.d. but probably 1962 as the text mentioned 114 years of suffering, box 1, folder 1, RLT Papers.

28. To my knowledge, the word showed up just once more in the English-language 1966 pamphlet *The Spanish Land Grant Question Examined*, which, based upon its pristine grammar, I doubt was written by Reies López Tijerina.

29. "La Voz de la Justicia," radio script, April 23, 1965, KAQB, box 1, folder 36, RLT Papers.

30. "El radio y los periódicos día a día nos están diciendo" and "Open letter statement," dated 1963 at top (but more likely 1965, 117 years from 1848), both box 1, folder 1, RLT Papers.

31. Gottheimer, *Ripples of Hope*, 314.

32. "Obligación de cada raza o pueblo," January 26, 1968, box 54, folder 8, RLT Papers.

33. Olivares, *International Studies in Honor of Tomás Rivera*, 149.

34. Tijerina, *Mi Lucha*, 276. Both Bancroft and Twitchell in their histories of New Mexico mention enslavement briefly and generally in the context of "just war doctrine," meaning that the Spanish empire justified enslavement as punishment for rebellion. See Bancroft, *History*, 142, 194; Twitchell, *Leading Facts*, 112, 326, 347, 355, 393.

35. "Open letter statement," RLT Papers.

36. El Pueblo Olvidado," September 11, 1964, box 52, folder 4, RLT Papers.

37. Menchaca, *Recovering History*, 89.

38. See Gómez, *Manifest Destinies*, 55, on this point.

39. Saldaña-Portillo, "'How Many Mexicans Is a Horse Worth?'"

40. In an August 20, 2017, email to the author, Maria Varela observed that not everyone was rushing to whiteness. At least some northern New Mexicans proudly boasted a bicultural heritage, both Pueblo Indian and Hispano, and sometimes trilingual abilities, English, Spanish, and, around Taos, for example, Tiwa.

41. As quoted in Swadesh, "Alianza Movement of New Mexico," 55.

42. Nieto-Phillips, *Language of Blood*, especially chapter 2, "Citizenship in the American Empire."

43. Montgomery, "Trap of Race and Memory."

44. "Portrayal of Courthouse Raid Still Stirs Anger," newspaper clipping in RLT Vertical File.

45. Bodine, "Tri-Ethnic Trap," 150.

46. P. Gonzales, *Forced Sacrifice as Ethnic Protest*.

47. Jose del Valle, "Poco a Poco" column, box 60, folder 9, RLT Papers.

48. 51. Tijerina, *Mi Lucha*, 70, 77.

49. Tijerina to Dennis Lovato, Santa Clara Pueblo, August 17, 1963, box 41, folder 40, RLT Papers. However, by 1972 Tijerina had made friends with Ernest L. Lovato, relation, if any, unknown, of the Santo Domingo Pueblo. See Ernest Lovato to Tijerina, handwritten thank-you note, August 17, 1962, box 47, folder 5, RLT Papers.

50. Tijerina to Burnette, March 25, 1964, box 47, folder 4, RLT Papers.

51. Members of Hopi House aligned themselves with people who called themselves "traditionalists" and opposed the Bureau of Indian Affairs–approved tribal council. See Geertz, *Invention of Prophecy*, 300.

52. "El Pueblo Olvidado," RLT Papers.

53. That assumption propelled Tijerina's 1964 request to President Johnson that Alianza members be extended the same courtesy regarding recognition of land claims that Native Americans enjoyed. Tijerina to Sr. Lindon B. Johnson, November 11, 1964, box 47, folder 19, RLT Papers.

54. Lucero, "*State v. Romero*," 677.

55. Swadesh to Knowlton, "10/24," Quintana Papers.

56. Knowlton, "Land-Grant Problems Among the State's Spanish-Americans," *New Mexico Business* 20 (June 1967): 3.

57. "La Alianza Federal de Mercedes Informa," September 17, 1963, box 1, folder 1, RLT Papers.

58. "Minorities Crusade against Gringos," *Newsweek*, January 3, 1966, 17.

59. "'Black Cult' Supremacy in the U.S.—How Much a Threat?," *U.S. News and World Report*, November 9, 1959, 112–14.

60. Joseph, *Waiting 'til the Midnight Hour*, 23.

61. Tijerina, *Mi Lucha*, 79. His brother Cristóbal indirectly confirmed the visit in a letter to Reies dated July 30, 1961. "I wish you very good luck in your dealings with the leader of the *negritos*," box 54, folder 27, RLT Papers.

62. "Century of Negro Progress," 58–59; Davis's obituary mentioning his career as an ad-man appeared in the *St. Louis Post-Dispatch*, November 29, 1999.

63. November 1, 1967, investigative report, box 1, folder "Investigative Reports," Blea Papers.

64. Foley, "Becoming Mexican American"; Guglielmo, "Fighting for Caucasian Rights."

65. For competition and prejudice, see Behnken, *Struggle in Black and Brown*. Mariscal mentioned ignorance in *Brown-Eyed Children*, 171–72.

66. González, *Spanish-Americans of New Mexico*, 103.

67. See especially *partida* 2, title 9, law 5, in Burns, *Las Siete Partidas*.

68. Receipt, May 11, 1966, box 41, folder 45, RLT Papers. The total was $14,750 pesetas with an exchange rate of 60 pesetas to the dollar at the time.

69. Frances L. Swadesh, "The Alianza Movement: Catalyst for Social Change in New Mexico," box 1, folder 12, p. 168, Quintana Papers.

70. *ABC* interview, RLT Papers.

71. "March Starts to NM Capital," *AT*, July 2, 1966, and "Land March Near Its End," *Hobbs (N.Mex.) Daily News-Sun*, July 4, 1966, news clippings in box 60, folder 5, RLT Papers.

72. Araiza, *To March for Others*, 34–38.

73. Mark Acuff, "12 Marchers Await Return of Governor," *SFNM*, July 6, 1966.

74. Acuff, "12 Marchers Await Return of Governor."

75. Edward M. McManus, "Spanish Americans Brave Heat," *AT*, July 4, 1966.

76. McManus, "Spanish Americans Brave Heat."

77. Marginalia signed JMC (Jack M. Campbell) on memo to governor from Thomas G. Trotter, October 5, 1964, box 80, folder 1, Jenkins Collected Papers.

78. Memo, no author's name, box 7, folder "Mug Shots," Blea Papers.

79. These statements appear within a stack of documents regarding Tijerina in box 7, untitled folder, Blea Papers.

80. "Campbell Hears Marchers," *AJ*, July 12, 1966; Mark Acuff, "Governor to Send Petition," *SFNM*, July 11, 1966. More news clippings about the march and meeting can be found in box 60, folder 5, RLT Papers.

81. Acuff, "Governor to Send Petition," *SFNM*, July 11, 1966.

82. "Civil Rights March, New Mexican Style," *Denver Post* news clipping dated July 7, 1966, box 60, folder 5, RLT Papers.

83. Biddle Duke, "Respected, Beloved Historian Myra Jenkins Dies," *SFNM*, June 24, 1993.

84. Jenkins memo to Campbell, July 11, 1966, box 7, untitled folder, Blea Papers.

85. Jenkins letter to David M. Brugge, July 18, 1966, box 80, folder 3, Jenkins Collected Papers.

86. Jenkins statement, box 80, folder 7, Jenkins Collected Papers.

87. Jenkins letter to Catron, December 22, 1966, box 80, folder 1, Jenkins Collected Papers.

88. Jenkins memo to Campbell, July 11, 1966, box 7, untitled folder, Blea Papers.

89. Jenkins's extensive work with Native American groups was reflected in her publications, including *History of the Laguna Pueblo Land-Claims*, and in her collection of papers donated to the Center for Southwest Studies at Fort Lewis, Colorado, which includes a set of records devoted to "Native American/Land Grants/Water Rights." Although she kept abreast of the Alianza activities, no similar category exists for Hispano land rights.

90. "Tijerina Says He's Not Making a 'Single Penny' from the Group," *SFNM*, July 14,

1966; "Alianza Slander Suit," *AJ*, July 22, 1966, news clipping, box 34, folder "Alianza news clippings," Cargo Papers.

91. All three letters are in box 41, folder 45, RLT Papers.

92. Knowlton, "Reies L. Tijerina," 136.

93. "Formal Editorial," box 41, folder 45, RLT Papers.

94. "Title Guaranteed," n.d., box 7, folder "Miscellaneous," Blea Papers.

95. "Claim Sought for Trenton," *SFNM*, July 10, 1966, news clipping in box 60, folder 5, RLT Papers.

96. "Distant Protest," *AJ*, July 6, 1966, news clipping, box 60, folder 5, RLT Papers.

97. "Tijerina Told of Old Claim," *AJ*, October 25, 1966, news clipping misdated "10-23-1966," box 60, folder 8, RLT Papers.

98. "Poco a Poco en la Tierra del Encanto," July 21, 1966, box 1, folder 2, Nabokov Papers.

99. Maria Varela made this observation in an email to author, August 20, 2017.

100. Deloria, *Playing Indian*.

101. Campbell letter to Lyndon B. Johnson, July 22, 1966, box 80, folder 1, Jenkins Collected Papers.

102. The voice of Jerry Noll can be heard during a recorded interview 1967, box 5, tape 13, Nabokov Papers. Noll's picture appeared in newspaper reports at the time, including the front page of the *AJ*, June 7, 1967. Another photo, taken after his arrest in 1967, contains his height and weight, box 7, folder "Mug Shots," Blea Papers.

103. "Cuarta Convención Nacional," 1966 Alianza conference agenda, box 1, folder 36; and convention speech, 1966, box 33, folder 16, both RLT Papers. Ramón A. Gutiérrez suggested that the notion of a "free city-state" borrowed from the lack of institutional structure and hierarchy that characterized Assemblies of God congregations. Gutiérrez, "Religious Origins," 299.

104. "Spanish-American Leads Fight to Regain Old Lands From U.S.," *Los Angeles Times*, April 24, 1966.

105. Noll to Tijerina, July 27, 1966, box 33, folder 16, RLT Papers.

106. Tijerina to Noll, August 1, 1966, box 33, folder 16, RLT Papers.

107. "*USA vs. Reies Lopez Tijerina, Cristobal Tijerina, Jerry Noll, Ezekial Dominguez and Alfonso Chavez*, Transcript of Testimony and Proceedings," November 8, 1967, p. 958, box 39, folder 6, RLT Papers. Perhaps Tijerina said something closer to "primer entre pares," which is what the court reporter wrote.

108. During a car ride with me from Albuquerque to Alcalde, N.Mex., to attend a fortieth anniversary commemoration, Rose mentioned the possibility of her marrying Noll and the start of a new American dynasty.

109. Reies López Tijerina phone conversation.

110. See, for example, John McMillion, "New Mexico Still Hearing Fairy Tales," *AJ*, February 26, 1968.

111. *The Spanish Land Grant Question Examined*, box 2, folder 1, RLT Papers.

112. Juan Valdez oral history interview.

113. See, for example, "Text of Speech, July 29, 1967," box 36, folder 16, RLT Papers.

114. The territorial law earned mention in a 1966 news clipping, "Land Grant Leader Wants All of City, to Start at Old Town," box 60, folder 9, RLT Papers. Passed by the territorial legislature shortly before the establishment of the Court of Private Land Claims,

it allowed community land grants to transform into corporations, Laws of New Mexico, 1891, chapter 86.

115. *Congressional Record*, May 12, 1944, 4462–63.

116. Photo is available on the website "Celebrating New Mexican Statehood."

117. "Finders/Keepers," *Newsweek*, November 11, 1966, 13.

118. "U.S. Forest Service Refuses to Recognize," *Rio Grande Sun*, October 20, 1966, news clipping, box 1, folder 6, Sánchez Papers.

119. "To Fight NM Claim for Land," *El Paso Times*, October 20, 1966, news clipping, box 60, folder 8, RLT Papers.

120. Testimony of Chris Zamora, box 39, folder 5, RLT Papers.

121. "Land Grant Seizure Strategy Meet. Held," October 18, 1966, news clipping, and *El Paso Times*, October 20, 1966, news clipping, both box 60, folder 8, RLT Papers.

122. Testimony of Phil Smith, box 39, folder 6, RLT Papers.

123. Testimony of Walter Taylor, box 39, folder 5, RLT Papers.

124. Testimony of Chris Zamora, box 39, folder 5, RLT Papers.

125. "U.S. Marshals Set to Oust Campers," *Amarillo Daily News*, October 27, 1966, news clipping, box 60, folder 8, RLT Papers.

126. Testimony of Martin Vigil, box 39, folder 6, RLT Papers.

127. Bob Beier, "Rangers Tells of Capture by Tijerina Followers," *AJ*, November 8, 1967; Gardner, *¡Grito!*, 131.

128. Scarborough, *Trespassers on Our Own Land*, 112.

129. "Land Grants 'Sitters' Score Major Victory," *SFNM*, October 23, 1966, news clipping, box 60, folder 8, RLT Papers.

130. Testimony of Walter Taylor, box 39, folder 5, RLT Papers.

131. Testimony of James H. Evans, box 39, folder 2, RLT Papers.

132. "Long Walks Are Healthy," *Rio Grande Sun*, October 20, 1966, news clipping, box 60, folder 8, RLT Papers.

133. *Taos News*, October 20, 1966, news clipping, box 60, folder 8, RLT Papers.

134. Typed paper about San Joaquín del Río de Chama land grant, box 79, folder 20, Jenkins Collected Papers.

135. Reade, "La Voz del Pueblo," 103.

136. Reade, 85.

137. Scarborough, *Trespassers on Our Own Land*, 111.

138. "Land Grant Leader Wants All of City, to Start at Old Town"; "Land Grant Alliance Quits Forest Claim," *Raton (N.Mex.) Daily Range*, news clipping, box 60, folder 8, both RLT Papers.

139. Bob Beier, "U.S. Takes Steps to Bar Alliance in Land Claim," *AJ*, October 26, 1966.

140. Martha Buddecke, "Alliance Members Abandon 'Republic,'" *AJ*, October 27, 1966, news clipping, box 60, folder 8, RLT Papers.

141. White Bear to Tijerina, December 12, 1966, box 34, folder 17, RLT Papers.

142. Tijerina letter to White Bear, box 34, folder 17, RLT Papers.

143. Robert McG. Thomas Jr., "Thomas Banyacya, 89, Teller of Hopi Prophecy to the World," *New York Times* obituary, February 15, 1999.

144. "Hopi Independent Nation" inscribed on letterhead, box 34, folder 17, RLT Papers.

145. "Order," October 26, 1966, box 47, folder 25, RLT Papers.

146. "FBI Agents Arrest Five Members of Land Alliance," UPI news clipping, October 27, 1966, box 60, folder 8, RLT Papers.

147. Beier, "U.S. Takes Steps to Bar Alliance in Land Claim."

148. Jim Neal, "Village Gossip," *SFNM*, October 23, 1966, news clipping, box 60, folder 8, RLT Papers.

149. "Alliance Vows Court Fight," *AT*, October 27, 1966, news clipping, box 60, folder 8, RLT Papers.

150. "FBI Agents Arrest Five Members of Land Alliance," RLT Papers.

151. "Old Town in Albuquerque Is Now Target of Alliance," *Carlsbad Current-Argus*, December 22, 1966, news clipping, box 60, folder 9, RLT Papers.

CHAPTER 8

1. Trouillot, *Silencing the Past*, especially chapter 3, "An Unthinkable History."

2. "Raid 'Terrific Success,' Declares Tijerina," *AJ*, June 11, 1967.

3. Scarborough, *Trespassers on Our Own Land*, 128.

4. "Sanchez Releases Confederation's Plans for a 'New Cuba in the North,'" *SFNM*, June 25, 1967.

5. Juan Valdez oral history interview.

6. "Manifesto," *AJ*, February 20, 1967.

7. Troy Kemper, "Sanity of Alliance Defendant is Questioned," *AJ*, March 31, 1967.

8. Letters from Victorino Chavez to the president, January 4 and 6, 1967, box 58, folder "Federal Issues/Alianza," Cargo Papers; Victorino Chavez, governor of San Joaquín, to the secretary of state, November 8, 1966, box 48, folder 30, RLT Papers; and Victorino Chavez to the president, January 3, 5, and 6, 1967, box 47, folder 19, RLT Papers. Another letter to the secretary of state in Noll's florid style appears in box 1, folder 6, Sánchez Papers. A letter with the official seal of the pueblo appears in box 41, folder 46, RLT Papers.

9. Tijerina to secretary of state, December 19, 1966, box 48, folder 30, RLT Papers.

10. Andrew H. Brenman to Ramona Brusseau, Governor's Office, May 23, 1967, RLT Papers.

11. Edwin L. Weisl Jr. to Tijerina, March 12, 1967, box 48, folder 26; and A. W. Greeley to Tijerina, April 19, 1967, box 48, folder 28, both in RLT Papers.

12. Letter from Tijerina to "Your Excellency," referring to previous March 2, 1967, letter, box 47, folder 19, RLT Papers.

13. "'Last Human Warning' Given by Heirs," *AT*, dated mid-April 1967, and "200 Alianza Members Parade at Statehouse," *SFNM*, April 18, 1967, news clippings in box 1, folder 4, Nabokov Papers.

14. Cargo, *Lonesome Dave*, 109, 119–20, 197.

15. "Cargo Can Understand the Purpose of the Alianza but Not Its Violence," *AJ*, June 4, 1967.

16. U.S. Congress, House, "Effect of Federal programs on rural America," 192.

17. Socio-economics Studies Foundation, "Northern New Mexico: A Special Survey for the Office of the Governor," June 23, 1967, box 58, folder "Alianza Socio-Economic Studies," Cargo Papers.

18. Gardner, *¡Grito!*, 140.

19. Gardner, 146.

20. "'Last Human Warning' Given by Heirs," Nabokov Papers.

21. "Cargo Assures Action on Land Grant Claims," news clipping marked "Item #6," box 1, folder 4, Nabokov Papers.

22. Nabokov, *Tijerina and the Courthouse Raid*, 21.

23. Typed yellow sheet that begins, "Back in March 22," box 1, folder 7, Nabokov Papers.

24. Jake Booher Jr., "Alliance Takes Battle for Land to Federals," news clipping marked *New Mexican*, December 14, 1966, box 2, folder 21, Nabokov Papers.

25. Vina Windes, "Governor Offers His Office as Avenue for Alianza," *SFNM*, April 23, 1967.

26. "Alianza will 'Enforce Certain Rights,'" *SFNM*, May 15, 1967, news clipping, box 1, folder 6, Nabokov Papers.

27. "U.S. Court Orders Alianza Members to Show Cause," *AJ*, April 26, 1967.

28. "Haystack Fires Hit Land Grant Area," *AJ*, May 20, 1967; "Cargo to Confer with Rio Arriba Police Officials," *AJ*, May 23, 1967.

29. New Mexico State Police report, May 17, 1967, for damage to Spill's car. That report and others detailing suspicious fires and fence-cutting are in box 34, folder 709, "State Police in Rio Arriba County," Cargo Papers.

30. "Call for Governor to Act on Suspected RA Arson," *SFNM*, May 19, 1967.

31. "Identified from G. Noll" to "Reies," May 9, 1967, box 33, folder 16, RLT Papers. With astounding foresight, Noll furthermore predicted the eventual fate of the organization. Given Tijerina's "inability to delegate authority," he asked, "Who is to carry on the Alianza while you are in prison?"

32. Troy Kemper, "Sanity of Alliance Defendant Is Questioned," *AJ*, March 31, 1967.

33. "Tijerina Quits as President of the Alianza," *SFNM*, May 25, 1967.

34. "Tijerina Quits as President of the Alianza."

35. "Tijerina Ordered to Court on Contempt Question," *SFNM*, May 31, 1967.

36. "Former Alliance Group Will Be Ready to Fight," *SFNM*, May 28, 1967.

37. "Land Grant Chief, Whole Staff Resign from Office," *AJ*, May 26, 1967.

38. "KOB-TV" announcement, dated "5/28/67," box 1, folder 7, Sánchez Papers.

39. "Former Alliance Grant May Try to Take Over Vast Southwest Areas," *AJ*, May 28, 1967.

40. FBI memo dated May 29, 1987, box 1, folder 7, Sánchez Papers.

41. Memoir, box 1, folder 7, Sánchez Papers; see also John McMillion, "No Illusions About Tijerina," *AJ*, June 7, 1967.

42. Copy of sign, box 1, folder 7, Sánchez Papers.

43. "Gas Station Enjoys Heavy Sales," *SFNM*, June 4, 1967; Alianza handbill, box 3, folder 7, RLT Papers.

44. F. Martinez police report, folder 8, and memoir, folder 7, both in box 1, Sánchez Papers.

45. Memoir, box 1, folder 7, Sánchez Papers.

46. "Friday June 2, 1967" notes by John Crenshaw, box 1, folder 6, Nabokov Papers.

47. "Tijerina Says Followers Fight-Ready," *SFNM*, May 29, 1967.

48. Handwritten notes, "5/31/67," box 1, folder 7, Sánchez Papers. Based on the hand-

writing, the author is probably Sánchez; the same note appears as "Item #7" in box 1, folder 6, Nabokov Papers.

49. Quinn to Sánchez, June 1, 1967, folder 8, and memoir, folder 7, both in box 1, Sánchez Papers.

50. Memoir and New Mexico State Police reports, November 7 and 9, 1966, all in box 1, folder 7, Sánchez Papers; Martha Buddecke, "Awaited 'Showdown' in Land Fight Fails," *AJ*, June 4, 1967.

51. Memoir, box 1, folder 7, Sánchez Papers.

52. Memoir, Sánchez Papers.

53. Handwritten notes, "5/15/67," box 1, folder 7, Sánchez Papers.

54. "Notice to all followers of Reyes López Tijerina," box 1, folder 8, Sánchez Papers.

55. John Crenshaw, "Federation of City States Meeting in Coyote Was a Big Bust," *SFNM*, June 4, 1967; Howard Graves, "Police Grab Guns in Land Issue," *AJ*, June 3, 1967.

56. "Sanchez Releases Confederation's Plan," *SFNM*, June 25, 1967; for actual maps with writing on them, see box 1, folder marked "oversized," Sánchez Papers.

57. McMillion, "No Illusions about Tijerina."

58. Reies López Tijerina phone conversation.

59. "Two Chama Men Question Arrest Procedures," news clipping marked "Item #5," n.d., Box 1, Folder 7, Nabokov Papers.

60. "Land Grant Feud Brings Arrests," *Gallup (N.Mex.) Independent*, June 3, 1967; injunction, box 46, folder 22, RLT Papers. Other accounts list Valdez as sixty-eight. Cruz was also Gregorita's husband.

61. Crenshaw, "Federation of City States Meeting in Coyote Was a Big Bust."

62. Buddecke, "Awaited 'Showdown' in Land Fight Fails."

63. Bud Jorgensen, "Governor's Role as a Mediator On Again, Off Again Affair," *AJ*, June 4, 1967.

64. "Arraignments in Tierra Amarilla Hoy," *SFNM*, June 5, 1967; Crenshaw, "Federation of City States Meeting in Coyote Was a Big Bust."

65. Howard Graves and Jake Booher, "Cargo Intervenes in Land Claims Showdown Crisis," *Hobbs Daily News-Sun*, June 4, 1967.

66. Crenshaw, "Federation of City States Meeting in Coyote Was a Big Bust."

67. Buddecke, "Awaited 'Showdown' in Land Fight Fails."

68. Trujillo conversation with author. At the National Association of Chicana/Chicano Studies in Denver, after a panel at which both Trujillo and I presented, he shared some of the stories his grandfather Ventura Chavez told about his participation in the courthouse raid and his Alianza activism in general.

69. Gardner, *¡Grito!*, 148.

70. "A Job Well Done at Coyote," *AJ*, June 4, 1967.

71. Buddecke, "Awaited 'Showdown' in Land Fight Fails."

72. Gardner, *¡Grito!*, 54.

73. Buddecke, "Awaited 'Showdown' in Land Fight Fails."

74. Buddecke, "Awaited 'Showdown' in Land Fight Fails."

75. Peter Nabokov, "The *New Mexican*'s Reporter Interviews Tijerina," *SFNM*, June 8, 1967.

76. Rose Tijerina oral history interview.

77. Rose Tijerina oral history interview.

78. Rose Tijerina oral history interview. In his account of that day, Juan Valdez, for example, contested almost every point of Rose's recollection. See Scarborough, *Trespassers on Our Own Land*, 128–36.

79. Escobar oral history interview.

80. Wayne S. Scott, "Guns Bristle at S.F. Court Hearing," *AJ*, June 8, 1967.

81. Mary Leyba oral history interview.

82. Escobar conversation with author, February 6, 2013.

83. Through the use of oral history, Reade's "La Voz del Pueblo" compiled by far the most detail about these men's lives and their family connections.

84. Leyba, "My Cow, She Was Almost Arrested," *El Grito del Norte*, April 29, 1970.

85. Juan Valdez oral history interview.

86. Mary Leyba oral history interview.

87. "Kidnapped Deputy Recalls Ordeal," *¡Salsa!*, the monthly supplement to the *Rio Grande Sun*, May 28, 1987, RLT Vertical File.

88. Reade, "La Voz del Pueblo," 176.

89. Gardner, *¡Grito!*, 158–60.

90. "Kidnapped Deputy Recalls Ordeal," RLT Vertical File.

91. Nabokov, *Tijerina and the Courthouse Raid*, 102.

92. Rose Tijerina oral history interview.

93. Martin Waldron, "New Mexico Band Eludes Pursuers," *New York Times*, June 7, 1967.

94. Waldron, "New Mexico Band Eludes Pursuers."

95. Carrol W. Cagle, "Tension in Governor's Office," *SFNM*, June 6, 1967.

96. Dick McAlpin, "Gunmen Raid Courthouse," *AJ*, June 6, 1967.

97. Cargo, *Lonesome Dave*, 199.

98. Howard Bryan, "Tanks, Guns, Trucks Pass Through Canjilón," and Pete Pence, "Guardsmen Take Over in Rio Arriba," *AT*, June 6, 1967; Doyle Akers, "Daylight Raiders Leave Bloody Path," *SFNM*, June 6, 1967; Dick McAlpin, "Gunmen Raid Courthouse," *AJ*, June 6, 1967. Also see "Civil Disturbance Rio Arriba County 5–8 June 1967," box 1, folder 18, Nabokov Papers.

99. Carrol W. Cagle, "Cargo Appeals to Fugitives," *SFNM*, June 7, 1967. In her oral history interview, Mary Leyba mentioned Noll grabbing some of her tortillas.

100. Scarborough, *Trespassers on Our Own Land*, 135–14; Reade, "La Voz del Pueblo," 217–18.

101. "The Word Is Revolution," *AT*, June 6, 1967.

102. "Bitter Fruits of Neglect," *SFNM*, June 6, 1967.

103. "Sanchez Claims Tijerina Dupes Latin Citizens in Alliance Movement," *AJ*, June 11, 1967.

104. John Crenshaw, "Judge OKs Attorney for Alianza People," *SFNM*, June 10, 1967.

105. Front page photo, *AJ*, June 11, 1967.

106. Dick McAlpin, "Armed Raiders Elude Searchers," *AJ*, June 7, 1967.

107. Carrol W. Cagle, "Cargo Appeals to Fugitives to Surrender to Authorities," *SFNM*, June 7, 1967.

108. John Crenshaw, "National Guard Withdrawn," *SFNM*, June 7, 1967.

109. "Gov. Cargo Fears Northern Trip Might Lead to More Bloodshed."

110. "News Release by Reies López Tijerina," box 58, folder "Alianza, Published Material," Cargo Papers; "Tijerina's Letter May Bring FBI to Search," *SFNM*, June 9, 1967.

111. "Letter Laid to Tijerina Makes Threats," *AT*, June 8, 1967.

112. "Governor, D.A. Locked in a Bitter Feud," *SFNM*, June 6, 1967; "State Police, Guardsmen Comb Forests for Gunmen," *Las Vegas Optic*, June 7, 1967.

113. "Governor Blamed by Sen. Delgado," *AJ*, June 6, 1967.

114. Jack D. Daum, "¿Revolución Aquí?," *Santa Fe News*, June 8, 1967, news clipping in box 55, folder 16, Knowlton Collection.

115. Joy Cook, "Rebels Seethe in North New Mexico," unidentified news clipping dated September 10, 1967, box 80, folder 4, Jenkins Collected Papers.

116. Gardner, *¡Grito!*, 200.

117. "Poverty War 'Experts' Ask for Amnesty," *AT*, June 7, 1967.

118. Peter Nabokov, "Long Ride Brings Reporter Interview with Tijerina," *SFNM*, June 8, 1967.

119. Larry Calloway, "Tijerina Caught in Son's Car," *AJ*, June 11, 1967.

120. "Raid 'Terrific Success,' Declares Tijerina," *AJ*, June 11, 1967.

121. Entire corrido in Reade, "La Voz del Pueblo," 316–18.

122. Scarborough, *Trespassers on Our Own Land*, 130.

123. Scarborough, 135.

124. Scarborough, 131.

125. David Steinberg, Tomas O. Martinez, and Thomas Day, "Memories of 'TA Raid' Vivid," *AJ*, June 5, 1977.

126. Calloway, "June 5, 1967."

127. John Crenshaw, "Angel Bars Threats," *SFNM*, February 2, 1968.

128. Steinberg, Martinez, and Day, "Memories of 'TA Raid' Vivid." When he was required to testify against Baltazar Martínez, the other hostage-taker, a sympathetic Calloway lived up to that reputation by deliberately trying to make the jury laugh and thus reduce the likelihood of conviction. He shared that story during a fiftieth anniversary commemoration of the courthouse raid on June 4, 2017, at the Center for Contemporary Arts in Santa Fe, New Mexico.

129. Nick Saiz testimony, June 11, 1968, box 2, folder "Investigative Reports," Blea Papers. According to Saiz and Rose Tijerina, the person making the threat was her younger brother Danny, although Rose remembered it as Fabian Duran intervening, not Juan Valdez. Rose Tijerina oral history interview. As for the nature of the intervention, Valdez either got between Saiz and the angry raider with a gun, essentially defending Saiz with his own life, or said something along the lines of, "Leave him alone, he is going to die anyway." The differing recollections of Valdez and Saiz also appeared in "Wounded Officer Went for Gun" and "'I'd Do It Again,' Says Raider," both in *¡Salsa!*, the monthly supplement to the *Rio Grande Sun*, May 28, 1987.

130. "Raid Surprised County Workers," *¡Salsa!*, monthly supplement to the *Rio Grande Sun*, May 28, 1987.

131. Susan Landon, "Rio Arriba Courthouse Raid Vivid Memory 20 Years Later," *AJ*, June 5, 1987.

132. Juan Valdez oral history interview.

133. Gardner, *¡Grito!*, 169.

134. Alex Leyba oral history interview.

135. Crenshaw, "National Guard Withdrawn."

136. June 15, 1967, "investigatory report" and "record of arrest," box 2, folder "Wilfred Garcia," Blea Papers; "Arraignment Date Now Not Certain," *SFNM*, June 14, 1967; "FBI Checking Claims of Rights Violations," *AJ*, June 16, 1967.

137. "Governor Gives Award to Baltazar Martinez's Mother," *SFNM*, July 9, 1967.

138. Tomas O. Martinez, "Veteran of Tierra Amarilla Raid Tries to Leave It All Behind," *AJ*, December 19, 1982.

139. "Tijerina Challenges 120 Years of Injustice," trifold flyer, box 2, folder 1, RLT Papers. The document added the children of Alianza members on trial for the Echo Amphitheater occupation to the final tally.

140. See 1970 correspondence from José A. Madril to El Presidente, box 42, folder 9, RLT Papers.

141. "Judge Rules Apodaca, 73, Incompetent for Trial," *AJ*, November 7, 1968.

142. "Found Innocent," *Las Cruces (N.Mex.) Sun-News*, August 18, 1969; "Albuquerque Jury Finds Valdez Guilty," *SFNM*, July 1, 1969.

143. "Rio Arriba Raid Figure Pardoned," *AJ*, March 28, 1973.

144. "AG Asks New Raid Case Funds," *AJ*, January 24, 1970.

145. Rosina Valdez oral history interview.

146. Scarborough, *Trespassers on Our Own Land*, 87.

CHAPTER 9

1. "'Poor People's March Starts at Slaying Site,'" *Tucson Citizen*, May 2, 1968; "Mrs. King Launches Poor People March," *AJ*, May 3, 1868, news clipping in box 61, folder 7, RLT Papers.

2. Nabokov, *Tijerina and the Courthouse Raid*, 222–23.

3. "Tijerina—A Mexican Malcom X," *The Movement*, August 1967, news clipping, RLT Vertical File.

4. Tijerina interview by Della Rossa, box 52, folder 5, RLT Papers.

5. Marx, *Critique*, 137. Thanks to Sudipta Sen for pointing out this helpful quotation.

6. Gardner, *¡Grito!*, 208.

7. Reprint of April 1968 KPFA interview in Rosales, *Testimonio*, 309.

8. Mantler, *Power to the Poor*, 92.

9. Chesly Manly, "'New Politics' Convention to Open Here," *Chicago Tribune*, August 27, 1967.

10. Bazian, "Revisiting MLK's Speech."

11. Gardner, *¡Grito!*, 141.

12. Varela to Tijerina, September 7, 1967, box 42, folder 1, RLT Papers. See also "Maria Varela Meets Reies Tijerina."

13. As quoted in Mantler, *Power to the Poor*, 1.

14. Bell Blawis, *Tijerina and the Land Grants*, 99.

15. Araiza, *To March for Others*, 66.

16. Bell Blawis, *Tijerina and the Land Grants*, 99.

17. Along the way, as a Young Christian Students representative, Varela helped draft the 1962 Port Huron Statement, the political manifesto that established Students for a Democratic Society as one of the leading student organizations of the decade. See Jenschke, "Maria Varela," 787–88; and Pycior, "Important but Neglected."

18. Maria Varela, "Time to Get Ready," in Holsaert, *Hands on the Freedom Plow*, 566, 569.

19. Varela, "Time to Get Ready," 567–68.

20. Araiza, *To March for Others*, 63.

21. Varela to Tijerina, September 7, 1967, box 42, folder 1, RLT Papers.

22. Tijerina to Varela, September 14, 1967, box 42, folder 1, RLT Papers.

23. Joy Cook, "Tijerina Says Alianza Will Unite with Black Muslims and Others," *AJ*, September 11, 1967.

24. Nabokov, *Tijerina and the Courthouse Raid*, 220.

25. Apparently so did Corky Gonzales. See Vigil, *Crusade for Justice*, 57.

26. November 1, 1967, investigative report, box 2, folder "Investigative Reports," Blea Papers.

27. Robert E. Huber, "Tijerina Preaches Racist Gospel, Calls Disciples New Breed," *AJ*, October 1, 1967; "Tijerina Charges U.S. Is Murdering Women, Children," *SFNM*, October 1, 1967.

28. Lehmberg, *Holy Faith of Santa Fe*, 22, 29, 31, 35.

29. For a defense of Tijerina, see "A Power of Healing?," box 1, folder 37, Nabokov Papers.

30. Gardner, *¡Grito!*, 213.

31. Reies López Tijerina phone conversation.

32. "Tijerina Charges U.S. Is Murdering Women, Children."

33. "La Unión de un Pueblo" dated "Marzo 10, 1966," box 53, folder 45, RLT Papers.

34. Bell Blawis, *Tijerina and the Land Grants*, 139.

35. This point is stressed by multiple authors, including Mariscal, *Brown-Eyed Children*; Araiza, *To March for Others*; and Mantler, *Power to the Poor*.

36. Araiza, *To March for Others*, 68.

37. Mantler, *Power to the Poor*, 76.

38. Both state police and the FBI compiled many of these details in reports on the conference. See "Re: Federal Alliance of Free States Convention Summary," box 2, folder "Investigators Reports," Blea Papers; "Alianza Federal de Mercedes" FBI report, box 2, folder 20, RLT Papers. Also see Nabokov, *Tijerina and the Courthouse Raid*, 224; Mariscal, *Brown-Eyed Children*, 192–93, and Gardner, *¡Grito!*, 223–24. Pictures of the "Che" sign and the attendees' dress appear in both Nabokov and Mariscal.

39. For quote, see "Confidential Oct. 21, 1967, 9:30," box 2, folder "Investigators Reports," Blea Papers. Additional details in works mentioned above.

40. "Re: Federal Alliance of Free States Convention Summary" mentioned Gutiérrez's pledge.

41. José Angel Gutiérrez, "La Raza and Revolution."

42. Nabokov, *Tijerina and the Courthouse Raid*, 222.

43. Nabokov, 159.

44. Gardner, *¡Grito!*, 222.

45. For the lack of women's participation, see Mantler, *Power to the Poor*, 78.

46. The pact was reprinted under the headline "Brown and Black Together," *La Raza* magazine, October 29, 1967.

47. "Brown and Black Together."

48. As quoted in Araiza, *To March for Others*, 59.

49. U.S. Inter-agency Committee on Mexican American Affairs, "Mexican American."

50. Vicente Ximenes to Alfonso Sánchez, July 17, 1958, and Hector P. Garcia to Alfonso Sánchez, November 8, 1958, box 1, folder 14, Sánchez Papers.

51. U.S. Inter-agency Committee on Mexican American Affairs, "Mexican American," 33, 236.

52. U.S. Inter-agency Committee on Mexican American Affairs, 223–25.

53. U.S. Inter-agency Committee on Mexican American Affairs, 36.

54. U.S. Inter-agency Committee on Mexican American Affairs, 233–38.

55. deBuys, *Enchantment and Exploitation*, 230.

56. Martha Buddecke, "Farm Chief Backs Views of the Spanish," *AJ*, October 28, 1967.

57. Buddecke, "Farm Chief Backs Views of the Spanish."

58. Rep. Thomas G. Morris to Wayne N. Aspinall, July 13, 1967, box 445, Montoya Papers; Wayne Macomber Jr. to Robert F. Kennedy, August 2, 1967, box 47, folder 28, RLT Papers.

59. A copy of the Plan de la Raza Unida appears in Rendón, *Chicano Manifesto*, 301–2.

60. I. García, *Chicanismo*, 9.

61. Muñoz, *Youth, Identity, Power*, 7–8. See also Gutiérrez, "Religious Origins."

62. Baldenegro's written comments, dated June 13, 2016, in author's possession.

63. Rosales, *Chicano!*

64. R. Rodriguez, *Next of Kin*.

65. Vasquez, *Enriqueta Vasquez*, 15.

66. "Corrido de Río Arriba" and "Me Vino del Corazón" in Reade, "La Voz del Pueblo," 309–10 and 316–18; Gardner, *¡Grito!*, 205–6.

67. Harris, "Bede and Gregory's Allusive Angles," 273.

68. "U.S. Asks to Cite Tijerina on Contempt," *AJ*, November 11, 1967.

69. Bob Beier, "Tijerina's Trial Will Open Today," *AJ*, November 6, 1967.

70. Tijerina testimony transcript, pp. 1151–1236, box 39, folder 7, RLT Papers.

71. "Jury Ponders Verdict in Trial of Tijerina," *AJ*, November 11, 1967.

72. "Tijerina, Followers Convicted," *AJ*, November 12, 1967. Jurors deadlocked on conspiracy charges.

73. "Tijerina Gets 2 Years, 4 Compadres Sentenced," *SFNM*, December 15, 1967.

74. "Tijerina, Followers Convicted."

75. Nabokov, *Tijerina and the Courthouse Raid*, 232–33; see also Van H. Fris, "Naranjo Asks Aid of FBI," *SFNM*, May 6, 1968.

76. "Deputy, Policeman File $1.5 Million Suit against Tijerina," *AJ*, December 17, 1967.

77. John McMillion, "Charge Two in Jailer's Death," *AJ*, January 4, 1968.

78. John McMillion, "Rio Arriba's Hate Festers, Jailer Dies," *AJ*, January 6, 1968.

79. Pedro Ribera Ortega, "Entre Nosotros," *Santa Fe News*, January 11, 1968.

80. "Governor's View: Keep Them in Jail," *SFNM*, January 4, 1968.

81. John Crenshaw, "Reies Soon Out on Bond," *SFNM*, February 8, 1968.

82. "Obligación de cada Raza o Pueblo," box 54, folder 8, RLT Papers.

83. "Court Actions Surround Tijerina, Followers," *AJ*, March 10, 1968; "Tijerina Conviction Upheld," *SFNM*, June 25, 1969,

84. Mario García, *Memories of Chicano History*, 253.

85. Bert Corona appeal, box 34, folder 7, RLT Papers.

86. Press release, November 18, 1967, box 34, folder 7, RLT Papers. Also see telegrams in box 58, folder "Alianza/Eulogio Salazar," and box 59, folder "Alianza, Citizens Letters I," both in Cargo Papers.

87. Mario García, *Memories of Chicano History*, 252–53.

88. Bell Blawis, *Tijerina and the Land Grants*, 67; Mario García, *Memories of Chicano History*, 253. Axelrod also developed a close relationship with Eldridge Cleaver, who became a Panther after his release from prison. The letters that the pair exchanged while Cleaver was incarcerated formed the basis for his best-selling memoir, *Soul on Ice*, which he dedicated to her.

89. FBI agents recorded the entire speech, box 3, folder 1, RLT Papers; Bloom and Martin, *Black against Empire*, 145.

90. FBI agents recorded the entire speech, RLT Papers.

91. "Negro Comedian May Be Candidate of Peace Party," *Santa Cruz Sentinel*, March 18, 1968; "Peace-Freedom Delegates Meet Tonight," *Santa Cruz Sentinel*, August 1, 1968; also see news clippings in box 61, folder 5, RLT Papers.

92. Nabokov, *Tijerina and the Courthouse Raid*, 229.

93. *Los Angeles Free Press* news clipping dated "3-15-68," box 61, folder 5, RLT Papers.

94. Pitti, "Chicano Cold Warriors," 293; Nabokov, *Tijerina and the Courthouse Raid*, 229.

95. Telegram dated March 5, 1968, box 4, folder 3, RLT Papers.

96. As quoted in Mantler, *Power to the Poor*, 115.

97. David Braaten, "State Doesn't Escape the Wrath of the Poor."

98. Poor People's Campaign of New Mexico news release, June 13, 1968, box 31, folder 28, RLT Papers.

99. Martin Weil, "West's Poor: A Proud People," *Washington Post*, May 28, 1968.

100. Statement of Purpose, Poor People's Campaign, Washington D.C., box 1, folder 30, Nabokov Papers.

101. Statement of Purpose, Nabokov Papers.

102. Mantler, *Power to the Poor*, 129.

103. Robert E. Huber, "Reies Arrested on Raid Counts," *Clovis News Journal*, April 28, 1968; Tijerina, *Mi Lucha*, 107.

104. Tijerina, *Mi Lucha*, 107.

105. The grand jury issued second-degree felony charges, whereas the defendants originally were accused of first-degree kidnapping, a capital offense in New Mexico. Bob Knight, "Tijerina, 3 Others Arrested," *SFNM*, April 28, 1968.

106. "4-28-68 Telegram," box 47, folder 35, RLT Papers; "Report on Action Proposed with Reies Being Jailed," by "M. Varela," box 31, folder 22, RLT Papers.

107. "Indians in Poor People's March Push Old Land Treaty Demands," *Greensville (Miss.) Delta-Democrat*, May 6, 1968. Also see "Report on Action Proposed with Reies Being Jailed," RLT Papers.

108. Nabokov, *Tijerina and the Courthouse Raid*, 246.

109. Bob Beier, "Ages, Faiths, Races Mingled in March," *AJ*, May 19, 1968.

110. Mantler, *Power to the Poor*, 146.

111. Frankie McCarty, "1000 March in Poor People Drive," *AJ*, May 19, 1968.

112. "Non-Negroes Feel Ignored in March," *Arizona Republic*, May 26, 1968.

113. Mantler, *Power to the Poor*, 149, 157.

114. "Poor Staying in Capital Despite Rain," *Hobbs Daily News-Sun*, May 31, 1968; Vigil, *Crusade for Justice*, 55–57; Mantler, *Power to the Poor*, 136, 150, 157–61; Bell Blawis, *Tijerina and the Land Grants*, 131–45.

115. Vigil, *Crusade for Justice*, 56.

116. "Abernathy Acts to Avert a Split," *New York Times*, May 28, 1968.

117. "Friction between Marchers Builds," *Clovis News Journal*, May 30, 1968.

118. Oropeza, *¡Raza Sí!*, 74.

119. Mantler, *Power to the Poor*, 8.

120. "Washington D.C., June 13, 1968," statement, box 32, folder 3, RLT Papers.

121. Press release, Poor People's Campaign of New Mexico, June 3, 1968, box 31, folder 21, RLT Papers.

122. "Washington D.C., June 13, 1968," box 32, folder 3, RLT Papers.

123. Transcript of James Mosby interview with Tijerina, box 51, folder 17, RLT Papers.

124. Mantler, *Power to the Poor*, 180–81.

125. Hand-drawn flyer announcing June 13, 1968, meeting, box 31, folder 21, RLT Papers.

126. Hand-drawn flyer announcing June 13, 1968 meeting, and flyer about June 5th anniversary, both in box 31, folder 21, RLT Papers.

127. Vigil, *Crusade for Justice*, 56.

128. Transcript of James Mosby interview, RLT Papers. For Tijerina's insistence that he be solely designated leader of the Southwest contingent, see Mantler, *Power to the Poor*, 285–86n89.

129. Vigil, *Crusade for Justice*, 61.

130. Dick McAlpin, "Tijerina Claim Upset Negro Marchers," *AJ*, June 3, 1968.

131. Varela was among four coauthors of a dense press release refuting the welfare advocate's criticism. See news release, June 3, 1968, box 31, folder 21, RLT Papers.

132. Mantler, *Power to the Poor*, 180.

133. Varela's comments appear in director Hector Galán's *Chicano!*, episode 1, "Quest for a Homeland."

134. Mantler, *Power to the Poor*, 179.

135. Solidarity Day speech, June 19, 1968, box 31, folder 23, RLT Papers.

136. Film footage of Tijerina in Galán, *Chicano!*, episode 1, "Quest for a Homeland."

137. Tijerina, *Mi Lucha*, 208.

138. Hank Adams to Tijerina, May 28, 1968, box 47, folder 4, Reies López Tijerina Papers.

139. Bell Blawis, *Tijerina and the Land Grants*, 126–27; Tijerina, *Mi Lucha*, 210–14; Mantler, *Power to the Poor*, 201, 216–17. For a version of this protest that highlights Gonzales's support of indigenous rights, see Vigil, *Crusade for Justice*, 57–58.

140. Press release, May 29, 1968, box 31, folder 21, RLT Papers.

141. Braaten, "State Doesn't Escape the Wrath of the Poor."

142. Paul W. Valentine, "Negroes Bar Coalition, Tijerina Says," *Washington Post* article reprinted in *SFNM*, July 31, 1968.

143. "Impugnan el Tratado Guadalupe Hidalgo ante Nuestro Embajador," news clipping, box 59, folder 68, RLT Papers.

144. "June 12, 1968 News Release," box 42, folder 3, RLT Papers.

145. Alianza handbill, box 3, folder 7, RLT Papers.

146. "Doc. 129 State Department," box 46, folder 4, RLT Papers; Griswold del Castillo, *Treaty of Guadalupe Hidalgo*, 33–38.

147. Mantler, *Power to the Poor*, 183; press release, July 20, 1968, box 31, folder 28, RLT Papers.

148. "Dear Friend" letter, n.d., box 34, folder 709, Cargo Papers.

149. Mario García, *Memories of Chicano History*, 253.

CHAPTER 10

1. Joline Daffner, "No Holiday for Tijerina Case Jurors," *AJ*, November 28, 1968; Joline Daffner, "Tijerina Maneuver Slows Trial Start," *AJ*, November 21, 1968. Along with day-to-day coverage of the trial in the state's newspapers, the trial also earned a chapter in Nabokov, *Tijerina and the Courthouse Raid*; and Gardner, *¡Grito!* The trial also merited inclusion in a popular anthology, *Great Courtroom Battles*, edited by Richard Rubenstein, about other famous trials such as those of Lizzie Borden and Al Capone.

2. Joline Daffner, "Deputy Says Tijerina Gave Raid Orders," *AJ*, December 3, 1968.

3. Rubenstein, *Great Courtroom Battles*, 211; Gardner, *¡Grito!*, 273. Also see Joline Daffner, "State Rests in Tijerina Raid Trial," *AJ*, December 4, 1968, for not imposing blame.

4. Joline Daffner, "Tijerina Found Not Guilty," *AJ*, December 14, 1968.

5. "Tijerina Case Jurors 'Explain' Acquittal," *AJ*, December 22, 1968.

6. Copy of a letter sent from the editor of the *Herald of St. John* to the editor of *El Hispano*, September 1968, box 42, folder 4, RLT Papers.

7. Stang, "Reies Tijerina."

8. Mulloy, *World of the John Birch Society*, 110, 124, 125–29.

9. "Speaker Claims Tijerina Wants to Set Up Separate Nation," *AJ*, November 10, 1967.

10. Stang, "'War on Poverty' Supports Castroite Terrorists"; Stang, "New Mexico."

11. Paul R. Wieck, "Montoya Calls Tijerina an 'Enemy,'" *AJ*, December 16, 1967; "Belated but Welcome," *AJ*, December 19, 1967. The feud between Montoya and Tijerina played out in subsequent articles. See Frankie McCarty, "Tijerina Denounces Sen. Joseph Montoya," *AJ*, December 24, 1967; and Vina Windes, "Reies Lacks Big Backing—Montoya," *SFNM*, December 29, 1967. For "phony," see "Not through Courts," *AJ*, June 14, 1968.

12. John McMillion, "Rio Arriba's Hate Festers, Jailer Dies," *AJ*, January 6, 1968.

13. "Tijerina the Wrong Choice," *AJ*, April 26, 1968.

14. "Not through Courts."

15. "Rules and Regulations of the People's Constitutional Party," box 32, folder 6, RLT Papers.

16. "This is my promise to God and to the Poor of New Mexico," in Spanish at the bottom of the page, box 32, folder 7, RLT Papers.

17. "The Alianza: What, Where, and Why," box 1, folder 1, RLT Papers.

18. "The Alianza: What, Where, and Why," RLT Papers.

19. Donation of salary mentioned in article announcing his candidacy, *AJ*, July 28, 1968.

20. For Salazar reward, see press release on topic, box 32, folder 7, RLT Papers.

21. "Tijerina to Sue School Officials," July 26, 1968, news clipping, box 61, folder 12, RLT Papers. The folder is full of news clippings about his candidacy.

22. "For Immediate Release," August 2, 1968, box 42, folder 12, RLT Papers.

23. Tijerina, *Mi Lucha*, 198.

24. Howard, *Men Like That*, 155–58. Two articles from the *Harvard Crimson* address Higgs's civil rights activism; see Oyama, "Students to Man Rights Project Organized by Meredith Lawyer"; and Hessler, "Bill Higgs."

25. A letter from Noll to Cristóbal Tijerina postmarked March 20, 1968, makes clear that he had moved back to Washington, box 33, folder 16, RLT Papers.

26. "Actas de la junta," box 42, folder 4, RLT Papers.

27. Newspaper coverage of the December 1968 courthouse raid trial mentioned Axelrod, but subsequent articles about the Alianza do not.

28. The judge contemplating the complaint against the Albuquerque school board questioned Tijerina's right to sue as a noncustodial parent before dismissing the case altogether for being too vague. See "Tijerina Suit Is Dismissed," *AJ*, December 6, 1969. Similarly, Tijerina's attempt to persuade U.S. attorney general Ramsey Clark to launch an antitrust investigation of the Albuquerque newspapers went nowhere. See Tijerina letter to Ramsey Clark, August 2, 1968, box 48, folder 6, RLT Papers.

29. "Sec'y of State Rules Tijerina Off of Ballot," *AJ*, October 8, 1968.

30. "Tijerina, 2 Others Ruled Off Ballot," *AJ*, October 29, 1968.

31. Evans to Witt, September 10, 1968, in box 7, folder "People's Constitutional Party," Blea Papers; "Opinion of Boston Witt," October 1, 1968, box 32, folder 7, RLT Papers.

32. Nabokov, *Tijerina and the Courthouse Raid*, 230–31. For the size of the report, see Wayne S. Scott, "Witt Report Attacks Garcia Acts during Search for Tijerina," *AJ*, December 12, 1967; and Gardner, *¡Grito!*, 233.

33. "PCP Candidates on Ballot," *AJ*, October 29, 1968.

34. "More Tijerina," news clipping, box 34, folder "Alianza news clippings," Cargo Papers.

35. "Voice from Above Tells Tijerina to Run for Governor," July 29, 1968, news clipping and others, box 61, folder 12, RLT Papers.

36. Chart of early tallies, *SFNM*, November 6, 1968.

37. James Kennedy, "More Tijerina," partial news clipping, n.d., folder: Alianza news clippings, box 34, Cargo Papers.

38. Joline Daffner, "Reies Tijerina Must Stand Trial Alone," *AJ*, November 19, 1968.

39. Joline Daffner, "Number of Tierra Amarilla Charges Will Be Reduced," *AJ*, October 3, 1968.

40. "Tijerina Maneuver Slows Trial," *AJ*, November 21, 1968.

41. Joline Daffer, "Tijerina Found Not Guilty," *AJ*, December 14, 1968.

42. "The Tijerina Trial," *SFNM*, December 16, 1968.

43. "Incoming DA Will Recommend That State Continue Criminal Case against Tijerina," *Alamogordo (Tex.) Daily News*, December 18, 1968.

44. Daffner, "Tijerina Found Not Guilty."

45. Patrick Lamb, "Man Loses Hand in Explosion," *AJ*, April 17, 1968.

46. New Mexico State Police report, March 11, 1968, box 48, folder 26, RLT Papers.

47. "Man Given BCMC [Bernalillo County Medical Center] Duty in Careless Driving," *AJ*, September 10, 1968.

48. "Vandals Break Glass in Alianza Building," *Clovis News Journal*, October 17, 1968.

49. "Alianza Building Target of Attack," *AJ*, December 7, 1968.

50. Dan Brumbelow, "Bomb Is Exploded at Tijerina Base," *AJ*, January 24, 1969.

51. "Taos Fire May Get State Look," *AJ*, February 4, 1969.

52. "Raza Attacked, Raza Fights Back," *El Grito del Norte* (Española, N.Mex.), March 28, 1969; "Explosions Are Directed at Alianza," *AJ*, March 16, 1969; "Tijerina Asks U.S. Aid in Study of Bombings," *AJ*, March 17, 1969.

53. Numerous Freedom of Information Act requests by Tijerina showed that the FBI kept close tabs on him and his associates, generating reports sufficient to fill box 2, folders 13–23; and box 3 and box 4, folders 1–9, RLT Papers.

54. FBI document dated "October 26, 1967," box 2, folder 22, RLT Papers.

55. As quoted in Correia, "'Rousers of the Rabble,'" 575.

56. Correia, "'Rousers of the Rabble,'" 573, 569.

57. U.S. Congress. Senate. Select Committee to Study Government Operations with Respect to Intelligence Activities, "Final Report."

58. January 24, 1969, memo from SAC (Special Agent in Charge) Albuquerque to Hoover, box 3, folder 17, RLT Papers, as quoted in Correia, "'Rousers of the Rabble,'" 576.

59. Correia, "'Rousers of the Rabble,'" 576.

60. Document dated "12-15-67" for "avowed racist and militant," folder "Tecolote"; document that begins, "Dear Mrs. Escobar," folder "Wilfred Garcia"; and November 15, 1967, letter to Thomas C. Donnelly, president of Highlands University from Boston Witt, folder "Alianza Correspondence," all in box 2, Blea Papers. A wealth of additional post-raid state police reports on Tijerina and other Alianza members appears in this box.

61. State police reports mention agents attending the wedding of Office of Economic Opportunity director Robert Garcia, in box 2, untitled folder, Blea Papers.

62. Box 2, folder "Investigators Reports," Blea Papers.

63. See report dated "November 1, 1967," box 2, folder "Investigators Reports," Blea Papers.

64. Tijerina, *Mi Lucha*, 207.

65. "El radio y los periódicos día a día nos están diciendo," dated "Marzo 25, 1964," and "Pueblos Mexicanos Quemados por Yanquís," both box 1, folder 1, RLT Papers; "La Voz de la Justicia," radio script, April 23, 1965, KABQ, box 1, folder 36, RLT Papers.

66. Black to Montoya, July 29, 1969, box 34, folder "State Police-Crime in Río Arriba County," Cargo Papers.

67. Police chased rumors of another raid or similar uprising. See, for example, confidential report with the date December 7, 1967, appearing on the first line, and December 11, 1967, U.S. memorandum from forest supervisor to district ranger, both box 1, folder "Investigators Reports," Blea Papers. The *SFNM* published these rumors on June 5, 1968.

68. May 14, 1968, state police report mentions both the sowing of discord and the importation of Cuban guerrillas, box 1, folder "Alianza," Blea Papers.

69. Chapa interview.

70. Chapa interview. Chapa, for example, described the fire at the Vincent ranch without knowing who the owners were.

71. "Death Suit Dismissal Is Upheld," *AJ*, September 12, 1974.

72. Guillermo Contreras, "Police Shooting to Stay Closed," *AJ*, April 12, 2000; "Families of Activists Want Old Cases Reviewed," *SFNM*, January 11, 2000; Matt Mygatt, "Court Upholds Ruling in Chicano Activists Lawsuit," *SFNM*, March 2, 2001.

73. Guillermo Contreras, "Suit: Activists Killed in '72 Police Plot," *AJ*, January 9, 2000.

74. See FBI files contained within boxes 2 and 3, RLT Papers.

75. Correia, "'Rousers of the Rabble,'" 575.

76. "The Most Hated Man in New Mexico," directed by Walter Miller, which appeared in 1969 as part of the NBC News program *First Tuesday*. A complete transcript of the show is available in box 1, folder 1, Reies López Tijerina News Reports, Kenneth Spencer Research Library, University of Kansas Libraries.

77. "Most Hated Man in New Mexico."

78. "Most Hated Man in New Mexico."

79. "Most Hated Man in New Mexico."

80. "Tijerina Loses Rehearing Appeal," *AJ*, April 19, 1969.

81. "Committee Plans 429th Anniversary," *El Paso Times Herald*, May 17, 1969, news clipping; "Parade Today Commemorates Spanish Speech," *AJ*, May 17, 1969, and "150 Take Part in Spanish Parade," *AJ*, May 18, 1969, news clippings, all in box 34, folder "Alianza news clippings," Cargo Papers.

82. "Telegram Sent December 28, 1968 to Premier Franco of Spain," box 42, folder 5, RLT Papers.

83. For a brief history of ownership, see Ghost Ranch, https://www.ghostranch.org/explore/our-story-mission/, accessed April 11, 2018. Letter from president, Supreme Council, Alianza Federal de Pueblos Libres, to Dr. William P. Thompson, Stated Clerk, Presbyterian Church, November 14, 1968, box 42, folder 5, RLT Papers.

84. Rees Lloyd, "Tijerina Sees Land Release 'Confusion,'" *AJ*, May 21, 1969.

85. "Presbyterian Board Told to Seek Ghost Ranch Land for Hispanos," *AJ*, May 20, 1969.

86. Jim Maldonado, "Tijerina Attacks Church," *SFNM*, June 2, 1969.

87. Nabokov, *Tijerina and the Courthouse Raid*, 272.

88. "Senate Group Gives Burger Quick OK as Tijerina 'Arrest' Fails," *AJ*, June 4, 1969.

89. "Tijerina to Arrest Nominee for Supreme Court," *AJ*, May 31, 1969.

90. "Tijerina Citizen's Arrest Attempt Unsuccessful," *SFNM*, June 8, 1969.

91. "Tijerina's Attorney's Open Case," *SFNM*, June 17, 1969.

92. Conflicting accounts of the confrontation can be found in police reports and Alianza witness accounts. For detailed pictures of the events in question, see Bailey, "Reies López Tijerina."

93. "'Hates Reies,' Officer Says at a Hearing," *AJ*, June 17, 1969.

94. ""Tijerina Conviction Upheld," *SFNM*, June 25, 1969.

95. Kathy Mason, "Tijerina Convicted in Burning," *AJ*, September 28, 1969.

96. "Tijerina Sentenced to 3 Years," *SFNM*, October 10, 1969.

97. Kathy Mason, "Court Upholds 5 Alianzans' Convictions," *AJ*, October 14, 1969.

98. Tomas O. Martinez, "Admirers Mob Reies Tijerina on His Return to New Mexico," *AJ*, July 27, 1971.

99. Tijerina, *Mi Lucha*, 308–9.

100. Letter dated "August 15–17, 1969," box 53, folder 46, RLT Papers. The letter was also published in *El Grito del Norte* on September 26, 1969.

101. Cisneros, *Border Crossed Us*, 67.

102. Letter dated "August 15–17, 1969," RLT Papers.

103. As quoted in Busto, *King Tiger*, 152.

104. Busto hypothesized that another dream revelation inspired by the June 1969 moon landing inspired Tijerina's change of tune between the first letter of mid-August and the second of mid-October; *King Tiger*, 154–55. Details of this dream, in which Tijerina matched the ability to travel in space with the arrival of a "fourth-dimensional language" to diminish conflict globally, concluded Nabokov, *Tijerina and the Courthouse Raid*, 279–80. Tijerina referred to this fourth dimension in a prison writing dated September 1969 that begins, "el Universo es la habitación de los seres angélicos," box 53, folder 46, RLT Papers.

105. Leslie Bottorff, "Convict Tijerina on Two Counts by Jury," *SFNM*, November 27, 1969.

EPILOGUE

1. Reies López Tijerina oral history interview.

2. Reies López Tijerina anniversary comments, Coyote, N.Mex., June 5, 2007.

3. "Deny Tijerina Appeal," *Hobbs Daily News-Sun*, June 11, 1969. Also see prison writings marked "La Tuna" in box 53, folder 46, RLT Papers.

4. Norman A. Carlson to R. H. Tijerina Jr., October 2, 1970, box 47, folder 20, RLT Papers.

5. Department of Corrections, memo, p. 8, dated August 18, 1970, box 58, folder "Alianza: Eulogio Salazar," Cargo Papers. In contrast, when Tijerina attended mandatory therapy sessions after his release, a mental health clinic in Albuquerque concluded the opposite: "no manifest psychiatric disorder." Francis Fernandez, MSW, to Joe Padilla, probation officer, June 19, 1975, box 47, folder 13, RLT Papers.

6. "Affidavit," September 3, 1970, box 41, folder 8, RLT Papers.

7. Tomas O. Martinez, "Admirers Mob Reies Tijerina on His Return to New Mexico," *AJ*, July 27, 1971.

8. Martinez, "Admirers Mob Reies Tijerina on His Return to New Mexico."

9. The Brotherhood Awareness efforts are archived in box 32, folders 21–40, RLT Papers. To promote the idea, Tijerina founded the Institute for the Research and Study of Justice, the purpose of which was "world harmony." See letterhead in box 32, folder 15, RLT Papers.

10. Jerry Danziger, KOB Television general manager, to Reies López Tijerina, August 14, 1972, box 43, folder 3; press release, n.d., box 32, folder 21; H.J. Resolution 1049, box 43, folder 10; S.J. Res. 215, box 32, folder 39; Fernando E. C. de Baca to Tijerina, April 9, 1975, box 47, folder 21; Sen. Pete Domenici to Tijerina, August 28, 1973, box 47, folder 32; 1973 proclamation of New Mexico governor Bruce King declaring "Brotherhood Awareness Week," all RLT Papers.

11. Reies H. Tijerina to Dennis Hopper, August 7, 1972, box 43, folder 3, RLT Papers. Muhammad Ali appears in a 1976 Brotherhood Awareness photo, numbered 76, at

the back of the massive finding aid for RLT's collection at the Center for Southwest Research, University of New Mexico.

12. Parole authorization note to Tijerina, March 9, 1973, box 43, folder 6, RLT Papers.

13. Tijerina to Wallace "Mad Bear" Anderson, January 2, 1973, box 47, folder 4, RLT Papers.

14. "Alianza Split Indicated by Canceled Meeting," *AJ*, April 15, 1972; "Alianza Election Held," *SFNM*, April 17, 1972. Tijerina blamed Bill Higgs, the lawyer, for the split. See "Pending Land Grant bill Bill Higgs Prime Concern," *SFNM*, May 1, 1972.

15. For a while, two Alianzas competed, as evinced in two sets of letterheads. See Alianza Federal de Mercedes letters, box 34, folder 710, Cargo Papers; and Alianza Federal de Pueblos Libres letters, which also indicate that Tijerina resumed the presidency, box 47, folder 24, RLT Papers.

16. See correspondence between Tijerina and two Mexican presidents detailing his visits during the 1970s, box 47, folders 25–26, RLT Papers.

17. For Texas effort, see box 4, folders 14–20, RLT Papers.

18. "A Personal Statement of Reies López Tijerina Regarding New Mexico State Police," dated "10-24-1967," box 42, folder 13, RLT Papers.

19. "AG: Rape Charge 'Spurious,'" *SFNM*, November 8, 1971; also see "Report on Accusations of Reies López Tijerina against Officers and Officials of the State of New Mexico," box 54, folder 11, RLT Papers.

20. "Tijerina Asks U.S. to Probe Assault Claim," *AJ*, November 15, 1971.

21. Rose Tijerina mentioned this incident to me during our phone conversation in 2012. Her father often included it in his tale of persecution. Press release dated April 22, 1982, box 2, folder 4, RLT Papers.

22. "Tijerina Files Suit against Ex-Policeman," *AJ*, March 20, 1974. According to Noe Tijerina's oral history, the family received a small sum; transcript of interview of Noe Tijerina by José Angel Gutiérrez, box 1, folder 1, Noe Tijerina Papers, Center for Southwest Research, University of New Mexico, Albuquerque.

23. Press release, April 22, 1982, box 2, folder 5, RLT Papers.

24. Noe Tijerina interview by José Angel Gutiérrez, Noe Tijerina Papers.

25. Denise Kessler, "Education Comes Home to the Kids," *SFNM* clipping dated February 21, 1982, RLT Vertical File.

26. For the meaning of Danitha, see personal writing dated August 10, 1974, box 59, folder 10, RLT Papers. As was the case with Noe and Ira de Alá, the names that Tijerina chose for all four of his children with Patsy Tijerina reflected his political preoccupations. Carlo Joaquín was named after Carlo V of Spain and the San Joaquín land grant that the Spanish king deeded. Isabel Iris's name referred to Queen Isabel of Spain as well as the symbol of the rainbow. Harmony was born in 1972 during the height of his brotherhood awareness organizing.

27. "Tijerina Welcomed at Home," *AJ*, June 30, 1974; "Friends, Family Welcome Tijerina," *AJ*, December 19, 1974.

28. The movie, *Chicano*, was directed by Jaime Casillas.

29. Tijerina, *Mi Lucha*.

30. "Tijerina Backers Killed Jailer, AG Says," *AJ*, August 17, 1977. The entire report is in box 80, folder 9, Jenkins Collected Papers. The report stated that "two or three" Alianza members killed the jailer but that they had acted without Tijerina's knowl-

edge. The report also stated that not enough evidence existed to bring charges against these unnamed suspects, mainly because key witnesses refused to testify. In a bizarre twist, the author of the report, a lawyer named Michael Francke, was himself murdered in January 1989 apparently without ever disclosing who he thought the suspects to be.

31. For "warring tribes," see Nabokov, *Tijerina and the Courthouse Raid*, 280. In my 2010 interview, Tijerina started by mentioning that it was not coincidence that Alianza members stormed the courthouse on the same day that the Six-Day War began in the Middle East, or that Robert F. Kennedy, whom Tijerina believed failed to back "the cause," died on June 5, 1968, the first-year anniversary of the raid. Also see Bowman, "Tixerina's Dream," copy in RLT Vertical File. The article also mentioned Tijerina's/Tixerina's ongoing interest in Middle Eastern affairs.

32. Simon Romero, "60's Latino Militant Now Pursues a Personal Quest," *New York Times*, May 5, 2006.

33. Steve Terrell, "Activist Says Arson Ruined Home," *SFNM*, November 6, 1993.

34. Romero, "60's Latino Militant Now Pursues a Personal Quest."

35. Personal writing, December 7, 1974, box 54, folder 10, RLT Papers.

36. Noe Tijerina interview by José Angel Gutiérrez, Noe Tijerina Papers.

37. Arturo Sandoval, "Stalwarts of Alianza Movement Diligently Work on Land Issues," *Albuquerque News*, August 22, 1979, news clipping in box 33, folder 12, RLT Papers.

38. The invitations appear in the "General Correspondence" folders from 1971, 1972, and 1973, boxes 42 and 43, RLT Papers.

39. "Temper Spirit Urges Tijerina," *Denton (Tex.) Record-Chronicle*, September 3, 1972. For change in tone, also see Pete Herrera, "Tijerina Abandons the Clenched Fist," *SFNM*, February 27, 1972.

40. Navarro, *La Raza Unida Party*, 243.

41. Sylvia Loomis to Bill Brown, October 25, 1970, box 43, folder 3, RLT Papers; Busto, *King Tiger*, 218.

42. Multiple version of this plan can be found online. A copy of the original version appears in Rosales, *Testimonio*, 361–63.

43. Joline Daffer, "Tijerina Pulls Out of Alianza," *AJ*, October 22, 1969.

44. Bebout, *Mythohistorical Interventions*, 91.

45. Daffer, "Tijerina Pulls Out of Alianza."

46. Tijerina objected to the title of Valdez and Steiner's *Aztlán: An Anthology of Mexican American Literature*, even though it included him. See Tijerina to John Risaliti, editor, Alfred Knopf, Inc., March 10, 1972, and Stan Steiner to Tijerina, March 14, 1972, both in box 42, folder 16, RLT Papers. For a Tijerina comment on the word "Chicano," see Mariscal, *Brown-Eyed Children*, 201, especially footnote 92. For more of Tijerina's impatience with "youngsters," see Navarro, *La Raza Unida Party*, 244.

47. Navarro, *La Raza Unida Party*, 244.

48. The entire run of *El Grito del Norte* is available at the University of California, Berkeley's Ethnic Studies Library.

49. This theme particularly comes through in tenth-anniversary commentaries; see 1977 news clippings, RLT Vertical file.

50. David Roybal, "Tierra Amarilla: Then and Now," *SFNM*, June 5, 1977.

51. For more information about the clinic, see La Cooperación del Pueblo de Tierra Amarilla Collection, in particular the twenty-fifth-anniversary booklet, box 1, folder 4.

52. Along with newspaper accounts, see Correia, *Properties of Violence*, 159–64; and Busto, *King Tiger*, 74.

53. "Congressman Asks Land Grant Validity Probe," *AJ*, March 15, 1969.

54. H.R. 9422, box 46, folder 5, and H.R. 9777, box 48, folder 31, both in RLT Papers.

55. The New Mexico House voted 56–0 on House Joint Resolution 15 to establish a Spanish-Mexican Land Claims Commission. The New Mexico Senate then approved this resolution, 35–0. See "Senate Oks Request for Land Claims Study, *AJ*, February 2, 1974; "Legislative Summary," *AJ*, February 8, 1974.

56. Montoya proposed Senate 4050 Bill, which called for establishing a temporary special commission on Treaty of Guadalupe-Hidalgo land rights, appears in box 46, folder 5, RLT Papers. Also see "Land Rights Bill Introduced by Montoya," *Gallup Independent*, September 27, 1974.

57. Patrick Armijo, "Udall Revives Land Grant Bill," *AJ*, February 3, 1999. Representative Bill Richardson, Democrat, also supported the legislation.

58. "Anderson Cool to Grant Bill," *AJ*, June 19, 1968.

59. Committee on Energy and Natural Resources, *Hearing before the Subcommittee on Forests and Public Land Management.*

60. U.S. General Accounting Office, "Report for Congressional Requestors." For expense, time, and staff numbers, see Ebright, "G.A.O. Land Grant Report"; and Benavides and Golten, "Righting the Record."

61. Scarborough, *Trespassers on Our Own Land*, 81.

62. Benavides and Golten, "Righting the Record."

63. Ebright, "G.A.O. Land Grant Report."

64. Clark S. Knowlton, "Spanish American Protest Movements in Northern New Mexico," n.d., Knowlton Vertical File.

65. Carolyn Zeleny to David Cargo, June 11, 1967, box 59, Folder "Alianza, Citizen Letters, II," Cargo Papers.

66. Cargo, "Effects of Federal Programs on Rural America," 192.

67. David King to Tijerina, December 27, 1970, box 46, folder 19, RLT Papers; White, Koch, Kelley, and McCarthy, *Land Title Study.*

68. Ebright, *Tierra Amarilla Land Grant.*

69. Dunbar-Ortiz, *Roots of Resistance.*

70. The University of New Mexico launched a New Mexico Land Grant Series for starters, featuring *Mercedes Reales*, Westphall's book on land grants, and Forrest's *Preservation of the Village.* Key edited volumes included Briggs and Van Ness, *Land, Water, and Culture*, and Kutsche, *Survival of Spanish American Villages.* Interest in the deeper roots of resistance also appeared early in Rosenbaum's *Mexicano Resistance in the Southwest.* Nostrand declared the region culturally distinct in *The Hispano Homeland.* In *Acequia*, Sylvia Rodríguez took a much closer and more careful look at the cultural significance of land and water.

71. See Westphall's *Thomas Benton Catron*, as well as p. 273 in his *Mercedes Reales.*

72. Gómez-Quiñones, "Toward a Perspective on Chicano History," 2.

73. Acuña, *Occupied America.* Another early publication, a 1973 anthology, fore-

grounded the relationship that Tijerina had taken so much care to foster. See De la Garza, Kruszewski, and Arciniega, *Chicanos and Native Americans*.

74. Camarillo, *Chicanos in a Changing Society*; and Montejano, *Anglos and Mexicans*.

75. Chávez-García, *Negotiating Conquest*; D. González, *Refusing the Favor*.

76. Limerick, *Legacy of Conquest*, 232.

77. Goldstein, *Formations of U.S. Colonialism*.

78. In addition to his expressed support of Puerto Rican independence, Tijerina saved an article, "Angry Hawaiians Seek Land Compensation," which appeared in *AJ*, November 11, 1973, box 47, folder 4, RLT Papers.

79. He too shall remain anonymous.

80. Reies López Tijerina oral history interview.

81. Ginzburg, *Cheese and the Worms*. Thanks to Ali Anooshahr for this reference.

82. Busto, *King Tiger*.

83. Guinn, *Road to Jonestown*.

84. King, *Autobiography*, 76.

85. Menchú, *I, Rigoberta Menchú*, especially chapter 18, "The Bible and Self-Defence: The Examples of Judith, Moses and David."

86. Warren, *God's Red Sun*.

87. Love, "La Raza," 283.

Bibliography

MANUSCRIPT COLLECTIONS

Archivo Genaro Estrada, Mexico City
Secretaría de Relaciones Exteriores de México
Archivo General de La Nación, Mexico City
Gobernación, Dirección General de Seguridad, Investigaciones Políticas y Sociales
Center for Southwest Research, University of New Mexico, Albuquerque
La Cooperación del Pueblo de Tierra Amarilla Collection
Clark S. Knowlton Vertical File
Joseph M. Montoya Papers
Peter Nabokov Papers
Frances León Quintana Papers
Alfonso Sánchez Papers
Noe Tijerina Papers
Reies López Tijerina Papers
Reies López Tijerina Vertical File
Center of Southwest Studies, Fort Lewis College, Colo.
Myra Ellen Jenkins Collected Papers
Kenneth Spencer Research Library, University of Kansas Libraries, Kansas City
Reies López Tijerina News Reports Collection
New Mexico State Records Center and Archives, Santa Fe
Eloy Blea Papers
David F. Cargo Papers
Bruce King Papers
Clark S. Knowlton Collection

INTERVIEWS

Aguilar, Cruz. Conversation with author. Plaza Blanca, N.Mex. September 1, 2007.
Aguilar, Gregorita. Conversation with author. Plaza Blanca, N.Mex. September 1, 2007.
Baldenegro, Salomón. Email to author. February 2, 2016.

Chapa, Tim. Interview with José Angel Gutiérrez. June 7, 2000.
DeLaTorre, Lillian. Interview with Laurie Coyle. Yuba City, Calif. January 11, 2015.
Escobar, Mary. Conversation with author. Albuquerque, N.Mex. November 6, 2006.
———. Conversation with author. Albuquerque, N.Mex. February 6, 2013.
———. Oral history interview with author. Albuquerque, N.Mex. November 6, 2006.
Laughlin, Ofelia Theresa Tijerina. Phone conversation with author. May 26, 2011.
Leyba, Alex. Conversation with author. Canjilón, N.Mex. June 4, 2007.
Leyba, Mary. Oral history interview with author. Canjilón, N.Mex. June 4, 2007.
Martínez, Elizabeth "Betita." Oral history interview with author. San Francisco, Calif. January 15, 1993.
Sánchez, Alfonso. Oral history interview with author. Santa Fe, N.Mex. February 2, 2013.
Tijerina, Rachel. Oral history interview with author. Las Cruces, N.Mex. April 8, 2010.
Tijerina, Rachel. Conversation with author. Albuquerque, N.Mex. April 17, 2012.
Tijerina, Reies López. Oral history interview with author. El Paso, Tex., and Las Cruces, N.Mex. April 8–9, 2010.
———. Phone conversation with author. August 6, 2007.
Tijerina, Rose. Email to author. September 12, 2012.
———. Oral history interview with author. Albuquerque, N.Mex. November 7, 2006.
———. Phone conversation with author. January 12, 2012.
Trujillo, Simón Ventura. Conversation with author. Denver, Colo. April 7, 2016.
Valdez, Juan. Oral history interview with author. Canjilón, N.Mex. June 8, 2007.
Valdez, Rosina. Conversation with author. Canjilón, N.Mex. June 8, 2007.
Valdez, Valentina. Oral history interview with author. Tierra Maria, N.Mex. August 22, 1997.
Varela, Maria. Email to author. August 20, 2017.

PERIODICALS

Alamogordo (Tex.) Daily News
Albuquerque Journal
Albuquerque Tribune
Albuquerque News Chieftain
Arizona Republic
Casa Grande (Ariz.) Dispatch
Chicago Tribune
El Defensor Chieftain (Socorro, N.Mex.)
Clovis (N.Mex.) News Journal
Denton (Tex.) Record-Chronicle
Denver Post
Forumeer: Official Publication of the American GI Forum (San Jose, Calif.)
Gallup (N.Mex.) Independent
Greensville (Miss.) Delta-Democrat
El Grito del Norte (Española, N.Mex.)
Hobbs (N.Mex.) Daily News-Sun
Las Cruces (N.Mex.) Sun-News

Los Angeles Times
New York Times
El Paso Herald Post
Pentecostal Evangel (Springfield, Ill.)
Raleigh (N.C.) News Observer
St. Louis Post-Dispatch
Santa Cruz (Calif.) Sentinel
Santa Fe New Mexican
Santa Fe News
Socorro News Chieftain
Sydney Herald
Tucson Daily Citizen
Washington Post

PUBLISHED SOURCES

Acuña, Rodolfo. *Occupied America: The Chicano's Struggle toward Liberation*. San Francisco: Canfield Press, 1972.

Adler, Renata. "Letter from the Palmer House." *New Yorker*, September 23, 1967, 56–58, 60, 62, 65, 79–82, 85–88.

Aikman, David. "How Billy Graham Killed Communism with Kindness." *Christianity Today*, February 2018. https://www.christianitytoday.com/ct/2018/billy-graham/how-billy-graham-killed-communism-kindness-iron-curtain.html, accessed July 27, 2018.

Alegre Robert F. *Railroad Radicals in Cold War Mexico: Gender, Class, and Memory*. Lincoln and London: University of Nebraska Press, 2013.

Alexander, Charles C. *Crusade for Conformity*. Houston: Texas Gulf Coast Historical Association, 1961.

Allit, Patrick. "Religion and Politics since 1945." In *The Concise Princeton Encyclopedia of American Political History*, edited by Michael Kazin, Rebecca Edwards, and Adam Rothman, 453–59. Princeton: Princeton University Press, 2011.

Anderson, Carol. *Eyes Off the Prize: The United States and the African American Struggle for Human Rights, 1944–1955*. New York: Cambridge University Press, 2003.

Anderson, Terry H. *The Movement and the Sixties*. 5th ed. Oxford: Oxford University Press, 1996.

Araiza, Lauren. *To March for Others: The Black Freedom Struggle and the United Farm Workers*. Philadelphia: University of Pennsylvania Press, 2014.

Avila, Rolando, and Pedro Santoni. "The Historiography of the Mexican-American War." In *The Encyclopedia of the Mexican-American War: A Political, Social, and Military History*, vol. 1, edited by Spencer C. Tucker, 301–4. Santa Barbara: ABC-CLIO, 2012

Bailey, M. G. "Reies López Tijerina September 21, 1926–January 19, 2015." *What's Wrong with This Picture* (blog), January 19, 2015. http://mgbralley-whatswrongwiththis picture.blogspot.com.

Balderrama, Francisco E., and Raymond Rodríguez. *Decade of Betrayal: Mexican Repatriation in the 1930s*. Rev. ed. Albuquerque: University of New Mexico Press, 2006.

Bancroft, Hubert Howe. *History of New Mexico and Arizona*. San Francisco: History Company, 1889.

Barba, Lloyd. "California's Cross: A Cultural History of Pentecostalism, Race and Agricuture." Ph.D. diss., University of Michigan Press, 2016.

Barrera, Mario, Charles Ornelas, and Carlos Muñoz. "The Barrio as an Internal Colony in an Urban Society." In *People and Politics in an Urban Society*, edited by Harland Hahn, 465–99. Beverly Hills: Sage, 1972.

Bazian, Hatem. "Revisiting MLK's Speech, 'The Three Evils of Society.'" Hatem Bazian, December 23, 2015. http://www.hatembazian.com/content/revisiting-mlks-speech-the-three-evils-of-society/.

Bebout, Lee. "Hero Making in El Movimiento: Reies López Tijerina and the Chicano Nationalist Imaginary." *Aztlán: Journal of the Social Sciences and the Arts* 32 (Fall 2007): 93–121.

Bebout, Lee. *Mythohistorical Interventions: The Chicano Movement and Its Legacies*. Minneapolis: University of Minnesota Press, 2011.

Behnken, Brian D. *The Struggle in Black and Brown: African American and Mexican American Relations during the Civil Rights Era*. Lincoln: University of Nebraska Press, 2012.

Bell Blawis, Patricia. *Tijerina and the Land Grants: Mexican Americans in Struggle for Their Heritage*. New York: International Publishers, 1971.

Bemis, Samuel Flagg. *A Diplomatic History of the United States*. New York: Henry Holt, 1936.

Benavides, David. "The General Accounting Office Report Preliminary Comments by The New Mexico Land Grant Forum and the Mexicano Land Education and Conservation Trust." *Southwest Books: Center for Land Grant Studies*, July 2004. http://www.southwestbooks.org/gaolgfresponse.htm.

Benavides, David, and Ryan Golten. "Righting the Record: A Response to the GAO's 2004 Report Treaty of Guadalupe Hidalgo: Findings and Possible Options Regarding Longstanding Community Land Grant Claims in New Mexico." *Natural Resources Journal* 48, no. 4 (Winter 2008): 857–926.

Berlet, Chip, and Matthew N. Lyons. *Right-Wing Populism in America: Too Close for Comfort*. New York: Guilford Press, 2000.

Blackhawk, Ned. *Violence over the Land*. Cambridge, Mass.: Harvard University Press, 2008.

Blanton, Carlos. "From Intellectual Deficiency to Cultural Deficiency: Mexican Americans, Testing, and Public School Policy in the American Southwest, 1920–1940." *Pacific Historical Review* 72 (2003): 39–62.

———. *George I. Sánchez: The Long Fight for Mexican American Integration*. New Haven: Yale University Press, 2015.

Bloom, Joshua, and Waldo E. Martin Jr. *Black against Empire: The History and Politics of the Black Panther Party*. Berkeley: University of California Press, 1985.

Blumhofer, Edith L. *Restoring the Faith: The Assemblies of God, Pentecostalism, and American Culture*. Champaign: University of Illinois Press, 1993.

Bodine, John J. "A Tri-ethnic Trap: The Spanish Americans of Taos." In *Spanish-Speak-*

ing People of the United States, edited by June Helm, 145–63. Seattle: University of Washington Press, 1968.

Bowden, J. J. "Socorro Grant." New Mexico Office of the State Historian. http://dev.newmexicohistory.org/filedetails.php?fileID=24686, accessed February 18, 2017.

Bowler, Kate. *Blessed: A History of the American Prosperity Gospel*. Oxford: Oxford University Press, 2013.

Bowman, Robert. "Tixerina's Dream." *Impact: A Magazine of the Albuquerque Journal*, November 1, 1983.

Boyer, Paul S. *When Time Shall Be No More: Prophecy Belief in Modern American Culture*. Cambridge, Mass.: Belknap Press of Harvard University Press, 1994.

Braaten, David. "State Doesn't Escape the Wrath of the Poor." *Washington Sunday Star*, June 16, 1968.

Brick, Howard, and Gregory Parker. *A New Insurgency: The Port Huron Statement and Its Times*. Ann Arbor: University of Michigan Press, 2012.

Briggs, Charles, and John R. Van Ness, eds. *Land, Water, and Culture: New Perspectives on Hispanic Land Grants*. Albuquerque: University of New Mexico Press, 1987.

Brooks, James F. *Captives and Cousins: Slavery, Kinship, and Community in the Southwest Borderlands*. Chapel Hill: University of North Carolina Press, 2002.

Brown, Stephen R. *1494: How a Family Feud in Medieval Spain Divided the World in Half*. New York: Thomas Dunne Books, 2012.

Burns, Robert I. *Las Siete Partidas*. Philadelphia: University of Pennsylvania Press, 2012.

Busto, Rudiger V. "'In the Outer Boundaries': Pentacostalism, Politics and Reies López Tijerina's Civic Activism." In *Latino Religions and Civic Activism in the United States*, edited by Gaston Espinosa, 65–75. New York: Oxford University Press, 2005.

———. *King Tiger: The Religious Vision of Reies López Tijerina*. Albuquerque: University of New Mexico Press, 2005.

Calloway, Larry Joseph. "June 5, 1967: The Courthouse Raid Recalled." LarryCalloway.com, Crestone Conglomerate from the Rio Grande West, July 28, 2001. http://larrycalloway.com/courthouse-raid/#more-55.

Camarillo, Albert. *Chicanos in a Changing Society: From Mexican Pueblos to American Barrios in Santa Barbara and Southern California, 1846–1930*. Cambridge, Mass.: Harvard University Press, 1979.

Cannon, Terrence, and Joseph A. Blum. "Introduction to THE MOVEMENT." Veterans of the Civil Rights Movement. http://www.crmvet.org/docs/mvmt/movement_intro.pdf, accessed January 29, 2018.

Cargo, David. *Lonesome Dave: The Story of New Mexico Governor David Francis Cargo*. Santa Fe: Sunstone Press, 2010.

Carmichael, Stokeley, and Charles Hamilton. *Black Power: The Politics of Liberation in America*. New York: Viking Press, 1967.

Carroll, Michael P. *The Penitente Brotherhood: Patriarchy and Hispano-Catholicism in New Mexico*. Baltimore: Johns Hopkins University Press, 2002.

Celebrating New Mexico Statehood. *"Pueblo Republica de San Joaquin del Rio de Chama."* https://nmstatehood.unm.edu/node/56302, accessed April 8, 2018.

The Center for Land Grant Studies. "Preliminary List of Grants from the Land Grant

Database Project." Southwest Books, March 21, 2005. http://www.southwestbooks.org/grantssz.htm.

"Century of Negro Progress." *Jet*, August 29, 1963, 58-59.

Chávez, Fray Angélico. *My Penitente Land: Reflections of Spanish New Mexico, 1974*. Santa Fe, NM: Sunstone Press, 2012.

Chávez-García, Miroslava. *Negotiating Conquest: Gender and Power in California, 1770s to 1880s*. Tucson: University of Arizona Press, 2004.

———. *States of Delinquency: Race and Science in the Making of California's Juvenile Justice System*. Berkeley: University of California Press, 2012.

Cisneros, Josue David. *The Border Crossed Us: Rhetorics of Borders, Citizenship, and Latina/o Identity*. Tuscaloosa: University of Alabama Press, 2013.

Coerver, Don M., Suzanne B. Pasztor, and Robert Buffington. *Mexico: An Encyclopedia of Contemporary Culture and History*. Santa Barbara: ABC-CLIO, 2004.

Cohen, Deborah. *Braceros: Migrant Citizens and Transnational Subjects in the Postwar United States and Mexico*. Chapel Hill: University of North Carolina Press, 2011.

Committee on Energy and Natural Resources. *Hearing before the Subcommittee on Forests and Public Land Management*. Washington, D.C.: U.S. Government Printing Office, 1999.

Correia, David. "From Agropastoralism to Sustained Yield Forestry: Industrial Restructuring, Rural Change, and the Land-Grant Commons in Northern New Mexico." *Capitalism Nature Socialism* 16, no. 1 (2005): 25–44.

———. "The Future of the Commons, Part II: The Origins of United States Forest Service Paternalism in Northern New Mexico." *La Jicarita: An Online Magazine of Environmental Politics in New Mexico*, June 27, 2012. http://lajicarita.wordpress.com/2012/06/27/the-future-of-the-commons-part-ii-the-origins-of-united-states-forest-service-paternalism-in-northern-new-mexico/.

———. "The Hijuelas of Tierra Amarilla." *La Jicarita News*, October–November 2008.

———. "Making Destiny Manifest: United States Territorial Expansion and the Dispossession of Two Mexican Property Claims in New Mexico, 1824–1899." *Journal of Historical Geography* 35. no. 1 (January 2009): 87–103.

———. *Properties of Violence*. Athens: University of Georgia Press, 2013.

———. "'Rousers of the Rabble' in the New Mexico Land Grant War: La Alianza Federal de Mercedes and the Violence of the State." *Antipode* 40, no. 4 (2008): 551–83.

———. "Who Is Reies López Tijerina? A Reappraisal of a Folk Hero." *Alibi*, June 13–19, 2013, http://alibi.com/news/44776/who-is-reies-lopez-tijerina.html.

"The Courthouse Raid: Twenty Years Later." *¡Salsa!* supplement to the *Río Grande Sun*, May 28, 1987.

Coyle, Laurie, dir. *Adios Amor: The Search for Maria Moreno*. Produced by Laurie Coyle and Jane Greenberg. 2017 (documentary).

Cozolino, Louis. *The Neuroscience of Human Relationships: Attachment and the Developing Brain*. 2nd. ed. New York: Norton, 2014.

"The Crown Prince Regent of Thulia, 1954." Museum of Hoaxes, June 28, 2012. http://hoaxes.org/weblog/comments/crown_prince_regent_of_thulia.

Crum, Steven. "Almost Invisible: The Brotherhood of North American Indians and the League of North American Indians." *Wicazo Sa Review* 21, no. 1 (2006): 50–53.

Cue Cánovas, Agustin. *Los Estados Unidos y el México Olvidado*. Mexico City: B. Costa-Amic, 1970.

DeBuys, William. *Enchantment and Exploitation: The Hard Times of a New Mexico Mountain Range*. Albuquerque: University of New Mexico Press, 1985.

De la Garza, Rodolfo O., Z. Anthony Kruszewski, and Tomás A. Arciniega. *Chicanos and Native Americans: The Territorial Minorities*. Englewood Cliffs, N.J.: Prentice Hall, 1973.

DeLay, Brian. *War of a Thousand Deserts: Indian Raids and the U.S.-Mexican War*. New Haven: Yale University Press, 2008.

Deloria, Philip J. *Playing Indian*. New Haven: Yale University Press, 1998.

Dugger, Ronnie. "The Segregation Filibuster of 1957." In *Fifty Years of the Texas Observer*, edited by Char Miller, 30–35. San Antonio: Trinity University Press, 2004.

Dunbar-Ortiz, Roxanne. *Roots of Resistance: Land Tenure in New Mexico, 1680–1980*. Los Angeles: Chicano Studies Research Center at University of California Los Angeles, 1980.

Ebright, Malcolm. "The G.A.O. Land Grant Report: A Whitewash and Slap in the Face." *La Jicarita News*, July 2004.

———. *Land Grants and Lawsuits in Northern New Mexico*. Santa Fe: Center for Land Grant Studies Press, 2008.

———. *The Tierra Amarilla Land Grant: A History of Chicanery*. Santa Fe: Center for Land Grant Studies, 1980.

Encinias, Mario. "Iratéo: World Destruction in the Life and Legacy of Reies López Tijerina." Master's thesis, University of New Mexico, 2002.

Espinosa, Gastón. "Brown Moses." In *Mexican American Religions: Spirituality, Activism, and Culture*, edited by Gastón Espinosa and Mario T. García, 263–95. Durham: Duke University Press, 2008.

———. "El Azteca: Francisco Olazábal and Latino Pentecostal Charisma, Power, and Faith Healing in the Borderlands." *Journal of the American Academy of Religion* 67, no. 3 (1999): 597–616.

Espinosa, Gastón, Virgilio Elizondo, and Jesse Miranda. *Latino Religions and Civic Activism in the United States*. Oxford: Oxford University Press, 2005.

Espinosa, Gilbert. "New Mexico Land Grants." *State Bar of New Mexico Journal* 1, no. 2 (1962): 3-13.

Farber, David. *The Age of Great Dreams: America in the 1960s*. New York: Hill and Wang, 1994.

———. *The Sixties: From Memory to History*. Chapel Hill: University of North Carolina Press, 1994.

Featherstone, Ralph. *Ralph Featherstone: Raised in Washington D.C., May 26, 1939–March 9, 1970*. SNCC Legacy Project. https://snccdigital.org/people/ralph-featherstone, accessed April 11, 2018.

Federal Bureau of Investigation. "Full Text of Rabble Rouser Index." Internet Archive. June 5, 2012. https://archive.org/stream/RabbleRouserIndex/DOCID-59161088_djvu.txt.

Findlay, John M., and Richard White, eds. *Power and Place in the North American West*. Seattle: University of Washington Press, 1999.

Foley, Neil. "Becoming Mexican American: Mexican Americans and the Faustian Bargain with Whiteness." In *Reflexiones 1997: New Directions in Mexican American Studies*, edited by Neil Foley, 53–70. Austin: Center for Mexican American Studies, The University of Texas, Austin, 1998.

———. *Quest for Equality: The Failed Promise of Black-Brown Solidarity*. Cambridge, Mass.: Harvard University Press, 2010.

———. *The White Scourge: Mexican, Blacks, and Poor Whites in Texas Cotton Culture*. Berkeley: University of California Press, 1999.

Forman, James. "Speech to Black Caucus of National Politics for New Politics." Civil Rights Movement Veterans, Tougaloo College, September 2, 1967. http://www.crmvet.org/info/6709_forman_ncnp.pdf.

Forrest, Suzanne. *The Preservation of the Village*. Albuquerque: University of New Mexico Press, 1989.

Fortuny-Loret de Mola, Patricia. "La Luz del Mundo Church." In *Encyclopedia of Global Religions*, edited by Mark Juergensmeyer and Wade Roof Clark, 683–85. Los Angeles: Sage, 2012.

Frank, Ross. *From Settler to Citizen: New Mexican Economic Development and the Creation of Vecino Society*. Berkeley: University of California Press, 2007.

Galán, Hector, dir. *Chicano! History of the Mexican American Civil Rights Movement*. Episode 1, "Quest for a Homeland." NLCC Educational Media. PBS, 1996.

Gannon, Raymond L., and Stanley H. Horton. *The Shifting Romance with Israel*. Shippensburg, PA: Destiny Image, 2011.

Ganz, Marshall. *Why David Sometimes Wins: Leadership, Organization, and Strategy in the California Farm Worker Movement*. Oxford: Oxford University Press, 2009.

García, Ignacio M. *Chicanismo: The Forging of a Militant Ethos among Mexican Americans*. Tucson: University of Arizona Press, 1997.

———. *United We Win: The Rise and Fall of La Raza Unida Party*. 2nd ed. Tucson: University of Arizona Press, 1989.

García, Mario. *Memories of Chicano History: The Life and Narrative of Bert Corona*. Berkeley: University of California Press, 1994.

———. *Mexican Americans: Leadership, Ideology, and Identity*. New Haven: Yale University Press, 1989.

Garcia, Matthew. *From the Jaws of Victory: The Triumph and Tragedy of Cesar Chavez and the Farm Worker Movement*. Berkeley: University of California Press, 2014.

García, Richard A. *Rise of the Mexican American Middle Class*. College Station: Texas A&M University Press, 1991.

Gardner, Richard M. *¡Grito! Reies Tijerina and the New Mexico Land Grant War of 1967*. Indianapolis: Bobbs-Merrill, 1970.

Geertz, Armin W. *Invention of Prophecy: Continuity and Meaning in Hopi Indian Religion*. Berkeley: University of California Press, 1994.

Ginzburg, Carlo. *The Cheese and the Worms: The Cosmos of a Sixteenth Century Miller*. Translated by John Tedeschi and Anne C. Tedeschi. Baltimore: Johns Hopkins University Press, 1980.

Gitlin, Todd. *The Sixties: Years of Hope, Days of Rage*. New York: Bantam Books, 1987.

Glassberg, David. *Sense of History: The Place of the Past in American History*. Amherst: University of Massachusetts Press, 2001.

Goldstein, Alyosha. *Formations of United States Colonialism*. Durham: Duke University Press, 2016.

———. *Poverty in Common: The Politics of Community Action during the American Center*. Raleigh: Duke University Press, 2012.

Gómez, Laura E. *Manifest Destinies: The Making of the Mexican American Race*. New York: New York University Press, 2007.

Gómez-Quiñones, Juan. "Toward a Perspective on Chicano History." *Aztlán: Journal of the Social Sciences and the Arts* 2, no. 2 (1971): 1–49.

Gómez-Quiñones, Juan, and Irene Vásquez. *Making Aztlán: Ideology and Culture of the Chicana and Chicano Movement*. Albuquerque: University of New Mexico Press, 2014.

Gonzales, Nicki Margaret. "Yo Soy Loco Por Esa Sierra: The History of Land Rights Activism in San Luis, Colorado, 1863–2002." Ph.D. diss., University of Colorado, Boulder, 2007.

Gonzales, Phillip B. *Forced Sacrifice as Ethnic Protest: The Hispano Cause in New Mexico and the Racial Confrontation of 1933*. 2nd ed. New York: Peter Lang, 2011.

Gonzalez, Christina. "Reies López Tijerina, a Chicano Leader's Lifetime of Achievement Is Honored." *Borderzine*, July 4, 2009. http://borderzine.com/2009/07/reies-lopez-tijerina-a-chicano-leader%E2%80%99s-lifetime-of-achievement-is-honored/.

González, Deena. *Refusing the Favor: The Spanish-Mexican Women of Santa Fe, 1880–1920*. Oxford: Oxford University Press, 1999.

Gonzalez, Gilbert G. "Racial Intelligence Testing and the Mexican People." *Explorations in Ethnic Studies* 5, no. 2 (1982): 36–49.

"González, Henry B." History, Art and Archives: U.S. House of Representatives. http://history.house.gov/People/Detail/13906, accessed May 12, 2017.

González, Nancie. *The Spanish-Americans of New Mexico: A Heritage of Pride*. Albuquerque: University of New Mexico Press, 1969.

Gordon, Linda. *The Great American Orphan Abduction*. Cambridge, Mass.: Harvard University Press, 2001.

Gottheimer, Josh. *Ripples of Hope: Great American Civil Rights Speeches*. New York: Basic Civitas Books, 2003.

Greenberg, Amy S. *A Wicked War: Polk, Clay, Lincoln, and the 1846 U.S. Invasion of Mexico*. New York: Alfred A. Knopf, 2012.

Griswold del Castillo, Richard. *The Treaty of Guadalupe Hidalgo: A Legacy of Conflict*. Norman: University of Oklahoma Press, 1990.

Güemes, Odena Lina. "En busca de la méxicanidad." In *Nueves Identidades Culturales en México*, edited by Guillermo Bonfil Batalla and Héctor M. Capello, 89–125. Mexico City: Dirección General de Publicaciónes del Consejo Nacional para la Cultura y las Artes, 1993.

Guglielmo, Thomas A. "Fighting for Caucasian Rights: Mexicans, Mexican Americans, and the Transnational Struggle for Civil Rights in World War II Texas." *Journal of American History* 92, no. 4 (2006): 1212–37.

Guinn, Jeff. *The Road to Jonestown: Jim Jones and the Peoples Temple*. New York: Simon and Schuster, 2017.

Gómez, Laura E. *Manifest Destinies: The Making of the Mexican American Race*. New York: New York University Press, 2007.

Gutiérrez, José Angel. "Chicanos and Mexicanos under Surveillance, 1940–1980." In

Renato Rosaldo Lecture Series Monographs 2: 1984–1985, edited by Ignacio M. García. Tucson: Mexican American Studies and Research Center, 1985.

———. "La Raza and Revolution: The Empirical Conditions of Revolution in Four South Texas Counties." Master's thesis, St. Mary's University, 1968.

Gutiérrez, José Angel, Michelle Meléndez, and Sonia Adriana Noyola. *Chicanas in Charge: Texas Women in the Public Arena*. Lanham, Md.: Altamira Press, 2007.

Gutiérrez, Ramón A. "The Religious Origins of Reies López Tijerina's Land Grant Activism in the Southwest." In *A New Insurgency: The Port Huron Statement and Its Times*, edited by Howard Brick and Gregory Parker, 289–300. Ann Arbor: University of Michigan Publishing, 2015.

———. *When Jesus Came*. Stanford: Stanford University Press, 1991.

Hammerback, John C., Richard Jensen, and José A. Guiterrez. *A War of Words: Chicano Protests in the 1960s and 1970s*. Westport, Conn: Praeger, 1985.

Harden, Paul. "Free State of Socorro." Visit Socorrow, October 17, 2013. https://www.socorronm.org/notable-local/free-state-socorro/.

Harrell, David Edwin. *Oral Roberts: An American Life*. New York: HarperCollins, 1987.

Harris, Stephen J. "Bede and Gregory's Allusive Angles." *Criticism* 44, no. 3 (2002): 271–89.

Hayden, Dolores. *The Power of Place: Urban Landscapes as Public History*. Cambridge: MIT Press, 1995.

Herman, Judith Lewis. *Father-Daughter Incest*. 2nd ed. Cambridge, Mass.: Harvard University Press, 2000.

———. *Trauma and Recovery: The Aftermath of Violence, from Domestic Abuse to Political Terror*. New York: Basic Books, 2015.

Hernández, Kelly Lytle. *Migra! A History of the U.S. Border Patrol*. Berkeley: University of California Press, 2009.

Herzog, Jonathan P. *The Spiritual-Industrial Complex: America's Religious Battle against Communism in the Early Cold War*. Oxford: Oxford University Press, 2011.

Hessler, Curtis. "Bill Higgs: Silhouette." *Harvard Crimson*, March 4, 1964. https://www.thecrimson.com/article/1964/3/4/bill-higgs-peight-years-ago-mississipian/.

Hietala, Thomas. "Expansionism and Imperialism." *U.S. Mexican War 1846–1848: Prelude to War*. PBS. https://www.pbs.org/kera/usmexicanwar/prelude/md_expansionism.html, accessed September 1, 2017.

———. *Manifest Design: Anxious Aggrandizement in Late Jacksonian America*. Ithaca: Cornell University Press, 1985.

Higginbotham, Evelyn Brooks. *The Women's Movement in the Black Baptist Church*. Cambridge, Mass.: Harvard University Press, 1993.

Hillerman, Tony. *The Great Taos Bank Robbery and Other Indian Country Affairs*. Albuquerque: University of New Mexico Press, 1973.

Hobsbawn, Eric. *Primitive Rebels*. New York: Norton, 1965.

Holsaert, Faith S., et al. *Hands on the Freedom Plow: Personal Accounts by Women in SNCC*. Champaign: University of Illinois Press, 2010.

Howard, John. *Men Like That: A Southern Queer History*. Chicago: University of Chicago Press, 1999.

Immerman, Richard H. *Empire for Liberty: A History of American Imperialism from Benjamin Franklin to Paul Wolfowitz*. Princeton: Princeton University Press, 2010.

Isserman, Maurice, and Michael Kazin. *America Divided: The Civil Wars of the 1960s*. Oxford: Oxford University Press, 2000.

Jelin, Elizabeth. *State Repression and the Labors of Memory*. Translated by Judy Reim and Marcial Godoy-Anativia. Minneapolis: University of Minnesota Press, 2003.

———. *Los Trabajos de la Memoria*. Madrid: Siglo XXI, 2001.

Jenkins, Myra Ellen. *History of the Laguna Pueblo Land-Claims*. New York: Garland, 1974.

Jenkinson, Michael. *Tijerina: Land Grant Conflict in New Mexico*. Agoura Hills: Paisano Press, 1968.

Jenschke, Callie. "Maria Varela." In *Latinas in the United States: A Historical Encyclopedia*, vol. 3, edited by Vicki L. Ruiz and Virginia Sánchez Korrol, 787–88. Bloomington: Indiana University Press, 2006.

Johnson, Benjamin Heber. *Revolution in Texas: How a Forgotten Rebellion and Its Bloody Suppression Turned Mexicans into Americans*. New Haven: Yale University Press, 2003.

Johnston, Dick. *The Taylor Ranch War: Property Rights Die*. Bloomington: AuthorHouse, 2006.

Joseph, Peniel E. *Waiting 'til the Midnight Hour: A Narrative History of Black Power in America*. New York: Henry Holt, 2006.

Julian, George W. "Land-Stealing in New Mexico." *North American Review* 145, no. 368 (1887): 17–31.

Kaufman, Herbert. *The Forest Ranger: A Study in Administrative Behavior*. Baltimore: Johns Hopkins University Press, 1960.

King, Martin Luther, Jr. *The Autobiography of Martin Luther King, Jr.* Edited by Clayborne Carson. New York: Warner Books, 1998.

Kino, Eusebio. *Historic Memoir of Pimería Alta*. Translated by Herbert Bolton. Vol. 1. Reprint of original 1919 edition. Bedford, Mass.: Applewood Books, 2011.

Kirby, Dianne. "The Cold War and American Religion." *Oxford Research Encyclopedia*. http://religion.oxfordre.com/view/10.1093/acrefore/9780199340378.001.0001/acrefore-9780199340378-e-398, accessed August 13, 2018.

Kirk, Lydia. "Letters from Moscow." *Ladies Home Journal*, March 1952, 46–47, 192–204, 206.

Kluckhohn, Florence Rockwood, and Fred L. Strodtbeck. *Variations in Value Orientations*. Evanston, Ill.: Peterson, 1961.

Knowlton, Clark S. "Chapter Thirteen, El Paso: 1962 1968 (Part Two)." *Autobiography of Clark S. Knowlton* (blog), December 22, 2013. http://clarksknowlton.blogspot.com/2013/12/chapter-thirteen-el-paso-1962–1968-part_3121.html, accessed August 18, 2016.

———. "Land-Grant Problems among the State's Spanish-Americans." *New Mexico Business* 3 (1967): 1–13.

———. "Reies L. Tijerina and the Alianza Federal de Mercedes: Seekers after Justice." *Wisconsin Sociologist* 22 (Fall 1985): 133–44.

Kosek, Jake. *Understories: The Political Life of Forests in Northern New Mexico*. Durham: Duke University Press, 2006.

Krogstad, Jens Manuel, and Mark Hugo Lopez. "For Three States, Share of Hispanic Population Returns to the Past." Pew Research Center, June 10, 2014. http://www.pewresearch.org/fact-tank/2014/06/10/for-three-states-share-of-hispanic-population-returns-to-the-past/.

Kutsche, Paul. *The Survival of Spanish American Villages*. Edited by Research Committee. Colorado Springs: Colorado College, 1979.

LaFeber, Walter. *The New Empire*. Ithaca: Cornell University Press, 1963.

Lamar, Howard. *The Far Southwest, 1846–1912: A Territorial History*. New Haven: Yale University Press, 1966.

Lampinen, Lily Gay. "The Poor People's Campaign." *International Socialism*, 1st ser., 34 (1968): 8–10.

"Land Areas of the National Forest Service." USDA Forest Service: Lands and Realty Management. https://www.fs.fed.us/land/staff/lar-index.shtml, accessed September 11, 2018.

Lane, Christopher. *Surge of Piety: Norman Vincent Peale and the Remaking of American Religious Life*. New Haven: Yale University Press, 2016.

Larson, Robert W. *New Mexico's Quest for Statehood*. Albuquerque: University of New Mexico Press, 1968.

Lehmberg, Stanford. *Holy Faith of Santa Fe: 1863–2000*. Los Ranchos de Albuquerque: LPD Press, 2004.

Lemke-Santangelo, Gretchen. *Daughters of Aquarius: Women of the Sixties Counterculture*. Lawrence: University of Kansas Press, 2009.

Leonard, David J., and Carmen R. Lugo. *Latino History and Culture: An Encyclopedia*. New York: Sharpe Reference, 2010.

LeSeur, Greta. *Not All Okies Are White: The Lives of Black Cotton Pickers in Arizona*. Columbia: University of Missouri Press, 2000.

Lewis, Sinclair. *Elmer Gantry*. New York: Harcourt, 1926.

Limerick, Patricia. *The Legacy of Conquest: The Unbroken Past of the American West*. New York: W. W. Norton, 1987.

Lopez, Andrew. "Minority Groups in New Mexico." Employment Security Commission of New Mexico, January 1969. U.S. Department of Health, Education, and Welfare. https://eric.ed.gov/?id=ED035475.

Love, Joseph. "La Raza: Mexican Americans in Rebellion." In *Pain and Promise: The Chicano Today*, edited by Edward Simmen, 271–85. Originally from *TRANS-action*, February 1969. New York: New American Library, 1972.

Lozano, Rosina. *An American Language: A History of Spanish in the United States*. Berkeley: University of California Press, 2018.

Lucero, Robert L. "*State v. Romero*: The Legacy of Pueblo Indian Land Grants and the Contours of Jurisdiction in Indian Country." *New Mexico Law Review* 37 (2007): 671–99.

Mantler, Gordon K. *Power to the Poor: Black-Brown Coalition and the Fight for Economic Justice, 1960–1974*. Chapel Hill: University of North Carolina Press, 2013.

"Maria Varela Meets Reies Tijerina at National Conference for New Politics." SNCC Digital Gateway. https://snccdigital.org/events/maria-varela-meets-reies-tijerina-at-national-new-politics-conference/, accessed January 11, 2018.

Mariscal, George. *Brown-Eyed Children of the Sun: Lessons from the Chicano Movement, 1965–1975*. Berkeley: University of California, 2005.

Martínez, Elizabeth (Betita). "A View from New Mexico: Recollections of the Movimiento Left." *Monthly Review: An Independent Socialist Magazine*, July 1, 2002. https://monthlyreview.org/2002/07/01/a-view-from-new-mexico/.

Marty, Martin E. *Modern American Religion: Volume 3, Under God, Indivisible, 1941–1960*. Chicago: University of Chicago Press, 1999.

Marx, Karl. *Critique of Hegel's "Philosophy of Right."* Cambridge: Cambridge University Press, 1977.

Matusow, Allen J. *The Unraveling of America: A History of Liberalism in the 1960s*. Repr., Athens: University of Georgia Press, 2009.

McKay, Robert R. "The Federal Deportation Campaign in Texas: Mexican Deportation from the Lower Rio Grande Valley during the Great Depression." *Borderlands Journal* 5 (1981): 95–109.

Meier, Matt S., and Feliciano Ribera. *The Chicanos: A History of Mexican Americans*. New York: Hill and Wang, 1972.

———. *Mexican Americans/American Mexicans: From Conquistadores to Chicanos*. Rev. ed. New York: Hill and Wang, 1993.

Menchaca, Martha. *Recovering History, Constructing Race: The Indian, Black, and White Roots of Mexican Americans*. Austin: University of Texas Press, 2010.

Menchú, Rigoberta. *I, Rigoberta Menchú: An Indian Woman in Guatemala*. Edited by Elisabeth Burgos-Debray and Ann Wright. London: Verso Press, 1984.

Metcalf, R. Warren. *Termination's Legacy: The Discarded Indians of Utah*. Lincoln: University of Nebraska Press, 2002.

Meyerowitz, Joanne Jane. *Not June Cleaver: Women and Gender in Postwar America, 1945–1960*. Philadelphia: Temple University Press, 1994.

Miller, Walter, dir. *Most Hated Man in New Mexico*. NBC News, 1969.

Mintz, S., and S. McNeil. "New Mexico Constitution, 1912." Digital History. http://www.digitalhistory.uh.edu/disp_textbook.cfm?smtID=3&psid=571, accessed November 10, 2013.

Mitchell, Don. *They Saved the Crops: Labor, Landscape, and the Struggle over Industrial Farming in Bracero-Era California*. Athens: University of Georgia Press, 2012.

Montejano, David. *Anglos and Mexicans in the Making of Texas, 1836–1986*. Austin: University of Texas Press, 1986.

Montgomery, Charles. "The Trap of Race and Memory: The Language of Spanish Civility on the Upper Rio Grande." *American Quarterly* 52 (Fall 2000): 478–513.

"Montoya, Joseph Manuel." History, Art and Archives: U.S. House of Representatives. http://history.house.gov/People/Detail/18432, accessed July 12, 2014.

Montoya, María E. *Translating Property: The Maxwell Land Grant and the Conflict over Land in the American West, 1940–1900*. Berkeley: University of California Press, 2002.

Mulloy, D. J. *The World of the John Birch Society: Conspiracy, Conservatism, and the Cold War*. Nashville: Vanderbilt University Press, 2014.

Mundy, Jim. "Rocks and Pine Stumps." *Bill Mundy Memorial* (blog), June 16, 2009. http://billmundymemorial.blogspot.com/2009/06/rocks-and-pine-stumps.html.

Muñoz, Carlos, Jr. *Youth, Identity, Power: The Chicano Movement*. New York: Verso Books, 1989.

Nabokov, Peter. *Tijerina and the Courthouse Raid*. Albuquerque: University of New Mexico Press, 1969.

Navarro, Armando. *La Raza Unida Party: A Chicano Challenge to the Two-Party Dictatorship*. Philadelphia: Temple University Press, 2000.

New Mexico Commission of Public Records. "Research Resources: Land Grants." New

Mexico State Records Center and Archives. http://www.nmcpr.state.nm.us/archives/research-resources/land-grants/, accessed October 11, 2017.

New Mexico Office of the State Historian. "Frances Swadesh Quintana." New Mexico History. http://newmexicohistory.org/people/frances-swadesh-quintana, accessed December 12, 2016.

———. "Land of Enchantment—1935." New Mexico History. http://newmexicohistory.org/people/land-of-enchantment-1935.

———. "One Land, Many Hands: The Story of the Sangre De Cristo Land Grant." New Mexico History. http://www.newmexicohistory.org/landgrants/sangre_de_cristo/english/grantees1.html, accessed August 31, 2017

Nieto-Phillips, John M. *The Language of Blood: The Making of Spanish-American Identity in New Mexico*. Albuquerque: University of New Mexico Press, 2004.

Nostrand, Richard L. *The Hispano Homeland*. Norman: University of Oklahoma Press, 1992.

Ochoa, Enrique. *Feeding Mexico: The Political Uses of Food*. New York: S. R. Books, Scholarly Resources, 2001.

Olivares, Julián. *International Studies in Honor of Tomás Rivera*. Houston: Arte Público Press, 1986.

O'Neill, William. *Coming Apart: An Informal History of America in the 1960s*. 1971. Repr., Chicago: Ivan R. Dee Publishers, 2004.

"Oral Roberts, 1918–2009, Legacy." *Tulsa World*, December 20, 2009.

Oropeza, Lorena. "The Heart of Chicano History: Reies López Tijerina as a Memory Entrepreneur." *The Sixties* 1, no. 1 (2008): 49–67.

———. *¡Raza Sí! ¡Guerra No!* Berkeley: University of California Press, 2005.

Orosco, José-Antonio. *Cesar Chavez and the Common Sense of Nonviolence*. Albuquerque: University of New Mexico Press, 2015.

Oyama, David L. "Students to Man Rights Project Organized by Meredith Lawyer." *Harvard Crimson*, April 15, 1963. https://www.thecrimson.com/article/1963/4/15/students-to-man-rights-project-organized/.

Pawel, Miriam. *The Crusades of Cesar Chavez: A Biography*. New York: Bloomsbury Press, 2014.

Peale, Norman Vincent. *The Power of Positive Thinking*. New York: Prentice Hall, 1952.

Pitti, Stephen. "Chicano Cold Warriors: César Chávez, American Politics, and California Farmworkers." In *In from the Cold: Latin America's New Encounter with the Cold War*, edited by Gilbert M. Joseph and Daniela Spenser, 273–307. Durham: Duke University Press, 2008.

Pitzer, Donald E. *America's Communal Utopias*. Chapel Hill: University of North Carolina Press, 1997.

Portelli, Alessandro. *The Order Has Been Carried Out: History, Memory, and the Meaning of a Nazi Massacre in Rome*. New York: Palgrave Macmillan, 2003.

Pulido, Laura. "Ecological Legitimacy and Cultural Essentialism: Hispano Grazing in the Southwest." *Capitalism Nature Socialism* 7, no. 4 (1996): 37–58.

Pycior, Julie Leininger. "Important but Neglected: Midwest Latino/a Biography and Memoir." 20th Anniversary Conference: Latino/a Communities in the Midwest. Julian Samora Research Institute, Michigan State University. https://jsri.msu.edu/upload/events/20thAnniversary/Pycior.pdf, accessed November 6, 2009.

———. *LBJ and Mexican Americans: The Paradox of Power.* Austin: University of Texas Press, 1997.

"Ralph Featherstone." SNCC Digital Gateway. https://snccdigital.org/people/ralph-featherstone/, accessed January 11, 2018.

Ramírez, Daniel. *Migrating Faith: Pentecostalism in the United States and Mexico.* Chapel Hill: University of North Carolina Press, 2017.

Reade, Federico A. "La Voz del Pueblo: A Narrative Analysis of the 1967 Tierra Amarilla Courthouse Raid." Ph.D. diss., University of New Mexico, 2005.

Rendón, Armando B. *Chicano Manifesto.* Repr., Berkeley: Ollin and Associates, 1996.

Reséndez, Andrés. *Changing National Identities at the Frontier: Texas and New Mexico, 1800–1850.* New York: Cambridge University Press, 2005.

———. *The Other Slavery: The Uncovered Story of Indian Enslavement in America.* New York: Houghton Mifflin Harcourt, 2016.

Riss, F. Richard. "The Latter Rain Movement of 1948." *Pneuma: The Journal of the Society for Pentecostal Studies* 4 (1982): 35-36.

Rodriguez, Richard T. *Next of Kin: The Family in Chicano/a Cultural Politics.* Durham: Duke University Press, 2009.

Rodríguez, Sylvia. *Acequia: Water Sharing, Sanctity, and Place.* Santa Fe: School of Advanced Research Press, 1997.

Romano-V, Octavio. "The Anthropology and Sociology of Mexican Americans." *El Grito: A Journal of Contemporary Mexican American Thought* 2 (1968): 13–26.

Roozen, David A., and C. Kirk Hadaway. *Church and Denominational Growth.* Hartford: Abingdon Press, 1993.

Rosales, F. Arturo. *Chicano! The History of the Mexican American Civil Rights Movement.* Houston: Arte Público Press, 1997.

———. *Testimonio: A Documentary History of the Mexican American Struggle for Civil Rights.* Houston: Arte Público Press, 2000.

Rosenbaum, Robert J. *Mexicano Resistance in the Southwest: The Sacred Right of Self-Preservation.* Austin: University of Texas Press, 1981.

Rowan, Helen. "A Minority Nobody Knows." *The Atlantic,* June 1967, 47–52.

Rubenstein, Richard E. *Great Courtroom Battles.* Chicago: Playboy Press, 1973.

Salazar, Eulogio. "New Mexico History Multimedia Audio File." New Mexico Office of the State Historian. http://newmexicohistory.org/images/uploads/audios/07_26_12_Eulogio%20Salazar.mp3, accessed October 1, 2016.

Saldaña-Portillo, María Josefina. "'How Many Mexicans Is a Horse Worth?' The League of United Latin American Citizens, Desegretation Cases, and Chicano Historiography." *South Atlantic Quarterly* 107, no. 4 (2008): 809–31.

Sánchez, George I. *Forgotten People: A Study of New Mexicans.* Albuquerque: University of New Mexico Press, 1940.

Sánchez, Joseph P., and Robert L. Spude. *New Mexico: A History.* Norman: University of Oklahoma Press, 2013.

Sánchez Walsh, Arlene M. *Latino Pentecostal Identity: Evangelical Faith, Self, and Society.* New York: Columbia University Press, 2003.

Sandoval, Richard. *One of Our Fifty Is Missing.* Albuquerque: University of New Mexico Press, 1986.

Savage, Kenzy. *The Spirit Bade Me Go.* Kearny, Neb.: Morris Publishing, 2000.

Scarborough, Mike. *Trespassers on Our Own Land: Structured as an Oral History of the Juan P. Valdez Family and of the Land Grants of Northern New Mexico.* Indianapolis: Dog Ear Publishing, 2011.

Schroeder, John H. *Mr. Polk's War: American Opposition and Dissent, 1846–1848.* Madison: University of Wisconsin Press, 1973.

Scott, Samuel Parsons. *Las Siete Partidas.* Edited by Robert Ignatius Burns. Philadelphia: University of Pennsylvania Press, 2000.

"Secession of Socorro." *Life*, June 8, 1953, 53–54.

Shaw, Randy. *Beyond the Fields: Cesar Chavez, the UFW, and the Struggle for Justice in the 21st Century.* Berkeley: University of California Press, 2010.

Simmen, Edward R., and Richard F. Bauerle. "Chicano: Origin and Meaning." *American Speech* 44, no. 3 (1969): 225–30.

Simmons, Marc. *The Last Conquistador.* Norman: Oklahoma University Press, 1991.

Sloan, David W., and Lisa Mullikin Parcell. *American Journalism: History, Principles, and Practices.* Jefferson, N.C.: McFarland, 2002.

Smith, Robert Charles. *We Have No Leaders: African Americans in the Post–Civil Rights Era.* Albany: SUNY Press, 1996.

Spencer, Robyn C. *The Revolution Has Come: Black Power, Gender, and the Black Panther Party of Oakland.* Durham: Duke University Press, 2016.

Spicer, Edward. *Cycles of Conquest.* Tucson: University of Arizona Press, 1962.

Stang, Alan. *It Is Very Simple: The True Story of Civil Rights.* Boston: Western Islands Press, 1965.

———. "New Mexico: The Coming Guerilla War." *American Opinion*, March 1969, 49–62.

———. "Reies Tijerina: The Communist Plot to Grab the Southwest." *American Opinion*, October 1967, 1–22.

———. "'War on Poverty' Supports Castroite Terrorists." *American Opinion*, March 1968, 1–17.

Steele, Thomas J. *The Alabados of New Mexico.* Albuquerque: University of New Mexico Press, 2005.

Swadesh, Frances L. "The Alianza Movement of New Mexico." In *Minorities and Politics*, edited by Henry J. Tobias and Charles E. Woodhouse, 19-23. Albuquerque: University of New Mexico Press, 1969.

"Tejas: Life and Times of the Caddo." Texas beyond History. http://www.texasbeyondhistory.net/tejas/, accessed April 24, 2017.

Tijerina, Reies López. *Mi Lucha por la Tierra.* Mexico City: Fondo de Cultura Economíca, 1978.

———. *They Called Me "King Tiger": My Struggle for the Land and Our Rights.* Edited by José Angel Gutiérrez. Translated by José Angel Gutiérrez. Houston: Arte Público Press, University of Houston, 2000.

Time to Get Ready: Civil Rights Photography of Maria Varela. Chicago: National Museum of Mexican Art, 2017. Exhibition catalogue, accessed January 23, 2019. http://latinocultural.uic.edu/events/time-to-get-ready-civil-rights-photography-of-maria-varela.

Tórrez, Robert J. "New Mexico State Archives Groundbreaking." New Mexico History. http://newmexicohistory.org/people/new-mexico-state-archives-groundbreaking, accessed October 8, 2012.

———. "Spanish and Mexican Land Grants." New Mexico Office of the State Historian.

http://dev.newmexicohistory.org/filedetails_docs.php?fileID=21447, accessed September 1, 2017.

Tórrez, Robert J., and Robert Trapp. *Rio Arriba: A New Mexico County*. Los Ranchos: Rio Grande Books, 2010.

Treviño, Jesús Salvador, and Barry Nye, dirs. *Yo soy Chicano*. Cinema Guild. PBS, 1972.

Trillin, Calvin. "U.S. Journal: A Little Cloud on the Title." *New Yorker*, April 26, 1976, 122, 125, 128, 131–32.

Trouillet, Michel-Rolph. *Silencing the Past: Power and the Production of History*. Boston: Beacon Press, 2015.

Tuan, Yi-Fu. *Space and Place: The Perspective of Experience*. Minneapolis: University of Minnesota Press, 1977.

Turner, Frederick Jackson. *The Significance of the Frontier in American History*. Essay delivered in 1893 to the American Histocial Association. https://www.historians.org/about-aha-and-membership/aha-history-and-archives/historical-archives/the-significance-of-the-frontier-in-american-history.

Twitchell, Ralph Emerson. *Leading Facts of New Mexico History*, vol 1. Cedar Rapids: Torch Press, 1911.

U.S. Bureau of the Census. "Number of Inhabitants, Arizona, 1950." In "Census of Population, Number of Inhabitants, Volume 1." https://www2.census.gov/library/publications/decennial/1950/population-volume-1/vol-01-06.pdf, accessed June 30, 2018.

———. "Nativity, Parentage, and Country of Origin of White Persons of Spanish Surname by Sex, for Five Southwestern States, Table 1." In "1960 Census Subject Reports: Persons of Spanish-Surname." https://www2.census.gov/library/publications/decennial/1960/population-volume-2/41927938v2p1a-1ech04.pdf.

U.S. Congress. House. Committee on Agriculture. Subcommitee on Rural Development. *Effect of Federal programs on rural America: hearings before the Subcommittee on Rural Development: hearings before the Subcommittee on Rural Development of the Committee on Agriculture, Ninetieth Congress, first session*. Washington, D.C.: U.S. Government Printing Office, 1967.

U.S. Congress. Senate. Select Committee to Study Governmental Operations with Respect to Intelligence Activities. *Final report of the Select Committee to Study Governmental Operations with Respect to Intelligence Activities, United States Senate: together with additional, supplemental, and separate views*. Washington: U.S. Govt. Print. Off., 1976.

U.S. Congress, 78th Cong., 2nd sess. *Congressional Record*, May 12, 1944, to June 12, 1944. https://www.govinfo.gov/content/pkg/GPO-CRECB-1944-pt4/pdf/GPO-CRECB-1944-pt4.pdf

U.S. Department of Labor. "One Hundred Years of Consumer Spending: Data for the Nation, New York City, and Boston, Report 991." Bureau of Labor Statistics, 2006. https://www.bls.gov/opub/uscs/report991.pdf, accessed May 1, 2018.

U.S. General Accounting Office. "Report for Congressional Requestors: Treaty of Guadalupe Hidalgo: Findings and Possible Options Regarding Longstanding Community Land Grant Claims in New Mexico." United States General Accounting Office, June 2004. https://www.gao.gov/new.items/d0459.pdf.

U.S. Inter-agency Committee on Mexican American Affairs. "The Mexican American, a New Focus on Opportunity: Testimony Presented at the Cabinet Committee

Hearings on Mexican American Affairs." El Paso, Tex., October 26–28, 1967. ERIC: Institute of Education Sciences. https://files.eric.ed.gov/fulltext/ED032950.pdf.
Urias, Robert V. "The Tierra Amarilla Grant, Reies Tijerina, and the Courthouse Raid." *Chicano-Latino Law Review* 16, no. 1 (Winter 1995): 141-52.
Vaca, Nick C. "The Mexican American in the Social Sciences." *El Grito: A Journal of Contemporary Mexican American Thought* 4, no. 1 (Fall 1970): 17–51.
Valdés, Dennis Nodin. *Al Norte: Agricultural Workers in the Great Lakes Region, 1917–1970*. Austin: University of Texas Press, 1991.
Valdez, Luis, and Stan Steiner. *Aztlán: An Anthology of Mexican American Literature*. New York: Vintage Books, 1972.
Varela, Maria. "Many Inheritances: One Legacy." Unpublished essay, December 2013.
Vasquez, Enriqueta. *Enriqueta Vasquez and the Chicano Movement: Writings from El Grito del Norte*. Edited by Lorena Oropeza and Dionne Espinoza. Houston: Arte Público Press, 2006.
Vasquez, Irene, and Juan Gómez-Quiñones. *Making Aztlán: Ideology and Culture of the Chicana and Chicano Movement*. Albuquerque: University of New Mexico Press, 2014.
Vigil, Ernesto B. *The Crusade for Justice: Chicano Militancy and the Government's War on Dissent*. Madison: University of Wisconsin Press, 1999.
Vincent, Carol Hardy, Laura A. Hanson, and Carla N. Argueta. "Federal Land Ownership: Overview and Data." Congressional Research Service, March 3, 2017. https://fas.org/sgp/crs/misc/R42346.pdf.
Walker, Ronald W. "'A Banner Is Unfurled': Mormonism's Ensign Peak." *Dialogue: A Journal of Mormon Thought* 26, no. 4 (1993): 71-91.
Wallace, Anthony F. C. "Revitalization Movements." *American Anthropologist* 58, no. 2 (1956): 264–81.
Wallis, Michael. *En Divina Luz: The Penitente Moradas of New Mexico*. Albuquerque: University of New Mexico Press, 1994.
Warren, Louis. *God's Red Sun: The Ghost Dance Religion and the Making of Modern America*. New York: Basic Books, 2017.
Waters, Frank. *Book of the Hopi*. New York: Penguin Press, 1963.
Weber, David. *The Spanish Frontier in North America*. New Haven: Yale University Press, 1992.
Weber, Max. *Economy and Society*. Edited by Guenther Roth and Claus Wittich. Berkeley: University of California Press, 1978.
Weigle, Marta. *Brothers of Light, Brothers of Blood: The Pentitentes of the Southwest*. Albuquerque: University of New Mexico Press, 1976.
Westphall, Victor. *Mercedes Reales: Hispanic Land Grants of the Upper Rio Grande Region*. Albuquerque: University of New Mexico Press, 1983.
———. *The Public Domain in New Mexico*. Albuquerque: University of New Mexico Press, 1965.
———. *Thomas Benton Catron and His Era*. Tucson: University of Arizona Press, 1973.
Weyerman, Debra. *Answer Them Nothing: Bringing Down the Polygamous Empire of Warren Jeffs*. Chicago: Chicago Review Press, 2011.
White, Koch, Kelley and McCarthy, Attorneys at Law. *Land Title Study*. Santa Fe: State Planning Office, 1971.

White, Richard. *It's Your Misfortune and None of My Own*. Norman: University of Oklahoma Press, 1991.

White, Richard, and John M. Findlay, eds. *Power and Place in the North American West*. Seattle: University of Washington Press, 1999.

Wilson, Dwight. *Armageddon Now! The Premillenarian Response to Russia and Israel since 1917*. 1977. Repr., Tyler, Tex.: Institute for Christian Economics, 1991.

Wilson, Jenny. "A Not-Quite National Holiday." *Time*, March 31, 2011.

Windes, Vina. "Governor Offers His Office as Avenue for Alianza." *Albuquerque Journal*, April 23, 1967.

Wolfe, Patrick. "Settler Colonialism and the Elimination of the Native." *Journal of Genocide Research* 8, no. 4 (2006): 387–409.

Wolin, Sheldon S. *Politics and Vision: Continuity and Innovation in Western Political Thought*. Princeton: Princeton University Press, 1960.

Wu, Judy Tzu-Chun. *Radicals on the Road: Internationalism, Orientalism, and Feminism during the Vietnam Era*. Ithaca: Cornell University Press, 2013.

Yavenditti, Michael J. "The American People and the Use of Atomic Bombs on Japan: The 1940s." *The Historian* 36 (1974): 224–47.

Zamora, Emilio. *The World of the Mexican Worker in Texas*. College Station: Texas A&M University Press, 1993.

Index

Page numbers in *italics* refer to illustrations.